D0876604

Black Women in
Nineteenth-Century American Life

BLACK WOMEN IN NINETEENTH-CENTURY AMERICAN LIFE

Their Words
Their Thoughts
Their Feelings

Edited with an Introduction by
Bert James Loewenberg
and **Ruth Bogin**

The Pennsylvania State University Press
University Park, Pennsylvania

Library of Congress Cataloging in Publication Date

Main entry under title:
Black women in nineteenth-century American life.

  Bibliography: p.333
  Includes index.
  1. Women, Negro—Biography. I. Loewenberg,
Bert James, 1905-1974. II. Bogin, Ruth.
E185.96.B54   920.72'0973   75-27175
ISBN 0-271-01207-2
ISBN 0-271-00507-6 (pbk.)

Eighth printing, 1996

To the memory of
BERT JAMES LOEWENBERG
teacher, friend, colleague
who did not live to see this work in print

Ruth Bogin

Contents

Preface

Neither a hall of fame for black women nor a narrative of the female side of black history, this volume presents a variety of life experiences of some articulate black women of the nineteenth century. Those included have been selected for their written or recorded observations, stemming from personal events or from participation in organized social or political movements.

Some of the lecturers and writers represented here are widely known, at least by name. The striking oratory of Sojourner Truth, the feats of Harriet Tubman, and the diary kept by Charlotte Forten Grimké have brought these women a measure of renown. Inclusion of less famous women and of materials not readily available shows that insight is not limited to the famous, nor is sensitivity to experience invariably wedded to distinguished achievement. While some of these individuals lived on well into the present century, we have had to omit many whose activities belong to the twentieth century rather than the nineteenth. Mary Church Terrell, to cite a single example, made major contributions to American life even following the Second World War.

Many black women of the nineteenth century not included in this book enriched the tapestry of American experience. Among leading women in the arts were Edmonia Lewis, black sculptor whose works achieved a measure of fame in her native land while she maintained her home and studio in Rome, and the concert singer Elizabeth Taylor Greenfield, heralded as "The Black Swan" in America and abroad. Pioneer women physicians included Caroline Still Anderson, daughter of a noted black abolitionist. Numerous black women demonstrated leadership capacities as founders of schools and other social institutions and as organizers of important social movements. Mary Burnett Talbert, for example, played a leading role in southern prison reform. These talented individuals in most instances left only fragmentary written evidence of their attitudes and reflections.

The present study is designed to amplify the historical understanding of American life. Using little-known sources, it reveals a segment of the American people whose story constitutes a distinctive part of this country's history. At the same time it is a study in individuality and diversity. It seeks to fathom the interactions of culture and personality within the special context of black experience in nineteenth-century America. Records prove that black women, despite their absence from the conventional histories, were in fact eloquently present. The sources were plumbed for evidence of how individual women developed unique qualities and capacities. High priority was given to the ideals and ideas from which the meaning and direction of their lives were forged. Documents were combed for hints and subtle inflections no less than for fully polished statements.

A courageous struggle is revealed within these pages. Countless black women found creative ways to transcend and to transform the often harrowing circumstances that constricted their lives. Their strivings for liberty, and for the liberty to grow, were personal and inward as well as public and declamatory. They drew upon all the strengths of womanhood including those deriving from their roles as wives and as mothers. For these women the universal struggle for survival and growth was hampered by a special set of barriers. Their words offer new insight into the variety of means by which these limitations on human potentiality were dissolved or overcome.

Twenty-four women are presented in this collection. All were born before the Civil War or during it. Ten were born free. Of these, one hailed from Maryland and one from Georgia; eight were of northern origin, born in New England, New York, New Jersey, or Pennsylvania. For more than half, slavery was a personal experience, including two who were born in the North. Of those who were slaves, six obtained their liberty as a result of the war; the remainder were emancipated in various ways. In three instances, escape from bondage was arranged by purchase. One father bought his daughter, an aunt bought her niece. One hoarded her meager earnings until she was able to buy herself. Mere chance accounted for the freeing of others. In one case, a master who for religious reasons made a fine distinction between enslavement for a term of years and enslavement for life manumitted his female servant. An owner's death brought a free lease of the future for another. Friction between one young slave and her mistress spurred the master to end her state of bondage. Anticipating the impact of New York's abolition law, one woman claimed her freedom a year in advance. Two daring individuals fled to safety.

Portions of the introductory essay have been adapted, with the permission of the *Sarah Lawrence Journal,* from our article, "American Negro Women: Four Nineteenth Century Selections" (Spring 1969): 27–52. The biographical sketch of Sarah Parker Remond is from a more extensive discussion in Ruth Bogin, "Sarah Parker Remond: Black Abolitionist from Salem," *Essex Institute Historical Collections* 110 (April 1974): 120–50, and is adapted here with the permission of the Essex Institute. Dr. Ray Allen Billington has allowed us to use excerpts from his edition of *The Journal of Charlotte L. Forten* (New York, 1953).

Many institutions and individuals have contributed to this investigation. Special mention must be made of the invaluable resources of the New York Public Library's Schomburg Center for Research in Black Culture, and of the generosity with which Mrs. Jean B. Hutson, director, and Mr. Ernest

Kaiser, her associate, gave their time, encouragement, and expertise. The Moorland-Spingarn Research Center of Howard University Library and its former curator, Mrs. Dorothy B. Porter, also made available a number of rare materials. The Library of Congress responded to numerous requests for information and for photocopying; research in its manuscript collections yielded valuable insights, especially regarding the education of black women in the District of Columbia and elsewhere.

We acknowledge with thanks the friendly cooperation of the following institutions in our pursuit of information: Trevor Arnett Library of Atlanta University; Augusta–Richmond County (Georgia) Public Library; Boston Public Library; Brockport (New York) Public Library; Chicago Public Library; Hartford Public Library; Astor, Lenox, and Tilden Foundations of the New York Public Library; Arthur and Elizabeth Schlesinger Library on the History of Women in America, Radcliffe College; Sophia Smith Collection, Smith College; and Friends Historical Library, Swarthmore College.

Several individuals who entered with especial enthusiasm into our search for obscure data deserve particular mention: Mrs. Juanita Hardy, Librarian of the Lucy Craft Laney High School, Augusta, Georgia; Mrs. Willis Knapp of Brockport, New York; Mr. H. Sass, Senior Librarian of the Buffalo and Erie County (New York) Historical Society; and Mrs. Flora Wester, Clerk of the Board of National Missions of the United Presbyterian Church in the United States of America. We are also grateful to the many librarians who searched in vain, hoping to uncover records that had eluded earlier cataloguers.

The Sarah Lawrence College Library, in recent years directed by Mrs. Elizabeth Seely, sustained our research with innumerable courtesies. Warm thanks are due to the entire staff for its continuing generosity and helpfulness. The library at the Pleasantville (New York) campus of Pace University contributed in many ways to completion of the study and it is a pleasure to acknowledge the assistance of Miss Maryvie Cramblitt and the other members of the staff. From the reference department of the Great Neck (New York) Public Library came many valuable suggestions to shorten the search for information.

For the careful reading of the manuscript by Professors Wilhelmena S. Robinson, Benjamin Quarles, and Irene Diggs we are particularly indebted. Many of their suggestions have been incorporated and have improved the presentation of our material. To Mrs. Dorothy W. Millner, Ms. Pamela DiPesa, and Ms. Ruth Lazar, who participated in the early stages of research on nineteenth-century black women, our sincere appreciation is now formally recorded. We also thank Mrs. Sylvia M. Halpern for her kind assistance in the later phases of our work.

Bert James Loewenberg
Ruth Bogin

Introduction
SELVES AND SOCIETY

Women, Blacks, History

"If the fifteenth century discovered America to the Old World," wrote Frances Ellen Watkins Harper in 1893, "the nineteenth century is discovering woman to herself."[1] This perceptive black woman, like others in the United States, was unswervingly devoted to the black cause, and to the cause of women of whatever color. To aid women in the discovery of themselves was in itself a powerful solvent of social imbalance. The bondage of chattel slavery for one sector of American womanhood was compounded by another bondage. All women in America were encumbered by a cultural tradition of inferiority and a social condition of second-class citizenship.

But the history of women is the other half of the history of the world. Equality of condition, first-class citizenship, is necessary for uniform opportunities in education, voting, and income. But fuller equality results in a larger diversity of human and cultural development, and it is furthered by the equal right of women to be themselves. "Today," continued Frances Harper, "we stand on the threshold of woman's era, and woman's work is grandly constructive."

The very word emancipation was an incantation to black womanhood. It was at once symbolic, reverent, and compelling. Emancipation meant the tireless quest of ideals, liberation from serfdom of whatever kind, freedom for women as people. "To be alive," exulted Anna Julia Cooper, "at such an epoch is a privilege, to be a woman . . . sublime." Women like this young black educator who gave themselves up to sundry social causes discovered themselves. They also discovered, in Julia Ward Howe's exciting words, "the addition of a new continent to the map of the world." Nor was it mere rhetoric to affirm, as did Anna Julia Cooper, that those who took a creative part in this discovery were endowed with "a heritage . . . unique in the ages."[2]

Emancipation from restraints has to do with the shifting course of historical events and the shifting frontiers of human potentiality. Culture

---

[1]Unless otherwise indicated, all the quotations in the introductions are from the readings.

[2]Anna Julia Cooper, A Voice From the South (Xenia, Ohio, 1892), p.143; Julia Ward Howe, Reminiscences, 1819–1899 (Boston and New York, 1900), pp. 372–73; Cooper, Voice, p. 144.

change and personality change evolve in continual interaction; each new convergence broadens the scope of the possible. If men and women are made by culture and individual attributes, they also remake them. Frances Watkins Harper, at the centennial of the Pennsylvania Society for the Abolition of Slavery in 1875, spoke of the fusion of personality and purpose: "It is the inner life that develops the outer, and if we are in earnest the precious things lie all around our feet."[3]

Yet history and historians are themselves events; historical analyses and understandings are parts of the historical process. They too derive from the merger of changes in culture and personality. Historical insight is deepened by every new cultural transformation, and historians are tutored by the creative rediscovery of the past. The philosopher Frederick J.E. Woodbridge was doubtless correct in describing historical reinterpretation as "genuinely progressive." Understandings of history are "worked out in the course of time, and the sequence of events ... progressively makes [them] clear." Historians, always limited, are not always perverse. Scholars can scarcely be censured for what they could not conceivably have known, nor can they ordinarily be expected to entertain viewpoints foreign to the culture that helped to form them.[4]

Historiography—the history of history—is itself a part of the record, reflecting a constant though jagged growth. One of the functions of the historian is to create new perspectives welding smaller fragments into larger wholes. Individuals and epochs see different things in different ways; what appears obvious to one generation is simply not within another's arc of perception. Events alter the significance of data, and experiences transform ideas.

Henry Adams made an important historical announcement at the turn of the century. New varieties of women, he proclaimed, "had been created since 1840; all were to show their meaning before 1940." Followers of Adams must account him right. Now it is apparent, as it could not have been before to the same degree, that a more complete history of the world has yet to be written. Women, whether American, European, African, or Asian, remain culturally wedded to the lands of their origin. They share an identity with their male compatriots but they also differ from them. As women they have an identity of their own.[5]

Women, like men, respond to the surges of history, but their responses are unique. Omission of woman's role and woman's story shrivels the evidence at hand for analysis and dilutes the full validity of the seg-

---

[3]Frances Ellen Watkins Harper, Address at Centennial Exercises, April 14, 1875, Pennsylvania Society for Promoting the Abolition of Slavery, *Centennial Anniversary* (Philadelphia, 1875), p. 32.

[4]Frederick J.E. Woodbridge, *The Philosophy of History* (New York, 1916), p. 17.

[5]Henry Adams, *The Education of Henry Adams*, Modern Library ed. (New York, 1931), p. 445.

ments presently available. Neglect of the history of black women—Harriet Tubman and Sojourner Truth are notable exceptions—is a crucial instance of distortion. Men have been granted a conceptual monopoly. Both the interpreters and those interpreted with few exceptions reflect a set of masculine attitudes, a cast of masculine thought. Persistent study of the institution of slavery has until recently ignored the obvious fact that slavery did not affect men and women in the same ways.[6] Historians writing of the black ministry, to cite another instance, depend upon an ordained ministry of men. They almost never treat of the spiritual and intellectual contributions of nonordained evangelical women whose very presence at the church altar, at revivals, and at religious meetings, brought solace to black men and women alike. These women preached a gospel of inner emancipation, a message that outlined proposed roads to freedom and peace. Though they used similar language and images, they preached from the wellsprings of feminine experience and from the hidden crevices of feminine hearts. Recovery of the black past is itself a force shaping the black future, yet the full range of experience of black women still awaits discovery and assessment.

"The difference between being a Negro woman and being a Negro man," remarks one anthropologist, "is not at all the difference between being a white woman and being a white man."[7] Some anthropologists and sociologists have made greater use of black historical materials than the majority of historians themselves. Not only do black women seldom appear in treatments of black history, but historians have been content to permit the male to represent the female in almost every significant category. Thus it is the male who is the representative abolitionist, fugitive slave, or political activist. The black male is the leader, the entrepreneur, the politician, the man of thought. When historians discuss black abolitionist writers and lecturers, they are men. David Walker, Charles Lenox Remond, and a procession of male stalwarts preempt the list in conventional accounts. Particularly later, when black history was consciously written, it was the male, not the female, who recorded it. Women are conspicuous by their silence.

The written history of black Americans remains both partial and partisan. Among other Americans, to paraphrase Ralph Ellison, black men and black women have lived their lives invisibly. Only within the past decade have historians in larger numbers launched a serious study of the black experience; still, the history of blacks, except for the so-called critical peri-

---

[6]Valuable recent studies shedding light on these differences include John W. Blassingame, *The Slave Community: Plantation Life in the Antebellum South* (New York, 1972); Eugene D. Genovese, *Roll Jordan Roll: The World the Slaves Made* (New York, 1974); George P. Rawick, *The American Slave: A Composite Autobiography*, Vol. 1: *From Sundown to Sunup: The Making of the Black Community* (Westport, Conn., 1972).

[7]Hortense Powdermaker, *After Freedom: A Cultural Study in the Deep South* (New York, 1939; paperback edition, 1967), p. 71.

ods, remains obscure. Paucity of evidence is itself an eloquent fact. Diaries, letters, autobiographies, essays and reportage, interviews and speeches—part of the evidence for understanding lives—were rare among blacks in the eighteenth and early nineteenth centuries. If individuals wrote, their writings were seldom salvaged, which testifies to patterns of life predominantly unsettled and unlettered.

Literacy itself was exceptional. While this was particularly true in the antebellum South, opportunities for education in the North as well were often minimal. If the black male's words, before the most recent period of ferment, were recorded only spasmodically, those of the black female were still less frequently set down on paper. And the more that black communities reared churches, schools, and institutions of family life on white America's models, the more it was the men, not the women, who gave expression to their history, their strivings, and their innermost feelings.

Some women, nevertheless, contrived to transmit their ideas in print. They form a distinctive group beyond the confines of slavery, peonage, and the crippling conditions of life that silenced numberless others. Free or freed, they were literate, or else their spoken words, valued by others, were preserved for posterity. And what they had to say was often distinctive. Differing in experience from white women, they spoke as blacks. Differing in experience from men who were black, they spoke as women. Differing from one another in their experience as black women, they spoke as individuals. Literacy made the aspirations of these women public and durable. Protestantism and the Bible gave a moral imprint to their lives.

Those who comprise this study were influenced by urban conditions. They represent neither the relatively closed circle of plantation existence nor the circumscribed living of the small southern town. A few were molded by the rural mode of life. But the circumstances of birth, the course of personal migration, or the fluctuations of slave ownership make this group of women predominantly an urban one. Even though the lives of blacks were differently affected by the city than those of whites, the black world and the white world overlapped in American cities.

At one crucial point, the contrast between the rural and the urban environment is radiantly clear. Despite the hardships of slavery, the city afforded advantages for growth. Despite the limitations even on black urban dwellers who were free, there was scope for self-enhancement. Nature was not yet out of reach in the nineteenth-century town nor had the city become the "concrete jungle" of the twentieth. Blacks on the fringe of survival had whatever benefits were obtainable both in the countryside and in the city. The plantation world was narrow and static, even when benign; the urban process immersed the black in the swiftly moving currents of a changing society. These disparities, long recognized by students of black history, were apparent to many blacks at the time. One young black girl of fourteen, who was later to be a leader among her black sisters, explained the situation to a Union officer who was startled to find her literate. Susie King Taylor ascribed her advantage to a simple fact: "they were reared in the country and I in the city."

In the early twentieth century, W.E.B. DuBois analyzed the attitudes of American blacks. His delineation, as apt then as now, distinguished three varieties of reaction to spiritual impoverishment and social constraint. Blacks are in the first place spurred by "a feeling of revolt and revenge" or, second, they are motivated "to adjust all thought and action to the will of the greater group." Third, they are inspired by an effort to realize themselves as full human beings, to achieve "self-development despite environing opinion."[8] Each of these attitudes emerged at different periods of Afro-American history; together they are among the persistent threads in the design of black American life. Although all these themes reverberate in the lives of the women in this study, the third appears as the most constant motif.

There were among these women individuals of eminence who were thrust by events into contact with the celebrated of their era. From them came not simply the chance to achieve ends otherwise doubtful of attainment, but the opportunity to rebuild attitudes and to solidify resolve. They took their place on the lecture platform and in the classroom, and they joined as pioneers in social, civic, and educational reform. They addressed large and influential audiences, traveled to Europe, and linked hands and hearts with others who found error and evil in the ways of man and the ways of society.

Eminence refers as much to magnificence of character as to splendor of success. Many black women lived out their lives in tortured quiet in the midst of searing events, leaving only an imprint "of simple lives, led in stormy periods."[9] Other women responded to internal motivations which shaped their actions. In their writings—or in their recorded words—they reveal their own uniqueness. Those who make up the bulk of this selection bespeak a sense of fulfillment that stems from their striving, an immersion in both the struggle for existence and the struggle to move beyond mere survival.

In their patterns of existence, four areas of self-expression are emphasized: social reform, education, religion, and family life. Some of the women made social reform the orbit of their public lives as speakers and lecturers; these are Maria Stewart, Nancy Prince, Harriet Tubman, Sarah Parker Remond, Sojourner Truth, Frances Ellen Watkins Harper, Ida Wells-Barnett, Fannie Barrier Williams. For others—Charlotte Forten Grimké, Lucy Craft Laney, Fanny Jackson Coppin, Anna Julia Cooper—education seemed the fulcrum for all social change. Another segment—Elizabeth, Jarena Lee, Amanda Berry Smith, and Ann Plato—found fulfillment in religious work

---

[8]W.E.B. DuBois, *The Souls of Black Folk* (Chicago, 1903; paperback reprint, 1961), pp. 45–46.

[9]Thomas Wentworth Higginson, Introduction, Susie King Taylor, *Reminiscences of My Life in Camp with the 33rd United States Colored Troops, late 1st S.C. Volunteers* (Boston, 1902), p. xii.

and religious themes. The struggle to retain a family—or regain one—was the very core of purpose for Silvia Dubois, Cornelia, Louisa Picquet, Elizabeth Keckley, Elleanor Eldridge, Susie King Taylor, Annie Louise Burton, and Ellen Craft as well as numerous women not represented here. The writings of the last group focus on social relationships between men and women and between women and children. The excerpts disclose how they made the straggling ends of their lives meet for themselves and their families. The minute details of black experience which they describe provide the basis for the wider conceptions spoken from the lecture platform and discussed in the reformer's essay.

But living is organic, and the selections spill over the edges of these categories. Women like Fanny Jackson Coppin in education and Fannie B. Williams in the organizations of women were deeply imbued with religious convictions and visualized their work as a mode of implementing Christian faith. The religious worker named Elizabeth tells as much about the cultural and psychological roots of her fervor as about religious belief as such. Indeed, the central theme within the writings and life patterns of some of these women is often elusive. It is the fusion of their concerns that warrants emphasis.

Awareness of options for independent action unifies the sentiment of the women in this collection. We tend to think of action in its dramatic or external forms, but the creation of a private domain beyond compulsion and limitation, for example, is also a mode of action. Brunó Bettelheim's psychological exploration of life in Nazi concentration camps, later utilized in Stanley M. Elkins' study of slavery, contributes to an understanding of black attitudes and black thought.[10] An inner citadel of strength and privacy may serve as a last haven of survival in an evil and destructive environment. The women in this sample were powerfully moved to preserve and nurture the spark of living. They were inspired to reject futility. They refused to accept individual collapse.

---

[10] Stanley M. Elkins, Slavery: A Problem in American Institutional and Intellectual Life (Chicago, 1959).

Sources of
Inner Wholeness

White assumptions of black inferiority maimed the personalities of black men and women. Slavery assumed white superiority, however considerate the master or however unthreatening the employer, neighbor, or fellow townsman. Long after emancipation, feelings of inferiority were part of the black cultural inheritance. Even benevolence is no substitute for social equality. Benevolence, concludes a modern investigator, "deprived Negroes of the opportunity for developing responsibility, competency, and autonomy; it made them unfit for maturity and independence; it rendered them incapable of assuming responsibility, of becoming adults."[11] Perhaps, as later history demonstrated, it did not render emancipated slaves incapable or less capable of responsibility or adulthood. Rather, it fitted them inadequately for swift adaptation toward either. But there were many exceptions: the father of Amanda Berry Smith, once he was able to formulate and to pursue aims of his own, "had an important and definite object before him, and was willing to sacrifice sleep and rest in order to accomplish it. It was not his own liberty alone, but the freedom of his wife and five children. For this he toiled day and night."

Yet servitude was likely to foster dependence rather than psychological poise. A spirit of independence on the plantation, unless miraculously attuned to the delicate shadings of the master's whim, was a hazard rather than a virtue. Nor did conditions fostering segregation after the Civil War make for the development of a full-blown humanity. In the study of black women there is a latent hypothesis which aids in understanding how some were able to salvage themselves from the incubus of slavery and from the later abasement of racism. Psychic wholeness, the evidence suggests, stemmed from a two-stage process. Fundamental was the childhood experience of being loved, but the precarious world of slavery and its aftermath made necessary a symbolic extension of this experience. Therefore it was crucial to the individual to acquire and absorb enduring concepts capable of

---

[11]Jessie Bernard, *Marriage and Family among Negroes* (Englewood Cliffs, N.J., 1966), p. 71.

replenishing a sense of worthiness and love. Numberless black women in surroundings often barren and cruel wrought creative miracles by providing such sustenance for themselves and for their children.

The crucial test of an integrated personality is awareness of a psychological center. A psychological center, in Paul Radin's words, is a "fixed point" from which an individual fashions an inner core, his ego or his individuality.[12] From this point a person may take soundings, establish directions, discern the self. Achievement of this fixed point may derive in its initial stages from a single parent or from two parents, from a parent substitute such as a grandparent, a blood relative, a close friend, a teacher, or in special cases a master or an employer. During later stages it may be fostered by religion, by education, by an evolving set of purposes or values. The goal in the case of a black slave woman might be that of freedom coupled with the yearning for a decent life and a decent job for herself and her family.

Slavery as a system endowed the acts of men with the force of acts of God. Under such a system, the social and cultural patterns of humanity, evolved to shelter the human spirit against the natural calamities of life and death, were warped. A normal progression toward wholeness, the interior process of becoming, was jeopardized by the absence of any psychological center. Slavery did not preclude the emergence of richly creative personalities, for religion, surrogate parents, and culture did exist among the slaves. But the possibilities of cultivating internal strength, if not withered, were curbed by servility and fear.

Religion was pivotal to black American life. Womanhood in each of its phases was sanctioned by religious values. The religious experience was a group heritage and a creative personal impetus. At once secular and holy, a religious sentiment suffused black thought and generated a dynamic for black action. If an eternal kinship with the divine "enabled them to keep on keeping on,"[13] eternal membership in the kingdom of God made secular ideals sacred. Both served as bases for social criticism and earthly hope. Although such commitments and aspirations were the same for scores of whites, they had a special meaning for black Americans.

Religion was a hardy fixed point in a social universe of uncontrollable flux. Human beings cannot live with flux alone; there must be points of departure and return to permit survival of the psyche. Men and women in slave society found meanings in the promises of Scripture; they became one with the Christian epic. The promise of Christianity permeates Afro-American culture. The moving words of song and spiritual and the rich imagery of Christianity gave countless slaves communion with imperishable stability.

---

[12]Paul Radin, "Status, Phantasy, and the Christian Dogma," in Fisk University Social Science Institute, God Struck Me Dead, Social Science Source Documents No. 2, Fisk University Social Science Institute (Nashville, 1945), p. vi.

[13]Benjamin Mays, The Negro's God as Reflected in His Literature (Boston, 1938; paperback ed., 1968), p. 26.

Ritual anchored fear and gave men and women the courage to dream. A Bible reading by a parent later remembered, a furtive prayer recited together merged God's blessing with parental love. Harriet Tubman's efforts for freedom were undertaken with the confidence that they were the commands of God.[14] Her security came from the religious training begun in childhood. Others experienced conversion later in life.

The Bible, patrimony of mankind, has been invoked and cited for purposes widely divergent. A black girl named Elizabeth, who in adulthood became an itinerant evangelist, recalled a vision experienced at the age of twelve. "I thought I heard a voice saying . . . 'Art thou willing to be saved in my way?' . . . I exclaimed, 'Yes Lord, in thy own way.' . . . I was filled with light and . . . shown the world lying in wickedness, and . . . told I must go there . . . and this message was as a heavy yoke upon me."

Enforced obedience to a cruel earthly master meant emotional bondage; voluntary obedience to a beneficent heavenly master offered redemption. Each kind of service imposed burdens. But the act of choosing—the liberty to be able to choose—gave this girl a sense of relief and a sense of mission. An enduring feeling of divine protection sheltered her, insulated her against the buffets of existence. After years of preaching she was threatened with arrest in slave territory. Asked by what authority she spoke, she replied: "Not by the commission of men's hands: if the Lord had ordained me, I needed nothing better."

Evidence of inhumanity, as often unconscious as conscious, is harrowingly abundant. The auction block, gifts made of slaves, the breaking up of families, exhausting labor, and premature death have all been documented. Elizabeth was separated from her mother in early childhood. At the moment of parting her mother told her there was "nobody in the wide world to look to but God," a farewell the child always remembered. Faith in divine guidance and purpose alone made grief bearable and softened the traumas of parting. Guilt and redemption were doctrines all the more satisfying because of the desperate need for acknowledgment as a person. "The ante-bellum Negro was not converted to God. He converted God to himself. . . . Within and outside of himself, he could see only vacillation and endless shifting. . . . The white Methodist and Baptist was asked to prove that Christ had forgiven his sins; the Negro Methodist and Baptist was asked to prove that Christ had recognized him and that he had recognized Christ."[15]

A private world inside the self, sustained by religious sentiment and religious symbolism, was fashioned to contain the world without. The faith, the feelings, the language of Biblical Christianity explained existence,

---

[14]"A deeply religious person," wrote John Hope Franklin, Harriet Tubman "never doubted that her actions were guided by divine commands." Notable American Women, ed. Edward T. James and Janet Wilson James (Cambridge, Mass., 1971), III, 482.

[15]Radin, "Status," pp. vi, viii.

forged attitudes, and conditioned behavior. They gave to black men and black women such tranquillity and dignity as people deprived of humanity by law and cultural pressure can attain.

Religion was basically Christian, Protestant, and evangelical.[16] Surviving fragments of African culture were sometimes fused with Christian practice. Although black denominations were founded in Northern cities soon after the Revolution, the essential quality of black religion in America stems from the South. The core of black tradition in this country, it remains the driving force of the contemporary black population. After emancipation, black religious thought moved north with the black migration, which is still continuing in some measure, although a reversal of this pattern may now be under way. Black women of the nineteenth century in leadership positions who lectured, wrote, and agitated were the legatees of this tradition and its trustees. The oneness of humanity derived from the fatherhood of God and the brotherhood of man. Said Maria Stewart: "Many think . . . that you are an inferior race of beings; but God does not consider you as such. He hath formed and fashioned you in his own glorious image . . . and according to the Constitution of these United States, he hath made all men free and equal."

Abolition of slavery was part of the black religion of the antebellum South. It was an unspoken prayer, an arsenal of faith. When Father Abraham freed the slaves in 1863, he appeared as the agent of divine intent. After emancipation, "it seemed to the freedman," said W.E.B. DuBois, "a literal coming of the Lord."[17] The Reverend Martin Luther King, Jr., dreamed a Christian dream, a revelation to be brought about by divine dispensation and by divine aid.

Black women were important carriers of black culture. They transmitted its message in the haunting music and inspiring lyrics of folk songs and the homely maxims of folk wisdom. They interpreted the anxieties of present life against the background of theology and heralded the future in the liturgy of fervent belief. Black women who spoke from the lecture platform or from the pages of books and essays emphasized, though mainly in secular terms, an almost identical code. They reared their children in the idiom of the Christian faith. As defenders of human dignity and human equality, they grounded their argument in appeals to religious sanctions. Their values were those of the western world, the ethical principles of the Judaic–Christian lineage.

---

[16]Roman Catholicism was, however, the adopted faith of blacks in numerous instances. The widow Madame Bernard Couvent exemplifies the Catholic orientation of the New Orleans black community in her 1836 will establishing L'Ecole des Orphelins Indigents, a school for poor black orphans to be run under clerical direction. See Rodolphe L. Desdunes, *Nos Hommes et Notre Histoire; Notices Biographiques Accompagnées de Reflexions et de Souvenirs Personnels, Hommage à la Population Créole, en Souvenir des Grands Hommes qu'elle a Produits et des Bonnes Choses qu'elle a Accomplies* (Montreal, 1911), pp. 28–30 and *passim.*

[17]DuBois, *Souls*, p. 148.

Although the vision of the coming of the Lord retained its heavenly meanings after freedom, it acquired more earthly connotations. Other aspects of black life, however, did alter. More blacks had homes, at least in name, more had families and known relatives who possessed full names and assignable location. Yet permanence in the social universe was still as rare as it had ever been. The yoke of slavery had been severed, but bondage of a different sort remained. The plantation was exchanged for the peonage of tenant farming. Dependence upon the unpredictable whims of the master was exchanged for the predictable behavior of scores of new masters: the money lender, the commission merchant, the boss, the agent in the company store. And there was the urban ghetto. By the late nineteenth century this often meant miles of littered concrete separating one slum alley from another. These mean streets were separated from the larger society by an invisible wall of segregation even more difficult to scale than if it had been a physical one. An inner world to contain the world outside was still the price of survival.

Religious experiences are peak experiences. In psychological language, they are parts of individual becoming. For the ancient evangelical preacher named Elizabeth, religious faith and its promise supplied the impetus for activity. "The presence of the Lord overshadowed" her wherever she went and permitted her to live with an almost uncrushable stability. "In every lonely place I found an altar," this former slave child later wrote. Maria Stewart seized identity through the promptings of Christian evangelicalism. For her, service to God and service to her black brothers and sisters were completely fused.

The "fixed point" of religion helped countless men and women find a sense of wholeness, but other sources also yielded psychic strength. Annie Burton described her mother's trials in reconstituting her family after the Civil War. It was a family fathered by two, perhaps three different men, of whom none was present.

> My mother took Henry in her arms, and my sister carried me on her back. We climbed fences and crossed fields, and after several hours came to a little hut. . . . We had no more than reached the place, and made a little fire, when master's two sons rode up and demanded that the children be returned. My mother refused to give us up. . . . There were six in our little family; my mother, Caroline, Henry, two other children that my mother had brought with her upon her return, and myself.

These siblings, sisters and brothers only by half, were fully accepted by the writer of this account. She could hardly forget her mother—a memory constantly refreshed by a heritage of love. Once, soon after emancipation, a white woman sought lodging and refuge in the little hut her mother had fashioned into a home. "I ain't got much," she recalled her mother saying, "but what I have got I will share with you." Recorded after four weary decades, the details may not be historically accurate. They contain a substantive truth in any case: united in recollection are the meal, the visitors, and the mother's protective affection.[18]

Fanny Jackson Coppin was bought out of slavery by an aunt and sent to New England to be raised in one of the free states. There she found the tendrils of life, among her relatives and in the care of a wealthy woman in whose home she was employed. The Calverts, kin of the famed Maryland clan, "had no children, and this gave me an opportunity to come very near to Mrs. Calvert, doing for her many things which otherwise a daughter would have done. I loved her and she loved me." Sources of spiritual nourishment were as diverse as they were unpredictable. Even a master could occasionally serve as a supportive influence. Silvia Dubois had a tyrannical mistress, but she met with kindness in her master. "He was a good man; and a great man, too; all the grand folks liked Minical Dubois. When the great men had their meetings, Minical Dubois was always invited to be with 'em. . . . I liked my master, and every body liked him. . . . I had good times when he was around, and he always done things right; but you mustn't get him mad."[19]

Phillis Wheatley, eighteenth-century black poet, found a substitute for the family of her earlier African childhood in that of her owners. While her life in slavery was hardly typical, she confided to a friend also kidnapped into bondage: "I have lately met with a great trial in the death of my mistress; let us imagine the loss of a parent, sister, or brother, the tenderness of all these were united in her. I was a poor little outcast and a stranger when she took me in; not only into her house, but I presently became a sharer in her most tender affections. I was treated by her more like her child than her servant."[20] She was then but twenty. Such a transfer of emotional response to the Wheatley family stemmed as much from their openness as from the shock of separation. Only a single vague memory permitted Phillis Wheatley to imagine her parents and her birthplace: the dawn in Massachusetts kept alive an image of her mother's ritualistic greeting of the morning sun. Imagery of this kind sometimes is a source of strength for the bereft. Sojourner Truth in one of her speeches gave similar evidence of her mother's gift for imparting such wisdom.

---

[18] A recent sociological study, given historical validity by stories like Annie Burton's, says that characteristics functional for "survival, development and stability," including strong kinship bonds and adaptability of family roles, though present among white families, are "manifested quite differently in the lives of black families because of the unique history of racial oppression." Robert B. Hill, *The Strengths of Black Families* (New York, 1972), p. 40.

[19] C. Wilson Larison, *Silvia Dubois. (Now 116 Years Old.) A Biography of the Slave who Whipped Her Mistress and Gained Her Freedom, as told to C.W. Larison, M.D.* (Ringoes, N.J., 1883), pp. 65–66.

[20] G. Herbert Renfro, *Life and Works of Phillis Wheatley* (Washington, D.C., 1916), pp. 29–30.

The black woman, says a sociologist who made a recent study of marriage and family among blacks, has "borne the major burden" of the race.[21] To help children to survive in a precarious world, to provide the inner strength they would need in their unknown future, symbols of stability had to be contrived. Impoverished women, denied life's comforts and society's conventional supports, were often sufficiently inventive to improvise the solutions to this basic human problem.

---

[21]Bernard, *Marriage*, p. x.

The Family

Disruption of black families under slavery was an ever-present threat. Denied legal status, a slave household existed at the pleasure of the master. Custom might honor the wishes of the slaves; economic purpose and family stability might often coincide. Yet antislavery records bulge with harrowing tales of children and parents sold away from one another. The consequences took a number of diverse forms, but they almost always inflicted paralyzing wounds beyond full mending. Frederick Douglass, bereft of a parental family and its comforts in childhood, felt like an aimless wanderer "without an intelligible beginning in the world." Harriet Tubman, to make good her escape from bondage, had to tear herself away from parents and home. A stranger in a strange land, she determined to reunite her family in the North. "I was free, and they should be free also," she resolved. "I would make a home for them in the North." Another refugee from the South, whose mother was the slave of her father, was said to be unable even to bear the thought of motherhood "under the wretched system of American slavery." For Ellen Craft, simply to contemplate the possibility "appeared to fill her very soul with horror."[22]

Fannie Barrier Williams, born in freedom in the North, evaluated the impact of slavery on the family.

> In nothing was slavery so savage and so relentless as in its attempted destruction of the family instincts of the negro [sic] race in America. Individuals, not families; shelters, not homes; herding, not marriages, were the cardinal sins in that system of horrors. Who can ever express in song or story the pathetic history of this race of unfortunate people when freedom came, groping about for their scattered offspring with only instinct to guide them, trying to knit together the broken ties of family kinship?

But the family in some form is universal. Patterns of course vary. Nevertheless, "In every known human society, everywhere in the world, the young male learns that when he grows up, one of the things which he must

---

[22]Frederick Douglass, *My Bondage and My Freedom* (New York and Auburn, N.Y., 1855), p.60.

do in order to be a full member of society is to provide food for some female and her young."[23] Blacks transplanted forcibly to American shores could not transplant their culture. The savage uprooting of individual lives was compounded by the severing of African cultural forms from their native sources. In Africa as elsewhere the family was the marrow of social organization. "As among other peoples," a leading historian of blacks in America writes, "the family was the basis of social organization in early Africa. At the basis even of economic and political life in Africa was the family with its inestimable influence over its individual members."[24] Cultural fatherhood is learned through a "delicate line of transmission."[25] While renewal of lost social forms may follow temporary disruption, catastrophic severance threatens disintegration. The history of the black population in America involved sustained and drastic catastrophe—tribal, linguistic, religious, economic. Disaster splintered the family. African cultural life was diverse in its patterns; a chaotic scrambling of populations resulting from the slave trade blocked the reemergence of those older patterns in America. New generations of black Americans were born to parents stripped of their old culture. These children were barred from full entry into the culture of their own native land. What kind of family bonds were they able to create?

Observers at the time and most modern students have cited the minimal role of the slave father, but account must be taken of contrary data. The inherent distortion in the conventional view of slave fatherhood has been emphasized by such recent black sociologists as Joyce Ladner, Andrew Billingsley, and Robert B. Hill. In a Fisk University interview with a former slave who grew up on a small Tennessee farm, a woman named Cornelia told of

> four families of slaves, that is, Aunt Caroline's family, Uncle Tom's family, Uncle Dave's family, and the family of which I was a member. . . . Each family had a cabin. . . . My father had a garden of his own around his little cabin, and he also had some chickens. . . . Master Jennings allowed his slaves to earn any money they could for their own use. . . . Every Sunday [he] would let pa take the wagon to carry watermelons, cider and ginger cookies to Spring Hill. . . . The white folks would buy from him as well as the free Negroes. . . . Pa was allowed to keep the money he made at Spring Hill, and of course Master Jennings didn't know about the little restaurant we had in our cabin.

The father in this instance participates fully in the social and economic life of his family. In addition to the parents and children, a maiden aunt was a part of the household, an arrangement traditionally associated with the

[23]Margaret Mead, *Male and Female: A Study of the Sexes in a Changing World*, rev. ed. (New York, 1955), p. 146.
[24]John Hope Franklin, *From Slavery to Freedom*, 3d ed. (New York, 1967), p. 28.
[25]Mead, *Male and Female*, p. 148.

white household of slavery times. In some slave households, it should be noted, male heads did function despite the appellation "Uncle."

One writer, Lucy Laney, etched a quite different portrait of slavery and the home.

> The home, with its fire-side training, mother's moulding, woman's care, was not only neglected but utterly disregarded. . . . During those two hundred and fifty years there was not a single marriage legalized in a single state. . . . Homes were only places in which to sleep, father had neither responsibility nor authority; mother, neither cares nor duties.

Such one-sided statements must be weighed against contradictory evidence. While the male as provider is bound up with the concept of fatherhood, such roles were seldom permitted to evolve within slavery in the traditional way. Sometimes slaves had no responsibility; sometimes they had more than their white owners. Amanda Berry Smith records: "After my father's master died, his young master . . . and himself, had all the charge of the place. They had been boys together, but as father was the older of the two, and was a trustworthy servant, his mistress depended on him, and much was entrusted to his care."

Individual characters were formed in many different ways. Cornelia says:

> Aunt Caroline . . . was very quiet and good-natured. . . . My mother was very different in nature from Aunt Caroline. Ma fussed, fought and kicked. . . . She was loud and boisterous. . . . Father was often the prey of her high temper. . . . "I can't tolerate you if you ain't got no backbone." Such constant warning to my father had its effect. My mother's unrest and fear of abuse spread gradually to my father. He seemed to have been made after the timid kind.

She does not, however, suggest that her father's timidity or her mother's temper was a typical male or female trait. Significantly, she notes her mother's desire for a husband who is stronger, and her father's partial development toward strength under her pressure.

During periods of crisis, "the primary unit may again become mother and child, the biologically given."[26] This pattern, where found in Afro-American life, represents a disruption of social form. Although some African societies followed a matriarchal pattern, there was always a responsible social role for adult males. In John Hope Franklin's words:

> Although the eldest male was usually the head of the family, there was the widespread practice of tracing relationships through the mother instead of the father. In areas where this latter practice was followed, children belonged solely to the family of the mother, her eldest brother

---

[26]Ibid., p. 149.

exercising the paternal rights and assuming all responsibility for the children's lives and actions.[27]

When individual blacks in America had the opportunity to reconstruct fully adult lives, they tended to adopt or adapt the pattern most visible and accessible, that sanctioned by Christianity and endorsed by the white world. This pattern also represented the pattern of freedom. This was one of the ways of identification with the values of the masters. Augmented and extended families were widely prevalent too.

The particular form of family structure is not psychologically controlling. Uprootings and separations, often depriving a family group of responsible adult men, encouraged compensatory forms. The life histories of the black women in these pages suggest that mother love and religious precept bridged the gap. The educational levels of parents, of other significant adults, or of the children themselves were not decisive in fostering the ego strength of the child. Neither the legality nor the common law paternity of the offspring nor absence of an identical paternity for all siblings made any meaningful difference. Even in instances where the identity of the father was not acknowledged, negative psychological consequences were not inevitable.

Children cherished by their mothers were able to surmount the handicaps imposed by the absence of a father. Mothers showed fierce tenacity in keeping their children with them during the slavery and the Reconstruction periods. They defied almost every hardship to build a home for themselves and their progeny. They persevered in doing so whether or not there was a paternal presence. The mother-child relationship, reciprocally beneficial to both, is more adequately revealed in this collection than the dynamic values of marriage. Selfhood was nourished for nineteenth-century black women, of course, through their husbands as well as their children. But for the black women of the nineteenth century the home rather than the relationship between man and woman was emphasized. Devotion to the home and its duties was not posed as an alternative to outside work. The principal stress was on better prospects for the generations to follow rather than on immediate satisfactions.

Christian standards placed a signal value on chastity, monogamy, and fidelity in family life. Nineteenth-century America took for granted parental love and care, filial love and obedience. Yet for those in bondage these ideals were denigrated, if not altogether out of reach. Abolitionists, black as well as white, women even more than men, demanded the end of those poignant and permanent separations of husbands from wives, children from parents, that wreaked such havoc on family life and family morality. They swore to eliminate the system that denied protection to black women and violated the sanctity of marriage. Slavery caused gross infringements on the

---

[27]Franklin, *From Slavery to Freedom*, p. 28.

standard of femininity as understood in western society. The position of the black woman as a worker, menial both in slave times and afterward, all but destroyed safeguards for chastity, safeguards for the ties between mother and child, the concept of woman's dignity, and the need for protection. Sojourner Truth's speech of 1851, included in this collection, is movingly explicit. The list of burdens she had been forced to endure was punctuated with the cry, "And ain't I a woman?" Ellen Craft testified that slavery destroyed femininity. None can wonder that she entertained strong feelings: "I had much rather starve in England, a free woman, than be a slave for the best man that ever breathed upon the American continent."[28]

Black feminists were not reticent about the sordid details of their experience. Anna Julia Cooper, addressing the World's Congress of Representative Women in 1893, scored the shameful denial of women's rights: "The painful, patient, and silent toil of mothers to gain a fee simple title [outright ownership; a term in the common law normally used with reference to land ownership] to the bodies of their daughters, the despairing fight . . . to keep hallowed their own persons, would furnish material for epics. . . . The majority of our women are not heroines—but I do not know that a majority of any race of women are heroines."

If concern and action by white clubwomen and white legislators were solicited, so too was sustained effort by blacks demanded. Decent work, decent education, a decent home life, and just laws adequately enforced were minimal needs. But blacks, black women especially, were not absolved from an obligation as solemn as it was inescapable. Anna Julia Cooper proclaimed: "Negro sentiment cannot remain callous and Negro effort nerveless in view of the imminent peril of the mothers of the next generation. 'I am my Sister's keeper!' should be the . . . response of every man and woman of the race."[29] Ida Wells-Barnett's reference was more acridly barbed. Miscegenation law of the 1890s, she rightly maintained, left "the white man free to seduce all the coloured girls he can, but it is death to the coloured man who yields to the force and advances of a similar attraction in white women." The black women of the nineteenth century were indeed their sisters' keepers.

---

[28]The statement by Mrs. Craft may be found in a letter to the British Anti-Slavery Standard, dated Ockham School near Ripley, Surrey, 26 October 1852, reprinted in Liberator, 17 December 1852, and from there reprinted in Carter G. Woodson, The Mind of the Negro as Reflected in Letters Written During the Crisis, 1800–1860 (Washington, D.C., 1926), p. 265.

[29]A Voice from the South (Xenia, Ohio, 1892), p. 32.

Responsibilities of Black Women

Three indefatigable black women appeared as speakers at the Congress of Representative Women in 1893. The Congress, meeting in conjunction with the Columbian Exposition at Chicago, had invited Fannie Barrier Williams to read a paper. She was joined by two other black women who addressed the assembly, Anna Julia Cooper and Frances Jackson Coppin. As guest of honor, Frederick Douglass, former slave and revered elder statesman of the black minority, was seated on the platform, and at the conclusion of the program he was invited to comment. His brief remarks contain a moving historical judgment. What he saw and heard in this mixed congress of noted females was a symbol of achievement for both blacks and whites, and it renewed his hope:

> I have heard tonight what I hardly expected to live to hear. I have heard refined, educated colored ladies addressing—and addressing success-fully—one of the most intelligent white audiences that I ever looked upon. It is the new thing under the sun, and my heart is too full to speak; my mind is too much illuminated with hope and with expecta-tion for the race in seeing this sign.[30]

Women began to make a public imprint on American society in the nineteenth century. During the 1830s and 1840s, antislavery agitation and other humanitarian movements enlisted devoted feminine support. White women operated on two pioneering fronts; black women necessarily oper-ated on three. White women, whatever the venture which inspired their effort, were simultaneously involved as women. Black women, whenever involved in activities, were engaged not only as women but as black women. The way to emancipation for white women was littered with obstacles: tradi-tion and prejudice conspired to impede them. Black women shared all the difficulties encountered by white women; in addition, they were black. "The white woman," wrote Anna Julia Cooper, herself a trained and articulate

---

[30]The full statement by Frederick Douglass is included following the Fannie Barrier Williams selection.

professional, "could at least plead for her own emancipation; the black woman, doubly enslaved, could but suffer and struggle and be silent."

American women, particularly black women, were still expected to be seen rather than heard. Afro-American women in leadership positions had little choice: as leaders, they were forced to give expression to black problems and black needs, to women's problems and women's needs. Priorities had to be established, and failure to set goals led to confusion.

Problems multiplied more readily than solutions. Should funds and energy go first to the careful and costly development of a leadership elite or to emergency assistance for the masses? Should existing institutions be altered to meet and accept black cultural patterns or should blacks be aided in adjusting to white mores in order to gain a readier acceptance?

Black women felt a unique responsibility to discover solutions. They understood their role long before the Civil War and long before Reconstruction. As early as 1832, Maria Stewart announced this to the newly formed Afric-American Female Intelligence Society: "O woman, woman! upon you I call; for upon your exertions almost entirely depends whether the rising generation shall be any thing more than we have been or not. O woman, woman! your example is powerful, your influence great; it extends over your husbands and over your children, and throughout the circle of your acquaintance."[31] The responsibility rested upon the already overburdened shoulders of the black mothers. They were enjoined to encourage a "thirst for knowledge" and a "love of virtue" in their children. If schools were lacking, as in most instances they were, it was the duty of mothers to commence the process themselves and later to seek private teachers. "Shall it any longer be said of the daughters of Africa, they have no ambition . . . ? Let us raise a fund . . . and at the end of one year and a half, we might be able to lay the cornerstone for the building of a High School."

Lucy Laney, founder of a Georgia school for black youth of both sexes, recognized the complexity of the black problem. Her appraisal of continuing southern needs made in 1899 was sensible and forward-looking. "We must," she admonished, "have better homes, and better homes mean better mothers, better fathers, better born children." This was elementary and could on no reasonable account be qualified. And it was woman's responsibility. Miss Laney said of women that they were "by nature fitted for teaching very young children. . . . The educated Negro woman, the woman of character and culture, is needed in the schoolroom not only in the kindergarten, and in the primary and the secondary school; but she is needed in high school, the academy, and the college." She had her own list of emergencies; each item was a feminine task, and almost every one was relevant to education. And she distinguished between present functions and future prospects; the generations were separate in her thought. "The educated Negro woman

---

[31]Maria W. Stewart, *Productions of Mrs. Maria W. Stewart* (Boston, 1835), p. 62. Excerpts of several other speeches are included in the present collection.

must teach the 'Black Babies;' she must come forward and inspire our men and boys to *make a successful onslaught upon sin, shame, and crime. . . .* We would prescribe: homes—better homes, clean homes, pure homes; schools—better schools; more culture; more thrift; and work in large doses. . . . Can woman do this work? She can; and she must." When W.E.B. DuBois spoke of black teachers and the transformation they were able to effect, he had the Lucy Laneys in mind. "In a single generation they put thirty thousand black teachers in the South; they wiped out the illiteracy of the majority of the black people of the land."[32] Lucy Laney put her finger on the reasons for the conclusions reached by DuBois and others. "Not alone in the schoolroom can the intelligent woman lend a lifting hand, but as a public lecturer she may give advice . . . that will change a whole community."

One woman splendidly fitted for teaching was Frances Jackson Coppin. Her student years at Oberlin from 1860 to 1865 coincided with the movement of freedmen into Ohio. During her senior year she organized an evening class for liberated blacks who wished to learn to read and write. "It was deeply touching to me to see old men painfully following the simple words of spelling; so intensely eager to learn." The Institute for Colored Youth in Philadelphia, established in 1837, secured her services as a teacher of classics. The school had been devised as a test of black capacity for "any considerable degree of education"; Mrs. Coppin's evidence was recorded with pride. "I was given the delightful task of teaching my own people, and how delighted I was to see them mastering Caesar, Virgil, Cicero, Horace, and Xenophon's Anabasis. We also taught New Testament Greek."

Fanny Jackson Coppin and her companions in spirit undermined the ancient prejudices; race was not a gauge of intelligence nor was color a measure of talent. Capacities were individual and talents various. Although the activities of black women—as teachers, writers, lecturers—could not alone dissolve prevailing assumptions, they demonstrated their falsity. The lives of such trained black women were clear evidence of their intelligence, their competence, and their talent for leadership.

The Emancipation Proclamation freed the slaves in law, but black Americans were not freed in fact. Laws cannot command love and affection. Laws cannot enact equality of the spirit. They can only enjoin prejudicial behavior and provide methods to cure the consequences of antisocial and inhumane acts. This is the sum of equality of condition. Equality in its wider sense, when it exists, resides in the attitudes of men.

Appomattox was succeeded by the chaos of the city and the social problems of the industrial revolution. There was no single answer to the complexities confronting blacks, and therefore to the complexities of society. Confusion was inescapable and unanimity impossible, for the problems were beyond immediate solution and beyond individual wisdom. "Since

---

[32]DuBois, *Souls*, pp. 79–80.

emancipation," observed Anna Julia Cooper, "we could not always tell whether we were going forward or groping in a circle." Concerned Americans faced the issues with such skills, resources, and good will as they had at their command. Black women, even when trained professionals and sincere humanitarians, had no marvels of method to offer, no panaceas for these great evils. They faced the dilemmas of their time, however, as women, and this fact often shaped both their methods and their goals.

Women's clubs, emerging in the decades following the Civil War, had joined to form the General Federation of Women's Clubs in 1890. Though black women in small numbers belonged to some of these clubs, exclusion of blacks was more typical. In organizing their own groups, black women had a distinctive purpose. They were less involved with their own personal growth and more concerned with uplift of the race. Mary Church Terrell, a highly educated woman, became the first national president of the National Association of Colored Women. For the sake of the children, she wrote at the end of the century, black women must know more about motherhood and homemaking. Moreover, they must not isolate themselves from those less well trained, even if they had the endurance and the good fortune to acquire training themselves. "The real solution of the race problem," she said, rested with the future of the children, "both so far as we who are oppressed and those who oppress us are concerned."

> If the women of the dominant race ... feel the need of a mother's congress, that they may be enlightened upon the best methods of rearing their children and conducting their homes, how much more do our women, from whom shackles have but yesterday been stricken, need information on the same vital subjects. ...
>
> Colored women of education and culture know that ... the call of duty, ... policy and self-preservation demand that they go down among the lowly, the illiterate and even the vicious, to whom they are bound by the ties of race and sex ... to reclaim them.[33]

Throughout the century the majority of blacks suffered privations of body and mind. Women capable of leadership strove to overcome the inertia and indifference that permitted this. They aimed to ignite the American conscience. "More than the changing of institutions we need the development of a national conscience, and the upbuilding of national character," said Mrs. Harper in 1893. "It is the women of a country who help to mold its character, and to influence if not determine its destiny."

---

[33]D.W. Culp, ed., *Twentieth Century Negro Literature; or, a Cyclopedia of Thought on the Vital Topics Relating to the American Negro, by One Hundred of America's Greatest Negroes* (Naperville, Ill., and Toronto, 1902), pp. 174–75.

Rights for Blacks,
Rights for Women

Before Abraham Lincoln's proclamation of emancipation in 1863, the abolition of slavery served as the overarching objective. Abolition enlisted the unstinting support of black women, who knew that artificial barriers must first be undermined before true growth was conceivable. The campaign to wipe out slavery bound thousands of Americans together. Abolition was for them indeed the work of God. Competing assumptions separated humanitarians and reformers on issues such as the place of women, the respective function of thought and action, the part assigned to the church, the role of various levels of government and social institutions. But human slavery and the moral compulsion to eradicate it assured a unison of intent.

Black and white, men and women were linked by despair, by anger, and by compassion. They feared the wrath stored up in celestial vineyards, they feared for the safety of the Republic, and they feared for the survival of the humanist faith. Abolition was a crusade, both secular and religious. Black men and black women made the movement their own. To make their brothers—and their sisters—free was to make America free.

A distinctly feminine note was occasionally sounded. Sarah Remond, one of those who carried the abolitionist message to Britain, made a profound impression because of her color and her womanhood. In a rousing speech in Dublin the year before Sumter, she made a special plea for the female slave, "the most deplorably and helplessly wretched of human sufferers." Her femininity underscored the appeal of male abolitionists, and enhanced her mission with large audiences, for whom a woman lecturer was a new experience.[34]

Diffidence among women was dispelled when some of them openly displayed bravery. A woman lecturer supplied a model for emulation. Sojourner Truth was one example; this extraordinary woman, whose unusual height and striking vocal range made her unforgettable when she spoke,

---

[34]Ruth Bogin, "Sarah Parker Remond: Black Abolitionist from Salem," *Essex Institute Historical Collections* 110 (April 1974): 120–50. Miss Remond's Dublin speech is printed below.

inspired many by her own courage. Black women who dared to say their piece about the evils of slavery gave heart to other women. For whites, the knowledge of bondage was second-hand at best, but liberty had an intimate, a personal, and a wholly individual meaning for blacks. "I have," Sarah Remond declared in 1859 soon after reaching Britain, "been received here as a sister by white women for the first time in my life. I have been removed from the degradation which overhangs all persons of my complexion."[35]

Maria Stewart had been alerted early to the powers of leadership black women could provide. When she learned in 1831 that the editors of the new *Liberator* were ready to recruit black women in the drive to extirpate slavery, the news "fired" her "with holy zeal." Holy was in truth the word. Religion and freedom were one, and she resolved to give her life in behalf of both. "Be no longer astonished," Mrs. Stewart charged her listeners in 1833, "that God at this eventful period should raise up your own females." An identical passion gripped Nancy Prince, who offered her aid to William Lloyd Garrison and other abolitionists.

The inconsistent views on female delicacy were targets of Maria Stewart's scorn. The femininity of black women was thought to bar them, like their white sisters, from entry into public life. Yet society found the drudgery of domestic work appropriate. "Where constitutional strength is wanting, labor of this kind, in its mildest form, is painful. And doubtless many are the prayers . . . from Afric's daughters for strength to perform their work. . . . And why are not our forms as delicate, and our constitutions as slender, as yours? Is not the workmanship as curious and complete? Have pity upon us." Not race or sex, she insisted, but individual capacities should point the direction and frame the boundaries of individual growth.

Fanny Jackson Coppin reinforced this precept from years of achievement as scholar and educator. "If we have been able to accomplish anything whatever in what are considered the higher studies . . . it is an unanswerable argument for every woman's claim." A devout president of Oberlin once asked her how she was growing in grace. To this she responded that long residence at the College had succeeded in making her forget her color, but that grace grew only "as fast as the American people" would permit.

To achieve a state of grace was easier for the Coppins than for many others, but the Coppins were unwilling to accept a world without it. Fannie Barrier Williams told the members of the Congress of Representative Women in 1893, "Liberty to be all that we can be, without artificial hindrances, is a thing no less precious to us than to women generally." Women—and men as well—were endowed with an inherent right to pursue their individual fulfillment.

Advancement in the field of education and elsewhere was marred by savage reversion in the South. Violence against blacks, particularly lynch-

---

[35]Sarah P. Remond, 2 February 1859, reprinted in *Liberator* (11 March 1859) from a report in *Warrington (England) Times* (February 1859).

ing, made other gains seem hollow. Civil rights appeared meaningless if the sanctity of life remained insecure and unprotected. The right to liberty is a delusion unless the right to life is guaranteed. Black women, South and North, could not be silent. Ida Wells-Barnett, as a young teacher and journalist, observed the means by which blacks were deprived of the equal protection of the laws. Then she investigated them, and tried to acquaint her fellow citizens with them. To attempt to do so was highly courageous: outspokenness on such topics might itself carry the penalty of lynching.

Militant in her approach, she marshaled the statistics on lynching. Wherever possible she documented her evidence from reports in the white press. Men were the principal victims and rape the principal charge. Rape, she quite reasonably suggested, was not the only basis for sex relations between black men and white women. Blame was placed where she believed it belonged, and most subsequent students have agreed. Those who resorted to violence, asserted Ida Wells-Barnett, were those usually classed as the "respectable" elements of society. "Threats of lynching were freely indulged—not by the lawless element upon which the devilry of the South is usually saddled, but by the leading business men, in their leading business centre [the Cotton Exchange Building]." A contemporary wrote of her: "Being protected by the respect which man endeavors to possess for woman she has been able to touch as well as treat at length articles upon which our man editors have shown the greatest reluctance."[36]

Frances Watkins Harper, reaching much wider audiences, vigorously indicted violence, lawlessness, and social disorder. At a meeting in 1875, celebrating the centennial of Pennsylvanian abolition effort, she shared a platform with Henry Wilson, Vice President of the United States. "I do not believe," she told her audience, "there is another civilized nation under Heaven where there are half so many people who have been brutally and shamefully murdered . . . as in this republic within the last ten years." And in 1891 she appealed to the National Council of Women: "Outside of America, I know of no other civilized country, Catholic, Protestant, or even Mahometan, where men are still lynched, murdered, and even burned for real or supposed crimes. . . . A government which has power to tax a man in peace, and draft him in war, should have power to defend his life in the hour of peril."[37]

Discriminatory legislation lacerated black sensitivity. Jim Crow was the ultimate in degradation. Lynching at least ended in death; Jim Crow was the slow torture of a lifetime. These laws were variously analyzed, explained, protested. But none save blacks themselves—and representatives of other groups subjected to parallel indignities—can truly be said to have felt

---

[36]M.A. Majors, Noted Negro Women: Their Triumphs and Activities (Chicago, 1893), p. 189.

[37]Pennsylvania Society for . . . the Abolition of Slavery, Centennial, p. 30.

them. Fannie Williams in an 1893 speech in Chicago made a muted reference to the incurable wounds of humiliation: "This social quarantine on all means of travel in certain parts of the country is guarded and enforced more rigidly against us than the quarantine regulations against cholera."

Protection of life and limb logically preceded maintenance of civil rights, but violations of either one flouted the Constitutional guarantees of all men and women. Ida Wells-Barnett was a militant woman, and Jim Crow quite naturally provoked a belligerent retort. She advocated methods against Jim Crow legislation similar to the bus boycott later to be led by Martin Luther King in Montgomery, Alabama. "The Afro-American citizens of Kentucky . . . have never had a separate car law until now. . . . Will the great mass of Negroes continue to patronize the railroad?" She proposed a combination of economic actions:

> To Northern capital and Afro-American labour the South owes its rehabilitation. If labour is withdrawn capital will not remain. The Afro-American is thus the backbone of the South. . . .

> I have shown how he [the Negro] may employ the "boycott," emigration, and the Press; and I feel that by a combination of all these agencies Lynch Law—the last relic of barbarism and slavery—can be effectively stamped out. "The gods help those who help themselves."

Ida Wells-Barnett believed men and women should defend themselves against abuse, and if it could not be done singly, people should join together to maintain security and order. Should boycott, pressure, emigration, and reason fail to avail them, she was prepared to endorse sterner measures: "Of the many inhuman outrages of this present year, the only case where the proposed lynching did not occur, was where the men armed themselves. . . . The lesson this teaches, and which every Afro-American should ponder well, is that a Winchester rifle should have a place of honour in every black home, and it should be used for that protection which the law refuses to give." Whites were not to be excluded from the struggle for equal rights, for the entire community bore the moral burden for immoral acts: "The men and women in the South who disapprove of lynching and remain silent . . . are particeps criminis—accomplices."

To respond to violence with violence was not the majority sentiment. Ida Wells-Barnett represented a minority attitude. The "hands of the negro [sic]," affirmed Frances Harper, "are not dripping with dynamite. We do not read of his flaunting the red banners of anarchy . . . nor plotting . . . to overthrow existing institutions, nor spitting on the American flag. Once that flag was to him an ensign of freedom. Let our Government resolve that . . . every American-born child shall be able to read upon its folds liberty for all and chains for none." Mrs. Harper's response to the American dilemma was formulated in the same spirit that Gunnar Myrdal was to proclaim during the Second World War and that the Kerner Report was to stress still later. The alternative was a nation divided in disaster. To avoid such disaster required "new attitudes, new understanding and, above all, new will."[38]

The disaster of division was elaborated by Anna Julia Cooper.

What the dark man wants . . . is merely to live his own life, in his own world, with his own chosen companions, in whatever of comfort, luxury, or emoluments his talent or his money can in an impartial market secure. Has he wealth, he does not want to be forced into inconvenient or unsanitary sections of cities to buy a home and rear his family. . . . Has he religion, he does not want to be made to feel that there is a white Christ and a black Christ, a white Heaven and a black Heaven, a white Gospel and a black Gospel, but the one ideal of perfect manhood and womanhood, the one universal longing for development and growth.[39]

The approach of these two leaders and their colleagues in reform was the philosophy of democracy. Frances Watkins Harper stated its assumptions with prayerful conviction. Few have ever stated them better. The Kerner Report, which followed by almost a century, only repeats the Harper faith. Mrs. Harper posed what was "the great problem to be solved by the American people . . . whether or not there is strength enough in democracy, virtue enough in our civilization, and power enough in our religion to have mercy and deal justly with four millions of people but lately translated . . . to the new commonwealth of freedom." The conclusion followed inexorably from the premises: "Upon the right solution of this question depends in a large measure the future strength, progress, and durability of our nation."[40]

Black American women were persuaded that new attitudes could in fact be nurtured. They wished to awaken new understanding among blacks as well as in the general population. Will they had in overflowing measure, and likewise a limitless faith in their own powers to quicken the feelings of others as they themselves had been stirred. They could hardly feel otherwise. They were Americans. They were democrats. And they were Christians.

Christianity and its Bible were their justifications for belief, the warrant for reform. One reform was the right of women to preach. Many felt with Jarena Lee that what they had to say burned "as a fire . . . in [their] bones." To preach the gospel would bring faith, solace, and strength. Said Jarena Lee, who was unwilling to take nay for an answer from male elders of the church when she already had a powerful yea within her: "And why should it be thought impossible, heterodox, or improper for a woman to preach? seeing the Saviour died for the woman as well as for the man. . . . Is

---

[38]National Advisory Commission on Civil Disorders, Report . . . [Preliminary Kerner Report](New York, 1968), p. 2. Gunnar Myrdal directed an earlier study culminating in a massive report, The American Dilemma, 2 vols. (New York, 1944).

[39]Cooper, Voice, pp. 112–13.

[40]For both quotations, see Pennsylvania Society for . . . the Abolition of Slavery, Centennial, pp. 29–30.

he not a whole Saviour, instead of a half one? as those who hold it wrong for a woman to preach, would seem to make it appear."

Amanda Berry Smith, showing an aptitude for this calling, met with the determined opposition of males within the church, but she preferred to bypass her opponents rather than confront them directly. She made her way from New York to Nashville in 1872 to attend the General Conference of the African Methodist Episcopal Church. The delegates and their ladies regarded her with unmasked apprehension, and she was greeted with something less than gracious welcome. "I was quite a curiosity to most of the visitors, especially the Southern brethren, in my very plain Quaker dress; I was eyed with suspicion as being there to agitate the question of the ordination of women." If the churchmen and their wives expected a tumultuous episode, they were disappointed. Amanda Smith did not attempt to argue the question of female ordination. Gifted with an extraordinarily moving voice and already well known among choral groups, she was recognized by some of the Fisk Jubilee singers. Instead of agitating, she sang. The music of her voice charmed the ministers and dissolved their fears. She was a woman with an innate sense of the occasion and her magnificent voice expressed her awareness of inner power.

The issue of women as preachers and ministers agitated both black and white religious organizations intermittently throughout the nineteenth century and into our own era. In 1891 a black bishop of the A.M.E. Zion Church proudly asserted that his denomination "guarantees to women all rights in common with men."[41]

Black women were thwarted by exclusion not only from professions like the ministry, but also from employment even in the comparatively restricted areas open to white women. "It is almost literally true," Fannie Barrier Williams reported as the century was ending, that "except teaching in colored schools and menial work, colored women can find no employment in this free America." This condition of affairs prompted her to ask: "Are these women not as thoroughly American in all the circumstances of citizenship as the best citizens of our country?" Whites, she inferred, feared social equality as the ultimate danger, which explained discrimination against black women.

The system of caste was overcome by some black women through their own efforts. They acquired responsibility, competence, and initiative. Generosity, self-discipline, steadfastness in the face of adversity were among the creative qualities black women brought into their own lives and the lives of those around them.

Elleanor Eldridge, free-born in antebellum New England, served as informal apprentice for five years in a prosperous family for whom her mother once worked. She became adept at all kinds of domestic activity,

---

[41]Bishop J.W. Hood, quoted in William J. Walls, The African Methodist Episcopal Zion Church: Reality of the Black Church (Charlotte, N.C., 1974), p. 479.

especially the art of spinning, including ornamental weaving. When she reached the age of sixteen she moved to another home. Here she performed at the loom for a year, when the labors of the dairy were entrusted to her. The extent of her management during eight years was considerable; she milked "from twenty-five to thirty cows" and made vast quantities of cheese. With this backlog of experience she was ready to engage in other enterprises. Together with a sister she began a business of weaving, spinning, nursing, and soap boiling. A careful entrepreneur, she saved enough to build a small house, which she rented. Her money invested, she moved to another city to enter into the trade of whitewashing, papering, and painting.

Initiative is but another name for determination. In the era of the plantation, skills such as these, or hard labor without skills, bought freedom, made good an escape, or lessened the dangers of existence. Then as now, the hoarding of pennies converted fantasies into realities for children, kinfolk, and friends. Unless an unforeseen calamity consumed the savings of years, it made the difference between futility and some form of change. Black women free enough to wield the privilege of leadership taught the virtue of independence. The virtue was not prized solely as an end in itself; it was what could be accomplished by means of independence.

Maria Stewart, in the 1830s, designed a program for free black women. "Do you ask, what can we do? Unite and build a store of your own. . . . Fill one side with dry goods, and the other with groceries. . . . Possess the spirit of independence. The Americans do, and why should not you?" Two black women born just after the Civil War gained prominence through economic leadership. Maggie Lena Walker became an insurance and banking executive in Richmond, Virginia, combining her business activities with fraternal and civic concerns. Sarah Breedlove Walker, better known as Madame C.J. Walker, devised a method of hair treatments for blacks who sought smooth hair styles; she developed the method and the manufacture of hair products into a million-dollar business, centered in Indianapolis but known throughout the United States and beyond.[42]

For black leaders, no reform seemed as promising as training itself. Education appeared as an answer both to immediate practical needs and to future progress. The antebellum struggle to acquire even a modicum of education, North or South, was arduous almost beyond belief. Some women described how they began their education. Amanda Berry Smith had her first training at home after her father had bought his family's freedom.

Father was the better reader. . . . Always on Sunday morning after breakfast he would call us children around and read the Bible to us. . . . I first taught myself to read by cutting out large letters from the newspapers my father would bring home. Then I would lay them on the window

---

[42]For brief summaries of their careers, see *Notable American Women*, III, 530–31 and 533–35.

[presumably the deep window sill of a Pennsylvania farm house] and ask mother to put them together for me to make words, so that I could read.

To learn one's letters, to conquer the alphabet, and to master reading was a triumph of fortunate circumstances. Amanda Smith had the good fortune to possess a parent with the blessing of literacy and the blessing of solicitude for a child's tomorrows. Another common pattern for elementary learning was the chance discovery of a willing mistress, another child's friendship, or the possibility of tutelage.

The preliminary stages of Frances Jackson Coppin's schooling were attained within similar chance happenings. An aunt in New Bedford, Massachusetts, "put me out to work at a place where I was allowed to go to school when I was not at work. But I could not go on wash day, nor ironing day, nor cleaning day, and this interfered with my progress." When she was fourteen and living in Newport, Rhode Island, she took a place with the Calvert family, which permitted an hour "every other afternoon in the week to take some private lessons. . . . After that, I attended for a few months the public colored school. . . . I thus prepared myself to enter . . . the Rhode Island State Normal School." To dream of a career, such as average white boys and white girls took for granted, entailed hard choices for a black youngster. Frances Coppin had to leave her employer who had warmly supported her ambition. Actually there was no real alternative: the life of service for which she yearned demanded unremitting academic work. Oberlin, already a pioneer toward equality, admitted her and she added luster to its proud record. "I never rose to recite in my classes at Oberlin but I felt that I had the honor of the whole African race upon my shoulders. . . . It was in me to get an education and to teach my people. . . . It must have been born in me."

Susie King Taylor's adventures in ideas were simpler when acquired, but more complex in achievement. Allowed to live with her free grandmother in Savannah, she contrived as a little slave girl to circumvent the laws against the education of bondsmen. "We were sent to a friend of my grandmother. . . . We went every day about nine o'clock, with our books wrapped in paper to prevent the police or white persons from seeing them. We went in, one at a time. . . . She had twenty-five or thirty children whom she taught." Ways were quickly found to supplement such primitive beginnings.

I had a white playmate . . . who lived on the next corner . . . and who attended a convent. One day she told me, if I would promise not to tell her father, she would give me some lessons. On my promise not to do so, and getting her mother's consent, she gave me lessons about four months, every evening. . . . Our landlord's son . . . was attending the High School, and was very fond of grandmother, so she asked him to give me a few lessons, which he did until the middle of 1861.

In the early days of Reconstruction, Annie Burton, then about six, was adopted into the white family of a music teacher who was the wife of a lawyer and the daughter-in-law of a former judge. The care of their little daughter was placed in her hands. She was sent to Sunday school where she acquired the ability to read, and her mistress instructed her in writing "at her knee." When she reached her early twenties, and with the added duty of caring for her own three young sisters and brothers, she went to live with "a colored woman, who adopted me and gave me her name. . . . While living with her, I went six months to Lewis' High School in Macon." At the age of forty-four, with desire and energy unabated, she enrolled in the Franklin School in Boston where evening classes were conducted.[43]

Educators like Fanny Coppin accented the urgency of industrial training for black youth threatened by unemployment and disenchantment with life. Shifts in population from the plantation to urban centers, including her own Philadelphia, affected whites and blacks in all sections of the country. Continuing migrations made Detroit, Chicago, and New York, as well as Atlanta, Nashville, and New Orleans the centers of black endeavor.[44] The metamorphosis of the blacks from a rural to an urban minority altered their predicament and that of American society. In the Philadelphia of Fanny Coppin's day (1879), "the only place a colored boy could learn a trade was in the House of Refuge, or the Penitentiary."

Mrs. Coppin offered explicit suggestions. "We should," she admonished, "make known to the good men and women who are so solicitous for our souls and our minds that we haven't quite got rid of our bodies yet, and until we do we must feed and clothe them." She would have black youth look to industrial employment as a first practical step. She approvingly quoted Frederick Douglass, who said it was easier "to get a colored boy into a lawyer's office than into a blacksmith's shop." The "inflexibility of the Trades Unions" were to blame, and it would be necessary "for us to have our own 'blacksmith shop,' " said Douglass. Accordingly, an industrial department was added at the Institute for Colored Youth of which Mrs. Coppin was the head. She never maintained that qualified boys and girls should not pursue academic programs, but she thought industrial education was expedient to meet a temporary emergency.

---

[43]The quotations are from Annie L. Burton, *Memories of Childhood's Slavery Days* (Boston, 1909), pp.13 and 17. Sabbath school often served as the sole approach to literacy for whites as well as for blacks, in both urban and rural settings. Catherine Ferguson, a former slave, is said to have been the moving force behind the Sabbath school of the Murray Street Church, the first such endeavor in New York City. Abigail Mott, *Narratives of Colored Americans* (New York, 1875), pp. 69–73.

[44]Fannie M. Richards, daughter of a free black family that migrated from Virginia to Detroit in 1851 when she was only ten, grew up to become a prominent educator in her adopted city; after segregated schooling was abolished in 1871 she taught mixed classes until her retirement in 1915. W.B. Hartgrove, "The Story of Maria Louise Moore and Fannie M. Richards," *Journal of Negro History* 1 (January 1916): 23–33.

Rural populations, of course, had their own continuing educational needs in this same period. Rural black women commanded the attention of a leading black minister in 1883. "A true civilization," said Dr. Alexander Crummell, "can only . . . be attained when the life of woman is reached." His speech was published as a pamphlet entitled *The Black Woman of the South: Her Neglects and her Needs*, of which half a million copies were circulated. Though he ardently endorsed higher education, a more basic step was essential, "the domestic training of the MASSES . . . the raising up [of] women meet to be the helpers of *poor* men, the RANK AND FILE of black society, all through the rural districts of the South."[45]

But Mrs. Coppin's flexible conception of education was remarkably foresighted. Learning was a process as diverse as people were different. Individual and social conditions altered, and needs changed. Backgrounds were not identical, and inner urges and desires were not the same. One person's goal was not shared by others. Women were not men. Scornful critics raised the question, "Why educate woman—what will she do with it?" Mrs. Coppin's answer took the form of another question: "What will she be with it?" Her response implied that women or men, blacks or whites, will try to become all that they can be. This was the function of education in a free society. Education was of many types and many levels, including self-education, for those capable of pursuing it.

Few champions of black womanhood were as persuasive as Anna Julia Cooper. Women in every sector, she insisted repeatedly, were entitled to equal consideration with men. A highly educated woman herself, she was anxious that other women of her race share the rewards of learning. She crossed debating swords with certain black clergymen who granted women something less than an even chance for knowledge. Black males, like white males, endorsed conventional standards. She was convinced that there was much work other than so-called women's work for which women had peculiar aptitudes.

> That great social and economic questions await her interference, that she could throw any light on problems of national import, that her intermeddling could improve the management of school systems, or elevate the tone of public institutions, or humanize and sanctify the far reaching influence of prisons and reformatories and improve the treatment of lunatics and imbeciles . . . I fear the majority of "Americans of the colored variety" are not yet prepared to concede.[46]

She did not wish to curtail higher education for males. Her motto was "not the boys less, but the girls more." She shrewdly identified the logic be-

---

[45]Alexander Crummell, *Africa and America: Addresses and Discourses* (Springfield, Mass., 1891), p. 82.

[46]Cooper, *Voice*, p. 135.

neath male hostility as more appropriate to the sixteenth century than the nineteenth.

Achievements of the talented and well-placed few were not enough. Anna Julia Cooper looked to the elevation of the many, and addressed the average woman instead of those especially privileged. To a group of black clergymen in Washington, she said in 1886 that "no man can represent the race." However celebrated, however noble or revered, no one could by himself vindicate the black people, given "the actual status of the race in America today. . . . Not by pointing to sun-bathed mountain tops do we prove that Phoebus warms the valleys. We must point to homes, average homes. . . . Only the BLACK WOMAN can say 'when and where I enter, in the quiet, undisputed dignity of my womanhood, without violence and without suing or special patronage, then and there the whole Negro race enters with me.' "[47]

There was progress. At the end of the century, Fannie Barrier Williams reported that "the mental development of the colored women as well as men has been little less than phenomenal. In twenty-five years, and under conditions discouraging in the extreme, thousands of our women have been educated as teachers." But these gains were only a beginning. They established the preconditions for further goals. Reform and struggle, rehabilitation and repair are without end. Mrs. Williams's hopes were disciplined by sanity and wisdom. "Today they feel strong enough to ask for but one thing . . . the same opportunity for the acquisition of all kinds of knowledge that may be accorded to other women. . . . Our women are ambitious to be contributors to all the great moral and intellectual forces that make for the greater weal of our common country."

The ambitions of black women as expressed by this sturdy woman were simply to provide living space for the will to grow and the desire to serve, the acknowledgment of black women as mature and responsible human beings.

---

[47]Ibid., pp. 30–31.

The Solidarity
of Humankind

Humanism in Afro-American life is the counterpart of American humanism. The history of black women is part of a larger whole. "We take our stand," Anna Julia Cooper proclaimed, "on the solidarity of humanity, the oneness of life. . . . Women's wrongs are . . . linked with all undefended woe." Black women did not acquire a knowledge of pain and sorrow vicariously. Fear and uncertainty, their lot in bondage, were no less their portion in freedom. "Long suffering has so chastened them that they are developing a special sense of sympathy for all who . . . fail of justice," said Fannie Barrier Williams. There was no hint of exclusiveness in the posture of black women reformers. They stood squarely for all mankind. "The cause of freedom is not the cause of a race or a sect, a party or a class—it is the cause of human kind, the very birthright of humanity."[48] If black American women in the forefront of reform were to have their way, the American promise would have been honored as much in deeds as in words.

Freedom was the ideal, before emancipation and after, in America and elsewhere. Maria Stewart took note of the European nationalist uprisings of the 1830s: "All the nations of the earth are crying out for Liberty and Equality. Away, away with tyranny and oppression!" She berated her fellow Americans who gave aid and comfort to the oppressed outside the country, but ignored oppression within it. "We know that you are raising contributions to aid the gallant Poles . . . you have befriended Greece and Ireland; and . . . rejoiced with France, for her heroic deeds of valor. You have acknowledged all the nations of the earth, except Hayti."

Black women addressed mankind. They spoke to all America about America: its issues, its evils, its meanings. They were partisans of every aspect of democratic reform: human rights, women's rights, black rights, the right to work, to vote, and to study. But they had a special mandate and a special trust. They were above all the spokeswomen for the essence of femininity: the pristine right of women to be women, the freedom to struggle toward the most complete development of their total selves. Femininity was

---

[48]Ibid., pp. 120–21.

for them the creative biological and psychological legacy of womankind. As such it was a means to nurture individual and social aims. The right of women to be women in every act of their lives implied a conscious and purposive cultivation of femaleness. It was a right sanctified by religious precept and by the philosophy of democracy.

The credo of femininity was articulated by Frances Watkins Harper during her address, "Woman's Political Future," delivered at the Congress of Representative Women. "The world has need of all the spiritual aid that woman can give for the social advancement and moral development of the human race." And Anna Julia Cooper's vision of the feminine calling is unparalleled in the literature of nineteenth-century black women. Subtle, learned, and unequivocal, she made precise the conditions which deprived civilization of women's substance. Wisdom and knowledge were of diverse kinds, and the male view taken alone was a distortion. To add women's attributes, women's experience, and women's knowledge would merely complete the "circle of the world's vision." While "it is no fault of man's that he has not been able to see truth" from a feminine standpoint, mankind "has had to limp along with the wobbling gait and one-sided hesitancy of a man with one eye."[49] Such astigmatism was curable by removing the blindfold from the other eye. Then, and only then, one would see a circle where before one could only see a segment. Both segments were needful for telling insights. "There is a feminine as well as a masculine side to truth . . . related not as inferior and superior, not as better and worse, not as weaker and stronger, but as complements . . . in one necessary and symmetric whole."

---

[49] Ibid., pp.121–23.

I

"TO KNIT TOGETHER
THE BROKEN TIES
OF FAMILY KINSHIP"

Affection and legality are hardly identical. Yet historians and social scientists have often entangled the two. To black and white scholars alike, the special aspects of legality regarding slave relationships have long produced confusion. Even the patterns existing outside the confines of slavery have been studied, until fairly recently, with inadequate or erroneous concepts. Current scholars are reassessing the evidence. New approaches for understanding the history of the black family are now beginning to take shape.

The women included in this volume testify to the presence of robust bonds of affection. Close companionship or long-sought reunions gave heightened meaning to individual lives, though death, sale, or employment starting in early childhood meant painful separations. Some wrote about these private areas of living yet gave more emphasis to other facets of existence. The stories of the eight women in this opening section reveal the intensity, variety, and significance of kinship ties.

Silvia Dubois

"I struck her a hell of a blow with my fist," recalled Silvia Dubois, and then she ran away. Silvia Dubois was a slave; the recipient of the blow was her mistress, a mean and impetuous woman who had treated Silvia cruelly. Slaves must have struck many blows, but the strikers were not always able to flee. Silvia, however, was an unusually large and powerful woman. She weighed over 200 pounds and stood five feet ten inches tall. In addition, the husband of the mistress was away on grand jury duty, and the score between the two women was an old and festering one.

The relationship between master and slave was unnatural. The language of the law, impersonal and relatively clear, defied the wisdom of the ages and the most elementary psychological insights. The prospect of violent eruption was latent in the bond, a prospect written into the most ancient laws and into the southern slave codes. Such eruptions, when confined to words, were usually monologues; the master or the overseer alone spoke. The response of the servant was silence, an inner contest of endurance no scale yet devised can accurately measure or record. If the soliloquy of the slave had been transmuted into dialogue, the range of probable consequences was certain. Docility, like physical strength, was a prime slave virtue, and methods were devised to encourage the one and to perpetuate the other. Deviations do not prove the rule; they suggest it. This particular fracas between slave and mistress, instead of bringing severe punishment, brought Silvia her freedom.

The circumstances of the Dubois case were exceptional. She was born in New Jersey about 1768, the offspring of slave parents, each of whom was the property of a different owner. Not confined to a plantation or to a small southern town, she was in the service of a small farmer in Pennsylvania in a region then considered frontier. Her master farmed his own land and also operated a tavern located at a ferry on the Susquehanna. As a woman of great bulk and one "willing to use her strength," she performed unusual work with ease; she often did work conventionally regarded as a man's. Once she took part in a local brawl. Without taking sides, she interposed her strength against anyone disposed to resume fighting. Her prowess gave her a sense of being both figuratively and literally above the fray. But the temperament of her mistress goaded her to sheer hate, and her feelings were no longer a matter of meditated choice. The master was not oblivious to his wife's unkindliness and conceivably had himself been the victim of her uncontrollable unpleasantness. When he returned, he separated Silvia from his wife and ended her slavery. "He told me," said Silvia many years later, "that . . . if I would take my child and go to New Jersey . . . he would give me free[dom]."

The biography of Silvia Dubois, published in 1883, was put together by a physician fascinated by the elderly inhabitants of his region. Dr. C.W. Larison asked for the privilege of interviewing her. She willingly consented, and he took down her story, later printed in "diacritic type following phonic orthography," another of the doctor's passions. His orthographic passion was likely to discourage any but the most curious readers. Silvia could not have been less interested in the type of her book, and when asked for permission to publish, she replied, "Most of folks think that niggers han't no account; but, if you think what I tell you is worth publishing, I will be glad if you do it. . . . I've lived a good while, and have seen a good deal." She had indeed seen much and had much to tell. The book, 124 pages in length, is a valuable document even when allowance is made for the unconscious adornment of memory.

Silvia Dubois's father was a veteran of the American Revolution. He served as a fifer and took part in the Battle of Princeton. If loyal service to his country gave him his freedom, it is not recorded, but he did nothing to extricate his wife and child from bondage. Her mother made repeated attempts to "buy her time" by mortgaging herself against a loan. She was unable to meet the payments as they accrued, thus becoming the slave of her creditor. One of these transactions separated the mother from her child, Silvia later being moved to Pennsylvania.

A formidable woman with a character of her own, Silvia was as courageous as she was colorful. With the obnoxious former mistress behind her, she made her way to freedom, carrying the baby in her arms. Her journey took her through primitive forests and across inhospitable rivers. When challenged at one place by a white man who demanded a pass, she bluntly refused to identify herself. "I'm no man's nigger," she retorted defiantly. "I belong to God." Fortunately, she grew up among Old Scotch Presbyterians whose theological precepts she appropriated. "He sends to you," she said of God, "whatever He wants you to have, and you've got to take it, and make the best of it." Silvia believed in this principle. Yet she needed the principle less than the experiences of her life and the will to survive in spite of them. "I've always got along somehow, and I always will —but sometimes it's pretty damned hard sledding."[1]

---

[1]C. Wilson Larison, *Silvia Dubois. (Now 116 Years Old.) A Biography of the Slave who Whipped Her Mistress and Gained Her Freedom* . . . (Ringoes, N.J., 1883), pp. 63, 32, 65, 37, 70, and 93, respectively.

Have you always lived on this mountain, Silvia?
No. I was born on this mountain in an old tavern that used to stand near the Rock Mills; it stood upon the land now owned by Richard Scott. The old hotel was owned and kept by Richard Compton; it was torn down a long while ago, and now you can't tell the spot on which it stood. My parents were slaves; and when my master moved down to Neshanic, I went along with them; and, when my master went to Great Bend [Pa.], on the Susquehanna, I went with him there. Afterwards I lived in New Brunswick, and in Princeton, and in other places. I came back to the mountain because I inherited a house and lot of land, at my father's death. That's what brought me back to the mountain.

Who was your father?
My father was Cuffee Bard, a slave to John Bard. He (Cuffee) was a fifer in the battle of Princeton. He used to be a fifer for the Minute Men, in the days of the Revolution.

Who was your mother?
My mother was Dorcas Compton, a slave to Richard Compton, the proprietor of the hotel, at Rock Mills. When I was two years old, my mother bought her time of Richard Compton, Minical Dubois going her security for the payment of the money. As my mother failed to make payment at the time appointed, she became the property of Minical Dubois. With this failure to make payment, Dubois was greatly disappointed and much displeased, as he did not wish to fall heir to my mother and her children, as slaves to him. So he treated mother badly—often times cruelly. On one occasion, when her babe was but three days old, he whipped her with an ox-gad, because she didn't hold a hog while he yoked it; it was in March; the ground was wet and slippery, and the hog proved too strong for her, under the circumstances. From the exposure and the whipping, she became severely sick with puerperal fever; but after a long while she recovered.

Under the slave laws of New Jersey, when the slave thought the

Source: C. Wilson Larison, *Silvia Dubois. (Now 116 Years Old.) A Biography of the Slave who Whipped Her Mistress and Gained Her Freedom, as told to C.W. Larison,* M.D. (Ringoes, N.J., 1883), pp. 43–52, 59, 62–65, 69–71. This book was set in diacritic type based on phonetic spelling. The portions excerpted have been rendered into standard spelling and customary type by the editors. Minor changes in punctuation have also been incorporated. For greater clarity, the questions of the interviewer are italicized. Although the interviewer claims to have written the responses "exactly as she related the facts to me," there are intermittent instances of sophisticated vocabulary undoubtedly supplied by Dr. Larison himself. All footnotes are the editors'.

master too severe, and the slave and the master did not get along harmoniously, the slave had a right to hunt a new master.[1] Accordingly, my mother Dorcas went in quest of a new master; and, as Mr. William Bard [the relationship between this man and John Bard, master of Silvia's father, is not made clear] used to send things for her and her children to eat, when Dubois neglected or refused to furnish enough to satisfy their craving stomachs, she asked him (Bard) to buy her. This he did. And she liked him well; but she was ambitious to be free. Accordingly, she bought her time of Bard, but failed to make payment, and returned to him his slave.

She was then sold to Miles Smith, who was a kind master, and a good man. But she was ambitious to be free—so, of Smith she bought her time, and went away to work, and to live with strangers. But, as she had failed to make payment at the appointed time, she was taken back a slave, and spent the remainder of her days with him, and was buried about 45 years ago upon his homestead.[2]

Of course, I remained a slave to Minical Dubois. He did not treat me cruelly. I tried to please him, and he tried to please me; and we got along together pretty well—excepting sometimes I would be a little refractory, and then he would give me a severe flogging. When I was about five years old, he moved upon a farm near the village of Flagtown. While there I had good times—aplenty to eat, aplenty of clothes, and aplenty of fun—only my mistress was terribly passionate, and terribly cross to me. I did not like her, and she did not like me; so she used to beat me badly. On one occasion, I did something that did not suit her. As usual, she scolded me. Then I was saucy. Hereupon, she whipped me until she marked me so badly that I will never lose the scars. You can see the scars here on my head, today; and I will never lose them, if I live another hundred years.

When I was about ten years old, the battle of Monmouth occurred [28 June 1778]. I remember very well when my master come home from that battle. Cherries were ripe, and we were gathering harvest. He was an officer; but I do not know his rank. He told great stories about the battle, and of the bravery of the New Jersey militia; and about the conduct of General Washington. He said they whipped the British badly—but it was a desperate fight. He told us that the battle occurred on the hottest day he ever saw; he said he came near perishing from the excess of heat and from thirst; and that a great many did die from want of water.

I also remember when my father and others returned from the battles of Trenton and Princeton [26 December 1776 and 3 January 1777], but I was

---

[1]This practice, while not infrequent, was not actually mandated by New Jersey law. See Arthur Zilversmit, *The First Emancipation: The Abolition of Slavery in the North* (Chicago, 1967), p. 29.

[2]Slavery was not entirely abolished in New Jersey until 1846. Silvia's mother may well have remained a slave throughout her life, if she died around 1838 as Silvia's recollection would indicate.

younger then, and only remember that it was winter, and that they complained that they had suffered so much from cold and exposure.

Before the battle of Princeton, my master had been a prisoner of war. He had been captured while fighting on the water, somewhere near New York. I used to hear him tell how he and several others were crowded into a very small room in a hold of a vessel—the trap-door securely fastened down, and the supply of fresh air so completely shut off, that almost all who were thus imprisoned, died in a few hours. In this place they were kept two days. Dubois, by breathing with his mouth in close contact with a nail-hole, held out until he was removed. Two or three others were fortunate enough to find some other defect in the wood-work, through which a scanty supply of air came.

When I was in my fourteenth year, my master moved from Flagtown to his farm along the Susquehanna River. This farm is the land on which the village called Great Bend has been built. When we moved upon the farm, there was but one other house in the settlement for the distance of several miles. These two houses were built of logs. The one upon my master's farm had been kept as a tavern; and when he moved into it, he kept it as a tavern. The place was known as Great Bend. It was an important stopping place for travelers on their way to the Lake Countries, and to other places westward. Also, it was a place much visited by boatmen going down and up the river. Here, too, came great numbers of hunters and drovers. In fact, even in these days, Great Bend was an important place.

In moving to Great Bend, we went in two wagons. We took with us two cows; these I drove all the way there. After we crossed the Delaware at Easton, the road extended through a great forest, with only here and there a clear patch, and a small log hut. Even the taverns were only log huts, sometimes with but one room downstairs and one upstairs. Then there would be two or three beds in the room upstairs, and one in the room downstairs.

The great forest was called the Beech Woods. It was so big that we was six days in going through it. Sometimes we would go a half day without passing a house, or meeting a person. The woods was full of bears, panthers, wildcats and the like. About these I had heard a great many wild stories. So I made sure to keep my cows pretty close to the wagon.

Usually, we stopped overnight at a hotel. But, as the houses were small, often it would happen that others had stopped before we arrived, and the lodging rooms would all be occupied. Then we would sleep in our wagons, or in the out-buildings. In those days, travelers had to get along the best way they could.

As my master saw that the site upon which he lived was favorable to business, during the third summer after our arrival, he erected a large new frame house—the first house, not built of logs, in Great Bend. Then he began to do a large business, and became a very prominent man there, as he was while he lived in New Jersey.

Already several people had moved to the neighborhood, had erected log houses, cleared the land, and began to cultivate fields and raise stock. Very soon, in the village, storehouses and mills were built. Indeed, Great Bend began to be the center of a large and thriving settlement.

At this time hunters used to come to this point to trade; to sell deer meat, bear meat, wild turkeys and the like, and to exchange the skins of wild animals for such commodities as they wished. At our tavern, they used to stay; and they were a jolly set of fellows; I liked to see them come—there was fun then.

There was a ferry across the Susquehanna at Great Bend. The boat upon our side was owned by my master; the one upon the other side was owned by Captain Hatch. I soon learned to manage the boat as well as any one could, and often used to ferry teams across alone. The folks who were acquainted with me, used to prefer me to take them across, even when the ferrymen were about. But Captain Hatch did not like me. I used to steal his customers. When I landed my boat upon his side, if anybody was there that wanted to come over to the Bend, before he knew it, I would hurry them into my boat and push off from the shore, and leave him swearing. You see the money I got for fetching back a load was mine; and I stole many a load from old Hatch; I always did, every time I could.

Along with the ferry boat, always were one or two skiffs. These we took along to have in readiness in case of accident. When the load was heavy, or when it was windy, two or more ferrymen were required. At such times, I would help them across, but I always come back alone in a skiff. In this way I got so that I could handle the skiff first rate, and was very fond of using it. Oftentimes I used to take single passengers over the ferry in a skiff; sometimes two or more at once. This I liked, and they used to pay me well to do it. I had a good name for managing the skiff. They used to say that in using the skiff I could beat any man on the Susquehanna, and I always did beat all that raced with me.

Oftentimes when the ferrymen were at dinner, someone would come to the ferry to cross. They would hullo to let us know that some one wanted to cross. Then there would be a race. I'd skip out, and down to the wharf so soon that I'd have 'em loaded and pushed off before anyone else could get there—and then I'd get the fee. I tell you, if they did not chuck knife and fork, and run at once, 'twas no use—they couldn't run with me—the fee was gone. I've got many a shilling that way, and many a good drink, too. . . .

Was your master willing that you should cheat the ferryman out of his fees in that way?
. . . He did not care; he thought I was smart for doing it. And sometimes, if I had not been in the habit of hurrying things up in this way, people would have waited at the ferry by the hour, but you see they didn't have to wait when I was about, and this is why they liked me, and why my master liked me, too. . . .

Well; your mistress was always kind to you, wasn't she?

Kind to me; why, she was the very devil himself. Why, she'd level me with anything she could get hold of—club, stick of wood, tongs, fire-shovel, knife, ax, hatchet; anything that was handiest; and then she was so damned quick about it, too. I tell you, if I intended [to] sass her, I made sure to be off aways.

Well; did she ever hit you?
Yes, often; once she knocked me till I was so stiff that she thought I was dead; once after that, because I was a little saucy, she leveled me with the fire-shovel and broke my pate. She thought I was dead then, but I wasn't.

Broke your pate?
Yes; broke my skull; you can put your fingers here, in the place where the break was, in the side of my head, yet. She smashed it right in—she didn't do things to the halves. . . .

Well, Silvia, what did your master say about such as was done by your mistress?
Say! Why he knew how passionate she was. He saw her kick me in the stomach one day so badly that he interfered. I was not grown up then; I was too young to stand such. He didn't tell her so when I was by; but, I have heard him tell her when they thought I was not listening, that she was too severe—that such work would not do—she'd kill me next.

Well, did his remonstrating with her make her any better?
Not a bit; made her worse—just put the devil in her. And then, just as soon as he was out of the way, if I was a little saucy, or a little neglectful, I'd catch hell again. But I fixed her—I paid her up for all her spunk; I made up my mind that when I grew up I would do it; and when I had a good chance, when some of her grand company was around, I fixed her.

Well, what did you do?
I knocked her down, and blamed near killed her.

Well; where and how did that happen?
It happened in the bar-room; there was some grand folks stopping there, and she wanted things to look pretty stylish; and so she set me to scrubbing up the bar-room. I felt a little grum, and didn't do it to suit her; she scolded me about it and I sassed her; she struck me with her hand. Thinks I, it's a good time now to dress you out, and damned if I won't do it; I set down my tools, and squared for a fight. The first whack, I struck her a hell of a blow with my fist. I didn't knock her entirely through the panels of the door; but her landing against the door made a terrible smash, and I hurt her so badly that all were frightened out of their wits, and I didn't know myself but that I'd killed the old devil.

[Was] there anyone in the bar-room, then?
It was full of folks; some of them were Jersey folks, who were going from the

Lake Countries home, to visit their friends; some were drovers, on their way to the west, and some were hunters and boatmen staying a while to rest.

What did they do when they saw you knock your mistress down?
Do! Why, they were going to take her part, of course; but I just sat down the slop bucket and straightened up, and smacked my fists at 'em, and told 'em to wade in, if they dared, and I'd thrash every devil of 'em; and there wasn't a damned one that dared to come.

Well, what next?
Then I got out, and pretty quick, too. I knew it wouldn't do to stay there; so I went down to Chenang Point [possibly Chenango Forks across the state line in New York]; and there went to work.

Where was your master, during this fracas?
He! He was gone to tend court at Wilkes-Barre. He was a grand-jury-man, and had to be gone a good many days. He often served as grand-jury-man, and then he was always gone a week or two. Things would have gone better if he had been home.

When he came home, what did he do?
He sent for me to come back.

Did you go?
Of course, I did, I had to go; I was a slave, and if I didn't go, he would have brought me, and in a hurry, too; in those days, the masters made the niggers mind; and when he spoke, I knew I must obey.

Them old masters, when they got mad, had no mercy on a nigger—they'd cut a nigger all up in a hurry—cut 'em all up into strings, just leave the life—that's all; I've seen 'em do it, many a time.

Well, what did your master say when you came back?
He didn't scold me much; he told me that, as my mistress and I got along so badly, if I would take my child and go to New Jersey, and stay there, he would give me free; I told him I would go. It was late at night; he wrote me a pass, gave it to me, and early the next morning I set out for Flagtown, New Jersey. . . .

How did you go to Flagtown?
On foot, to be sure; I came right down through the Beech Woods, all alone, excepting my young one in my arms; sometimes I didn't see a person for half a day; sometimes I didn't get half enough to eat, and never had any bed to sleep in; I just slept anywhere. My baby was about a year and a half old, and I had to carry it all the way. The wood was full of panthers, bears, wildcats and wolves; I often saw 'em in the daytime, and always heard 'em howling in the night. Oh! that old panther—when he howled, it made the hair stand up all over my head.

At Easton, I went on board of a raft to go down the Delaware. A man by the name of Brink had his wife and family on board of a raft, bound for Philadelphia; I went on board to help the wife, for my passage; they were nice folks, and I had a good time; I left the raft not far from Trenton, but I do not know exactly where—there was no town at the place at which I got off the raft.

Then I proceeded directly to Flagtown, to see my mother; I did not find her there—she had moved to New Brunswick. On my way, a man called to me, asking me, "Whose nigger are you?" I replied, I'm no man's nigger—I belong to God—I belong to no man.

He then said: Where are you going? I replied: That's none of your business—I'm free; I go where I please.

He came toward me; I sat down my young one, showed him my fist, and looked at him; and I guess he saw 'twas no use; he mosied off, telling me that he would have me arrested as soon as he could find a magistrate.

You see that in those days, the Negroes were all slaves, and they were sent nowhere, nor allowed to go anywhere without a pass; and when anyone met a Negro who was not with his master, he had a right to demand of him whose Negro he was; and if the Negro did not show his pass, or did not give good evidence whose he was, he was arrested at once, and kept until his master came for him, paid whatever charges were made, and took him away. You see, in those days, anybody had authority to arrest vagrant Negroes. They got paid for arresting them, and charged for their keeping till their master redeemed them. But, he didn't arrest me—not a bit.

When I got to New Brunswick, I found my mother; soon after, I went to work, and remained in New Brunswick several years.

Cornelia

A close family unit is depicted in this narrative by a former slave. On the small farm where Cornelia (she gave no further name) was born in Tennessee, each family occupied its own cabin. The legal right of the master to disrupt these households, though ever present, was seldom invoked. Cornelia lived with her father and mother, three younger children, and her mother's aunt who had never married and had no children. The father was handy at all the skills required on the premises; he was a good provider for his family through gardening and hunting permitted on his own time. The mother, as the child remembered her, was able at everything from housework to field work. Together the parents devised a variety of means, some of them on the sly, to augment their diet and improve their life.

The interview with Cornelia was conducted in 1929 or 1930 by a Fisk University sociologist as part of a large-scale study of the experiences and recollections of elderly men and women who had begun their lives as slaves. Not necessarily reflecting precise historical truth, the narratives are valid in revealing the experiential world of the persons interviewed. Cornelia's reconstruction of a network of significant relationships presents her own awareness of distinct personalities and the circumstances in which they were shaped. The anguish of a lengthy separation from her parents and its happy conclusion remained vivid across a span of many decades.

I began to exist in the year 1844, in a small town in Tennessee. Eden, Tennessee, was between Nashville and Memphis, and was located on a branch of the Memphis River. There were no more than four hundred people there, including the slaves. There was a post office, two stores and a hotel in the town. The hotel was owned by Mr. Dodge, who was the uncle of my master.

Source: Cornelia, "My Mother was the Smartest Black Woman in Eden," *Unwritten History of Slavery: Autobiographical Accounts of Negro Ex-Slaves*, ed. by Ophelia Settle Egypt, J. Masuoka, and Charles S. Johnson, Social Science Source Documents No. 1, Fisk University Social Science Institute (Nashville, 1945), pp. 283–90. Mimeographed.

I was the personal property of Mr. Jennings, who was a well-polished southern man. He was portly in build, lively in step, and dignified in manner. Mr. Jennings was a good man. There was no disputing that. He seemed to always be in debt, and I reasoned that he was too easy, that people took advantage of his good nature. He had married a woman of the same mold, and they had three children.

I did not have the honor or dishonor of being born on a large plantation. Master Jennings had a small farm. We did not cultivate any cotton; we raised corn, oats, hay and fruits. Most of Master Jennings' slaves were hired out. He had four families of slaves, that is, Aunt Caroline's family, Uncle Tom's family, Uncle Dave's family, and the family of which I was a member. None of these others were related by blood to us. My father had several brothers who lived on other places.

Aunt Caroline, a big mulatto woman, was very quiet and good-natured. I don't remember ever hearing her fuss. Each family had a cabin, and there were but four cabins on the place. Aunt Mary, my mother's aunt, stayed with us in our cabin. She had never married or had any children.

My mother was the smartest black woman in Eden. She was as quick as a flash of lightning, and whatever she did could not be done better. She could do anything. She cooked, washed, ironed, spun, nursed and labored in the field. She made as good a field hand as she did a cook. I have heard Master Jennings say to his wife, "Fannie has her faults, but she can outwork any nigger in the country. I'd bet my life on that."

My mother certainly had her faults as a slave. She was very different in nature from Aunt Caroline. Ma fussed, fought, and kicked all the time. I tell you, she was a demon. She said that she wouldn't be whipped, and when she fussed, all Eden must have known it. She was loud and boisterous, and it seemed to me that you could hear her a mile away. Father was often the prey of her high temper. With all her ability for work, she did not make a good slave. She was too high-spirited and independent. I tell you, she was a captain.

The one doctrine of my mother's teaching which was branded upon my senses was that I should never let anyone abuse me. "I'll kill you, gal, if you don't stand up for yourself," she would say. "Fight, and if you can't fight, kick; if you can't kick, then bite." Ma was generally willing to work, but if she didn't feel like doing something, none could make her do it. At least, the Jennings couldn't make, or didn't make her.

"Bob, I don't want no sorry nigger around me. I can't tolerate you if you ain't got no backbone." Such constant warning to my father had its effect. My mother's unrest and fear of abuse spread gradually to my father. He seemed to have been made after the timid kind. He would never fuss back at my mother, or if he did, he couldn't be heard above her shouting. Pa was also a sower of all seeds. He was a yardman, houseman, plowman, gardener, blacksmith, carpenter, keysmith, and anything else they chose him to be.

I was the oldest child. My mother had three other children by the time I was about six years old. It was at this age that I remember the almost daily talks of my mother on the cruelty of slavery. I would say nothing to her, but I was thinking all the time that slavery did not seem so cruel. Master and Mistress Jennings were not mean to my mother. It was she who was mean to them.

Master Jennings allowed his slaves to earn any money they could for their own use. My father had a garden of his own around his little cabin, and he also had some chickens. Mr. Dodge, who was my master's uncle, and who owned the hotel in Eden, was pa's regular customer. He would buy anything my pa brought to him; and many times he was buying his own stuff, or his nephew's stuff. I have seen pa go out at night with a big sack and come back with it full. He'd bring sweet potatoes, watermelons, chickens and turkeys. We were fond of pig roast and sweet potatoes, and the only way to have pig roast was for pa to go out on one of his hunting trips. Where he went, I cannot say, but he brought the booty home. The floor of our cabin was covered with planks. Pa had raised up two planks, and dug a hole. This was our storehouse. Every Sunday, Master Jennings would let pa take the wagon to carry watermelons, cider and ginger cookies to Spring Hill, where the Baptist Church was located. The Jennings were Baptists. The white folks would buy from him as well as the free Negroes of Trenton, Tennessee. Sometimes these free Negroes would steal to our cabin at a specified time to buy a chicken or barbecue dinner. Mr. Dodge's slaves always had money and came to buy from us. Pa was allowed to keep the money he made at Spring Hill, and of course Master Jennings didn't know about the little restaurant we had in our cabin.

One day my mother's temper ran wild. For some reason Mistress Jennings struck her with a stick. Ma struck back and a fight followed. Mr. Jennings was not at home and the children became frightened and ran upstairs. For half hour they wrestled in the kitchen. Mistress, seeing that she could not get the better of ma, ran out in the road, with ma right on her heels. In the road, my mother flew into her again. The thought seemed to race across my mother's mind to tear mistress' clothing off her body. She suddenly began to tear Mistress Jennings' clothes off. She caught hold, pulled, ripped and tore. Poor mistress was nearly naked when the storekeeper got to them and pulled ma off.

"Why, Fannie, what do you mean by that?" he asked.

"Why, I'll kill her, I'll kill her dead if she ever strikes me again."

I have never been able to find out the why of the whole thing. My mother was in a rage for two days, and when pa asked her about it and told her that she shouldn't have done it, it was all that Aunt Caroline could do to keep her from giving him the same dose of medicine.

"No explaining necessary. You are chicken-livered, and you couldn't understand." This was all ma would say about it.

Pa heard Mr. Jennings say that Fannie would have to be whipped by law. He told ma. Two mornings afterwards, two men came in at the big gate, one with a long lash in his hand. I was in the yard and I hoped they couldn't find ma. To my surprise, I saw her running around the house, straight in the direction of the men. She must have seen them coming. I should have known that she wouldn't hide. She knew what they were coming for, and she intended to meet them halfway. She swooped upon them like a hawk on chickens. I believe they were afraid of her or thought she was crazy. One man had a long beard which she grabbed with one hand, and the lash with the other. Her body was made strong with madness. She was a good match for them. Mr. Jennings came and pulled her away. I don't know what would have happened if he hadn't come at that moment, for one man had already pulled his gun out. Ma did not see the gun until Mr. Jennings came up. On catching sight of it, she said, "Use your gun, use it and blow my brains out if you will."

Master sent her to the cabin and he talked with the man for a long time. I had watched the whole scene with hands calmly clasped in front of me. I felt no urge to do anything but look on.

That evening Mistress Jennings came down to the cabin. She stopped at the door and called my mother. Ma came out.

"Well, Fannie," she said, "I'll have to send you away. You won't be whipped, and I'm afraid you'll get killed. They have to knock you down like a beef."

"I'll go to hell or anywhere else, but I won't be whipped," ma answered.

"You can't take the baby, Fannie, Aunt Mary can keep it with the other children."

Mother said nothing at this. That night, ma and pa sat up late, talking over things, I guess. Pa loved ma, and I heard him say, "I'm going too, Fannie." About a week later, she called me and told me that she and pa were going to leave me the next day, that they were going to Memphis. She didn't know for how long.

"But don't be abused, Puss." She always called me Puss. My right name was Cornelia. I cannot tell in words the feelings I had at that time. My sorrow knew no bound. My very soul seemed to cry out, "Gone, gone, gone forever." I cried until my eyes looked like balls of fire. I felt for the first time in my life that I had been abused. How cruel it was to take my mother and father from me, I thought. My mother had been right. Slavery was cruel, so very cruel.

Thus my mother and father were hired to Tennessee. The next morning they were to leave. I saw ma working around with the baby under her arms as if it had been a bundle of some kind. Pa came up to the cabin with an old mare for ma to ride, and an old mule for himself. Mr. Jennings was with him.

"Fannie, leave the baby with Aunt Mary," said Mr. Jennings very quietly.

At this, ma took the baby by its feet, a foot in each hand, and with the baby's head swinging downward, she vowed to smash its brains out before she'd leave it. Tears were streaming down her face. It was seldom that ma cried, and everyone knew that she meant every word. Ma took her baby with her.

With ma gone, there was no excitement around the place. Aunt Mary was old and very steady in her ways; Aunt Caroline was naturally quiet, and so were all the rest. I didn't have much to do around the place, and I thought about ma more than anyone around there knew. Yes, ma had been right. Slavery was chuck full of cruelty and abuse. During this time I decided to follow my mother's example. I intended to fight, and if I couldn't fight I'd kick; and if I couldn't kick, I'd bite. The children from the big house played with my brothers, but I got out of the bunch. I stopped playing with them. I didn't care about them, so why play with them. At different times I got into scraps with them. Everyone began to say, "Cornelia is the spit of her mother. She is going to be just like Fannie." And I delighted in hearing this. I wanted to be like ma now.

An uneventful year passed. I was destined to be happily surprised by the return of my mother and father. They came one day, and found me sitting by the roadside in a sort of trance. I had not seen them approaching; neither was I aware of their presence until ma spoke. Truly, I had been thinking of ma and pa at the time. I had dreams of seeing them again, but I thought that I would have to go to them. I could hardly believe that ma and pa were standing before my very eyes. I asked myself if I was still dreaming. No, I was not dreaming. They were standing over me. Ma was speaking to me.

"Puss, we've come back, me and pa, and we've come to stay."

"Oh, Ma," I exclaimed, "I was a praying to see you."

She and pa embraced and caressed me for a long time. We went to the cabin, and Master Jennings was there nearly as soon as we were.

"Hello, Fannie. How did you get along?" he asked.

"Why, Mr. Jennings, you know that I know how to get along," she answered.

"Well, I'm glad to hear that, Fannie."

Ma had on new clothes, and a pair of beautiful earrings. She told Aunt Mary that she stayed in Memphis one year without a whipping or a cross word.

Pa had learned to drink more liquor than ever, it seemed. At least, he was able to get more of it, for there were many disagreements between pa and ma about his drinking. Drinkers will drink together, and Mr. Jennings was no exception. Pa would have the excuse that Master Jennings offered him liquor, and of course he wouldn't take it from anybody else. It was common to see them together, half drunk, with arms locked, walking around and around the old barn. Then pa would put his hands behind him and let out a big whoop which could be heard all over Eden.

My temper seemed to be getting worse and worse. I was always fighting with my younger brothers, and with Aunt Caroline's kids. I went around with a chip on my shoulder all the time. Mrs. Jennings had me to nurse Ellen, her youngest child, for a while, but I was mean to her, and she stopped me. I could do plenty of work in a short time, but I had such an ugly temperament. Pa would scold me about being so mean, but ma would say, "Bob, she can't help it. It ain't her fault because she's made like that."

Our family was increased by the arrival of a baby girl. Ma was very sick, and she never did get well after that. She was cooking for Mistress Jennings one day when she came home and went to bed. She never got up. I guess ma was sick about six months. During that time she never hit a tap of work. She said she had brought five children in the world for the Jennings, and that was enough; that she didn't intend to work when she felt bad.

Louisa Picquet

When Louisa Picquet reached the age of twenty-two, she had already changed location four times. Free blacks and slaves residing in towns or cities possessed a limited mobility; otherwise movement was involuntary. The sale and resale of slaves was an economic aspect of human bondage; but there were other aspects, social, psychological, familial. Environmental hostility to family stability often made black men and women the irredeemable hostages of anonymity. Fathers, if lost in the beginning, might never be regained. Mothers, by their own pathetic but usually constricted struggles, sometimes retained or recovered some of their children. In other cases a child was restored to its mother after long separation and effort. The record of Louisa Picquet invests the history of slavery with added pathos. It is the history of a series of individual migrations, of replanted roots pulled up before fruitage, of hopeless quests for parents and family.

Louisa Picquet's mulatto mother was no more than a child herself when at fifteen she gave birth to her. The owner's wife had an infant of her own, but Louisa so much resembled her white half-sister that, for obvious reasons, the slave mother and child were sold. A Georgia cotton planter became their new master. Later, for financial reasons he ran off to Mobile, Alabama, with a few choice slaves, leaving his plantation to the mercy of creditors. Among the slaves who accompanied him were Louisa and her mother. Both were hired out to earn revenue; the mother continued to bear additional children belonging to the planter. Louisa, fourteen, worked in a boarding house where he was living. He attempted to coerce Louisa to join the ranks of his select consorts, but she managed to resist his solicitations. Before he was able to reach an inevitable conquest, he failed in business. To satisfy his creditors, under bankruptcy proceedings, Louisa was sold. While she escaped from her master, she was parted from her mother and her brother.

Louisa, now in New Orleans, became the concubine of her new owner, who was separated from his wife. The establishment consisted of three sons of his original marriage and four children of their own. The master, ill and with little left to life, promised to set her free at his death on condition that she leave for New York with her own brood. When he died she was claimed by a brother of the owner because he had advanced money toward her purchase for which he had never been repaid. Nevertheless, true to his dead brother's bond, he aided her by disposing of bits of furniture belonging to the estate. With the proceeds, she left the South. There were funds enough to reach Cincinnati in the free state of Ohio. There she met and married Henry Picquet. Picquet was a mulatto whose mother and children had been freed and sent to Cincinnati by a white Georgia father who had taken a legal wife.

During twenty years in slavery and freedom Louisa Picquet had been searching for her mother. Search for a lost slave parent or other relation was a difficult undertaking. There were no detectives for slaves to hire; records of sale did not readily yield to enslaved petitioners; whites, outside of anti-slavery communities, could not be expected to offer much help. Discovery of her mother's whereabouts opened up another series of negotiations to bring them together. Though easier than locating a missing slave, it was still an extremely arduous proceeding. With Louisa's husband as an active partner, a long and circuitous correspondence ensued and severe financial sacrifices were involved. To purchase the aging mother, a public solicitation of funds was made. Mother and daughter were finally united just before the outbreak of the Civil War.

The campaign to raise money resulted in the publication of Louisa Picquet's story. She herself was illiterate. Her account appeared following interviews between Louisa and a pastor interested in her case. The Reverend H. Mattison of the American Methodist Episcopal Church acted as her scribe. But the Reverend Mr. Mattison was prompted by other considerations than history. His tract was written as an instrument of pressure to be used at the General Conference of the denomination already under way in May 1860 at Buffalo. Mattison and others here and abroad wished the conference to take a strong antislavery stand. Thus he may have given overabundant weight to certain events, but the general authenticity of the account is not to be doubted. Louisa Picquet and the minister met after the solicitation of funds had already begun and the documentation of her narrative was compiled and completed. At most, it was a convergence of objective.

I was born in Columbia, South Carolina. My mother's name was Elizabeth. She was a slave owned by John Randolph,[1] and was a seamstress in his family. She was fifteen years old when I was born. Mother's mistress had a child only two weeks older than me. Mother's master, Mr. Randolph, was my father. So mother told me. She was forbid to tell who was my father, but

---

[1]What "John Randolph" this was, we know not; but suppose it was not the celebrated "John Randolph of Roanoke," though it may have been, and probably was, one of the same family. A gentleman in Xenia, Ohio, told Mrs. P. that if she could only make it out that her mother was one of John Randolph's slaves, there was money somewhere, now, of John Randolph's estate, to buy her mother and brother.

Source: Rev. H. Mattison, Louisa Picquet, the Octoroon: A Tale of Southern Slave Life (New York, 1861), pp. 6–53. The questions in italic type are those of Rev. Mattison.

I looked so much like Madame Randolph's baby that she got dissatisfied, and mother had to be sold. Then mother and me was sent to Georgia, and sold. I was a baby—don't remember at all, but suppose I was about two months old, may be older. . . .

Then I was sold to Georgia, Mr. Cook bought mother and me. When mother first went to Georgia she was a nurse, and suckled Madame Cook's child, with me. Afterward, she was a cook. I was a nurse. I always had plenty to do. Fast as one child would be walkin', then I would have another one to nurse.

Did your master ever whip you?
Oh, very often; sometimes he would be drunk, and real funny, and would not whip me then. He had two or three kinds of drunks. Sometimes he would begin to fight at the front door, and fight every thing he come to. At other times he would be real funny.

He was a planter, was he?
Yes; he had a large cotton plantation, and warehouse where he kept all the cotton in, and stores up the country, in a little town—Monticello [Ga.]—and then he had some in Georgia. He used to give such big parties, and every thing, that he broke up. Then his creditors came, you know, and took all the property; and then he run off with my mother and me, and five other slaves, to Mobile [Ala.], and hired us all out. He was goin' to have enough to wait on him, for he could not wait on his self. I was hired out to Mr. English. He was a real good man; I wouldn't care if I belonged to him, if I had to belong to any body. I'd like to swap Mr. Cook for him. Mr. English and his wife were very clever to me. They never whipped me. Mother had a little baby sister when we first went to Mobile—a little girl just running round. She died in Alabama. She had one before that, while she was in Georgia; but they all died but me and my brother, the oldest and the youngest.

Had she any one she called her husband while she was in Georgia?
No.

Had she in Mobile?
No.

Had she any children while she lived in Mobile?
None but my brother, the baby when we were all sold.

Who was the father of your brother, the baby you speak of?
I don't know, except Mr. Cook was. Mother had three children while Mr. Cook owned her.

Was your mother white?
Yes, she pretty white; not white enough for white people. She have long hair, but it was kind a wavy. . . .

[Louisa, first "hired out" to Mr. English, was later sent to work for a family named Bachelor, who kept a boardinghouse. Her owner, Mr. Cook, was now boarding there, having sent his wife and legitimate children to stay with her sister in Georgia. Mrs. Bachelor tried to protect the fourteen-year-old Louisa from Mr. Cook's demand, reinforced with gifts of money, that she come to his room; but Louisa's pretext of forgetting his commands led to severe whippings, and there seemed to be no escape for her. However, just at this time his bankrupt condition led to the sale of his slaves. For Louisa this meant permanent separation from her family, who had at least been in the same community, when she was sold to a Mr. Williams.]

Who was Mr. Williams?
I didn't know then, only he lived in New Orleans. Him and his wife had parted, some way—he had three children, boys. When I was going away I heard some one cryin', and prayin' the Lord to go with her only daughter, and protect me. I felt pretty bad then, but hadn't no time only to say good-bye. I wanted to go back and get the dress I bought with the half-dollars, I thought a good deal of that; but Mr. Williams would not let me go back and get it. He said he'd get me plenty of nice dresses. Then I thought mother could cut it up and make dresses for my brother, the baby. I knew she could not wear it; and I had a thought, too, that she'd have it to remember me.

It seems like a dream, don't it?
No; it seems fresh in my memory when I think of it—no longer than yester-day. Mother was right on her knees, with her hands up, prayin' to the Lord for me. She didn't care who saw her: the people all lookin' at her. I often thought her prayers followed me, for I never could forget her. Whenever I wanted any thing real bad after that, my mother was always sure to appear to me in a dream that night, and have plenty to give me, always.

Have you never seen her since?
No, never since that time. I went to New Orleans, and she went to Texas. So I understood.

Well, how was it with you after Mr. Williams bought you?
Well, he took me right away to New Orleans.

How did you go?
In a boat, down the river. Mr. Williams told me what he bought me for, soon as we started for New Orleans. He said he was getting old, and when he saw me he thought he'd buy me, and end his days with me. He said if I behave myself he'd treat me well: but, if not, he'd whip me almost to death.

How old was he?
He was over forty; I guess pretty near fifty. He was gray headed. That's the reason he was always so jealous. He never let me go out anywhere.

Did you never go to church?
No, sir; I never darken a church door from the time he bought me till after he died. I used to ask him to let me go to church. He would accuse me of some

object, and said there was more rascality done there than anywhere else. He'd sometimes say, "Go on, I guess you've made your arrangements; go on, I'll catch up with you." But I never dare go once.

Had you any children while in New Orleans?
Yes; I had four.

Who was their father?
Mr. Williams.

Was it known that he was living with you?
Everybody knew I was housekeeper, but he never let on that he was the father of my children. I did all the work in his house—nobody there but me and the children.

What children?
My children and his. You see he had three sons.

How old were his children when you went there?
I guess the youngest was nine years old. When he had company, gentlemen folks, he took them to the hotel. He never have no gentlemen company home. Sometimes he would come and knock, if he stay out later than usual time; and if I did not let him in in a minute, when I would be asleep, he'd come in and take the light, and look under the bed, and in the wardrobe, and all over, and then ask me why I did not let him in sooner. I did not know what it meant till I learnt his ways.

Were your children mulattoes?
No, sir! They were all white. They look just like him. The neighbors all see that. . . .

Well, now tell me about your life in New Orleans.
Well, when Mr. Williams bought me he told me where I was goin', to New Orleans, and what he bought me for. Then I thought of what Mrs. Cook told me; and I thought, now I shall be committin' adultery, and there's no chance for me, and I'll have to die and be lost. Then I had this trouble with him and my soul the whole time.

Did you ever say anything to him about this trouble?
Yes, sir; I told him often. Then he would dam' at it. He said he had all that to answer for himself. If I was only true to him, then I could get religion—that needn't hinder me from gettin' religion. But I knew better than that. I thought it was of no use to be prayin', and livin' in sin.

I begin then to pray that he might die, so that I might get religion; and then I promise the Lord one night, faithful, in prayer, if he would just take him out of the way, I'd get religion and be true to Him as long as I lived. If Mr. Williams only knew *that*, and get up out of his grave, he'd beat me half to death. Then it was some time before he got sick. Then, when he did get sick, he was sick nearly a year. Then he begin to get good, and talked kind to me. I could see there was a change in him. He was not all the time accusin' me of other people. Then, when I saw that he was sufferin' so, I begin to get sorry, and begin to pray that he might get religion first before he died. I felt sorry to see him die in his sins. I pray for him to have religion, when I did not have it myself. I thought if he got religion and then died, I knew that I could get religion.

It seems he did get religion, because he was so much changed in his way; but he said he wanted to see his way clearer.

Was he rich?
Oh no, sir. He had to borrow some of the money of his brother to buy me.

What kind of a house did you live in?
Why, it was a rented house. When he got up, one mornin', I got him up in a chair by the fire—it was cold weather—then he told me he was goin' to die, and that he could not live; and he said that if I would promise him that I would go to New York, he would leave me and the children free. He was then writin' to a table—had a little table to the side of him. Then he told me how to conduct myself, and not to live as I had lived with him, with any person. He told me to come out this way (North), and not to let any one know who I was, or that I was colored. He said no person would know it, if I didn't tell it; and, if I conducted myself right, some one would want to marry me, but warned me not to marry any one but a mechanic—some one who had trade, and was able to take care of me and the children.

How many children had you then?
Only two. I had four, but two had died. Then I promised him to go to New York. Then he said, just as soon as he died I must go right to New York; and he said he would leave me the things. He hadn't any thing to leave me but the things.

What things?
The things in the house—the beds, and tables, and such things

Then, in about a month or three weeks, he died. I didn't cry nor nothin', for I was glad he was dead; for I thought I could have some peace and happiness then. I was left *free*, and that made me so glad I could hardly believe it myself.

Then, on Sunday, I dressed myself and went out to go to church; and that was the first time I had been to church in six years. I used to go to the colored church in Georgia, with my mother, in the afternoon. When I got there, to the church in New Orleans, the minister talked just as though he knew all about me, and talked about the vows I had made to the Lord about my husband. Then I said in my mind, he wan't my husband; but then I determined to go there to church. Then I asked the people what church it was, and they said, a Methodist church. Then Mr. Williams' brother came, and told me I must go out of that house, because he would not pay the rent. Then a woman there, a friend of mine, let me come in one of her rooms. She was very kind to me, and used to give me victuals when I did not know where to get it.

Who was this woman?
Her name was Helen Hopkins; she was a colored woman that used to take in washing. I never knew how it was that she was so kind to me. I always thought it was the Lord takin' care of the widow and the fatherless.

One day I met Mr. Williams' brother, and he asked me what I was doin'; and I told him, nothin'. He said that by rights I belonged to him, because his brother had not paid him the money that he borrowed to help buy me. Mr. Williams—John Williams—had said before that he would give me somethin' for the children. Then he asked me why I did not go away, as his brother told me. Then I told him it was because I had not money enough to go with, and asked him to give me some. Then he said I had better thank God for my freedom; and that his brother had got enough from him. Then I told this friend of mine, who had given me victuals, and she advised me to get away as soon as I could.

Then Mr. John Williams sent the things I had to a second-hand furniture store, and sold them all; and I took the money and my two children, and went to Cincinnati. I had just money enough to get there, and a little bit over.

What made you stop at Cincinnati?
Because I had no money to go further [if she traveled by water up the Mississippi and Ohio rivers from New Orleans, Cincinnati was probably the first free city she would reach offering the sanctuary of a sizable black community]; and I met all my friends there that I knew, when I was small, in Georgia. One of them was a Mrs. Nelson, who was once a slave in Georgia with my mother. Her husband had bought her, and she was livin' with him in Cincinnati. I went right to her house. Then, when I saw her free, and was free myself, I began to think more about my mother.

When had you seen your mother last?
At the auction, where we were all sold. It is now most twenty years ago.

Had you never heard from her?
Yes. I had one letter from her when I was in New Orleans. Mr. Williams read the letter to me, and told me that my mother wanted me to send her some tea and sugar. That was just like the mornin' we parted. It grieved me so to think that she was where she could have no sugar and tea. She could always get it in Georgia, if she had to take in workin' and do it at night. But I had no money, and could not send her any thing; and I felt bad to think my mother could not have any of these things. Whenever I set down to eat ever since, I always think of my mother. When Mr. Williams was sick, before he died, he promised me, if he ever got up off from that bed, he would buy my mother, and set us all free. But he never did it.

Are the two children you brought with you from New Orleans now living?
No; one of them died soon after I got to Cincinnati. I have only one of them livin'—a daughter, about eighteen years old.

Is she as white as you are?
Oh yes; a great deal whiter. . . .

Have you any other children?
Yes; three others. I been in Cincinnati near twelve years. Three years after I came there, I married Mr. Picquet, my husband.

Is he a white man or colored?
He's a mulatto. His mother is brown skin, and his father white, and that makes a mulatto, you know.

Who was his father?
He was a Frenchman, in Georgia. He bought my husband's mother, and live with her public. I knew all about it there, before I left Georgia. She had four other children beside my husband.

Were they all slaves?
Yes. They all belong to Mr. Picquet, but he never uses them as slaves. They are his children.

How did they get free?
Why, when he got married, he sent them all to Cincinnati, the mother and five children. It would be unpleasant for them all to stay there together (i.e., his wife, and concubine and her children).

Had your husband ever been married before?
Yes; he married a slave-woman there.

How do the slaves get married?
In a general way they ask the owners, and the owner says yes; and they get married.

Do they have a minister to marry them out on the plantations?
No; not one out of three plantations. They ask the master, and then have little bit of frolic, and sometimes they don't have that. . . .

How was it with Henry, your husband?
Why, he hired Eliza, and rented a house, and put her in. She was a slave-woman, and took in washin'.

How came they to part?
Why, you see, she belong to heirs, and the property was sold for the money to be divided. Then a gentleman in Macon bought Eliza for himself. Then Henry felt so bad about it that, pretty soon, he went to see her. He went there with the intention of buyin' her and her baby, which was Henry's. Mr. Picquet, Henry's father, was goin' to let him have the money. So, when he got there, he found it different from what he expected. He found he could

not have her any more for his wife. You see, the gentleman had bought her for himself. So my husband writ to his father that he could not get his wife, but he could buy the child. Then his father, Mr. Picquet, sent on the money, and he bought the child, and brought it away. It was about three months old, and he raised it on a bottle, work all day, and then worry with the child all night.

Is that child yet living?
Oh yes; she is livin' with us in Cincinnati, and the smartest one we got too. She is about thirteen or fourteen.

Is she as white as your children?
Oh no; she is the darkest one in the house. But her hair is straight, only little bit wavy. . . .

How came you to find out where your mother was?
Well, I hear she was in Texas, and I keep writin' to Texas, and supposed it was one place, but never got no answer. But I kept prayin', and always believed that I should see her or hear from her, before I died.

You kept up praying all this time, did you?
Yes; but when I came to Cincinnati, I thought more about my mother—to think I was free, and so many others that I knew in Georgia, and she was still in slavery! It was a great weight on my mind; and I thought if I could get religion I should certainly meet her in heaven, for I knew she was a Christian woman. . . .

Well, how did you find out where your mother was?
Well, I have made it a business for about eleven years, to inquire of every one I saw, almost, about my mother. If any fugitives came through, I made it my business to get to see them, and inquire. A great many fugitives come through Cincinnati. I have had lots of them in my house. . . .

I used to take in washin', and one day a gentleman, Mr. B., a good friend of ours in Cincinnati, sent some shirts there to be done up, and said he was goin' to Texas. Then my husband inquired, and found out that he knew Mr. Horton, in Texas, and told us what kind of a lookin' man he was. Then I remembered how he looked when he bought my mother in Mobile, and I knew it was the same man. Then he told us how to send a letter, and where to mail it. (There is a kink about mailing a letter, so as to have it reach a slave, that we never before dreamed of; but Mrs. P. does not wish it published, for fear it will hinder her from getting her letters.) Then I wrote a letter (got one written), and in three weeks I had a letter from my mother.

What became of the first letter you had from your mother, while you were in New Orleans?
I never saw that. Mr. Williams only told me he got it, and what was in it. I only knew she was in Texas. I thought it was all Texas.

Have you the first letter you received from your mother?
Yes; up stairs. Shall I go and get it?

Here the letter was brought. It is on a tough blue paper, well soiled and worn; but yet quite legible. . . .

LETTER FROM A SLAVE MOTHER.

WHARTON, March 8, 1859

MY DEAR DAUGHTER,

"I a gane take my pen in hand to drop you a few lines.

"I have written to you twice, but I hav not yet received an answer from you I can not imagin why you do not writ I feel very much troubel I fear you hav not recived my letters or you would hav written; I sent to my little grand children a ring also a button in my first letter I want you to writ to me on recept of this letter, whether you hav ever received the letters and presents or not I said in my letter to you that Col. Horton would let you have me for 1000 dol. or a woman that could fill my place; I think you could get one cheaper where you are[2] that would fill my place than to pay him the money; I am anxios to hav you to make this trade. you hav no Idea what my feelings are. I hav not spent one happy moment since I received your kind letter. it is true I was more than rejoyest to hear from you my Dear child; but my feelings on this subject are in Expressible. no one but a mother can tell my feelings. in regard to your Brother John Col. Horton is willing for you to hav him for a boy a fifteen years old or fifteen hundred dol I think that 1000 dollars is too much for me you must writ very kind to Col Horton and try to Get me for less money; I think you can change his Price by writing Kindly to him aske him in a kind manner to let you hav me for less I think you can soften his heart and he will let you hav me for less than he has offered me to you for.

"you Brother John sends his love to you and 100 kisses to your little son; Kiss my Dear little children 100 times for me particuler Elizabeth say to her that sho must writ to her grand mar ofton; I want you to hav your ambrotipe [ambrotype was an early photographic process in which the image was deposited on glass] taken also your children and send them to me I would giv this world to see you and my sweet little children; may God bless you my Dear child and protect you is my prayer.

"Your affectionate mother,
"ELIZABETH RAMSEY.

"direct your letter to Gov. A.C. Horton Wharton Wharton contey texas."

The reader will understand that the brother John, mentioned in this

[2]For particular reasons the letter was dated at St. Louis, where so many slaves are bought for Texas and Alabama; and this letter came first to St. Louis, and was forwarded by a friend to Cincinnati. Thus all the letters come and go.

letter, was the "baby" sold with the mother some twenty years ago, in Mobile, whose slips were made of Louisa's pink dress bought with the half-dollars. Louisa's mother never would take the name of Randolph or Cook—the name of her owner—as other slaves do, so she still sticks to her first name of Ramsey, as when she lived in South Carolina thirty-five years ago.

This letter is dated at Wharton. Mrs. P. says it is "in the country, where they go in the winter, and live at Matagorda in the summer." By looking upon a map of Texas it may be seen that Matagorda is at the mouth of the Colorado River, on the Gulf of Mexico; and Wharton about forty miles northwest, on the same river, both in Southern Texas.

. . . The letter is, of course, written by some white person, and is printed exactly as it is written.

There is a fact worth recording in regard to the first letter that reaches Mrs. Ramsey. It is thus described by Mrs. Picquet:

"I had been tryin' hard to find out where my mother was twelve years, after I came to Cincinnati; and when I get that letter written, I just put my trust in the Lord to go with it. I had tried so long, and could not get no word at all. I prayed to the Lord to go with each seal. There was three envelopes: one to take the letter to my friend at St. Louis, to mail the letter that was in it to Matagorda for me. That letter was directed to the postmaster in Texas; and a letter to him in it, asking him, if Col. Horton was alive, to send it to him, and, if not, to send it to some of his children. And I prayed the Lord that he would work in the hearts of the man in St. Louis, and the postmaster at Matagorda, that my letter might reach my mother.

"In that letter I ask Mr. Horton if he would please to read it to my mother, to let her know that I was yet alive; and, if he did not feel disposed to read it to her, would he be so kind as to drop me a few lines, just to let me know if she was alive; and, if she was dead, how long ago, and how she died; and, if she was livin', if she was well, and how she looked—just to ease my mind, for I had been weighed down with sorrow to see her for many years. I told him I had no silver nor gold to pay him; but I trust the Lord would reward him for his kindness, if he would do that much for me. I told him I had great faith in the Lord; and I would pray that his last days might be his best. I tell him if she was livin', and he would sell her, I would try to buy her. If I thought she would die the next week, it would be a great comfort for me to have her here to bury her."

Thus it seems that the Lord did go with the letter, and that Mrs. Horton read the letter to Louisa's mother. She then wrote two letters, but they did not reach Mrs. P. One of them, the one containing the button and the ring, was afterward found in the post-office in Matagorda, by Mrs. Ramsey. It was probably either not stamped, or not properly directed.

As soon as Mrs. P. got the first letter from her mother, she wrote two letters back, one to her mother, and the other to Mr. Horton, and both dated and mailed as before. In a short time she received another from her mother, written but a few days after the first received by Mrs. P.; and as it throws some additional light upon the question whether or not slaves have any proper affection for their offspring, we transcribe and print that also.

SECOND LETTER FROM THE SLAVE MOTHER.

"WARTON, Warton County, March 13,'59.

"MY DEAR DAUGHTER,

"Your very kind and affectionate letters dated at St. Louis, One in January the other in Febuary has been received and contents partickularly notist, I had them read often creating in me both Sorrow and Joy. Joy that you were living & a doing wel so far as the comforts of this world are concerned and you seem to have a bright prospect in the World to come, this the brightest of all other prospects, If a Person should gain the whole world & lose there Soul they have lost all, My Dear Daughter you say a great deal to me about instructing your Brother in his duty, I endeavor to set a good example before him it is all that I can do John is a good disposed Boy & a favorite with his Master, Arthur, Jim & Mary [slaves bought along with Mrs. Ramsey when Mr. Cook's property was sold, and hence known to Louisa Picquet] are all members of the Babtist Church, they are all well and a doing well, In your first letter you spoke of trying to purchase me & your Brother, the proposition was made to you to exchang Property of equal value, or to take One Thousand Dollars for me, & Fifteen Hundred for your Brother this may seem an extravagant price to you but it is not an average price for Servants, I know of nothing on this earth that would gratify me so much as to meet with My Dear & only daughter, I fear that I should not be able to retain my senses on account of the great Joy it would create in me, But time alone will develup whether this meeting will tak plasc on oarth or not Hope keeps the soul alive, but my Dear Daughter if this should not be our happy lot, I pray God that we may be able to hold fast to the end, & be the Happy recipients of the promise made to the faithful. There will be no parting there, but we shall live in the immediate presence and smiles of our God. It is not in our power to comply with your request in regard to the Degeurrotypes [daguerrotype was another early photographic process, in which the image was deposited on a silver or copper plate] this tim, we shall move to Matagorda shortly, there I can comply with your request. Arthur, Jim, Mary and your brother desire to be very kindly remembered to you, Answer this at as early a date as convenient Direct your letter to Goven A.C. Horton, Matagorda, Texas.

"May God guide and protect you through Life, & Finally save You in Heaven is the prayer of your affectionate mother,

"ELIZABETH RAMSEY."

Before this second letter was received Mrs. P. writes to Mr. Horton, reminding him that her mother was growing old, and that it would be better for him to sell her cheaper, and buy a younger person. In answer to this letter the following was received from Mr. Horton himself.

LETTER FROM THE OWNER OF ELIZABETH.

MATAGORDA, June 17, 1859.
"LOUISA,

"I have your favor of 16th April last, and contents duly noticed.

"You seem to think that I ask you too much for your mother. Money would not induce me to sell her, were it not for existing circumstances. You know that she is as fine a washer, cook, and ironer as there is in the United States. It's true she is getting old, but she carries her age well, and looks as young as she did twenty years ago. I only ask you to place another of her quality and qualifications in her stead. You can not complain of this, if it's not of your power to comply with the terms. I write you to come and see her, and I pledge myself you shall not be molested either directly or indirectly, but protected to the utmost extent.

"I send you by this mail a Daguerreotype likeness of your mother and brother, which I hope you will receive. Your mother received yours in a damaged condition. Your mother and all your acquaintance are in fine health, and desire to be remembered, and would be pleased to see you.

"Respec'y yours,
"A.C. HORTON."

The Daguerreotype mentioned above was duly received, in perfect order, and is now in the hands of Mrs. Picquet. They are both taken on one plate, mother and son, and are set forth in their best possible gear, to impress us in the north with the superior condition of the slave over the free colored people. . . .

From the date of the last of the preceding letters, Mrs. Picquet has received letters from her mother nearly every month, but nothing further from Mr. Horton himself, though Mrs. P. has often written him, importuning him to take less for her mother. At length, in March, 1860, she wrote to Mrs. Horton, appealing to her regard for her own mother, to talk to Col. Horton, her husband, and see if he would take less than one thousand dollars for Mrs. Ramsey. Of the results of this appeal we shall learn hereafter.

[Louisa Picquet undertook to raise the money first by getting her husband to borrow his next two years' wages and by reducing her household expenses to the absolute minimum; then by public solicitation of funds, using a subscription-book into which she pasted newspaper notices identifying her and supporting her cause. This seemed especially necessary because of her white appearance, which created some suspicion that her appeal was fraudulent. Some of the delegates at the General Conference of the Methodist Episcopal Church meeting in Buffalo, where she had gone to further her campaign, were so doubtful about her that an inquiry was telegraphed to a banking firm in Cincinnati which Mrs. Picquet named as a reference.]

The telegraph operator kindly sent the message (amounting to nearly three dollars) gratuitously, and the next mail brought the following letter from W.T. DRAKE, Esq., of the firm of Evans & Co., and one of the first subscribers upon Mrs. Picquet's book:

JASON EVANS, BRIGGS SWIFT.	EVANS & CO., BANKERS.	H.W. HUGHES, W.T. DRAKE.

CINCINNATI, 22nd May, 1860.
"H.H. MATTISON, Esq., Buffalo, N. York.
   "*Dear Sir*,—I am in receipt of your telegram of 21st inst., and hasten to reply.
   "I *know* Mrs. Picquet has a mother in bondage in Texas, for whom she is trying to raise sufficient money to purchase her freedom.
   "I know, also, Mrs. Picquet to be a truthful, and, I trust, Christian woman. You can, therefore, place the utmost confidence in her representations to you.
   "I cordially commend her to your charity, in assisting her in the humane and filial endeavor of purchasing a mother from the curse of slavery.
   "A mother! Who would not brave any danger, toil, and hardship for that dear name!
                                          "I am, very truly,
                                             "W.T. DRAKE.

   "I have just seen the husband of Mrs. Picquet. He hands me two letters from Mrs. P.'s mother, received since she has been gone. Will you please hand them to her, after reading. The master of this woman has agreed to take $100 less than his former price."

MORE LETTERS FROM THE MOTHER.

                                          "APRIL 15th,'60.
"DEAR DAUGHTER,
   "I have been looking for some time for a letter from you.
   "I wrote to you on the business you wrote to me a bout; I have never herd if you received the letter or not.
   "I received a letter from you that was written to Mrs Horton a few

days since. She red it and then sent it to me. I ask her what she would do for us. She said that she was willing for him to take less

"I had a talk with Col Horton yesterday he told me that he would not take less than nine hundred dollars & no less   this is hard but we can not help it so you must make your self easy & dont fret any more than you can help.

"I would help you but my Situation is such that I cant.

"You must come and see me soon   your brother was well when I heard from him last   kiss my little grand children for me   your affectionate mother,

"ELIZABETH RAMSEY."

"MATAGORDA, April 21,1860.

"DEAR DAUGHTER,

"I received your kind & affectionate letter, & was glad to hear that you was well, & getting along very well. I was sorry to learn that you were disappointed in raising the amount of money required to purchase me. In a conversation with my master on the subject he says he is willing to take a woman in exchange for me, of my age and capasity or he will under the circumstances take nine hundred dollars in *cash* for me he says he would not part with me except under existing circumstances. he also says that money cannot buy either Arthur or John   he is a training John to take charge of one of his Plantations   he has unlimited confidence in him & will not part with him untel death parts them. I should be very happy to see you My Dear Daughter as well as my Grandchildren. I hope there will be a way provided for us to meet on earth once more before we die. Cant you come and see us My Master will give all the protection you require whilst with us. This you may rest assured of. Your Brother John is well and desires to be very kindly remembered to you. Arthur wishes to be kindly remembered to you.

"Farewell My Dear Daughter. May God protect you from All evil, is the prayer of your affectionate Mother.

"ELIZABETH RAMSEY."

This Arthur, it must be remembered, is the coachman sold with Mrs. Ramsey in Mobile, and bought by Col. Horton twenty years before; and John is the "baby" sold with its mother—the brother of Mrs. Picquet. Arthur is now, and has long been, Mrs. Ramsey's husband; and yet he is entirely willing she should go, if she can only be "free;" and she is willing to leave her husband and son forever, if she can only enjoy the precious boon of freedom. Oh, how sweet is LIBERTY! The Daguerreotype shows John to be as white as one in a hundred of our white fellow-citizens.

These two letters we took to Mrs. P., as directed, and read them to her;

and the tide of emotion they created in her bosom, we can never describe. Joy, mingled with intense sorrow—the one, to learn that her mother could be bought for $100 less than the former price; and sorrow, to learn, at the same time, that *her brother could not be bought out of bondage at any price.* These two conflicting currents seemed to sweep over her soul in a mingled flood of joy and sorrow.

But all this only showed the importance of every proper effort to restore the mother to freedom, even if the brother was obliged to remain in life-long bondage. . . .

UNEXPECTED GOOD TIDINGS!

Since the preceding was stereotyped, the following has been sent us, marked in the *Cincinnati Daily Gazette* of October 15, 1860:

NOTICE—The undersigned takes this the first opportunity of expressing her thanks to those ladies and gentlemen residing in Cincinnati and elsewhere, that having accomplished through their kind aid the freedom of her mother, Elizabeth Ramsey, from slavery, by paying to her owner, Mr. A.C. Horton, of Texas, cash in hand, the sum of $900, collected by myself in small sums from different individuals, residing in this city and States of Ohio and New York.

I beg leave further to express my gratitude by thanking you all for your kindness, which will be engraved on my heart until death. My mother also desires to say that she is also most grateful to you all, and that if any of those friends who have assisted her to her freedom, feel disposed to call on her at my residence on Third Street, near Race (No. 135), she will be happy to see them, and thank them personally.

Very respectfully, yours, etc.

LOUISA PICQUET.

Cincinnati, October 13, 1860.

Elizabeth Keckley

Elizabeth Keckley's early life was hardly outstanding. Like countless other black women, she worked her way to freedom. Like others, she became expert at a negotiable skill. Many another like herself, uncertain of her father's identity, had reason to think it was her mother's master. What set Elizabeth Keckley apart was her connection with Abraham Lincoln's White House. As modiste to Mary Todd Lincoln, "Madam Elizabeth," as the President called her, was witness to many epochal events.

Decades of struggle led to this distinction. Born around 1818 in Virginia to a slave whose husband belonged to another master, the child saw little of her supposed father before he was removed permanently to the West. When Elizabeth was about eighteen she was placed with a white man in North Carolina by whom she conceived a son. Her Virginia owner later moved to Missouri with his slaves, taking Elizabeth, her mother, and her child to live in St. Louis. The master failed to prosper in this new locale, and Elizabeth determined to protect her family. Arranging to find work as a seamstress, she brought in enough money to keep her owner's household intact.

She married a man she had known in Virginia, who turned out to be a slave although alleging to be free. Irresponsible and dissolute, James Keckley provided her with little but anguish, and the marriage collapsed some eight years later. If she had looked to him to help her out of bondage, she was now forced back into self-reliance.

So fully had this slave woman absorbed the teachings of American society that, earnestly as she longed for freedom, she wished to obtain it according to law. Persistent in work, she reached her objective; she purchased freedom for herself and her son. In 1860 Elizabeth Keckley went to Washington. Setting up as a dressmaker, she soon established an elegant clientele. Ironically, Mrs. Jefferson Davis was an early patron, but the new First Lady became her most cherished client.

Grasping the essentials of organization for communal needs as well as for personal goals, Elizabeth Keckley helped in 1862 to start the Contraband Relief Association. She served as its first president, holding the post for a number of successive terms. She also shared in founding the Home for Destitute Women and Children, the Washington institution where she spent her own declining years.

Mary Todd Lincoln made a confidante of Mrs. Keckley. Each had known grief, each was yet to know more. Elizabeth Keckley's son, by then a student at Wilberforce University, had enlisted in the Union forces. He was killed in battle in August 1861. In the sad days following the assassination of the President, new bonds of tender sympathy drew the two women closer. Though later disrupted by the indiscretions of a ghostwritten Keckley autobiography (Behind the Scenes appeared in 1868), the friendship had prompted mutual growth and mutual support.

Mrs. Keckley's understanding grew from long experience with suffering. Two selections from Behind the Scenes serve as illustrations. One depicts the complex ties of her adult life in slavery. The second shows her intuitive response when she learned of the fatal attack on Lincoln. [1]

. . . My troubles in North Carolina were brought to an end by my unexpected return to Virginia, where I lived with Mr. Garland, who had married Miss Ann Burwell, one of my old master's daughters. His life was not a prosperous one, and after struggling with the world for several years he left his native State, a disappointed man. He moved to St. Louis, hoping to improve his fortune in the West; but ill luck followed him there, and he seemed to be unable to escape from the influence of the evil star of his destiny. When his family, myself included, joined him in his new home on the banks of the Mississippi, we found him so poor that he was unable to pay the dues on a letter advertised as in the post-office for him. The necessities of the family were so great, that it was proposed to place my mother out at service. The idea was shocking to me. Every gray hair in her old head was dear to me, and I could not bear the thought of her going to work for strangers. She had been raised in the family, had watched the growth of each child from infancy to maturity; they had been the objects of her kindest care. . . . They had been the central figures in her dream of life—a dream beautiful to her, since she had basked in the sunshine of no other. . . . My mother, my poor aged mother, go among strangers to toil for a living! No, a thousand times no! I would rather work my fingers to the bone, bend over my sewing till the film of blindness gathered in my eyes; nay, even beg from street to street. I told Mr. Garland so, and he gave me permission to see what I could do. I was fortunate in obtaining work, and in a short time I had acquired something of a reputation as a seamstress and dress-maker. The best ladies in St. Louis were my patrons, and when my reputation was once established I

[1]Elizabeth Keckley, Behind the Scenes; or, Thirty Years a Slave and Four Years in the White House (New York, 1868); John E. Washington, They Knew Lincoln (New York, 1942), pp. 205–44.
Source: Elizabeth Keckley, Behind the Scenes; or Thirty Years a Slave and Four Years in the White House (New York, 1868), pp. 43–51, 54–55, 182–93.

never lacked for orders. With my needle I kept bread in the mouths of seventeen persons for two years and five months. While I was working so hard that others might live in comparative comfort, and move in those circles of society to which their birth gave them entrance, the thought often occurred to me whether I was really worth my salt or not; and then perhaps the lips curled with a bitter sneer. . . . The heavy task was too much for me, and my health began to give way. About this time Mr. Keckley, whom I had met in Virginia, and learned to regard with more than friendship, came to St. Louis. He sought my hand in marriage, and for a long time I refused to consider his proposal; for I could not bear the thought of bringing children into slavery—of adding one single recruit to the millions bound to hopeless servitude, fettered and shackled with chains stronger and heavier than manacles of iron. I made a proposition to buy myself and son; the proposition was bluntly declined, and I was commanded never to broach the subject again. I would not be put off thus, for hope pointed to a freer, brighter life in the future. Why should my son be held in slavery? I often asked myself. He came into the world through no will of mine, and yet, God only knows how I loved him. . . . Much as I respected the authority of my master, I could not remain silent on a subject that so nearly concerned me. One day, when I insisted on knowing whether he would permit me to purchase myself, and what price I must pay for myself, he turned to me in a petulant manner, thrust his hand into his pocket, drew forth a bright silver quarter of a dollar, and proffering it to me, said:

"Lizzie, I have told you often not to trouble me with such a question. If you really wish to leave me, take this: it will pay the passage of yourself and boy on the ferry-boat, and when you are on the other side of the river you will be free. It is the cheapest way that I know of to accomplish what you desire."

I looked at him in astonishment, and earnestly replied: "No, master, I do not wish to be free in such a manner. If such had been my wish, I should never have troubled you about obtaining your consent to my purchasing myself. I can cross the river any day, as you well know, and have frequently done so, but will never leave you in such a manner. By the laws of the land I am your slave—you are my master, and I will only be free by such means as the laws of the country provide." He expected this answer, and I knew that he was pleased. Some time afterwards he told me that he had reconsidered the question; that I had served his family faithfully; that I deserved my freedom, and that he would take $1200 for myself and boy.

This was joyful intelligence for me, and the reflection of hope gave a silver lining to the dark cloud of my life—faint, it is true, but still a silver lining.

Taking a prospective glance at liberty, I consented to marry. The wedding was a great event in the family. The ceremony took place in the parlor, in the presence of the family and a number of guests. Mr. Garland gave me away, and the pastor, Bishop Hawks, performed the ceremony, who had solemnized the bridals of Mr. G.'s own children. The day was a happy one, but it faded all too soon. Mr. Keckley—let me speak kindly of his faults—proved dissipated, and a burden instead of a helpmate. More than all, I learned that he was a slave instead of a free man, as he represented himself to be. With the simple explanation that I lived with him eight years, let charity draw around him the mantle of silence.

I went to work in earnest to purchase my freedom, but the years passed, and I was still a slave. Mr. Garland's family claimed so much of my attention—in fact, I supported them—that I was not able to accumulate anything. In the mean time Mr. Garland died, and Mr. Burwell, a Mississippi planter, came to St. Louis to settle up the estate. He was a kind-hearted man, and said I should be free, and would afford me every facility to raise the necessary amount to pay the price of my liberty. Several schemes were urged upon me by my friends. At last I formed a resolution to go to New York, state my case, and appeal to the benevolence of the people. . . .

. . . A carriage stopped in front of the house; Mrs. Le Bourgois, one of my kind patrons, got out of it and entered the door. She seemed to bring sunshine with her handsome cheery face. She came to where I was, and in her sweet way said:—

"Lizzie, I hear that you are going to New York to beg for money to buy your freedom. I have been thinking over the matter, and told Ma it would be a shame to allow you to go North to beg for what we should give you. You have many friends in St. Louis, and I am going to raise the twelve hundred dollars required among them. I have two hundred dollars put away for a present; am indebted to you one hundred dollars; mother owes you fifty dollars, and will add another fifty to it; and as I do not want the present, I will make the money a present to you. Don't start for New York now until I see what I can do among your friends."

. . . Mrs. Le Bourgois, God bless her dear good heart, was more than successful. The twelve hundred dollars were raised, and at last my son and myself were free. Free, free! what a glorious ring to tho word. Free! the bitter heart-struggle was over. Free! the soul could go out to heaven and to God with no chains to clog its flight or pull it down. Free! the earth wore a brighter look, and the very stars seemed to sing with joy. Yes, free! free by the laws of man and the smile of God—and Heaven bless them who made me so!

• • •

. . . During my residence in the Capital I made my home with Mr. and Mrs. Walker Lewis, people of my own race, and friends in the truest sense of the word.

The days passed without any incident of particular note disturbing the current of life. On Friday morning, April 14th—alas! what American does not remember the day—I saw Mrs. Lincoln but for a moment. She told me that she was to attend the theatre that night with the President, but I was not summoned to assist her in making her toilette. Sherman had swept from the northern border of Georgia through the heart of the Confederacy down to the sea, striking the death-blow to the rebellion. Grant had pursued General Lee beyond Richmond, and the army of Virginia, that had made such stubborn resistance, was crumbling to pieces. Fort Sumter had fallen;—the stronghold first wrenched from the Union, and which had braved the fury of Federal guns for so many years, was restored to the Union; the end of the war was near at hand, and the great pulse of the loyal North thrilled with joy. The dark war-cloud was fading, and a white-robed angel seemed to hover in the sky, whispering "Peace—peace on earth, good-will toward men!" Sons, brothers, fathers, friends, sweethearts were coming home. Soon the white tents would be folded, the volunteer army be disbanded, and tranquillity again reign. Happy, happy day!—happy at least to those who fought under the banner of the Union. There was great rejoicing throughout the North. From the Atlantic to the Pacific, flags were gayly thrown to the breeze, and at night every city blazed with its tens of thousand lights. But scarcely had the fireworks ceased to play, and the lights been taken down from the windows, when the lightning flashed the most appalling news over the magnetic wires. "The President has been murdered!" spoke the swift-winged messenger, and the loud huzza died upon the lips. A nation suddenly paused in the midst of festivity, and stood paralyzed with horror—transfixed with awe.

Oh, memorable day! Oh, memorable night! Never before was joy so violently contrasted with sorrow.

At 11 o'clock at night I was awakened by an old friend and neighbor, Miss M. Brown, with the startling intelligence that the entire Cabinet had been assassinated, and Mr. Lincoln shot, but not mortally wounded. When I heard the words I felt as if the blood had been frozen in my veins, and that my lungs must collapse for the want of air. Mr. Lincoln shot! the Cabinet assassinated! What could it mean? The streets were alive with wondering, awe-stricken people. Rumors flew thick and fast, and the wildest reports came with every new arrival. The words were repeated with blanched cheeks and quivering lips. I waked Mr. and Mrs. Lewis, and told them that the President was shot, and that I must go to the White House. I could not remain in a state of uncertainty. I felt that the house would not hold me. They tried to quiet me, but gentle words could not calm the wild tempest. They quickly dressed themselves, and we sallied out into the street to drift with the excited throng. We walked rapidly towards the White House, and on our way passed the residence of Secretary Seward, which was surrounded by armed soldiers, keeping back all intruders with the point of the bayonet. We hurried on, and as we approached the White House, saw that it too was surrounded with soldiers. Every entrance was strongly guarded, and no one was permitted to pass. The guard at the gate told us that Mr. Lincoln had not been brought home, but refused to give any other information. More excited than ever, we wandered down the street. Grief and anxiety were making me weak, and as we joined the outskirts of a large crowd, I began to feel as meek and humble as a penitent child. A gray-haired old man was passing. I caught a glimpse of his face, and it seemed so full of kindness and sorrow that I gently touched his arm, and imploringly asked:

"Will you please, sir, to tell me whether Mr. Lincoln is dead or not?"

"Not dead," he replied, "but dying. God help us!" and with a heavy step he passed on.

"Not dead, but dying! then indeed God help us!"

We learned that the President was mortally wounded—that he had been shot down in his box at the theatre, and that he was not expected to live till morning; when we returned home with heavy hearts. I could not sleep. I wanted to go to Mrs. Lincoln, as I pictured her wild with grief; but then I did not know where to find her, and I must wait till morning. Never did the hours drag so slowly. Every moment seemed an age, and I could do nothing but walk about and hold my arms in mental agony.

Morning came at last, and a sad morning was it. The flags that floated so gayly yesterday now were draped in black, and hung in silent folds at half-mast. The President was dead, and a nation was mourning for him. Every house was draped in black, and every face wore a solemn look. People spoke in subdued tones, and glided whisperingly, wonderingly, silently about the streets.

About eleven o'clock on Saturday morning a carriage drove up to the door, and a messenger asked for "Elizabeth Keckley."

"Who wants her?" I asked.

"I come from Mrs. Lincoln. If you are Mrs. Keckley, come with me immediately to the White House."

I hastily put on my shawl and bonnet, and was driven at a rapid rate to the White House. Everything about the building was sad and solemn. I was quickly shown to Mrs. Lincoln's room, and on entering, saw Mrs. L. tossing uneasily about upon a bed. The room was darkened, and the only person in it besides the widow of the President was Mrs. Secretary Welles, who had spent the night with her. Bowing to Mrs. Welles, I went to the bedside.

"Why did you not come to me last night, Elizabeth—I sent for you?" Mrs. Lincoln asked in a low whisper.

"I did try to come to you, but I could not find you," I answered, as I laid my hand upon her hot brow.

I afterwards learned, that when she had partially recovered from the first shock of the terrible tragedy in the theatre, Mrs. Welles asked:

"Is there no one, Mrs. Lincoln, that you desire to have with you in this terrible affliction?"

"Yes, send for Elizabeth Keckley. I want her just as soon as she can be brought here."

Three messengers, it appears, were successively despatched for me, but all of them mistook the number and failed to find me.

Shortly after entering the room on Saturday morning, Mrs. Welles excused herself, as she said she must go to her own family, and I was left alone with Mrs. Lincoln.

She was nearly exhausted with grief, and when she became a little quiet, I asked and received permission to go into the Guests' Room, where the body of the President lay in state. When I crossed the threshold of the room, I could not help recalling the day on which I had seen little Willie lying in his coffin where the body of his father now lay. I remembered how the President had wept over the pale beautiful face of his gifted boy, and now the President himself was dead. The last time I saw him he spoke kindly to me, but alas! the lips would never move again. The light had faded from his eyes, and when the light went out the soul went with it. What a noble soul was his—noble in all the noble attributes of God! Never did I enter the solemn chamber of death with such palpitating heart and trembling footsteps as I entered it that day. No common mortal had died. The Moses of my people had fallen in the hour of his triumph. Fame had woven her choicest chaplet for his brow. Though the brow was cold and pale in death, the chaplet should not fade, for God had studded it with the glory of the eternal stars.

When I entered the room, the members of the Cabinet and many distinguished officers of the army were grouped around the body of their fallen chief. They made room for me, and, approaching the body, I lifted the white cloth from the white face of the man that I had worshipped as an idol—looked upon as a demi-god. Notwithstanding the violence of the death of the President, there was something beautiful as well as grandly solemn in the expression of the placid face. There lurked the sweetness and gentleness of childhood, and the stately grandeur of godlike intellect. I gazed long at the face, and turned away with tears in my eyes and a choking sensation in my throat. Ah! never was man so widely mourned before. The whole world bowed their heads in grief when Abraham Lincoln died.

Returning to Mrs. Lincoln's room, I found her in a new paroxysm of grief. Robert was bending over his mother with tender affection, and little Tad was crouched at the foot of the bed with a world of agony in his young face. I shall never forget the scene—the wails of a broken heart, the unearthly shrieks, the terrible convulsions, the wild, tempestuous outbursts of grief from the soul. I bathed Mrs. Lincoln's head with cold water, and soothed the terrible tornado as best I could. Tad's grief at his father's death was as great as the grief of his mother, but her terrible outbursts awed the boy into silence. Sometimes he would throw his arms around her neck, and exclaim, between his broken sobs, "Don't cry so, Mamma! don't cry, or you will make me cry, too! You will break my heart."

Mrs. Lincoln could not bear to hear Tad cry, and when he would plead to her not to break his heart, she would calm herself with a great effort, and clasp her child in her arms.

Every room in the White House was darkened, and every one spoke in subdued tones, and moved about with muffled tread. The very atmosphere breathed of the great sorrow which weighed heavily upon each heart. Mrs. Lincoln never left her room, and while the body of her husband was being borne in solemn state from the Atlantic to the broad prairies of the West, she was weeping with her fatherless children in her private chamber. She denied admittance to almost every one, and I was her only companion, except her children, in the days of her great sorrow.

Elleanor Eldridge

Memoirs of Elleanor Eldridge, published in 1838, is the basic source of reference for the life of its subject. A helpful bibliography of American autobiography lists this treatment as the work of its author.[1] The account is written in the third person, which by itself raises no question of authenticity. But since 1849, if not before, authorship has been ascribed to a white woman, Frances Whipple Green, a Rhode Island poet, journalist, and essayist.[2] Did Elleanor Eldridge exist or was she the fictional creation of Frances Green? An Ellen Eldridge, listed in the 1830 census of free blacks in Providence, Rhode Island, seems clearly to have been the person in question. There can be little doubt of her existence. The volume was certainly written about her, although some fictitious elements cling to the narrative.

Elleanor Eldridge was born in Rhode Island in 1785, free by the grace of a year—Rhode Island enacted a bill for gradual emancipation in 1784. Warwick is a small town some fifteen miles from Providence on the peninsula knifing into the sea. Her father was an African captured as a child together with his whole family. He is alleged to have won his freedom fighting for it during the American Revolution. Elleanor's mother was of Indian extraction. With both parents present as well as a cluster of siblings, their family pattern matched the American norm.

Frances Green composed and published the book for a purpose: to bail the woman out of financial entanglements which restricted her business activity. The Memoirs achieved Frances Green's intent. Elleanor Eldridge's property was restored to her, although at a heavy price. Respectable and respected, she lived until her eightieth year.

---

[1]Louis Kaplan, A Bibliography of American Autobiographies (Madison, Wisc., 1961), p. 92.

[2]Rufus W. Griswold, The Female Poets of America, 2d ed. (Philadelphia, 1849), p. 123.

Source: [Frances Whipple Green(e)], Memoirs of Elleanor Eldridge (Providence, 1838), pp. 11–22, 29–31, 42–43, 62–93.

Elleanor Eldridge, on the one hand, is the inheritress of African blood, with all its heirship of wo [sic] and shame; and the subject of wrong and banishment, by her Indian maternity on the other. Fully, and sadly, have these titles been redeemed. It seems, indeed, as if the wrongs and persecutions of both races had fallen upon Elleanor.

She was born at Warwick, R.I., March 26, 1785. Her paternal grandfather was a native African. He was induced, with his family, to come on board an American slaver, under pretence of trade. With a large quantity of tobacco, prepared for barter, the simple-hearted African stepped fearlessly on board the stranger's ship, followed by his wife and little ones.

For some time he continued a friendly exchange of his staple commodity, for flannels and worsted bindings of gay and various colors. Already, in imagination, had his wife decorated herself with the purchased finery, and walked forth amid the villages, the envy and admiration of all the belles of Congo; and already had the honest African, himself, rivaled in splendor the princes of his land. Having finished his bargains, Dick, for that was the name of the Congo chieftain,[1] proposed to return; but his hospitable entertainers would, on no account, allow him to depart without further attentions. Refreshments were handed freely about, with many little presents of small value. Then all the wonders of the ship, with the mysteries of operating its machinery, were to be explained to the intelligent, but uninformed stranger; while appropriate curiosities were displayed before the wondering eyes of his wife and children. By these means the confidence of the simple Africans was completely won. . . .

. . . Still the chief was detained; and still remained unsuspecting; until, to his utter horror, he found that his detainers, under pretence of illustrating some operation, had carefully weighed anchor, and were putting out to sea

. . . They were chained, and ordered below; where the sight of hundreds of wretches, stolen, wronged, wretched as themselves, only showed them that they were lost forever.

No tongue can depict the horrors of that passage. No imagination can form even a faint outline of its sufferings. Physical torture wrought its work. Humanity was crushed within them; and they were presented for sale, more than half brutalized for the brutal market. Few minds ever rise from this state, to any thing of their former rigor. The ancestor of Elleanor had one of

---

Source: [Frances Whipple Green(e)], Memoirs of Elleanor Eldridge (Providence, 1838), pp. 11–22, 29–31, 42–43, 62–93.

[1]The English language was known to some extent along the coast of Africa, and the use of English names by Africans was entirely possible. See, e.g., Nancy Prince, Narrative of the Life and Travels . . . (Boston, 1853), p. 6, reprinted below. (BJL and RB)

these few; and though his pride was crushed, and his hopes forever extinguished, still he felt, and acted as a man.

But little more than the foregoing particulars is known to the subject of this narrative, concerning her ancestor, save that his African name was Dick; and that he had four children; one daughter Phillis; and three sons; Dick, George, and Robin; of whom the latter was her father.

At the commencement of the American Revolution, Robin Eldridge [the surname presumably reflects ownership after arrival in the New World] with his two brothers, presented themselves as candidates for liberty. They were promised their freedom, with the additional premium of 200 acres of land in the Mohawk country [unsettled land in what is now western New York] apiece.

These slaves fought as bravely, and served as faithfully, under the banner of Freedom, as if they had always breathed her atmosphere, and dwelt forever in her temple; as if the collar had never bowed down their free heads, nor the chain oppressed their strong limbs. What were toils, privations, distresses, dangers? Did they not already see the morning star of FREEDOM, glimmering in the east? Were they not soon to exhibit one of the most glorious changes in nature? Were they not soon to start up from the rank of goods and chattels, into MEN? . . .

At the close of the war they were pronounced FREE; but their services were paid in the old Continental money, the depreciation, and final ruin of which, left them no wealth but the one priceless gem, LIBERTY.—They were free.—Having no funds, they could not go to take possession of their lands on the Mohawk. And, to this day, their children have never been able to recover them; though, by an act of Congress, it was provided, that all soldiers' children who were left incapable of providing for themselves, should "inherit the promises" due to their fathers. The subject of this memoir, attracted by an advertisement to this effect, attempted to recover something for a young brother and sister; but with the success which too often attends upon honest poverty, struggling with adverse circumstances. Her efforts were of no avail.

The spirit of Robin Eldridge was not to be broken down. Before entering the army he had married Hannah Prophet; and he now settled in Warwick, near the Fulling-Mill; where, by his honest industry, and general good character, he was always held in esteem. He soon became able to purchase land and build a small house; when he reared a large family, all of whom inherit their father's claims to the kindness and respect of those about them. He had, by this marriage, nine children; of whom Elleanor was the last of seven successive daughters. Of these children only five lived to mature age.

It may now be proper to look back a little, in order to glance at Elleanor's maternal ancestry. Her maternal grandmother, Mary Fuller, was a native Indian, belonging to the small tribe, or clan, called the Fuller family; which was probably a portion of the Narragansett tribe. Certain it is that this tribe, or family, once held great possessions in large tracts of land; with a portion of which Mary Fuller purchased her husband Thomas Prophet; who, until his marriage, had been a slave. Mary Fuller, having witnessed the departing glories of her tribe, died in extreme old age, at the house of her son, Caleb Prophet; being 102 years old [a remarkable age, though not impossible, for a woman whose daughter was still of child-bearing age]. She was buried at the Thomas Greene burying place in Warwick, in the year 1780. Her daughter Hannah, as we have said before, had been married to Robin Eldridge, the father of Elleanor.

Our heroine had the misfortune to lose her mother at the age of ten years; when she launched out boldly into the eventful life which lay before her, commencing, at once, her own self government, and that course of rigorous and spirited action, for which she has since been so much distinguished.

During her mother's life, it had often been her practice to follow washing, at the house of Mr. Joseph Baker, of Warwick; a daughter of whom, Miss Elleanor Baker, gave her own name to the little one she often carried with her; and always continued to take great interest in her little colored name-sake. Not long after the death of her mother, this young lady called on Elleanor, and invited her to come and reside with her, at her father's, offering her a home. She asked permission of her father, who consented, but with this remark, that she would not stay a week. The young heroine was not, however, to be so discouraged; but bravely collected herself, and began by making a definite BARGAIN with Miss Baker, before she consented to put herself under her protection; evincing, by this single act, a degree of prudence and wisdom entirely beyond her years. She fixed her price at 25 cents per week, and agreed to work for one year. . . .

With this kind family she remained five years and nine months. During that time she learned all the varieties of house-work, and every kind of spinning; and in the last year she learned plain, double, and ornamental weaving, in which she was considered particularly expert. . . . This double weaving, as it is called—i.e. carpets, old fashioned coverlets, damask, and bed-ticking, is said to be a very difficult and complicated process. . . . Yet she was, at the expiration of the year, pronounced a competent and fully-accomplished weaver.

In the commencement of her sixteenth year, Elleanor took leave of her kind patrons, and went to live next at Capt. Benjamin Greene's, at Warwick Neck, to do their spinning for one year.

At the expiration of the year she was engaged as dairy woman. It appears really wonderful that any person should think of employing a girl, but just entering her seventeenth year, in this nice and delicate business. Yet so it was; and the event proves that their judgment was correct. Elleanor continued in this situation eight years. She took charge of the milk of from twenty-five to thirty cows; and made from four to five thousand weight of cheese annually. Every year our heroine's cheese was distinguished by A PREMIUM.

We acknowledge to the sentimentalist that these matters are not very poetical; but to the lover of truth, they are important, as giving a distinct idea of the capacity, which early distinguished our subject. . . .

At the age of nineteen, Elleanor was again called to mourn over the departure of another kind parent. She lost her father; and a sad loss it was to her; for Robin Eldridge had the art, which many white fathers have not, that of commanding, at once, respect and affection.

As the deceased had left property, letters of administration were taken out; but it was soon found that the estate could not be settled, without some legal advices from a daughter, then residing in the north-western part of Massachusetts. In this crisis, what was to be done? The delays and difficulties attending a communication by mail, were of themselves sufficiently objectionable; and to hire a person to go there, would be a greater expense than the little estate would justify. At this point Elleanor came forward and offered her services, which were gladly accepted.

With a spirit worthy one of the nation of Miantonomies, she set off, on foot and alone, to make a journey of 180 miles. . . .

Eleanor remained at Capt. Greene's until 1812, being then twenty-seven years old. At this time the death of Capt. G. occasioned alterations in the family; so our heroine returned home to live with her oldest sister Lettise, who had been appointed by the Court of Probate, as guardian to the younger children; and filled a mother's place in the care of the whole family.

Eleanor now, with her sister, entered into a miscellaneous business, of weaving, spinning, going out as nurse, washer, &c.—in all of which departments she gave entire satisfaction. . . . She also, with her sister, entered considerably into the soap boiling business. Of this article they every year made large quantities, which they brought to the Providence market, together with such other articles as they wished to dispose of, or as were, with suitable commissions, supplied by their neighbors. By this time the earnings of Eleanor had amounted to a sum sufficient to purchase a lot and build a small house, which she rented for forty dollars a year. . . .

She remained with her sister three years;—and was then induced by another sister . . . to come to Providence; where she soon arrived and commenced a new course of business, viz—white-washing, papering, and painting; which she has followed for more than twenty years, to the entire satisfaction of her numerous employers.

The above occupations she generally followed nine or ten months in the year; but commonly, during the most severe cold of winter, she engaged herself for high wages, in some private family, hotel, or boarding house. . . . It is worthy of remark, and alike creditable to herself, and her employers, that ELLEANOR HAS ALWAYS LIVED WITH GOOD PEOPLE. . . .

. . . About sixteen years ago, Eleanor, having six hundred dollars on hand, bought a lot, for which she paid one hundred dollars, all in silver money, as she has herself assured me. She then commenced building a house, which cost seventeen hundred dollars. This house was all paid for, with no encumbrance whatever. After it had been built three or four years, she built an addition on the east side, to live in herself; and subsequently one on the west side, to accommodate an additional tenant. This house rented for one hundred and fifty dollars per annum.—About this time there were two lots of land for sale, of which Elleanor wished to become the purchaser. Not having money enough she hired of a gentleman of Warwick, two hundred and forty dollars. For this she was to pay interest at the rate of ten per cent; and, by agreement, so long as she could do so, she might be entitled to keep the money; i.e. she was to pay the interest, and renew the note annually.

Elleanor had completed her house, which with its two wings, and its four chimneys, wore quite an imposing aspect; and in the honest pride and joy of her heart, she looked upon it with delight; as well she might do, since it was all earned by her own honest labors, and afforded the prospect of a happy home, and a comfortable income in her old age. Attached to this house, and belonging to a Mrs.—— was a gangway which Elleanor wished very much to obtain possession of, as she was entirely cut off from outdoor privileges, without it. She had hired it for five years; and had often spoken to Mrs.—— in regard to the purchase. But what was her surprise to find, that just before the term of her lease had expired, Mrs.—— had sold it. Mr. C—— then, who owned the house and premises adjoining her own, came directly forward and offered to sell to Elleanor, and as she felt very anxious to secure the privilege of the gang-way, she finally determined to do so; although, by doing so, she was obliged to involve herself considerably. This house had been built by Mr. C——, who, being unable to pay for it, had given a mortgage of the premises. At this time Elleanor had five hundred dollars in her possession, which she had been wishing to dispose of to the best advantage. She finally came to a bargain with Mr. C——, agreeing to give two thousand dollars for the house. She paid the five hundred dollars down; and then gave a mortgage on the house to Mr. Greenold, for fifteen hundred dollars. This was to be paid in four years; which, if she had received the least indulgence, she might easily have done; or rather if she had not, in her own honesty of heart, been led to confide in the PROMISE of ONE, who had more regard for his PURSE, than for his HONOR, or his CHRISTIAN CHARACTER, as we shall soon see.

. . . Elleanor was . . . seized with the typhus fever, which left her in so low a state of health, that her friends and herself feared she was falling into a decline. With a strong impression of this feeling upon her mind, she wished much to see her friends in Massachusetts again; and finally she persuaded her brother to accompany her on a journey thither.

She went out to Warwick, and remained there six weeks, until she believed she had regained her health, so far as to undertake the journey; when she returned to Providence, and, with her brother George, made arrangements for her departure. Accordingly, in October, Elleanor having left all her affairs in a good train, with her brother, set off for Adams.

For the first day she seemed somewhat invigorated with the ride, and the change of air and scene; but the unusual fatigue on the second and third days, quite overcame her.

They stopped for the night at Angell's tavern, in Hadley, where Elleanor found herself very ill. In the morning, her brother, finding she did not rise, tapped on her chamber door, and asked her if she felt well enough to pursue her journey. She replied that she was sick, and could not go any further that day. Her brother went to the land-lady, and requested permission to remain through the day, as his sister was too ill to proceed. From this circumstance—this trifling fact—sprang all the subsequent troubles of Elleanor. It so happened that there were two persons from Providence, within the hearing of George Eldridge, when he made the above named request; and as they had some knowledge of his sister, they made their report, when they returned to Providence. This, she being very sick, like a gathering snow-ball, grew as it went the rounds of gossip, into exceedingly dangerous illness— the point of death; and finally, by the simple process of accumulation, it was resolved into death itself. . . .

[After a day's rest Elleanor and her brother resumed the journey to visit their relatives. George found work in Massachusetts and they both remained there for some months, delaying their return to Rhode Island until spring.]

On the evening of the third day they arrived at Elleanor's house, in Providence; and, after having laid off her travelling dress, our heroine prepared for supper.

It was just at dusk when she ran across the street for bread. She stepped in at the door, as usual, and asked for bread. But the baker's boy, instead of supplying her, ran back into the entry, with an appearance of great alarm; and, having stood gazing at her a moment, with his arms extended in a horizontal line, and mouth and eyes laid open to their full extent, with the most querulous and misgiving tones, he called out: "Is that you Ellen?—Why I thought you was—dead!" . . .

This was the first that Elleanor knew of the story of her death; though she heard of it repeatedly during the evening, and the next morning. Her brother heard also at the hotel, where he went to put up his horse, that his sister's property had been attached, and was advertised to be sold, in consequence of a report concerning her death; but he did not mention it to Elleanor that evening, knowing her to be very much fatigued; and, as he expected to take her directly out to Warwick the next day, it seemed unnecessary; for then, and not till then, would she be able to see the gentleman; and, as he hoped, make some arrangements with him. . . .

As soon as the news of their arrival had gone about, the gentleman who had laid an attachment on Ellen's property, in order to procure the liquidation of the two hundred and forty dollar note before alluded to, came directly to see her; and that too altogether of his own accord. This gentleman was not the original creditor; who had deceased, leaving his brother as his sole heir.

The gentleman told Ellen what he had done; at the same time saying, that he should never have done it, had he not been told that she was dead. "But," said he, "I am glad you have returned, safe and well; and though I want the money, I WILL NEVER DISTRESS YOU FOR IT."

Ellen had the simplicity to believe this, because the man—perhaps I ought to say GENTLEMAN—was a member of a church; and was CALLED a christian [sic]. Poor, simple-hearted, honest Ellen: she did not know then that she had met "the wolf in sheep's clothing!" . . .

Elleanor had given Mr.—— a conditional promise that she would raise a hundred dollars for him in April; but it so happened that she could not procure the money; and, relying on his promise of indulgence, which his honor as a gentleman, and his christian character, alike conspired to strengthen; while, at the same time, his great wealth, or entire independence, placed him altogether above any temptation to uncharitableness.

In about a week she returned to Providence, satisfied that, in the withdrawal of his suit, Mr.—— had fairly "buried the hatchet," she commenced her summer's work with renewed vigor. This was the cholera season, which brought so much of terror with it, as to be long remembered. Ellen's usual business was somewhat modified by the prevailing sickness; and being a skilful and fearless person, she went much among the sick; and by her zealous attentions to the wants of the suffering, she won the kindest regard of all who were so fortunate as to obtain her valuable services.

In August Mrs. T——, having a daughter who was pronounced to be either afflicted with, or liable to, the cholera, left town for her country residence, in Pomfret, Connecticut. She engaged Elleanor to accompany her in the capacity of nurse and attendant.

In order to make all secure before leaving town, Ellen paid up all that was due on the mortgage: but she did not pay Mr.—— because she could not do so without great loss, and difficulty; and concerning this she felt no uneasiness, because there had been an express understanding between herself and the deceased Mr.——, that she should have the money so long as she could pay the interest of ten per cent on the note: and besides her well-known character for integrity and industry, seemed to secure the promise of indulgence, which had been voluntarily given.

Ellen's last step was to go round among her families [the families renting quarters on her property], and request them to be careful and prudent in all things, making no disturbance, and committing no trespass; and she assured them that if she heard any complaint from her neighbors, she should turn out the offenders, as soon as she returned.

Intent only upon her new duties, Elleanor then entered zealously into the service of Mrs. T.; and with that lady, and her family, left town for Pomfret, a distance of only thirty miles. . . .

In about two months, the family of Mrs. T. having recovered, and the cholera panic having somewhat subsided, that lady determined to return to Providence. On arriving in the city, she stopped at the Franklin House, still retaining Ellen in attendance. The next morning after their arrival, a lady came in and told Mrs. T.——that the property of Elleanor was all attached, and sold; and to the latter, the sad intelligence was speedily announced; but she found it very difficult to believe a story, at once, so entirely opposed to all her convictions of right, and so fraught with distress and anguish to herself; yet, upon enquiry, she found that one half the truth had not been told.

Mr.——, of Warwick, had attached and sold property, which a few months before had been valued at four thousand dollars, for the pitiful sum of two hundred and forty dollars.—Why he wished to attach so large a property, for so small a debt, is surprising enough; since Elleanor had then in her possession two house lots, and the little house and lot at Warwick; either of which would have been sufficient to liquidate the debt. There seems to be a spirit of wilful malignity, in this wanton destruction of property, which it is difficult to conceive of as existing in the bosom of civilized man.

One after another, all the aggravating particulars came to the knowledge and notice of Ellen. In the first place, the attachment, as we have before said, was entirely disproportioned to the debt; which the general good character, integrity, and PROPERTY of the debtor, rendered perfectly secure. In the second place, the sheriff never legally advertised the sale, or advertised it all, as can be learned. In the third place, the auctioneer, having, doubtless, ascertained the comfortable fact, that the owner was a laboring colored woman, who was then away, leaving no friend to protect her rights, struck it off, almost at the first bid; and at little more than one third its value; it being sold for only fifteen hundred dollars, which was the exact amount of the mortgage. In the fourth place, the purchaser, after seeing the wrongfulness of the whole affair, and after giving his word three successive times, that he would settle and restore the property for a given sum, twice meanly flew from his bargain, successively making larger demands. . . .

Thus, as we have seen, was Ellen, in a single moment, by a single stroke of the hammer, deprived of the fruits of all her honest and severe labors—the labors of years; and, not only so, but actually thrown in debt for many small bills, for repairs and alterations on her houses, which she had the honor and honesty to discharge, even against the advices of some of her friends, after the property by which they had been incurred had been so cruelly taken away. Elleanor has traits of character, which, if she were a white woman, would be called NOBLE. And must color so modify character, that they are not still so?

On visiting the premises, sad, indeed was the sight which the late owner witnessed. The two wings of her first house, which she had herself built, with their chimneys, had been pulled down: and it seemed as if the spirit of Ruin had been walking abroad. All her families had been compelled to leave, at a single week's notice; and many of them, being unable to procure tenements, were compelled to find shelter in barns and out-houses, or even in the woods. But THEY WERE COLORED PEOPLE—So thought he, who so unceremoniously ejected them from their comfortable homes; and he is not only a PROFESSED friend to their race, but "AN HONORABLE MAN." . . .

After a time, a ray of hope dawned on the dark path of Ellen. She consulted Mr. Greene, the State's attorney, and found that she might bring forward a case of "Trespass and Ejectment," against the purchaser of her property. She had hope to repudiate the whole sale and purchase, on the ground of the illegal or non-advertisement of the sale. This case was brought before the Court of Common Pleas, in January, 1837.

Of course, the whole success of it turned on the point of the sheriff's oath, in regard to the advertisement. When the oath was administered, the sheriff appeared strangely agitated, and many, then present in court, even the judge, thought it was the perturbation of guilt. Nevertheless he attested upon oath, that he had put up the notification in three public places;—viz. at Manchester's tavern bar-room, on the Courthouse door in time of Court, and on Market square. There were three men who came prepared to take their oath, that the notice was never put up at Manchester's; thus invalidating that part of his testimony; but it was found that the oaths of common men could not be taken against that of the High Sheriff. So the case was decided against the plaintiff.

Ellen's next step was to hire two men, whom she fee'd liberally, to make enquiries throughout the city, in regard to those notifications.—They went about, two days, making all possible search for light in regard to the contested notifications, calling upon all those who frequented public places. But no person could be found, who had either seen them, or heard of their being seen. A fine advertisement, truly! And here, let me ask, why was not this sale advertised in the public papers? The same answer that has been given before, will suffice now. THE OWNER OF THE PROPERTY WAS A LABORING COLORED WOMAN. Is not this reply, TRUTH as it is, a LIBEL on the character of those who wrought the work of evil?

Elleanor then brought an action against the sheriff, tending to destroy his testimony in the late case; and on the very day when it was to be laid before the court, Mr.——, the purchaser, came forward and told Ellen's attorney, that he would restore the property for twenty-one hundred dollars, and two years' rent. Ellen then withdrew her case, and set herself about procuring the money. This she raised; and it was duly tendered to Mr.——. But mark HIS regard for his word. He then said that Ellen had been so long[2] in procuring the money, that he must have twenty-three hundred dollars.

---

[2]She had great difficulty in obtaining it, as it was then the period of the greatest pressure; and it was next to impossible to get money at all. [During the Panic of 1837 many banks suspended specie payments.] That Elleanor was able to procure twenty-one hundred dollars, upon her own credit, at such a time, in the space of six weeks, of itself shows the esteem in which she was held, as well as the energy and perseverance, for which she has always been remarkable.

The additional two hundred dollars were then raised, but the gentleman, in consequence of repairs and alterations, which he could have had no right to make, and require pay for, as the case stood, next demanded twenty-five hundred dollars, with six months' rent.

The suspended action had, in the mean time, been again brought forward; and was to have been tried before the Circuit Court. But so anxious was Ellen again to possess the property, that she once more withdrew her action, and came to the exorbitant terms of Mr.——. She again hired the additional two hundred dollars; and finally effected a settlement.

This conduct, on the part of the purchaser, requires no comment; for its meanness, not to say dishonesty, is self-evident in the simplest statement of the facts themselves. But this is not all. The sheriff had informed Mr.——, that he could sue Elleanor for house rent, as her goods had never been removed from the tenement she had occupied. This he actually did, and laid an attachment on her furniture, which was advertised to be sold at public auction: and it would have been, had not a gentleman who had the management of her business, gone forward and settled with Mr.——.

The whole affair, from beginning to end, in all its connections and bearings, was A WEB OF INIQUITY. It was a wanton outrage upon the simplest and most evident principles of justice. But the subject of this wrong, or rather of this accumulation of wrongs, was a woman, and therefore weak—a COLORED WOMAN—and therefore contemptible. No MAN ever would have been treated so; and if A WHITE WOMAN had been the subject of such wrongs, the whole town—nay, the whole country, would have been indignant: and the actors would have been held up to the contempt they deserve!—The story would have flown upon the wings of the wind to the most remote borders of our land. Newspaper editors would have copied, and commented on it, till every spirit of honor, of justice, and of chivalry, would have been roused. At home benevolent SOCIETIES would have met, and taken efficient means to relieve the sufferer; while every heart would have melted in kindness, and every bosom have poured out its sympathy. Is this wrong the less a wrong, because the subject of it is weak and defenceless? By the common laws of HONOR, it is cowardice to strike the unarmed and the weak. By the same rule, HE WHO INJURES THE DEFENCELESS, ADDS MEANNESS TO CRIME. ... Then will not every reader of this little book, recommend it to the notice of the humane, and endeavor to promote its sale; not for its own sake, but for the sake of her, who depends upon its success, for deliverance from the difficulties in which she is involved. Ellen has yet a large debt to liquidate, before her estate is freed from its incumbrance. With a little timely help, together with her earnings, she may be able to do this.

Susie King Taylor

Susie King Taylor's reminiscences of her dramatic life open with a recita-
tion of her ancestry. Pride in having knowledge of her early forebears, even
though imprecise, makes her account important. If the longevity she attributes to her great-great-grandmother appears unlikely, it is not beyond the
bounds of possibility.

The remarkable, not the conventional, was characteristic of the lives
of black American women in the nineteenth century. Unheralded experiences that seem trivial in the retelling were frequently decisive. Differences
of birth, of circumstance, or of chance divided possibility from stagnation.
Susie King Taylor, who early displayed initiative, resourcefulness, and self-
confidence, was rescued from a commonplace existence by such a series of
events. She was born on an island off the coast of Savannah, Georgia, in
1848 to a mother who was a favored house slave in one of its established
families. The child had a personal history, roots, and identifiable relations.
At the age of seven she and a brother were permitted to stay in Savannah
with her maternal grandmother, apparently a free black who had a guardian
rather than a master. The guardian was the master of Susie's mother, of
herself, and of two other siblings.

Hers was an urban environment during adolescence, and under its
influence she matured swiftly. A smuggled education, described in her
Reminiscences, was the principal boon of her surroundings. Environment
and education combined to produce an astonishing sensibility. Not yet fourteen, she found herself in charge of some forty children who had escaped to
the Georgia Sea Islands in the early stages of the Civil War to seek the
protection of the Union Army. A city training, in her own estimation, was
the chief explanation of her capacities. Later in that same year, 1862, she
married Edward King, also a literate urban black. When the First South
Carolina Volunteers became the first black regiment, King joined it. His wife
"was enrolled as a laundress." She also was a nurse, and if there was time,
she taught many of the men when off duty to read and to write. Each
achievement served as a springboard for new competence.

Finally the peace came and Susie and her husband returned to Savannah. They began life afresh, the wife operating a private school, the
husband contracting for the unloading of ships in port. Before their first

child was born in 1866, King died. The widow was able to support herself with income from the school until public instruction became available for blacks, drying up that source of revenue. She then moved to Boston, entered domestic service, and remarried in 1879. In 1898 her son became ill in Louisiana where he was traveling with a theatrical company. She returned to the South to be with him. Near death, he needed specialist care and the solace of home, but Jim Crow laws prevented her from bringing him back to Boston. "There are," she wrote bitterly, "many people who do not know what some of the colored women did during the war. . . . These things should be kept in history before the people."[1]

My great-great-grandmother was 120 years old when she died. She had seven children, and five of her boys were in the Revolutionary War. She was from Virginia, and was half Indian. She was so old she had to be held in the sun to help restore or prolong her vitality.

My great-grandmother, one of her daughters, named Susanna, was married to Peter Simons, and was one hundred years old when she died, from a stroke of paralysis in Savannah. She was the mother of twenty-four children, twenty-three being girls. She was one of the noted mid-wives of her day. In 1820 my grandmother was born, and named after her grandmother, Dolly, and in 1833 she married Fortune Lambert Reed. Two children blessed their union, James and Hagar Ann. James died at the age of twelve years.

My mother was born in 1834. She married Raymond Baker in 1847. Nine children were born to them, three dying in infancy. I was the first born. I was born on the Grest Farm (which was on an island known as Isle of Wight), Liberty County, about thirty-five miles from Savannah, Ga., on August 6, 1848, my mother being waitress for the Grest family. I have often been told by mother of the care Mrs. Grest took of me. She was very fond of me, and I remember when my brother and I were small children, and Mr. Grest would go away on business, Mrs. Grest would place us at the foot of her bed to sleep and keep her company. Sometimes he would return home earlier than he had expected to; then she would put us on the floor.

When I was about seven years old, Mr. Grest allowed my grandmother to take my brother and me to live with her in Savannah [the grandmother was apparently a free black, living under the guardianship of the man who was master of her daughter and grandchildren; it is not clear how she came

[1]Susie King Taylor, *Reminiscences of My Life in Camp with the 33rd United States Colored Troops, late 1st S.C. Volunteers* (Boston, 1902), pp. 15, 67–68.

Source: Susie King Taylor, *Reminiscences of My Life in Camp with the 33rd United States Colored Troops, late 1st S.C. Volunteers* (Boston, 1902), pp. 1–11.

to be free]. There were no railroad connections in those days between this place and Savannah; all travel was by stagecoaches. I remember, as if it were yesterday, the coach which ran in from Savannah, with its driver, whose beard nearly reached his knees. His name was Shakespeare, and often I would go to the stable where he kept his horses, on Barnard Street in front of the old Arsenal, just to look at his wonderful beard.

My grandmother went every three months to see my mother. She would hire a wagon to carry bacon, tobacco, flour, molasses, and sugar. These she would trade with people in the neighboring places, for eggs, chickens, or cash, if they had it. These, in turn, she carried back to the city market, where she had a customer who sold them for her. The profit from these, together with laundry work and care of some bachelors' rooms, made a good living for her.

The hardest blow to her was the failure of the Freedmen's Savings Bank in Savannah, for in that bank she had placed her savings, about three thousand dollars, the result of her hard labor and self-denial before the war, and which, by dint of shrewdness and care, she kept together all through the war. She felt it more keenly, coming as it did in her old age, when her life was too far spent to begin anew; but she took a practical view of the matter, for she said, "I will leave it all in God's hand. If the Yankees did take all our money, they freed my race; God will take care of us."

In 1888 she wrote me here (Boston), asking me to visit her, as she was getting very feeble and wanted to see me once before she passed away. I made up my mind to leave at once, but about the time I planned to go, in March, a fearful blizzard swept our country, and travel was at a standstill for nearly two weeks; but March 15 I left on the first through steamer from New York, en route for the South, where I again saw my grandmother, and we felt thankful that we were spared to meet each other once more. This was the last time I saw her, for in May, 1889, she died. . . .

I was born under the slave law in Georgia, in 1848, and was brought up by my grandmother in Savannah. There were three of us with her, my younger sister and brother. My brother and I being the two eldest, we were sent to a friend of my grandmother, Mrs. Woodhouse, a widow, to learn to read and write. She was a free woman and lived on Bay Lane, between Habersham and Price streets, about half a mile from my house. We went every day about nine o'clock, with our books wrapped in paper to prevent the police or white persons from seeing them. We went in, one at a time, through the gate, into the yard to the L kitchen, which was the schoolroom. She had twenty-five or thirty children whom she taught, assisted by her daughter, Mary Jane. The neighbors would see us going in sometimes, but they supposed we were there learning trades, as it was the custom to give children a trade of some kind. After school we left the same way we entered, one by one, when we would go to a square, about a block from the school, and wait for each other. We would gather laurel leaves and pop them on our hands, on our way home. I remained at her school for two years or more, when I was sent to a Mrs. Mary Beasley, where I continued until May, 1860, when she told my grandmother she had taught me all she knew, and grandmother had better get some one else who could teach me more, so I stopped my studies for a while.

I had a white playmate about this time, named Katie O'Connor, who lived on the next corner of the street from my house, and who attended a convent. One day she told me, if I would promise not to tell her father, she would give me some lessons. On my promise not to do so, and getting her mother's consent, she gave me lessons about four months, every evening. At the end of this time she was put into the convent permanently, and I have never seen her since.

A month after this, James Blouis, our landlord's son, was attending the High School, and was very fond of grandmother, so she asked him to give me a few lessons, which he did until the middle of 1861, when the Savannah Volunteer Guards, to which he and his brother belonged, were ordered to the front under General Barton. In the first battle of Manassas, his brother Eugene was killed, and James deserted over to the Union side, and at the close of the war went to Washington, D.C., where he has since resided.

I often wrote passes for my grandmother, for all colored persons, free or slaves, were compelled to have a pass; free colored people having a guardian in place of a master. These passes were good until 10 or 10.30 P.M. for one night or every night for one month. The pass read as follows:—

SAVANNAH, GA., March 1st, 1860.

Pass the bearer————from 9 to 10.30. P.M.

VALENTINE GREST.

Every person had to have this pass, for at nine o'clock each night a bell was rung, and any colored persons found on the street after this hour were arrested by the watchman, and put in the guard-house until next morning, when their owners would pay their fines and release them. I knew a number of persons who went out at any time at night and were never arrested, as the watchman knew them so well he never stopped them, and seldom asked to see their passes, only stopping them long enough, sometimes, to say "Howdy," and then telling them to go along.

About this time I had been reading so much about the "Yankees" I was very anxious to see them. The whites would tell their colored people not to go to the Yankees, for they would harness them to carts and make them pull the carts around, in place of horses. I asked grandmother, one day, if this was true. She replied, "Certainly not!" that the white people did not want slaves to go over to the Yankees, and told them these things to frighten them. "Don't you see those signs pasted about the streets? one reading, 'I am a rattlesnake; if you touch me I will strike!' Another reads, 'I am a wild-cat! Beware,' etc. These are warnings to the North; so don't mind what the white people say." I wanted to see these wonderful "Yankees" so much, as I heard my parents say the Yankee was going to set all the slaves free. Oh, how those people prayed for freedom! I remember, one night, my grandmother went out into the suburbs of the city to a church meeting, and they were fervently singing this old hymn,—

"Yes, we all shall be free,
Yes, we all shall be free,
Yes, we all shall be free,
When the Lord shall appear,"—

when the police came in and arrested all who were there, saying they were planning freedom, and sang "the Lord," in place of "Yankee," to blind any one who might be listening. Grandmother never forgot that night, although she did not stay in the guard-house, as she sent to her guardian, who came at once for her; but this was the last meeting she ever attended out of the city proper.

On April 1, 1862, about the time the Union soldiers were firing on Fort Pulaski, I was sent out into the country to my mother. I remember what a roar and din the guns made. They jarred the earth for miles. The fort was at last taken by them [10–11 April 1862]. Two days after the taking of Fort Pulaski, my uncle took his family of seven and myself to St. Catherine Island. We landed under the protection of the Union fleet, and remained there two weeks, when about thirty of us were taken aboard the gunboat P——, to be transferred to St. Simon's Island; and at last, to my unbounded joy, I saw the "Yankee."

After we were all settled aboard and started on our journey, Captain Whitmore, commanding the boat, asked me where I was from. I told him Savannah, Ga. He asked if I could read; I said, "Yes!" "Can you write?" he next asked. "Yes, I can do that also," I replied, and as if he had some doubts of my answers he handed me a book and a pencil and told me to write my name and where I was from. I did this; when he wanted to know if I could sew. On hearing I could, he asked me to hem some napkins for him. He was surprised at my accomplishments (for they were such in those days), for he said he did not know there were any negroes in the South able to read or write. He said, "You seem to be so different from the other colored people who came from the same place you did." "No!" I replied, "the only difference is, they were reared in the country and I in the city, as was a man from Darien, Ga., named Edward King." [Later that year she and Edward King were married.] That seemed to satisfy him, and we had no further conversation that day on the subject.

In the afternoon the captain spied a boat in the distance, and as it drew nearer he noticed it had a white flag hoisted, but before it had reached the Putumoka he ordered all passengers between decks, so we could not be seen, for he thought they might be spies. The boat finally drew alongside of our boat, and had Mr. Edward Donegall on board, who wanted his two servants, Nick and Judith. He wanted these, as they were his own children. Our captain told him he knew nothing of them, which was true, for at the time they were on St. Simon's, and not, as their father supposed, on our boat. After the boat left, we were allowed to come up on deck again. . . .

Next morning we arrived at St. Simon's, and the captain told Commodore Goldsborough [probably Commodore John R. Goldsborough, brother of the more famous Louis M. Goldsborough who was raised to the rank of rear-admiral in July 1862] about this affair, and his reply was, "Captain Whitmore, you should not have allowed them to return; you should have kept them." After I had been on St. Simon's about three days, Commodore Goldsborough heard of me, and came to Gaston Bluff to see me. I found him very cordial. He said Captain Whitmore had spoken to him of me, and that he was pleased to hear of my being so capable, etc., and wished me to take charge of a school for the children on the island. I told him I would gladly do so, if I could have some books. He said I should have them, and in a week or two I received two large boxes of books and testaments from the North. I had about forty children to teach, beside a number of adults who came to me nights, all of them so eager to learn to read, to read above anything else.

Annie Louise Burton

Annie Louise Burton was born in 1859 or 1860 on an Alabama plantation. Her father was a neighboring plantation owner who never acknowledged her. Her mother was a cook, reared in childhood alongside the girl who was to become her mistress.

Annie Burton's mother quarreled with the first lady of the manor and earned her first whipping. Her mother's reaction to the lash, it may be assumed, was not much different from that of any human being, but she contrived to accomplish what was comparatively unusual: she ran away. Annie's mother not only ran away, she remained among the missing for three long years. Escape—amounting psychologically to abandonment plus thirty-six months of privation—could not but imprint itself on a very young child who doubtless was often reminded that her wicked parent had deserted.

The maternal flight occurred after the Civil War had begun, which probably made it easier to disappear and remain undiscovered. When the war was over, the mother suddenly reappeared at the old homestead to reclaim her brood. Appomattox and the Emancipation Proclamation notwithstanding, some Alabama planters wished to hold on to their slaves. Violations of the peace and the proclamation were not confined to Alabama. Many former slaveholders simply did not inform their erstwhile slaves. Since most of the latter were illiterate, the transmission wires of rumor, gossip, and the federal authorities were the sole means of communication.

Annie's former master might well have succeeded had not her mother managed to steal them away. Victorious in this artful and perilous adventure, she was also successful in establishing a home and a family life. The home was simple; the family consisted of Annie's mother and her children to which two new ones had been added. Her husband, she later told a visitor, had died soon after the war, and the nature of this relationship as well as its location was never revealed.

Annie Burton's life in reconstituted form now begins. By this time she was between six and seven years of age. When a white household in the neighborhood required the services of a young nursemaid, Annie secured the place. She was at once adopted into the family, although her mother continued to care for her well-being and never thereafter relinquished her *maternal duties. But here Annie had her first schooling and, little though it was by present day standards, it moved her into the slim minority of black women who took pride in literacy. She was instructed by her white family; she went to Sunday school; she learned to read and to write. At the age of twenty, when she had shifted her residence to Georgia, she spent six months in a Macon high school.*

This was only the formal equipment with which Annie Burton met the collisions of life. There was also her slave experience, her mother, her white employer, and the employer's menage, as well as the emotional sustenance of living with her relations. Her half-brothers and half-sisters were the hub of her private life; to all of them she was protective, kind, and affectionate. Annie Burton's life was a tribute to the education given her by her mother, and to the strength of her own character and will.

Copious energy and resourcefulness enabled her to operate a restaurant, a boarding house, and other business establishments. Money was never plentiful, and she was barely able to keep her head above the deluge of want. But she provided. When an orphaned nephew, long under her protection as a member of her household, went off to the Hampton Institute, Annie Burton was verging on thirty. At this point, she permitted herself to marry. Jobs in resort hotels for herself and her husband sustained them.

At forty-four she went back to school. Now living in Boston, she attended evening classes at the Franklin Institute. One of her teachers, fascinated by the history of her life, offered to assist her in the writing of an autobiography. After years of labor, Memories of Childhood's Slavery Days *appeared in print in 1909. This ninety-seven page volume is the chief source of knowledge about her. For Annie Burton it was a creative experiment in self-realization.*

The memory of my happy, care-free childhood days on the plantation, with my little white and black companions, is often with me. Neither master nor mistress nor neighbors had time to bestow a thought upon us, for the great Civil War was raging. That great event in American history was a matter wholly outside the realm of our childish interests. Of course we heard our elders discuss the various events of the great struggle, but it meant nothing to us.

On the plantation there were ten white children and fourteen colored children. Our days were spent roaming about from plantation to plantation, not knowing or caring what things were going on in the great world outside our little realm. Planting time and harvest time were happy days for us. How

---

Source: Annie L. Burton, *Memories of Childhood's Slavery Days* (Boston, 1909), pp. 3–12, 39–45, 49–51, 46.

often at the harvest time the planters discovered cornstalks missing from the ends of the rows, and blamed the crows! We were called the "little fairy devils." To the sweet potatoes and peanuts and sugar cane we also helped ourselves.

Those slaves that were not married served the food from the great house, and about half-past eleven they would send the older children with food to the workers in the fields. Of course, I followed, and before we got to the fields, we had eaten the food nearly all up. When the workers returned home they complained, and we were whipped.

The slaves got their allowance every Monday night of molasses, meat, corn meal, and a kind of flour called "dredgings" or "shorts." Perhaps this allowance would be gone before the next Monday night, in which case the slaves would steal hogs and chickens. Then would come the whipping-post. Master himself never whipped his slaves; this was left to the overseer.

We children had no supper, and only a little piece of bread or something of the kind in the morning. Our dishes consisted of one wooden bowl, and oyster shells were our spoons. This bowl served for about fifteen children, and often the dogs and the ducks and the peafowl had a dip in it. Sometimes we had buttermilk and bread in our bowl, sometimes greens or bones.

Our clothes were little homespun cotton slips, with short sleeves. I never knew what shoes were until I got big enough to earn them myself.

If a slave man and woman wished to marry, a party would be arranged some Saturday night among the slaves. The marriage ceremony consisted of the pair jumping over a stick. If no children were born within a year or so, the wife was sold.

At New Year's, if there was any debt or mortgage on the plantation, the extra slaves were taken to Clayton and sold at the court house. In this way families were separated.

When they were getting recruits for the war, we were allowed to go to Clayton to see the soldiers.

I remember, at the beginning of the war, two colored men were hung in Clayton; one, Caesar King, for killing a blood hound and biting off an overseer's ear; the other, Dabney Madison, for the murder of his master. Dabney Madison's master was really shot by a man named Houston, who was infatuated with Madison's mistress, and who had hired Madison to make the bullets for him. Houston escaped after the deed, and the blame fell on Dabney Madison, as he was the only slave of his master and mistress. The clothes of the two victims were hung on two pine trees, and no colored person would touch them. Since I have grown up, I have seen the skeleton of one of these men in the office of a doctor in Clayton. . . .

At one time, when they were building barns on the plantation, one of the big boys got a little brandy and gave us children all a drink, enough to make us drunk. Four doctors were sent for, but nobody could tell what was the matter with us, except they thought we had eaten something poisonous. They wanted to give us some castor oil, but we refused to take it, because we thought that the oil was made from the bones of the dead men we had seen. Finally, we told about the big white boy giving us the brandy, and the mystery was cleared up.

Young as I was then, I remember this conversation between master and mistress, on master's return from the gate one day, when he had received the latest news: "William, what is the news from the seat of war?" "A great battle was fought at Bull Run, and the Confederates won," he replied. "Oh, good, good," said mistress, "and what did Jeff Davis say?" "Look out for the blockade. I do not know what the end may be soon," he answered. "What does Jeff Davis mean by that?" she asked. "Sarah Anne, I don't know, unless he means that the niggers will be free." "O, my God, what shall we do?" "I presume," he said, "we shall have to put our boys to work and hire help." "But," she said, "what will the niggers do if they are free? Why, they will starve if we don't keep them." "Oh, well," he said, "let them wander, if they will not stay with their owners. I don't doubt that many owners have been good to their slaves, and they would rather remain with their owners than wander about without home or country."

My mistress often told me that my father was a planter who owned a plantation about two miles from ours. He was a white man, born in Liverpool, England. He died in Lewisville, Alabama, in the year 1875.

I will venture to say that I only saw my father a dozen times, when I was about four years old; and those times I saw him only from a distance, as he was driving by the great house of our plantation. Whenever my mistress saw him going by, she would take me by the hand and run out upon the piazza, and exclaim, "Stop there, I say! Don't you want to see and speak to and caress your darling child? She often speaks of you and wants to embrace her dear father. See what a bright and beautiful daughter she is, a perfect picture of yourself. Well, I declare, you are an affectionate father." I well remember that whenever my mistress would speak thus and upbraid him, he would whip up his horse and get out of sight and hearing as quickly as possible. My mistress's action was, of course, intended to humble and shame my father. I never spoke to him, and cannot remember that he ever noticed me, or in any way acknowledged me to be his child.

My mother and my mistress were children together, and grew up to be mothers together. My mother was the cook in my mistress's household. One morning when master had gone to Eufaula, my mother and my mistress got into an argument, the consequence of which was that my mother was whipped, for the first time in her life. Whereupon, my mother refused to do any more work, and ran away from the plantation. For three years we did not see her again.

Our plantation was one of several thousand acres, comprising large level fields, upland, and considerable forests of Southern pine. Cotton, corn, sweet potatoes, sugar cane, wheat, and rye were the principal crops raised on the plantation. It was situated near the P—— River, and about twenty-three miles from Clayton, Ala.

One day my master heard that the Yankees were coming our way, and he immediately made preparations to get his goods and valuables out of their reach. The big six-mule team was brought to the smoke-house door, and loaded with hams and provisions. After being loaded, the team was put in the care of two of the most trustworthy and valuable slaves that my master owned, and driven away. It was master's intention to have these things taken to a swamp, and there concealed in a pit that had recently been made for the purpose. But just before the team left the main road for the by-road that led to the swamp, the two slaves were surprised by the Yankees, who at once took possession of the provisions, and started the team toward Clayton, where the Yankees had headquarters. The road to Clayton ran past our plantation. One of the slave children happened to look up the road, and saw the Yankees coming, and gave warning. Whereupon, my master left unceremoniously for the woods, and remained concealed there for five days. The niggers had run away whenever they got a chance, but now it was master's and the other white folks' turn to run.

The Yankees rode up to the piazza of the great house and inquired who owned the plantation. They gave orders that nothing must be touched or taken away, as they intended to return shortly and take possession. My mistress and the slaves watched for their return day and night for more than a week, but the Yankees did not come back.

One morning in April, 1865, my master got the news that the Yankees had left Mobile Bay and crossed the Confederate lines, and that the Emancipation Proclamation had been signed by President Lincoln [news of the Emancipation Proclamation traveled very slowly to this rural outpost, from January 1863, or else became believable only after the military collapse of the South]. Mistress suggested that the slaves should not be told of their freedom; but master said he would tell them, because they would soon find it out, even if he did not tell them. Mistress, however, said she could keep my mother's three children, for my mother had now been gone so long.

All tho slaves left the plantation upon the news of their freedom, except those who were feeble or sickly. With the help of these, the crops were gathered. My mistress and her daughters had to go to the kitchen and to the washtub. My little half-brother, Henry, and myself had to gather chips, and help all we could. My sister, Caroline, who was twelve years old, could help in the kitchen.

After the war, the Yankees took all the good mules and horses from the plantation, and left their old army stock. We children chanced to come across one of the Yankees' old horses, that had "U.S." branded on him. We called him "Old Yank" and got him fattened up. One day in August, six of us children took "Old Yank" and went away back on the plantation for watermelons. Coming home, we thought we would make the old horse trot. When "Old Yank" commenced to trot, our big melons dropped off, but we couldn't stop the horse for some time. Finally, one of the big boys went back and got some more melons, and left us eating what we could find of the ones that had been dropped. Then all we six, with our melons, got on "Old Yank" and went home. We also used to hitch "Old Yank" into a wagon and get wood. But one sad day in the fall, the Yankees came back again, and gathered up their old stock, and took "Old Yank" away.

One day mistress sent me out to do some churning under a tree. I went to sleep and jerked the churn over on top of me, and consequently got a whipping.

My mother came for us at the end of the year 1865, and demanded that her children be given up to her. This, mistress refused to do, and threatened to set the dogs on my mother if she did not at once leave the place. My mother went away, and remained with some of the neighbors until supper time. Then she got a boy to tell Caroline to come down to the fence. When she came, my mother told her to go back and get Henry and myself and bring us down to the gap in the fence as quick as she could. Then my mother took Henry in her arms, and my sister carried me on her back. We climbed fences and crossed fields, and after several hours came to a little hut which my mother had secured on a plantation. We had no more than reached the place, and made a little fire, when master's two sons rode up and demanded that the children be returned. My mother refused to give us up. Upon her offering to go with them to the Yankee headquarters to find out if it were really true that all negroes had been made free, the young men left, and troubled us no more.

The cabin that was now our home was made of logs. It had one door, and an opening in one wall, with an inside shutter, was the only window. The door was fastened with a latch. Our beds were some straw.

There were six in our little family; my mother, Caroline, Henry, two other children that my mother had brought with her upon her return, and myself. . . .

Right after the war when my mother had got settled in her hut, with her little brood hovered around her, from which she had been so long absent, we had nothing to eat, and nothing to sleep on save some old pieces of horse-blankets and hay that the soldiers gave her. The first day in the hut was a rainy day; and as night drew near it grew more fierce, and we children had gathered some little fagots to make a fire by the time mother came home, with something for us to eat, such as she had gathered through the day. It was only corn meal and pease and ham-bone and skins which she had for our supper. She had started a little fire, and said, "Some of you close that door," for it was cold. She swung the pot over the fire and filled it with the pease and ham-bone and skins. Then she seated her little brood around the fire on the pieces of blanket, where we watched with all our eyes, our hearts filled with desire, looking to see what she would do next. She took down an old broken earthen bowl, and tossed into it the little meal she had brought, stirring it up with water, making a hoe cake. She said, "One of you draw that griddle out here," and she placed it on the few little coals. Perhaps this griddle you have never seen, or one like it. I will describe it to you. This griddle was a round piece of iron, quite thick, having three legs. It might have been made in a blacksmith's shop, for I have never seen one like it before or since. It was placed upon the coals, and with an old iron spoon she put on this griddle half of the corn meal she had mixed up. She said, "I will put a tin plate over this, and put it away for your breakfast." We five children were eagerly watching the pot boiling, with the pease and ham-bone. The rain was pattering on the roof of the hut. All at once there came a knock at the door. My mother answered the knock. When she opened the door, there stood a white woman and three little children, all dripping with the rain. My mother said, "In the name of the Lord, where are you going on such a night, with these children?" The woman said, "Auntie, I am travelling. Will you please let me stop here to-night, out of the rain, with my children?" My mother said, "Yes, honey. I ain't got much, but what I have got I will share with you." "God bless you!" They all came in. We children looked in wonder at what had come. But my mother scattered her own little brood and made a place for the forlorn wanderers. She said, "Wait, honey, let me turn over that hoe cake." Then the two women fell to talking, each telling a tale of woe. After a time, my mother called out, "Here, you, Louise, or some one of you, put some fagots under the pot, so these pease can get done." We couldn't put them under fast enough, first one and then another of us children, the mothers still talking. Soon my mother said, "Draw that hoe cake one side, I guess it is done." My mother said to the woman, "Honey, ain't you got no husband?" She said, "No, my husband got killed in the war." My mother replied, "Well, my husband died right after the war. I have been away from my little brood for four years. With a hard struggle, I have got them away from the Farrin plantation, for they did not want to let them go. But I got them. I was determined to have them. But they would not let me have them if they could have kept them. With God's help I will keep them from starving. The white folks are good to me. They give me work, and I know, with God's help, I can get along." The white woman replied, "Yes, Auntie, my husband left me on a rich man's plantation. This man promised to look out for me until my husband came home; but he got killed in the war, and the Yankees have set his negroes free and he said he could not help me any more, and we would have to do the best we could for ourselves. I gave my things to a woman to keep for me until I could find my kinsfolk. They live about fifty miles from here, up in the country. I am on my way there now." My mother said, "How long will it take you to get there?" "About three days, if it don't rain." My mother said, "Ain't you got some way to ride there?" "No, Auntie, there is no way of riding up where my folks live, the place where I am from."

We hoped the talk was most ended, for we were anxiously watching that pot. Pretty soon my mother seemed to realize our existence. She exclaimed, "My Lord! I suppose the little children are nearly starved. Are those pease done, young ones?" She turned and said to the white woman, "Have you-all had anything to eat?" "We stopped at a house about dinner

time, but the woman didn't have anything but some bread and buttermilk."
My mother said, "Well, honey, I ain't got but a little, but I will divide with
you." The woman said, "Thank you, Auntie. You just give my children a
little; I can do without it."

Then came the dividing. We all watched with all our eyes to see what
the shares would be. My mother broke a mouthful of bread and put it on
each of the tin plates. Then she took the old spoon and equally divided the
pea soup. We children were seated around the fire, with some little wooden
spoons. But the wooden spoons didn't quite go round, and some of us had to
eat with our fingers. Our share of the meal, however, was so small that we
were as hungry when we finished as when we began.

My mother said, "Take that rag and wipe your face and hands, and
give it to the others, and let them use it, too. Put those plates upon the
table." We immediately obeyed orders, and took our seats again around the
fire. "One of you go and pull that straw out of the corner and get ready to go
to bed." We all lay down on the straw, the white children with us, and my
mother covered us over with the blanket. We were soon in the "Land of
Nod," forgetting our empty stomachs. The two mothers still continued to
talk, sitting down on the only seats, a couple of blocks. A little back against
the wall my mother and the white woman slept.

Bright and early in the morning we were called up, and the rest of the
hoe cake was eaten for breakfast, with a little meat, some coffee sweetened
with molasses. The little wanderers and their mother shared our meal, and
then they started again on their journey towards their home among their
kinsfolk, and we never saw them again. My mother said, "God bless you! I
wish you all good luck. I hope you will reach your home safely." Then
mother said to us, "You young ones put away that straw and sweep up the
place, because I have to go to my work." But she came at noon and brought
us a nice dinner, more satisfactory than the supper and breakfast we had
had. We children were delighted that there were no little white children to
share our meal this time. . . .

In 1875 I was taken sick [the author was fifteen or sixteen years old at
this time]. I thought I was going to die, and I promised the Lord I would
serve Him if he would only spare my life. When I got well again, however, I
forgot all about my promise. Then I was taken sick again. It seemed I had to
go through a dark desert place, where great demons stood on either side. In
the distance I could just see a dim light, and I tried to get to this light, but
could not reach it. Then I found myself in a great marsh, and was sinking. I
threw up my hands and said, "Lord, if Thou wilt raise me from this pit, I
will never fail to serve Thee." Then it seemed as if I mounted on wings into
the air, and all the demons that stood about made a great roaring. My flight
ended on the top of a hill. But I was troubled because I could not find the
light. All at once, at the sound of a loud peal of thunder, the earth opened,
and I fell down into the pits of hell. Again I prayed to God to save me from
this, and again I promised to serve Him. My prayer was answered, and I was

able to fly out of the pit, on to a bank. At the foot of the little hill on which I sat were some little children, and they called to me to come down. But I could not get down. Then the children raised a ladder for me, and I came down among them. A little cherub took me by the hand and led me in the River of Badjied of Jordan. I looked at my ankles and shoulders and discovered I had little wings. On the river was a ship. The children, the cherub and I got into the ship. When we reached a beautiful spot, the little cherub made the ship fast, and there opened before us pearly gates, and we all passed through into the golden street. The street led to the throne of God, about which we marched. Then the cherub conducted us to a table where a feast was spread. Then the children vanished. The cherub took me by the hand, and said, "Go back into the world, and tell the saints and sinners what a Savior you have found, and if you prove faithful I will take you to Heaven to live forever, when I come again." . . .

Five years ago, I began to go to the Franklin evening school. Mr. Guild was the master. At one time he requested all the pupils to write the story of their lives, and he considered my composition so interesting he said he thought if I could work it up and enlarge upon it, I could write a book. He promised to help me. My teacher was Miss Emerson, and she was interested in me. But the next year Miss Emerson gave up teaching, and Mr. Guild died. . . .

. . . I worked on. On this, my 49th birthday, I can say I believe that the book is close to the finish.

Ellen Craft

Escapes to freedom, heroic and spectacular, were not the dominant response to slavery. The odds against such escapes were overwhelming. Ellen Craft defeated the odds, but she did not do it alone. The story of Ellen Craft cannot be told apart from the story of her husband, for their plan was jointly conceived and executed. Though dramatic in the telling, every break for freedom was a gamble—desperate, frightening, and unbearably hard. Unless such breaks were impulsive and therefore thoughtless, they had to be carefully designed in as much minute detail as imagination and wit allowed. The Craft adventure was bold in conception; it required courage, ability, and faith.

Ellen was born as a slave in Georgia about 1827, where William Craft was also born two years before. Ellen's father was the owner of her mother. William's master, after moving to Macon, apprenticed him to a cabinet-maker to learn the trade. He became a skilled worker who could be hired out for wages, which went to the master. Valuable in this capacity, William was mortgaged to a bank as security against a loan for cotton speculation. When the master was unable to repay the loan, the bank auctioned its human property to the highest bidder. William was purchased by the bank cashier and continued in his work at the cabinet shop.

Urban slave life gave William Craft some access to money and to the comparatively free use of his own time beyond the hours of his shop work. He grew accustomed to independence of thought and action beyond the range permitted most men who were slaves.

Ellen and William fell in love. Marriage was postponed since her mother's history taught her that without legal freedom there could be no security for mother and child. And Macon, Georgia, was a long way from free soil. Prospects for escape seemed vain and they finally decided upon a "slave marriage." They also determined to be on the alert should any hope of escaping present itself.

The Crafts were able to benefit from unusual circumstances. She was a favored house slave and with her husband lived in the privacy of a one-room cottage on the grounds of the family home. With a house to themselves and William's freedom of movement, the impossible began to seem feasible. Gossamer fragments of hope were woven into a plot.

They left Macon at dawn on 21 December 1848 and arrived in Philadelphia on Christmas morning. Antislavery Quakers, abolitionists, and free blacks were prepared for the advent of fugitives. Philadelphia Friends welcomed them, afforded them shelter, and taught them to read and write. They also conferred with other collaborators to prepare for the journey to New England. The editors of the Liberator were kept informed and lines of contact were extended. Boston gave them a home, and the learned and kindly Unitarian minister Theodore Parker married them according to law. William led the simple life of an artisan's assistant for the next two years.

Enthusiasm for the Crafts among antislavery elements in the North was matched by the determination of southern partisans to apprehend them. The Liberator celebrated the escape and its participants in the issue of 12 January 1849. These reports, read as avidly by slave hunters as by abolitionists, led to a concerted search for the Crafts. With the new Fugitive Slave Act of 1850 to justify such action, agents representing the Macon owners appeared in Boston to begin legal proceedings.

Close Boston friends conspired with abolitionists to arrange for passage abroad. In England antislavery groups protected the Crafts and enlisted others in their support. Lord Byron's widow helped to facilitate their education and to arrange conditions for their comfort. Life began anew. The safety of England gave them peace and the fulfillment of rearing a family in freedom.

RUNNING A THOUSAND MILES FOR FREEDOM.

Part I.

My wife and myself were born in different towns in the State of Georgia, which is one of the principal slave States. It is true, our condition as slaves was not by any means the worst; but the mere idea that we were held as chattels, and deprived of all legal rights—the thought that we had to give up our hard earnings to a tyrant, to enable him to live in idleness and luxury— the thought that we could not call the bones and sinews that God gave us our own: but above all, the fact that another man had the power to tear from our cradle the new-born babe and sell it in the shambles like a brute, and then scourge us if we dared to lift a finger to save it from such a fate, haunted us for years. . . .

My wife's first master was her father, and her mother his slave, and the latter is still the slave of his widow.

Source: William Craft, Running a Thousand Miles for Freedom; or, the Escape of William and Ellen Craft from Slavery (London, 1860), pp. 1–2, 15–16, 27–37, 40–62, 68, 74–93, 107–9.

Notwithstanding my wife being of African extraction on her mother's side, she is almost white—in fact, she is so nearly so that the tyrannical old lady to whom she first belonged became so annoyed, at finding her frequently mistaken for a child of the family, that she gave her when eleven years of age to a daughter, as a wedding present. This separated my wife from her mother, and also from several other dear friends. But the incessant cruelty of her old mistress made the change of owners or treatment so desirable, that she did not grumble much at this cruel separation. . . .

From having been myself a slave for nearly twenty-three years, I am quite prepared to say, that the practical working of slavery is worse than the odious laws by which it is governed.

At an early age we were taken by the persons who held us as property to Macon, the largest town in the interior of the State of Georgia, at which place we became acquainted with each other for several years before our marriage; in fact, our marriage was postponed for some time simply because one of the unjust and worse than Pagan laws under which we lived compelled all children of slave mothers to follow their condition. . . .

My wife was torn from her mother's embrace in childhood, and taken to a distant part of the country. She had seen so many other children separated from their parents in this cruel manner, that the mere thought of her ever becoming the mother of a child, to linger out a miserable existence under the wretched system of American slavery, appeared to fill her very soul with horror; and as she had taken what I felt to be an important view of her condition, I did not, at first, press the marriage, but agreed to assist her in trying to devise some plan by which we might escape from our unhappy condition, and then be married. . . .

But, after puzzling our brains for years, we were reluctantly driven to the sad conclusion, that it was almost impossible to escape from slavery in Georgia, and travel 1,000 miles across the slave States. We therefore resolved to get the consent of our owners, be married, settle down in slavery, and endeavour to make ourselves as comfortable as possible under that system; but at the same time ever to keep our dim eyes steadily fixed upon the glimmering hope of liberty, and earnestly pray God mercifully to assist us to escape from our unjust thraldom.

We were married, and prayed and toiled on till December, 1848, at which time . . . a plan suggested itself that proved quite successful, and in eight days after it was first thought of we were free from the horrible trammels of slavery, and glorifying God who had brought us safely out of a land of bondage.

Knowing that slaveholders have the privilege of taking their slaves to any part of the country they think proper, it occurred to me that, as my wife was nearly white, I might get her to disguise herself as an invalid gentleman, and assume to be my master, while I could attend as his slave, and that in this manner we might effect our escape. After I thought of the plan, I suggested it to my wife, but at first she shrank from the idea. She thought it was almost impossible for her to assume that disguise, and travel a distance of 1,000 miles across the slave States. However, on the other hand, she also thought of her condition. She saw that the laws under which we lived did not recognize her to be a woman, but a mere chattel, to be bought and sold, or otherwise dealt with as her owner might see fit. Therefore the more she contemplated her helpless condition, the more anxious she was to escape from it. So she said, "I think it is almost too much for us to undertake; however, I feel that God is on our side, and with his assistance, notwithstanding all the difficulties, we shall be able to succeed. Therefore, if you will purchase the disguise, I will try to carry out the plan."

But after I concluded to purchase the disguise, I was afraid to go to any one to ask him to sell me the articles. It is unlawful in Georgia for a white man to trade with slaves without the master's consent. But, notwithstanding this, many persons will sell a slave any article that he can get the money to buy. Not that they sympathize with the slave, but merely because his testimony is not admitted in court against a free white person.

Therefore, with little difficulty I went to different parts of the town, at odd times, and purchased things piece by piece, (except the trowsers which she found necessary to make,) and took them home to the house where my wife resided. She being a ladies' maid, and a favourite slave in the family, was allowed a little room to herself; and amongst other pieces of furniture which I had made in my overtime, was a chest of drawers; so when I took the articles home, she locked them up carefully in these drawers. No one about the premises knew that she had anything of the kind. So when we fancied we had everything ready the time was fixed for the flight. But we knew it would not do to start off without first getting our master's consent to be away for a few days. Had we left without this, they would soon have had us back into slavery, and probably we should never have got another fair opportunity of even attempting to escape.

Some of the best slaveholders will sometimes give their favourite slaves a few days' holiday at Christmas time; so, after no little amount of perseverance on my wife's part, she obtained a pass from her mistress, allowing her to be away for a few days. The cabinet-maker with whom I worked gave me a similar paper, but said that he needed my services very much, and wished me to return as soon as the time granted was up. I thanked him kindly; but somehow I have not been able to make it convenient to return yet; and, as the free air of good old England agrees so well with my wife and our dear little ones, as well as with myself, it is not at all likely we shall return at present to the "peculiar institution" of chains and stripes.

On reaching my wife's cottage she handed me her pass, and I showed mine, but at that time neither of us were able to read them. It is not only unlawful for slaves to be taught to read, but in some of the States there are heavy penalties attached, such as fines and imprisonment, which will be vigorously enforced upon any one who is humane enough to violate the so-called law. . . .

However, at first, we were highly delighted at the idea of having gained permission to be absent for a few days; but when the thought flashed across my wife's mind, that it was customary for travellers to register their names in the visitors' book at hotels, as well as in the clearance or Custom-house book at Charleston, South Carolina—it made our spirits droop within us.

So, while sitting in our little room upon the verge of despair, all at once my wife raised her head, and with a smile upon her face, which was a moment before bathed in tears, said, "I think I have it!" I asked what it was. She said, "I think I can make a poultice and bind up my right hand in a sling, and with propriety ask the officers to register my name for me." I thought that would do.

It then occurred to her that the smoothness of her face might betray her; so she decided to make another poultice, and put it in a white handkerchief to be worn under the chin, up the cheeks, and to tie over the head. This nearly hid the expression of the countenance, as well as the beardless chin. . . .

My wife, knowing that she would be thrown a good deal into the company of gentlemen, fancied that she could get on better if she had something to go over the eyes; so I went to a shop and bought a pair of green spectacles. This was in the evening.

We sat up all night discussing the plan, and making preparations. Just before the time arrived, in the morning, for us to leave, I cut off my wife's hair square at the back of the head, and got her to dress in the disguise and stand out on the floor. I found that she made a most respectable looking gentleman.

My wife had no ambition whatever to assume this disguise, and would not have done so had it been possible to have obtained our liberty by more simple means; but we knew it was not customary in the South for ladies to travel with male servants; and therefore, notwithstanding my wife's fair complexion, it would have been a very difficult task for her to have come off as a free white lady, with me as her slave; in fact, her not being able to write would have made this quite impossible. We knew that no public conveyance would take us, or any other slave, as a passenger, without our master's consent. This consent could never be obtained to pass into a free state. My wife's being muffled in the poultices, &c., furnished a plausible excuse for avoiding general conversation, of which most Yankee travellers are passionately fond. . . .

When the time had arrived for us to start, we blew out the lights, knelt down, and prayed to our Heavenly Father mercifully to assist us, as he did his people of old, to escape from cruel bondage; and we shall ever feel that God heard and answered our prayer. Had we not been sustained by a kind, and I sometimes think special, providence, we could never have overcome the mountainous difficulties which I am now about to describe.

After this we rose and stood for a few moments in breathless silence,—we were afraid that some one might have been about the cottage listening and watching our movements. So I took my wife by the hand, stepped softly to the door, raised the latch, drew it open, and peeped out. Though there were trees all around the house, yet the foliage scarcely moved; in fact, everything appeared to be as still as death. I then whispered to my wife, "Come my dear, let us make a desperate leap for liberty!" But poor thing, she shrank back, in a state of trepidation. I turned and asked what was the matter; she made no reply, but burst into violent sobs, and threw her head upon my breast. This appeared to touch my very heart, it caused me to enter into her feelings more fully than ever. We both saw the many mountainous difficulties that rose one after the other before our view, and knew far too well what our sad fate would have been, were we caught and forced back into our slavish den. Therefore on my wife's fully realizing the solemn fact that we had to take our lives, as it were, in our hands, and contest every inch of the thousand miles of slave territory over which we had to pass, it made her heart almost sink within her. . . .

However, the sobbing was soon over, and after a few moments of silent prayer she recovered her self-possession, and said, "Come, William, it is getting late, so now let us venture upon our perilous journey."

We then opened the door, and stepped as softly out as "moonlight upon the water." I locked the door with my own key, which I now have before me, and tiptoed across the yard into the street. . . .

We shook hands, said farewell, and started in different directions for the railway station. I took the nearest possible way to the train, for fear I should be recognized by some one, and got into the negro car in which I knew I should have to ride; but my master (as I will now call my wife) took a longer way round, and only arrived there with the bulk of the passengers. He obtained a ticket for himself and one for his slave to Savannah, the first port, which was about two hundred miles off. My master then had the luggage stowed away, and stepped into one of the best carriages.

But just before the train moved off I peeped through the window, and, to my great astonishment, I saw the cabinet-maker with whom I had worked so long, on the platform. He stepped up to the ticket-seller, and asked some question, and then commenced looking rapidly through the passengers, and into the carriages. Fully believing that we were caught, I shrank into a corner, turned my face from the door, and expected in a moment to be dragged out. The cabinet-maker looked into my master's carriage, but did not know him in his new attire, and, as God would have it, before he reached mine the bell rang, and the train moved off.

I have heard since that the cabinet-maker had a presentiment that we were about to "make tracks for parts unknown;" but, not seeing me, his suspicions vanished, until he received the startling intelligence that we had arrived safely in a free State.

As soon as the train had left the platform, my master looked round in the carriage, and was terror-stricken to find a Mr. Cray—an old friend of my wife's master, who dined with the family the day before, and knew my wife from childhood—sitting on the same seat.

The doors of the American railway carriages are at the ends. The passengers walk up the aisle, and take seats on either side; and as my master was engaged in looking out of the window, he did not see who came in.

My master's first impression, after seeing Mr. Cray, was, that he was there for the purpose of securing him. However, my master thought it was not wise to give any information respecting himself, and for fear that Mr. Cray might draw him into conversation and recognise his voice, my master resolved to feign deafness as the only means of self-defence.

After a little while, Mr. Cray said to my master, "It is a very fine morning, sir." The latter took no notice, but kept looking out of the window. Mr. Cray soon repeated this remark, in a little louder tone, but my master remained as before. This indifference attracted the attention of the passengers near, one of whom laughed out. This, I suppose, annoyed the old gentleman; so he said, "I will make him hear;" and in a loud tone of voice repeated, "It is a very fine morning, sir."

My master turned his head, and with a polite bow said, "Yes," and commenced looking out of the window again.

One of the gentlemen remarked that it was a very great deprivation to be deaf. "Yes," replied Mr. Cray, "and I shall not trouble that fellow any more." This enabled my master to breathe a little easier, and to feel that Mr. Cray was not his pursuer after all. . . .

We arrived at Savannah early in the evening, and got into an omnibus, which stopped at the hotel for the passengers to take tea. I stepped into the house and brought my master something on a tray to the omnibus, which took us in due time to the steamer, which was bound for Charleston, South Carolina.

Soon after going on board, my master turned in; and as the captain and some of the passengers seemed to think this strange, and also questioned me respecting him, my master thought I had better get out the flannels and opodeldoc [camphorated soap liniment] which we had prepared for the rheumatism, warm them quickly by the stove in the gentleman's saloon, and bring them to his berth. We did this as an excuse for my master's retiring to bed so early. . . .

. . . I took it to my master's berth, remained there a little while, and then went on deck and asked the steward where I was to sleep. He said there was no place provided for coloured passengers, whether slave or free. So I paced the deck till a late hour, then mounted some cotton bags, in a warm place near the funnel, sat there till morning, and then went and assisted my master to get ready for breakfast.

He was seated at the right hand of the captain, who, together with all the passengers, inquired very kindly after his health. As my master had one hand in a sling, it was my duty to carve his food. But when I went out the captain said, "You have a very attentive boy, sir; but you had better watch him like a hawk when you get on to the North. He seems all very well here, but he may act quite differently there. I know several gentlemen who have lost their valuable niggers among them d——d cut-throat abolitionists." . . .

On my master entering the cabin he found at the breakfast-table a young southern military officer, with whom he had travelled some distance the previous day.

After passing the usual compliments the conversation turned upon the old subject,—niggers.

The officer, who was also travelling with a man-servant, said to my master, "You will excuse me, Sir, for saying I think you are very likely to spoil your boy by saying 'thank you' to him. I assure you, sir, nothing spoils a slave so soon as saying, 'thank you' and 'if you please' to him. The only way to make a nigger toe the mark, and to keep him in his place, is to storm at him like thunder, and keep him trembling like a leaf. Don't you see, when I speak to my Ned, he darts like lightning; and if he didn't I'd skin him."

Just then the poor dejected slave came in, and the officer swore at him fearfully, merely to teach my master what he called the proper way to treat me.

After he had gone out to get his master's luggage ready, the officer said, "That is the way to speak to them. If every nigger was drilled in this manner, they would be as humble as dogs, and never dare to run away."

The gentleman urged my master not to go to the North for the restoration of his health, but to visit the Warm Springs in Arkansas.

My master said, he thought the air of Philadelphia would suit his complaint best; and, not only so, he thought he could get better advice there.

The boat had now reached the wharf. The officer wished my master a safe and pleasant journey, and left the saloon.

There were a large number of persons on the quay waiting the arrival of the steamer: but we were afraid to venture out for fear that some one might recognize me; or that they had heard that we were gone, and had telegraphed to have us stopped. However, after remaining in the cabin till all the other passengers were gone, we had our luggage placed on a fly, and I took my master by the arm, and with a little difficulty he hobbled on shore, got in and drove off to the best hotel, which John C. Calhoun, and all the other great southern fire-eating statesmen, made their head-quarters while in Charleston.

On arriving at the house the landlord ran out and opened the door: but judging, from the poultices and green glasses, that my master was an invalid, he took him very tenderly by one arm and ordered his man to take the other.

My master then eased himself out, and with their assistance found no trouble in getting up the steps into the hotel. The proprietor made me stand on one side, while he paid my master the attention and homage he thought a gentleman of his high position merited.

My master asked for a bed-room. The servant was ordered to show a good one, into which we helped him. The servant returned. My master then handed me the bandages, I took them downstairs in great haste, and told the landlord my master wanted two hot poultices as quickly as possible. He rang the bell, the servant came in, to whom he said, "Run to the kitchen and tell the cook to make two hot poultices right off, for there is a gentleman upstairs very badly off indeed!"

In a few minutes the smoking poultices were brought in. I placed them in white handkerchiefs, and hurried upstairs, went into my master's apartment, shut the door, and laid them on the mantel-piece. As he was alone for a little while, he thought he could rest a great deal better with the poultices off. However, it was necessary to have them to complete the remainder of the journey. I then ordered dinner, and took my master's boots out to polish them. While doing so I entered into conversation with one of the slaves. I may state here, that on the sea-coast of South Carolina and Georgia the slaves speak worse English than in any other part of the country. This is owing to the frequent importation, or smuggling in, of Africans, who mingle with the natives. Consequently the language cannot properly be called English or African, but a corruption of the two. . . .

At the proper time my master had the poultices placed on, came down, and seated himself at a table in a very brilliant dining-room, to have his dinner. I had to have something at the same time, in order to be ready for the boat; so they gave me my dinner in an old broken plate, with a rusty knife and fork, and said, "Here, boy, you go in the kitchen." I took it and went out, but did not stay more than a few minutes, because I was in a great hurry to get back to see how the invalid was getting on. On arriving I found two or three servants waiting on him; but as he did not feel able to make a very hearty dinner, he soon finished, paid the bill, and gave the servants each a trifle, which caused one of them to say to me, "Your massa is a big bug"—meaning a gentleman of distinction—"he is the greatest gentleman dat has been dis way for dis six months." I said, "Yes, he is some pumpkins," meaning the same as "big bug."

When we left Macon, it was our intention to take a steamer at Charleston through to Philadelphia; but on arriving there we found that the vessels did not run during the winter, and I have no doubt it was well for us they did not; for on the very last voyage the steamer made that we intended to go by, a fugitive was discovered secreted on board, and sent back to slavery. However, as we had also heard of the Overland Mail Route, we were all right. So I ordered a fly to the door, had the luggage placed on; we got in, and drove down to the Custom-house Office, which was near the wharf where we had to obtain tickets, to take a steamer for Wilmington, North Carolina. When we reached the building, I helped my master into the office, which was crowded with passengers. He asked for a ticket for himself and one for his slave to Philadelphia. This caused the principal officer—a very mean-looking, cheese-coloured fellow, who was sitting there—to look up at us very suspiciously, and in a fierce tone of voice he said to me, "Boy, do you belong to that gentleman?" I quickly replied, "Yes, sir" (which was quite correct). The tickets were handed out, and as my master was paying for them the chief man said to him, "I wish you to register your name here, sir, and also the name of your nigger, and pay a dollar duty on him."

My master paid the dollar, and pointing to the hand that was in the poultice, requested the officer to register his name for him. This seemed to offend the "high-bred" South Carolinian. He jumped up, shaking his head; and, cramming his hands almost through the bottom of his trousers pockets, with a slave-bullying air, said, "I shan't do it."

This attracted the attention of all the passengers. Just then the young military officer with whom my master travelled and conversed on the steamer from Savannah stepped in, somewhat the worse for brandy; he shook hands with my master, and pretended to know all about him. He said, "I know his kin (friends) like a book;" and as the officer was known in Charleston, and was going to stop there with friends, the recognition was very much in my master's favour.

The captain of the steamer, a good-looking jovial fellow, seeing that the gentleman appeared to know my master, and perhaps not wishing to lose us as passengers, said in an off-hand sailor-like manner, "I will register the gentleman's name, and take the responsibility upon myself." He asked my master's name. He said, "William Johnson." The names were put down, I think, "Mr. Johnson and slave." The captain said, "It's all right now, Mr. Johnson." He thanked him kindly, and the young officer begged my master to go with him, and have something to drink and a cigar; but as he had not acquired these accomplishments, he excused himself, and we went on board and came off to Wilmington, North Carolina. . . .

We reached Wilmington the next morning, and took the train for Richmond, Virginia. I have stated that the American railway carriages (or cars, as they are called), are constructed differently to those in England. At one end of some of them, in the South, there is a little apartment with a couch on both sides for the convenience of families and invalids; and as they thought my master was very poorly, he was allowed to enter one of these apartments at Petersburg, Virginia, where an old gentleman and two handsome young ladies, his daughters, also got in, and took seats in the same carriage. But before the train started, the gentleman stepped into my car, and questioned me respecting my master. He wished to know what was the matter with him, where he was from, and where he was going. I told him where he came from, and said that he was suffering from a complication of complaints, and was going to Philadelphia, where he thought he could get more suitable advice than in Georgia.

The gentleman said my master could obtain the very best advice in Philadelphia. Which turned out to be quite correct, though he did not receive it from physicians, but from kind abolitionists who understood his case much better. The gentleman also said, "I reckon your master's father hasn't any more such faithful and smart boys as you." "O, yes, sir, he has," I replied, "lots on 'em." Which was literally true. This seemed all he wished to know. He thanked me, gave me a ten-cent piece, and requested me to be attentive to my good master. I promised that I would do so, and have ever since endeavoured to keep my pledge. During the gentleman's absence, the ladies and my master had a little cosy chat. But on his return, he said, "You seem to be very much afflicted, sir." "Yes, sir," replied the gentleman in the poultices. "What seems to be the matter with you, sir; may I be allowed to ask?" "Inflammatory rheumatism, sir." "Oh! that is very bad, sir," said the kind gentleman: "I can sympathize with you; for I know from bitter experience what the rheumatism is." If he did, he knew a good deal more than Mr. Johnson.

The gentleman thought my master would feel better if he would lie down and rest himself; and as he was anxious to avoid conversation, he at once acted upon this suggestion. The ladies politely rose, took their extra shawls, and made a nice pillow for the invalid's head. My master wore a fashionable cloth cloak, which they took and covered him comfortably on the couch. After he had been lying a little while the ladies, I suppose, thought he was asleep; so one of them gave a long sigh, and said, in a quiet fascinating tone, "Papa, he seems to be a very nice young gentleman." But before papa could speak, the other lady quickly said, "Oh! dear me, I never felt so much for a gentleman in my life!" To use an American expression, "they fell in love with the wrong chap."

After my master had been lying a little while he got up, the gentleman assisted him in getting on his cloak, the ladies took their shawls, and soon all were seated. They then insisted upon Mr. Johnson taking some of their refreshments, which of course he did, out of courtesy to the ladies. All went on enjoying themselves until they reached Richmond, where the ladies and their father left the train. But, before doing so, the good old Virginian gentleman, who appeared to be much pleased with my master, presented him with a recipe, which he said was a perfect cure for the inflammatory rheumatism. But the invalid not being able to read it, and fearing he should hold it upside down in pretending to do so, thanked the donor kindly, and placed it in his waistcoat pocket. My master's new friend also gave him his card, and requested him the next time he travelled that way to do him the kindness to call; adding, "I shall be pleased to see you, and so will my daughters." Mr. Johnson expressed his gratitude for the proffered hospitality, and said he should feel glad to call on his return. I have not the slightest doubt that he will fulfil the promise whenever that return takes place. After changing trains we went on a little beyond Fredericksburg, and took a steamer to Washington. . . .

We left our cottage on Wednesday morning, the 21st of December, 1848, and arrived at Baltimore, Saturday evening, the 24th (Christmas Eve). Baltimore was the last slave port of any note at which we stopped.

On arriving there we felt more anxious than ever, because we knew not what that last dark night would bring forth. It is true we were near the goal, but our poor hearts were still as if tossed at sea; and, as there was another great and dangerous bar to pass, we were afraid our liberties would be wrecked, and . . . go down for ever just off the place we longed to reach.

They are particularly watchful at Baltimore to prevent slaves from escaping into Pennsylvania, which is a free State. . . .

We thought of this plan about four days before we left Macon; and as we had our daily employment to attend to, we only saw each other at night. So we sat up the four long nights talking over the plan and making preparations.

We had also been four days on the journey; and as we travelled night and day, we got but very limited opportunities for sleeping. I believe nothing in the world could have kept us awake so long but the intense excitement, produced by the fear of being retaken on the one hand, and the bright anticipation of liberty on the other.

We left Baltimore about eight o'clock in the evening; and not being aware of a stopping-place of any consequence between there and Philadelphia, and also knowing that if we were fortunate we should be in the latter place early the next morning, I thought I might indulge in a few minutes' sleep in the car; but I, like Bunyan's Christian in the arbour, went to sleep at the wrong time, and took too long a nap. So, when the train reached Havre de Grace, all the first-class passengers had to get out of the carriages and into a ferry-boat, to be ferried across the Susquehanna river, and take the train on the opposite side.

The road was constructed so as to be raised or lowered to suit the tide. So they rolled the luggage-vans on to the boat, and off on the other side; and as I was in one of the apartments adjoining a baggage-car, they considered it unnecessary to awaken me, and tumbled me over with the luggage. But when my master was asked to leave his seat, he found it very dark, and cold, and raining. He missed me for the first time on the journey. On all previous occasions, as soon as the train stopped, I was at hand to assist him. This caused many slaveholders to praise me very much: they said they had never before seen a slave so attentive to his master: and therefore my absence filled him with terror and confusion; the children of Israel could not have felt more troubled on arriving at the Red Sea. So he asked the conductor if he had seen anything of his slave. The man being somewhat of an abolitionist, and believing that my master was really a slaveholder, thought he would tease him a little respecting me. So he said, "No, sir; I haven't seen anything of him for some time: I have no doubt he has run away, and is in Philadelphia, free, long before now." My master knew that there was nothing in this; so he asked the conductor if he would please to see if he could find me. The man indignantly replied, "I am no slave-hunter; and as far as I am concerned everybody must look after their own niggers." He went off and left the confused invalid to fancy whatever he felt inclined. My master at first thought I must have been kidnapped into slavery by some one, or left, or perhaps killed on the train. He also thought of stopping to see if he could hear anything of me, but he soon remembered that he had no money. That night all the money we had was consigned to my own pocket, because we thought, in case there were any pickpockets about, a slave's pocket would be the last one they would look for. However, hoping to meet me some day in a land of liberty, and as he had the tickets, he thought it best upon the whole to enter the boat and come off to Philadelphia, and endeavour to make his way alone in this cold and hollow world as best he could. The time was now up, so he went on board and came across with feelings that can be better imagined than described.

After the train had got fairly on the way to Philadelphia, the guard came into my car and gave me a violent shake, and bawled out at the same time, "Boy, wake up!" I started, almost frightened out of my wits. He said, "Your master is scared half to death about you." That frightened me still more—I thought they had found him out; so I anxiously inquired what was the matter. The guard said, "He thinks you have run away from him." This made me feel quite at ease. I said, "No, sir; I am satisfied my good master doesn't think that." So off I started to see him. He had been fearfully nervous, but on seeing me he at once felt much better. He merely wished to know what had become of me.

On returning to my seat, I found the conductor and two or three other persons amusing themselves very much respecting my running away. So the guard said, "Boy, what did your master want?"[1] I replied, "He merely wished to know what had become of me." "No," said the man, "that was not it; he thought you had taken French leave, for parts unknown. I never saw a fellow so badly scared about losing his slave in my life. Now," continued the guard, "let me give you a little friendly advice. When you get to Philadelphia, run away and leave that cripple, and have your liberty." "No, sir," I indifferently replied, "I can't promise to do that." "Why not?" said the conductor, evidently much surprised; "don't you want your liberty?" "Yes, sir," I replied; "but I shall never run away from such a good master as I have at present."

One of the men said to the guard, "Let him alone; I guess he will open his eyes when he gets to Philadelphia, and see things in another light." After giving me a good deal of information, which I afterwards found to be very useful, they left me alone.

I also met with a coloured gentleman on this train, who recommended me to a boarding-house that was kept by an abolitionist, where he thought I would be quite safe, if I wished to run away from my master. I thanked him kindly, but of course did not let him know who we were. Late at night, or rather early in the morning, I heard a fearful whistling of the steam-engine; so I opened the window and looked out, and saw a large number of flickering lights in the distance, and heard a passenger in the next carriage—who also had his head out of the window—say to his companion, "Wake up, old horse, we are at Philadelphia!"

---

[1] I may state here that every man slave is called boy till he is very old, then the more respectable slaveholders call him uncle. The women are all girls till they are aged, then they are called aunts. This is the reason why Mrs. Stowe calls her characters Uncle Tom, Aunt Chloe, Uncle Tiff, &c.

The sight of those lights and that announcement made me feel almost as happy as Bunyan's Christian must have felt when he first caught sight of the cross. I, like him, felt that the straps that bound the heavy burden to my back began to pop, and the load to roll off. I also looked, and looked again, for it appeared very wonderful to me how the mere sight of our first city of refuge should have all at once made my hitherto sad and heavy heart become so light and happy. As the train speeded on, I rejoiced and thanked God with all my heart and soul for his great kindness and tender mercy, in watching over us, and bringing us safely through.

As soon as the train had reached the platform, before it had fairly stopped, I hurried out of my carriage to my master, whom I got at once into a cab, placed the luggage on, jumped in myself, and we drove off to the boarding-house which was so kindly recommended to me. On leaving the station, my master—or rather my wife, as I may now say—who had from the commencement of the journey borne up in a manner that much surprised us both, grasped me by the hand, and said, "Thank God, William, we are safe!" then burst into tears, leant upon me, and wept like a child. The reaction was fearful. So when we reached the house, she was in reality so weak and faint that she could scarcely stand alone. However, I got her into the apartments that were pointed out, and there we knelt down, on this Sabbath, and Christmas-day,—a day that will ever be memorable to us,—and poured out our heartfelt gratitude to God, for his goodness in enabling us to overcome so many perilous difficulties, in escaping out of the jaws of the wicked.

Part II.

After my wife had a little recovered herself, she threw off the disguise and assumed her own apparel. We then stepped into the sitting-room, and asked to see the landlord. The man came in, but he seemed thunderstruck on finding a fugitive slave and his wife, instead of a "young cotton planter and his nigger." As his eyes travelled round the room, he said to me, "Where is your master?" I pointed him out. The man gravely replied, "I am not joking, I really wish to see your master." I pointed him out again, but at first he could not believe his eyes; he said "he knew that was not the gentleman that came with me."

But, after some conversation, we satisfied him that we were fugitive slaves, and had just escaped in the manner I have described. We asked him if he thought it would be safe for us to stop in Philadelphia. He said he thought not, but he would call in some persons who knew more about the laws than himself. He then went out, and kindly brought in several of the leading abolitionists[2] of the city, who gave us a most hearty and friendly

---

[2]Among them was William Still, who later described the episode in The Underground Rail Road (Philadelphia, 1872), p. 370. (BJL and RB)

welcome amongst them. As it was in December, and also as we had just left a very warm climate, they advised us not to go to Canada as we had intended, but to settle at Boston in the United States. It is true that the constitution of the Republic has always guaranteed the slaveholders the right to come into any of the so-called free States, and take their fugitives back to southern Egypt. But through the untiring, uncompromising, and manly efforts of Mr. Garrison, Wendell Phillips, Theodore Parker,[3] and a host of other noble abolitionists of Boston and the neighbourhood, public opinion in Massachusetts had become so much opposed to slavery and to kidnapping, that it was almost impossible for any one to take a fugitive slave out of that State.

So we took the advice of our good Philadelphia friends, and settled at Boston. I shall have something to say about our sojourn there presently.

Among other friends we met with at Philadelphia, was Robert Purves, Esq., a well educated and wealthy coloured gentleman, who introduced us to Mr. Barkley Ivens, a member of the Society of Friends, and a noble and generous-hearted farmer, who lived at some distance in the country.[4]

This good Samaritan at once invited us to go and stop quietly with his family, till my wife could somewhat recover from the fearful reaction of the past journey. We most gratefully accepted the invitation, and at the time appointed we took a steamer to a place up the Delaware river, where our new and dear friend met us with his snug little cart, and took us to his happy home. This was the first act of great and disinterested kindness we had ever received from a white person.

The gentleman was not of the fairest complexion, and therefore, as my wife was not in the room when I received the information respecting him and his anti-slavery character, she thought of course he was a quadroon like herself. But on arriving at the house, and finding out her mistake, she became more nervous and timid than ever.

As the cart came into the yard, the dear good old lady, and her three charming and affectionate daughters, all came to the door to meet us. We got out, and the gentleman said, "Go in, and make yourselves at home; I will see after the baggage." But my wife was afraid to approach them. She stopped in the yard, and said to me, "William, I thought we were coming among coloured people?" I replied, "It is all right; these are the same." "No," she said, "it is not all right, and I am not going to stop here; I have no confidence whatever in white people, they are only trying to get us back to slavery." She turned round and said, "I am going right off." The old lady then came out, with her sweet, soft, and winning smile, shook her heartily by the hand,

---

[3]Wendell Phillips (1811–1884) was an orator and activist in abolition and other liberal movements; Theodore Parker (1810–1860) was a liberal Boston clergyman and active abolitionist who ministered to the fugitive slaves of Boston. (BJL and RB)

[4]Robert Purvis (incorrectly spelled in the text) (1810–1898) was for many years president of the Pennsylvania Anti-Slavery Society and an active supporter of the Underground Railroad; Barkley Ivens was a member of Falls Monthly Meeting at the present town of Fallsington, across the Delaware River from Trenton, N.J. (BJL and RB)

and kindly said, "How art thou, my dear? We are all very glad to see thee and thy husband. Come in, to the fire; I dare say thou art cold and hungry after thy journey."

We went in, and the young ladies asked if she would like to go upstairs and "fix" herself before tea. My wife said, "No, I thank you; I shall only stop a little while." "But where art thou going this cold night?" said Mr. Ivens, who had just stepped in. "I don't know," was the reply. "Well, then," he continued, "I think thou hadst better take off thy things and sit near the fire; tea will soon be ready." "Yes, come Ellen," said Mrs. Ivens, "let me assist thee;" (as she commenced undoing my wife's bonnet-strings;) "don't be frightened, Ellen, I shall not hurt a single hair of thy head. We have heard with much pleasure of the marvellous escape of thee and thy husband, and deeply sympathise with thee in all that thou hast undergone. I don't wonder at thee, poor thing, being timid; but thou needs not fear us; we would as soon send one of our own daughters into slavery as thee; so thou mayest make thyself quite at ease!" These soft and soothing words fell like balm upon my wife's unstrung nerves, and melted her to tears; her fears and prejudices vanished, and from that day she has firmly believed that there are good and bad persons of every shade of complexion.

After seeing Sally Ann and Jacob, two coloured domestics, my wife felt quite at home. After partaking of what Mrs. Stowe's Mose and Pete called a "busting supper," the ladies wished to know whether we could read. On learning we could not, they said if we liked they would teach us. To this kind offer, of course, there was no objection. But we looked rather knowingly at each other, as much as to say that they would have rather a hard task to cram anything into our thick and matured skulls.

However, all hands set to and quickly cleared away the tea-things, and the ladies and their good brother brought out the spelling and copy books and slates, &c., and commenced with their new and green pupils. We had, by stratagem, learned the alphabet while in slavery, but not the writing characters; and, as we had been such a time learning so little, we at first felt that it was a waste of time for any one at our ages to undertake to learn to read and write. But, as the ladies were so anxious that we should learn, and so willing to teach us, we concluded to give our whole minds to the work, and see what could be done. By so doing, at the end of the three weeks we remained with the good family we could spell and write our names quite legibly. They all begged us to stop longer; but, as we were not safe in the State of Pennsylvania, and also as we wished to commence doing something for a livelihood, we did not remain.

When the time arrived for us to leave for Boston, it was like parting with our relatives. We have since met with many very kind and hospitable friends, both in America and England; but we have never been under a roof where we were made to feel more at home, or where the inmates took a deeper interest in our well-being, than Mr. Barkley Ivens and his dear family. May God ever bless them, and preserve each one from every reverse of fortune!

We finally, as I have stated, settled at Boston, where we remained nearly two years, I employed as cabinet-maker and furniture broker, and my wife at her needle; and, as our little earnings in slavery were not all spent on the journey, we were getting on very well, and would have made money, if we had not been compelled by the General Government, at the bidding of the slaveholders, to break up business, and fly from under the Stars and Stripes to save our liberties and our lives.

In 1850, Congress passed the Fugitive Slave Bill, an enactment too infamous to have been thought of or tolerated by any people in the world, except the unprincipled and tyrannical Yankees. . . .

Our old masters sent agents to Boston after us. They took out warrants, and placed them in the hands of the United States Marshal to execute. But the following letter from our highly esteemed and faithful friend, the Rev. Samuel May, of Boston, to our equally dear and much lamented friend, Dr. Estlin of Bristol, will show why we were not taken into custody.[5]

"21, *Cornhill, Boston,*
"*November 6th,* 1850.

"My dear Mr Estlin,

"I trust that in God's good providence this letter will be handed to you in safety by our good friends, William and Ellen Craft. They have lived amongst us about two years, and have proved themselves worthy, in all respects, of our confidence and regard. The laws of this republican and Christian land (tell it not in Moscow, nor in Constantinople) regard them only as slaves—chattels—personal property. But they nobly vindicated their title and right to freedom, two years since, by winning their way to it; at least, so they thought. But now, the slave power, with the aid of Daniel Webster and a band of lesser traitors, has enacted a law, which puts their dearly-bought liberties in the most imminent peril; holds out a strong temptation to every mercenary and unprincipled ruffian to become their kidnapper; and has stimulated the slaveholders generally to such desperate acts for the recovery of their fugitive property, as have never before been enacted in the history of this government.

"Within a fortnight, two fellows from Macon, Georgia, have been in Boston for the purpose of arresting our friends William and Ellen. A writ was served against them from the United States District Court; but it was not served by the United States Marshal; why not, is not certainly known: perhaps through fear, for a general feeling of indignation, and a cool determina-

---

[5]Samuel May (1797–1871) was a minister and antislavery leader who was a member of the Vigilance Committee of Boston at this time; John Bishop Estlin (1785–1855) of Bristol, England, was a noted surgeon and reformer. (BJL and RB)

tion not to allow this young couple to be taken from Boston into slavery, was aroused, and pervaded the city. It is understood that one of the judges told the Marshal that he would not be authorised in breaking the door of Craft's house. Craft kept himself close within the house, armed himself, and awaited with remarkable composure the event. Ellen, in the meantime, had been taken to a retired place out of the city. The Vigilance Committee (appointed at a late meeting in Fanueil Hall) enlarged their numbers, held an almost permanent session, and appointed various subcommittees to act in different ways. One of these committees called repeatedly on Messrs. Hughes and Knight, the slave-catchers, and requested and advised them to leave the city. At first they peremptorily refused to do so, ''till they got hold of the niggers.' On complaint of different persons, these two fellows were several times arrested, carried before one of our county courts, and held to bail on charges of 'conspiracy to kidnap,' and of 'defamation,' in calling William and Ellen 'slaves.' At length, they became so alarmed, that they left the city by an indirect route, evading the vigilance of many persons who were on the look-out for them. Hughes, at one time, was near losing his life at the hands of an infuriated coloured man. While these men remained in the city, a prominent whig gentleman sent word to William Craft, that if he would submit peaceably to an arrest, he and his wife should be bought from their owners, cost what it might. Craft replied, in effect, that he was in a measure the representative of all the other fugitives in Boston, some 200 or 300 in number; that, if he gave up, they would all be at the mercy of the slave-catchers, and must fly from the city at any sacrifice; and that, if his freedom could be bought for two cents, he would not consent to compromise the matter in such a way. This event has stirred up the slave spirit of the country, south and north; the United States government is determined to try its hand in enforcing the Fugitive Slave law; and William and Ellen Craft would be prominent objects of the slaveholders' vengeance. Under these circumstances, it is the almost unanimous opinion of their best friends, that they should quit America as speedily as possible, and seek an asylum in England! Oh! shame, shame upon us, that Americans, whose fathers fought against Great Britain, in order to be FREE, should have to acknowledge this disgraceful fact! God gave us a fair and goodly heritage in this land, but man has cursed it with his devices and crimes against human souls and human rights. Is America the 'land of the free, and the home of the brave?' God knows it is not; and we know it too. A brave young man and a virtuous young woman must fly the American shores, and seek, under the shadow of the British throne, the enjoyment of 'life, liberty, and the pursuit of happiness.'

"But I must pursue my plain, sad story. All day long, I have been busy planning a safe way for William and Ellen to leave Boston. We dare not allow them to go on board a vessel, even in the port of Boston; for the writ is yet in the Marshal's hands, and he *may* be waiting an opportunity to serve it; so I am expecting to accompany them to-morrow to Portland, Maine, which is beyond the reach of the Marshal's authority; and there I hope to see them on board a British steamer.

"This letter is written to introduce them to you. I know your infirm health; but I am sure, if you were stretched on your bed in your last illness, and could lift your hand at all, you would extend it to welcome these poor hunted fellow-creatures. Henceforth, England is their nation and their home. It is with real regret for our personal loss in their departure, as well as burning shame for the land that is not worthy of them, that we send them away, or rather allow them to go. But, with all the resolute courage they have shown in a most trying hour, they themselves see it is the part of a foolhardy rashness to attempt to stay here longer.

"I must close; and with many renewed thanks for all your kind words and deeds towards us,

"I am, very respectfully yours,
"SAMUEL MAY, JUN."

Our old masters, having heard how their agents were treated at Boston, wrote to Mr. Filmore [sic], who was then President of the States, to know what he could do to have us sent back to slavery. Mr. Filmore said that we should be returned. He gave instructions for military force to be sent to Boston to assist the officers in making the arrest. Therefore we, as well as our friends (among whom was George Thompson, Esq.,[6] late M.P. for the Tower Hamlets—the slave's long-tried, self-sacrificing friend, and eloquent advocate) thought it best, at any sacrifice, to leave the mock-free Republic, and come to a country where we and our dear little ones can be truly free.— "No one daring to molest or make us afraid." But, as the officers were watching every vessel that left the port to prevent us from escaping, we had to take the expensive and tedious overland route to Halifax [actually a journey by land and water to the safety of Canada].

We shall always cherish the deepest feelings of gratitude to the Vigilance Committee of Boston (upon which were many of the leading abolitionists), and also to our numerous friends, for the very kind and noble manner in which they assisted us to preserve our liberties and to escape from Boston, as it were like Lot from Sodom, to a place of refuge, and finally to this truly free and glorious country; where no tyrant, let his power be ever so absolute over his poor trembling victims at home, dare come and lay violent hands upon us or upon our dear little boys (who had the good fortune to be born upon British soil), and reduce us to the legal level of the beast that perisheth. . . .

My wife and myself were both unwell when we left Boston, and, having taken fresh cold on the journey to Halifax, we were laid up there under the doctor's care, nearly the whole fortnight. I had much worry about

---

[6] George Thompson (1804–1878), former member of Parliament, made several visits to the United States on behalf of the antislavery cause. (BJL and RB)

getting tickets, for they baffled us shamefully at the Cunard office. They at first said that they did not book till the steamer came; which was not the fact. When I called again, they said they knew the steamer would come full from Boston, and therefore we had "better try to get to Liverpool by other means." Other mean Yankee excuses were made; and it was not till an influential gentleman, to whom Mr. Francis Jackson,[7] of Boston, kindly gave us a letter, went and rebuked them, that we were able to secure our tickets. So when we went on board my wife was very poorly, and was also so ill on the voyage that I did not believe she could live to see Liverpool.

However, I am thankful to say she arrived; and, after laying up at Liverpool very ill for two or three weeks, gradually recovered.

It was not until we stepped upon the shore at Liverpool that we were free from every slavish fear. . . .

In a few days after we landed, the Rev. Francis Bishop[8] and his lady came and invited us to be their guests; to whose unlimited kindness and watchful care my wife owes, in a great degree, her restoration to health.

We enclosed our letter from the Rev. Mr. May to Mr. Estlin, who at once wrote to invite us to his house at Bristol. On arriving there, both Mr. and Miss Estlin received us as cordially as did our first good Quaker friends in Pennsylvania. . . . It was principally through the extreme kindness of Mr. Estlin, the Right Hon. Lady Noel Byron, Miss Harriet Martineau, Mrs. Reid, Miss Sturch, and a few other good friends,[9] that my wife and myself were able to spend a short time at a school in this country, to acquire a little of that education which we were so shamefully deprived of while in the house of bondage. The school is under the supervision of the Misses Lushington, daughters of the Right Hon. Stephen Lushington, D.C.L. [Doctor of Civil Law]. During our stay at the school we received the greatest attention from every one; and I am particularly indebted to Thomas Wilson, Esq., of Bradmore House, Chiswick, (who was then the master,) for the deep interest he took in trying to get me on in my studies.

---

[7] Francis Jackson (1789–1861) was another member of Boston's Vigilance Committee. (BJL and RB)

[8] Francis Bishop was a Liverpool clergyman active in the antislavery movement. (BJL and RB)

[9] Lady Noel Byron, widow of the poet, was a friend of the writer Harriet Martineau and other British antislavery activists. (BJL and RB)

II

"AN ARROW
FROM THE BENT BOW
OF THE GOSPEL"

Religion was central to black tradition in America. It was an inner experience and a social bond, a beacon of hope and a solace for the hopeless. Though some blacks embraced Catholicism, the dominant pattern was Protestant and evangelical. Whatever its admixture of African elements, the religion of blacks was mainly a southern variety of evangelical Christianity. For those in bondage the Christian faith and its Scripture, especially the Old Testament chapter of Exodus, carried the compelling imagery of deliverance.

Christian conversion entailed an affirmation of self. The gift of devotion meant a free act by the donor. This in itself enhanced the dignity of human beings who may in all other respects have been degraded. To believe that each humble individual was dear to a divine Creator was to claim one's membership in the human family. While this applied equally to other worshippers, it was crucial for the blacks, enslaved or nominally free.

Conversion to many meant a specific emotional transformation. It was more than adherence to a church and to a faith. This was a moment of recognition: the event was a felt encounter, a sense of the literal presence of God. To encourage preparation for this sanctifying experience, itinerant preachers carried the holy message of redemption from town to town and into rural byways. If professors in schools of religion found it untouched by learning, those who preached it touched the lives of their hearers. Somewhat apart from the organized church establishments, such wanderers might be white or black. They might also be female.

This section brings together three women for whom religious evangelism was a dominant purpose. Although virtually all black women knew religion, the evangelists made the saving of souls their life's work. In their vision the cares of the world could be transcended. Heaven was bright with the promise of forgiveness, joy, and peace. A fourth individual is included in this grouping. Though her occupation was teaching, Ann Plato was mainly concerned with the preparation of souls. Haunted by the premature death of various friends, this young woman wrote memorial poems suffused with sadness. The extracts from her slender volume presented here are also threaded with a funereal tone. "This world," she wrote, "is only a place to prepare for another and a better."

Elizabeth

The *Philadelphia Quakers* issued a tract in 1889 called *Elizabeth, A Colored Minister of the Gospel, born in Slavery. Of her they said in appraisal:* "Against spiritual wickedness in high places she seemed to feel herself especially bound to testify, without fear of man, and the integrity of her speech not infrequently brought upon her much suffering, from such as held the form of godliness without the power."[1] Elizabeth never possessed more than her Christian name to identify her among her fellows. But the name of Christianity sustained her. Faith supplied her with the fortitude to minister without ordination to the wants of others, and her belief gave her the courage to preach fearlessly against slavery. This, as the Friends were pleased to say, was to lay bare a "spiritual wickedness in high places." To castigate the peculiar institution was to criticize the existing culture, including its leaders secular and divine. Officials in the sovereign state of Virginia challenged her freedom to preach and threatened her with imprisonment. Asked if she was ordained, she answered serenely, "Not by the commission of men's hands: if the Lord has ordained me, I need nothing better." She did not go to jail.

Elizabeth, who reputedly lived until one hundred and one, was born in 1766 of slave parents, in a Maryland family both religious and literate. She had an early childhood exposure to Sabbath Bible reading, but she could "read but little," even after forty. Separation from her family occurred when she was eleven, and her devout mother at parting gave her up to the care of God. There was in hard fact no one on earth. The very next year, when she was twelve, she experienced a vision, and as a result the protection of the Lord was substituted for the protection of her parent.

A conscientious Presbyterian who became her master freed her on religious grounds. She was then thirty and she began to preach. Direct social action was not her purpose; it was an immediate communication with divinity and personal salvation that she wished to achieve. She was almost ninety when she gave up her godly travels and settled in Philadelphia to spend her final years among the Quakers who were her friends.

---

[1]Philadelphia, 1889, p. 12.

I was born in Maryland in the year 1766. My parents were slaves. Both my father and mother were religious people, and belonged to the Methodist Society. It was my father's practice to read in the Bible aloud to his children every sabbath morning. At these seasons, when I was but five years old, I often felt the overshadowing of the Lord's Spirit, without at all understanding what it meant; and these incomes and influences continued to attend me until I was eleven years old, particularly when I was alone, by which I was preserved from doing anything that I thought was wrong.

In the eleventh year of my age, my master sent me to another farm several miles from my parents, brothers and sisters, which was a great trouble to me. At last I grew so lonely and sad I thought I should die, if I did not see my mother. I asked the overseer if I might go, but being positively denied, I concluded to go without his knowledge. When I reached home my mother was away. I set off and walked twenty miles before I found her. I staid with her for several days, and we returned together. Next day I was sent back to my new place, which renewed my sorrow. At parting, my mother told me that I had "nobody in the wide world to look to but God." These words fell upon my heart with ponderous weight, and seemed to add to my grief. I went back repeating as I went, "none but God in the wide world." On reaching the farm, I found the overseer was displeased at me for going without his liberty. He tied me with a rope, and gave me some stripes, of which I carried the marks for weeks.

After this time, finding as my mother said, I had none in the world to look to but God, I betook myself to prayer, and in every lonely place I found an altar. I mourned sore like a dove and chattered forth my sorrow, moaning in the corners of the field, and under the fences.

I continued in this state for about six months, feeling as though my head were waters, and I could do nothing but weep. I lost my appetite, and not being able to take enough food to sustain nature, I became so weak I had but little strength to work; still I was required to do all my duty. One evening, after the duties of the day were ended, I thought I could not live over the night, so threw myself on a bench, expecting to die, and without being prepared to meet my Maker; and my spirit cried within me, must I die in this state, and be banished from Thy presence forever? I own I am a sinner in Thy sight, and not fit to live where thou art. Still it was my fervent

Source: Elizabeth, A Colored Minister of the Gospel, born in Slavery (Philadelphia, 1889), pp. 2–12. This note precedes the original text: "In the following narrative of 'Old Elizabeth,' which was taken mainly from her own lips in her ninety-seventh year, her simple language has been adhered to as strictly as was consistent with perspicuity and propriety."

desire that the Lord would pardon me. Just at this season, I saw with my
spiritual eye, an awful gulf of misery. As I thought I was about to plunge
into it, I heard a voice saying, "rise up and pray," which strengthened me. I
fell on my knees and prayed the best I could the Lord's prayer. Knowing no
more to say, I halted, but continued on my knees. My spirit was then taught
to pray, "Lord have mercy on me—Christ save me." Immediately there appeared a director, clothed in white raiment. I thought he took me by the
hand and said, "come with me." He led me down a long journey to a fiery
gulf, and left me standing upon the brink of this awful pit. I began to scream
for mercy, thinking I was about to sink to endless ruin. Although I prayed
and wrestled with all my might, it seemed in vain. Still I felt all the while
that I was sustained by some invisible power. At this solemn moment, I
thought I saw a hand from which hung, as it were, a silver hair, and a voice
told me that all the hope I had of being saved was no more than a hair; still,
pray and it will be sufficient. I then renewed my struggle, crying for mercy
and salvation, until I found that every cry raised me higher and higher, and
my head was quite above the fiery pillars. Then I thought I was permitted to
look straight forward and saw the Saviour standing with his hand stretched
out to receive me. An indescribably glorious light was in Him, and He said,
"peace, peace, come unto me." At this moment I felt that my sins were
forgiven me, and the time of my deliverance was at hand. I sprang forward
and fell at his feet, giving Him all the thanks and highest praises, crying,
Thou hast redeemed me—Thou hast redeemed me to thyself. I felt filled
with light and love. At this moment I thought my former guide took me
again by the hand and led me upward, till I came to the celestial world and
to heaven's door, which I saw was open, and while I stood there, a power
surrounded me which drew me in, and I saw millions of glorified spirits in
white robes. After I had this view, I thought I heard a voice saying, "Art
thou willing to be saved?" I said, "Yes Lord." Again I was asked, "Art thou
willing to be saved in my way?" I stood speechless until he asked me again,
"Art thou willing to be saved in my way?" Then I heard a whispering voice
say, "If thou art not saved in the Lord's way, thou canst not be saved at all;"
at which I exclaimed, "Yes Lord, in thy own way." Immediately a light fell
upon my head, and I was filled with light and I was shown the world lying
in wickedness, and was told I must go there, and call the people to repentance, for the day of the Lord was at hand; and this message was as a heavy
yoke upon me, so that I wept bitterly at the thought of what I should have to
pass through. While I wept, I heard a voice say, "weep not, some will laugh
at thee, some will scoff at thee, and the dogs will bark at thee, but while
thou doest my will, I will be with thee to the ends of the earth."

I was at this time not yet thirteen years old. The next day, when I had
come to myself, I felt like a new creature in Christ, and all my desire was to
see the Saviour.

I lived in a place where there was no preaching, and no religious
instruction; but every day I went out amongst the hay-stacks, where the

presence of the Lord overshadowed me, and I was filled with sweetness and joy, and was as a vessel filled with holy oil. In this way I continued for about a year; many times while my hands were at my work, my spirit was carried away to spiritual things. One day as I was going to my old place behind the hay-stacks to pray, I was assailed with this language, "Are you going there to weep and pray? what a fool! there are older professors than you are, and they do not take that way to get to heaven; people whose sins are forgiven ought to be joyful and lively, and not be struggling and praying." With this I halted and concluded I would not go, but do as other professors did and so went off to play; but at this moment the light that was in me became darkened, and the peace and joy that I once had, departed from me.

About this time I was moved back to the farm where my mother lived, and then sold to a stranger. Here I had deep sorrows and plungings, not having experienced a return of that sweet evidence and light with which I had been favored formerly; but by watching unto prayer, and wrestling mightily with the Lord, my peace gradually returned, and with it a great exercise and weight upon my heart for the salvation of my fellow-creatures; and I was often carried to distant lands and shown places where I should have to travel and deliver the Lord's message. Years afterwards, I found myself visiting those towns and countries that I had seen in the light as I sat at home at my sewing,—places of which I had never heard.

Some years from this time I was sold to a Presbyterian for a term of years, as he did not think it right to hold slaves for life. Having served him faithfully my time out, he gave me my liberty, which was about the thirtieth year of my age.

As I now lived in a neighborhood where I could attend religious meetings, occasionally I felt moved to speak a few words therein; but I shrank from it—so great was the cross to my nature.

I did not speak much till I had reached my forty-second year, when it was revealed to me that the message which had been given to me I had not yet delivered, and the time had come. As I could read but little, I questioned within myself how it would be possible for me to deliver the message, when I did not understand the Scriptures. I went from one religious professor to another, enquiring of them what ailed me; but of all these I could find none who could throw any light upon such impressions. They all told me there was nothing in Scripture that would sanction such exercises. It was hard for men to travel, and what would women do? These things greatly discouraged me, and shut up my way, and caused me to resist the Spirit. After going to all that were accounted pious, and receiving no help, I returned to the Lord, feeling that I was nothing, and knew nothing and wrestled and prayed to the Lord that He would fully reveal his will, and make the way plain.

Whilst I thus struggled, there seemed a light from heaven to fall upon me which banished all my desponding fears, and I was enabled to form a new resolution to go on to prison and to death, if it might be my portion: and the Lord showed me that it was his will I should be resigned to die any death that might be my lot, in carrying his message, and be entirely crucified to the world, and sacrifice *all* to his glory that was then in my possession, which his witnesses, the holy Apostles, had done before me. It was then revealed to me that the Lord had given me the evidence of a clean heart, in which I could rejoice day and night, and I walked and talked with God, and my soul was illuminated with heavenly light, and I knew nothing but Jesus Christ, and Him crucified.

One day, after these things, while I was at my work, the Spirit directed me to go to a poor widow, and ask her if I might have a meeting at her house, which was situated in one of the lowest and worst streets in Baltimore. With great joy she gave notice, and at the time appointed I appeared there among a few colored sisters. When they had all prayed, they called upon me to close the meeting, and I felt an impression that I must say a few words; and while I was speaking, the house seemed filled with light; and when I was about to close the meeting, and was kneeling, a man came in and stood till I arose. It proved to be a watchman. The sisters became so frightened, they all went away except the one who lived in the house, and an old woman; they both appeared to be much frightened, fearing they should receive some personal injury, or be put out of the house. A feeling of weakness came over me for a short time, but I soon grew warm and courageous in the Spirit. The man then said to me, "I was sent here to break up your meeting. Complaint has been made to me that the people round here cannot sleep for the racket." I replied, "a good racket is better than a bad racket. How do they rest when the ungodly are dancing and fiddling till midnight? Why are not they molested by the watchmen? and why should we be for praising God, our Maker? Are we worthy of greater punishment for praying to Him? and are we to be prohibited from doing so, that sinners may remain slumbering in their sins?" Speaking several words more, he turned pale and trembled, and begged my pardon, acknowledging that it was not his wish to interrupt us, and that he would never disturb a religious assembly again. He then took leave of me in a comely manner and wished us success.

Our meeting gave great offence, and we were forbid holding any more assemblies. Even the elders of our meeting joined with the wicked people, and said such meetings must be stopped, and that woman quieted. But I was not afraid of any of them and continued to go, and burnt with a zeal not my own. The old sisters were zealous sometimes, and at other times would sink under the cross. Thus they grew cold, at which I was much grieved. I proposed to them to ask the elders to send a brother, which was concluded upon.

We went on for several years, and the Lord was with us with great power it proved, to the conversion of many souls, and we continued to grow stronger.

I felt at times that I must exercise in the ministry, but when I rose upon my feet I felt ashamed, and so I went under a cloud for some time, and endeavored to keep silence; but I could not quench the Spirit. I was rejected by the elders and rulers, as Christ was rejected by the Jews before me, and while others were excused in crimes of the darkest dye, I was hunted down in every place where I appointed a meeting. Wading through many sorrows, I thought at times I might as well be banished from this life, as to feel the Almighty drawing me one way, and man another; so that I was tempted to cast myself into the dock. But contemplating the length of eternity, and how long my sufferings would be in that unchangeable world, compared with this, if I endured a little longer, the Lord was pleased to deliver me from this gloomy, melancholy state in his own time; though while this temptation lasted I roved up and down, and talked and prayed.

I often felt that I was unfit to assemble with the congregation with whom I had gathered, and had sometimes been made to rejoice in the Lord. I felt that I was despised on account of this gracious calling, and was looked upon as a speckled bird by the ministers to whom I looked for instruction, and to whom I resorted every opportunity for the same; but when I would converse with them, some would cry out, "You are an enthusiast;" and others said, "the Discipline did not allow of any such division of the work;" until I began to think I surely must be wrong. Under this reflection, I had another gloomy cloud to struggle through; but after awhile I felt much moved upon by the Spirit of the Lord, and meeting with an aged sister I found upon conversing with her that she could sympathize with me in this spiritual work. She was the first one I had met with, who could fully understand my exercises. She offered to open her house for a meeting, and run the risk of all the church would do to her for it. Many were afraid to open their houses in this way, lest they should be turned out of the church.

I persevered, notwithstanding the opposition of those who were looked upon as higher and wiser. The meeting was appointed, and but few came. I felt much backwardness, and as though I could not pray, but a pressure upon me to arise and express myself by way of exhortation. After hesitating for some time whether I would take up the cross or no, I arose, and after expressing a few words, the Spirit came upon me with life, and a victory was gained over the power of darkness, and we could rejoice together in his love.

As for myself, I was so full I hardly knew whether I was in the body, or out of the body—so great was my joy for the victory on the Lord's side. But the persecution against me increased, and a complaint was carried forward, as was done formerly against Daniel, the servant of God, and the elders came out with indignation for my holding meetings contrary to discipline—being a woman. . . .

Again I felt encouraged to attend another and another appointment. At one of these meetings, some of the class-leaders were present, who were constrained to cry out, "Surely the Lord has *revealed* these things to her," and ask one another if they ever heard the like? I look upon man as a very selfish being, when placed in a religious office, to presume to resist the work of the Almighty; because He does not work by man's authority. I did not faint under discouragement, but pressed on.

Under the contemplation of these things, I slept but little, being much engaged in receiving the revelations of the Divine will concerning this work, and the mysterious call thereto.

I felt very unworthy and small, notwithstanding the Lord had shown himself with great power, insomuch that conjecturers and critics were constrained to join in praise to his great name; for truly, we had times of refreshing from the presence of the Lord. At one of the meetings, a vast number of the white inhabitants of the place, and many colored people, attended—many no doubt from curiosity to hear what the old colored woman had to say. One, a great scripturian, fixed himself behind the door with pen and ink, in order to take down the discourse in short-hand; but the Almighty Being anointed me with such a portion of his Spirit, that he cast away his paper and pen, and heard the discourse with patience, and was much affected, for the Lord wrought powerfully on his heart. After meeting, he came forward and offered me his hand, with solemnity on his countenance, and handed me something to pay for my conveyance home.

I returned, much strengthened by the Lord's power, to go on to the fulfilment of his work, although I was again pressed by the authorities of the church to which I belonged, for imprudency; and so much condemned, that I was sorely tempted by the enemy to turn aside into the wilderness. I was so embarrassed and encompassed, I wondered within myself whether all that were called to be mouth-piece for the Lord suffered such deep wadings as I experienced.

I now found I had to travel still more extensively in the work of the ministry, and I applied to the Lord for direction. I was often invited to go hither and thither, but felt that I must wait for the dictates of his Spirit.

At a meeting which I held in Maryland, I was led to speak from the passage, "Woe to the rebellious city," &c. After the meeting, the people came where I was, to take me before the squire; but the Lord delivered me from their hands.

I also held meetings in Virginia. The people there would not believe that a colored woman could preach. And moreover, as she had no learning, they strove to imprison me because I spoke against slavery: and being brought up, they asked by what authority I spake? and if I had been ordained? I answered, not by the commission of men's hands: if the Lord had ordained me, I needed nothing better.

As I travelled along through the land, I was led at different times to converse with white men who were by profession ministers of the gospel. Many of them, up and down, confessed they did not believe in revelation, which gave me to see that men were sent forth as ministers without Christ's authority. In a conversation with one of these, he said, "You think you have these things by revelation, but there has been no such thing as revelation since Christ's ascension." I asked him where the apostle John got his revelation while he was in the Isle of Patmos. With this, he rose up and left me, and I said in my spirit, get thee behind me Satan.

I visited many remote places, where there were no meeting-houses, and held many glorious meetings, for the Lord poured out his Spirit in sweet effusions. I also travelled in Canada, and visited several settlements of colored people, and felt an open door amongst them.

I may here remark, that while journeying through the different States of the Union, I met with many of the Quaker Friends, and visited them in their families. I received much kindness and sympathy, and no opposition from them, in the prosecution of my labors.

On one occasion, in a thinly settled part of the country, seeing a Friend's meeting-house open, I went in; at the same time a Friend and his little daughter followed me. We three composed the meeting. As we sat there in silence, I felt a remarkable overshadowing of the Divine presence, as much so as I ever experienced anywhere. Toward the close, a few words seemed to be given me, which I expressed, and left the place greatly refreshed in Spirit. From thence I went to Michigan, where I found a wide field of labor amongst my own color. Here I remained four years. I established a school for colored orphans, having always felt the great importance of the religious and moral agriculture of children, and the great need of it, especially amongst the colored people. Having white teachers, I met with much encouragement.

My eighty-seventh year had now arrived, when suffering from disease, and feeling released from travelling further in my good Master's cause, I came on to Philadelphia, where I have remained until this time, which brings me to my ninety-seventh year. When I went forth, it was without purse or scrip,—and I have come through great tribulation and temptation— not by any might of my own, for I feel that I am but as dust and ashes before my almighty Helper, who has, according to his promise, been with me and sustained me through all, and gives me now firm faith that He will be with me to the end, and, in his own good time, receive me into his everlasting rest.

Jarena Lee

In a single year Jarena Lee, unordained female preacher, traveled 2,325 miles and delivered 178 sermons. Two thousand miles of travel in 1827 was a considerable amount for a black woman over forty. If Jarena Lee always felt "it better to wear out than to rust out," it was because she believed herself a servant of the Lord's will to whose work she had irrevocably been called. The destiny of fellow blacks moved her, but she was more devoted to their souls than to their bodies. Yet to truly reach her racial kinsmen was to save them. Salvation forged a protective armor shielding them from ills to which they were presently subject, as well as preparing them for a future life of which she told them.

Probably born free at Cape May, New Jersey, in 1783, she went to live as a servant about sixty miles from her home. The distance meant separation from her family. She was only seven when this break occurred. Her parents encircled the heart of her life and she made contact with them whenever she could. After an absence of fourteen years she returned to Cape May to visit her aging mother, as she did again eleven years later. According to her own log book of contact, there were two more reunions. Thus she saw her mother four times after she was seven and one of her sisters, "long lost," twice in forty-two or forty-three years.

The consolations of religion substituted for the consolations of the family. She was twenty-one in 1804 when, moving in church groups in the area of her employment as a house servant, she was uplifted by the preaching of a local minister. The Reverend Richard Allen, founder and leader of the African Methodist Episcopal Church movement, became the fixed center of her Philadelphia period. An ecstatic religious experience and a subsequent vision brought her back to Allen of whom she requested permission to preach. He was not averse to women leading prayer meetings, but he drew the conservative theological line against female preaching. Without the firm resolution she later developed, she accepted the verdict. Shortly thereafter, in 1811, she married Joseph Lee, pastor of a society located a short distance from Philadelphia.

There were tragic incidents in her private life. Lee survived but seven years after their marriage; in addition, four other members of her family died. She was left with a child of two and a six-month infant. After these events she began to preach, first on occasions when the pastor "lost the spirit." Richard Allen, now Bishop of the African Methodist Episcopal Church, endorsed her desire to preach and she was soon, rightly or wrongly, to describe herself as "the first female preacher of the First African Methodist Episcopal Church."[1]

Her ministry was now her whole existence. Her detailed journal catalogs the years and miles and meetings. Each episode confirmed Mrs. Lee in her calling. She could hardly write too often of the people she affected, "tears rolling down their cheeks, the signs of contrition and repentance towards God." Even her enthusiasm for abolition bore the stamp of evangelism. Her concern with the earthly oppression of the slaves was outstripped by her desire that they have access to the Christian gospel.

I was born February 11th, 1783, at Cape May, State of New Jersey. At the age of seven years I was parted from my parents, and went to live as a servant maid, with a Mr. Sharp, at the distance of about sixty miles from the place of my birth.

My parents being wholly ignorant of the knowledge of God, had not therefore instructed me in any degree in this great matter. Not long after the commencement of my attendance on this lady, she had bid me do something respecting my work, which in a little while after she asked me if I had done, when I replied, Yes—but this was not true.

At this awful point, in my early history, the Spirit of God moved in power through my conscience, and told me I was a wretched sinner. On this account so great was the impression, and so strong were the feelings of guilt, that I promised in my heart that I would not tell another lie.

But notwithstanding this promise my heart grew harder, after a while, yet the Spirit of the Lord never entirely forsook me, but continued mercifully striving with me, until his gracious power converted my soul. . . .

The man who was to speak . . . was the Rev. Richard Allen,[1] since bishop of the African Episcopal Methodists in America. During the labors of

---

[1]Jarena Lee, Religious Experience and Journal of Mrs. Jarena Lee, Giving an Account of Her Call to Preach the Gospel (Philadelphia, 1849), p. 98.

Source: Religious Experience and Journal of Mrs. Jarena Lee, Giving an Account of Her Call to Preach the Gospel (Philadelphia, 1849), pp. 3–17.

[1]Richard Allen, together with Absalom Jones, cofounder of the Free African Society, withdrew from the Methodist Episcopal Church in Philadelphia in 1787 when efforts were made to segregate black worshipers. They became the leaders of separate black denominations. In 1816 the Reverend Mr. Allen was elected bishop of the African Methodist Episcopal Church, which united separate churches in a number of cities. The conversion experience described by Mrs. Lee occurred around 1805. (BJL and RB)

this man that afternoon, I had come to the conclusion, that this is the people to which my heart unites, and it so happened, that as soon as the service closed he invited such as felt a desire to flee the wrath to come, to unite on trial with them—I embraced the opportunity. Three weeks from that day, my soul was gloriously converted to God, under preaching, at the very outset of the sermon. The text was barely pronounced, which was "I perceive thy heart is not right in the sight of God," when there appeared to my view, in the centre of the heart, one sin; and this was *malice* against one particular individual, who had strove deeply to injure me, which I resented. At this discovery I said, *Lord* I forgive *every* creature. That instant, it appeared to me as if a garment, which had entirely enveloped my whole person, even to my fingers' ends, split at the crown of my head, and was stripped away from me, passing like a shadow from my sight—when the glory of God seemed to cover me in its stead.

That moment, though hundreds were present, I did leap to my feet and declare that God, for Christ's sake, had pardoned the sins of my soul. Great was the ecstacy of my mind, for I felt that not only the sin of *malice* was pardoned, but all other sins were swept away together. That day was the first when my heart had believed, and my tongue had made confession unto salvation—the first words uttered, a part of that song, which shall fill eternity with its sound, was *glory to God.* For a few moments I had power to exhort sinners, and to tell of the wonders and of the goodness of Him who had clothed me with *His* salvation. During this the minister was silent, until my soul felt its duty had been performed, when he declared another witness of the power of Christ to forgive sins on earth, was manifest in my conversion. . . .

By the increasing light of the Spirit, I had found there yet remained the root of pride, anger, self-will, with many evils, the result of fallen nature. . . . I was now greatly alarmed, lest I should fall away from what I knew I had enjoyed; and to guard against this I prayed almost incessantly. . . .

. . . I had struggled long and hard, but found not the desire of my heart. When I rose from my knees, there seemed a voice speaking to me, as I yet stood in a leaning posture—"Ask for sanctification." When to my surprise, I recollected that I had not even thought of it in my whole prayer. It would seem Satan had hidden the very object from my mind, for which I had purposely kneeled to pray. But when this voice whispered in my heart, saying, "Pray for sanctification," I again bowed in the same place, at the same time, and said "Lord *sanctify* my soul for Christ's sake." That very instant, as if lightning had darted through me, I sprang to my feet, and cried, "The Lord has sanctified my soul!" There was none to hear this but the angels who stood around to witness my joy—and Satan, whose malice raged the more. That Satan was there, I knew; for no sooner had I cried out "The Lord has sanctified my soul," than there seemed another voice behind me, saying "No, it is too great a work to be done." But another spirit said "Bow down for the witness—I received it—*thou art sanctified!*" The first I knew of myself after that, I was standing in the yard with my hands spread out, and looking with my face toward heaven.

I now ran into the house and told them what had happened to me, when, as it were a new rush of the same ecstacy came upon me, and caused me to feel as if I were in an ocean of light and bliss.

During this, I stood perfectly still, the tears rolling in a flood from my eyes. So great was the joy, that it is past description. There is no language that can describe it, except that which was heard by St. Paul, when he was caught up to third heaven, and heard words which it was not lawful to utter. . . .

Between four and five years after my sanctification, on a certain time, an impressive silence fell upon me, and I stood as if some one was about to speak to me, yet I had no such thought in my heart.—But to my utter surprise there seemed to sound a voice which I thought I distinctly heard, and most certainly understand, which said to me, "Go preach the Gospel!" I immediately replied aloud, "No one will believe me." Again I listened, and again the same voice seemed to say—"Preach the Gospel; I will put words in your mouth, and will turn your enemies to become your friends."

At first I supposed that Satan had spoken to me, for I had read that he could transform himself into an angel of light for the purpose of deception. Immediately I went into a secret place, and called upon the Lord to know if he had called me to preach, and whether I was deceived or not; when there appeared to my view the form and figure of a pulpit, with a Bible lying thereon, the back of which was presented to me as plainly as if it had been a literal fact.

In consequence of this, my mind became so exercised, that during the night following, I took a text and preached in my sleep. I thought there stood before me a great multitude, while I expounded to them the things of religion. So violent were my exertions and so loud were my exclamations, that I awoke from the sound of my own voice, which also awoke the family of the house where I resided. Two days after I went to see the preacher in charge of the African Society, who was the Rev. Richard Allen, the same before named in these pages, to tell him that I felt it my duty to preach the gospel. But as I drew near the street in which his house was, which was in the city of Philadelphia, my courage began to fail me; so terrible did the cross appear, it seemed that I should not be able to bear it. Previous to my setting out to go to see him, so agitated was my mind, that my appetite for my daily food failed me entirely. Several times on my way there, I turned back again; but as often I felt my strength again renewed, and I soon found that the nearer I approached to the house of the minister, the less was my fear. Accordingly, as soon as I came to the door, my fears subsided, the cross was removed, all things appeared pleasant—I was tranquil.

I now told him, that the Lord had revealed it to me, that [I] must preach the gospel. He replied, by asking, in what sphere I wished to move in? I said, among the Methodists. He then replied, that a Mrs. Cook, a Methodist lady, had also some time before requested the same privilege; who, it was believed, had done much good in the way of exhortation, and holding prayer meetings; and who had been permitted to do so by the verbal license of the preacher in charge at the time. But as to women preaching, he said that our Discipline knew nothing at all about it—that it did not call for women preachers. This I was glad to hear, because it removed the fear of the cross—but no sooner did this feeling cross my mind, than I found that a love of souls had in a measure departed from me; that holy energy which burned within me, as a fire, began to be smothered. This I soon perceived.

O how careful ought we to be, lest through our by-laws of church government and discipline, we bring into disrepute even the word of life. For as unseemly as it may appear now-a-days for a woman to preach, it should be remembered that nothing is impossible with God. And why should it be thought impossible, heterodox, or improper for a woman to preach? seeing the Saviour died for the woman as well as for the man.

If the man may preach, because the Saviour died for him, why not the woman? seeing he died for her also. Is he not a whole Saviour, instead of a half one? as those who hold it wrong for a woman to preach, would seem to make it appear.

Did not Mary first preach the risen Saviour, and is not the doctrine of the resurrection the very climax of Christianity—hangs not all our hope on this, as argued by St. Paul? Then did not Mary, a woman, preach the gospel? for she preached the resurrection of the crucified Son of God.

But some will say that Mary did not expound the Scripture, therefore, she did not preach, in the proper sense of the term. To this I reply, it may be that the term preach in those primitive times, did not mean exactly what it is now made to mean; perhaps it was a great deal more simple then, than it is now—if it were not, the unlearned fishermen could not have preached the gospel at all, as they had no learning.

To this it may be replied, by those who are determined not to believe that it is right for a woman to preach, that the disciples, though they were fishermen and ignorant of letters too, were inspired so to do. To which I would reply, that though they were inspired, yet that inspiration did not save them from showing their ignorance of letters, and of man's wisdom; this the multitude soon found out, by listening to the remarks of the envious Jewish priests. If then, to preach the gospel, by the gift of heaven, comes by inspiration solely, is God straitened: must he take the man exclusively? May he not, did he not, and can he not inspire a female to preach the simple story of the birth, life, death, and resurrection of our Lord, and accompany it too with power to the sinner's heart. As for me, I am fully persuaded that the Lord called me to labor according to what I have received, in his vineyard. If he has not, how could he consistently bear testimony in favor of my poor labors, in awakening and converting sinners?

In my wanderings up and down among men, preaching according to my ability, I have frequently found families who told me that they had not for several years been to a meeting, and yet, while listening to hear what God would say by his poor female instrument, have believed with trembling —tears rolling down their cheeks, the signs of contrition and repentance towards God. I firmly believe that I have sown seed, in the name of the Lord, which shall appear with its increase at the great day of accounts, when Christ shall come to make up his jewels. . . .

In the year 1811, I changed my situation in life, having married Mr. Joseph Lee, pastor of a Society at Snow Hill, about six miles from the city of Philadelphia. It became necessary therefore for me to remove. This was a great trial at first, as I knew no person at Snow Hill, except my husband, and to leave my associates in the society, and especially those who composed the *band* of which I was one. None but those who have been in sweet fellowship with such as really love God, and have together drank bliss and happiness from the same fountain, can tell how dear such company is, and how hard it is to part from them.

At Snow Hill, as was feared, I never found that agreement and close-ness in communion and fellowship, that I had in Philadelphia, among my young companions, nor ought I to have expected it. The manners and cus-toms at this place were somewhat different, on which account I became discontented in the course of a year, and began to importune my husband to remove to the city. But this plan did not suit him, as he was the Pastor of the Society, he could not bring his mind to leave them. This afflicted me a little. But the Lord showed me in a dream what his will was concerning this matter.

I dreamed that as I was walking on the summit of a beautiful hill, that I saw near me a flock of sheep, fair and white, as if but newly washed; when there came walking toward me a man of a grave and dignified countenance, dressed entirely in white, as it were in a robe, and looking at me, said emphatically, "Joseph Lee must take care of these sheep, or the wolf will come and devour them." When I awoke I was convinced of my error, and immediately, with a glad heart, yielded to the right spirit in the Lord. . . .

For six years from this time I continued to receive from above, such baptisms of the Spirit as mortality could scarcely bear. About that time I was called to suffer in my family, by death—five, in the course of about six years, fell by his hand; my husband being one of the number, which was the greatest affliction of all.

I was now left alone in the world, with two infant children, one of the age of about two years, the other six months, with no other dependence than the promise of Him who hath said—I will be the widow's God, and a father to the fatherless. Accordingly, he raised me up friends, whose liberality comforted and solaced me in my state of widowhood and sorrows. . . .

It was now eight years since I had made application to be permitted to preach the gospel, during which time I had only been allowed to exhort, and even this privilege but seldom. This subject now was renewed afresh in my mind; it was as a fire shut up in my bones. About thirteen months passed on, while under this renewed impression. During this time, I had solicited of the Rev. Bishop, Richard Allen, who at this time had become Bishop of the African Episcopal Methodists in America, to be permitted the liberty of holding prayer meetings in my own hired house, and of exhorting as I found liberty, which was granted me. By this means, my mind was relieved, as the house soon filled when the hour appointed for prayer had arrived. . . .

. . . Soon after this, as above related, the Rev. Richard Williams was to preach at Bethel Church, where I with others were assembled. He entered the pulpit, gave out the hymn, which was sung, and then addressed the throne of grace; took his text, passed through the exordium, and commenced to expound it. The text he took is in Jonah, 2d chap. 9th verse,—"Salvation is of the Lord." But as he proceeded to explain, he seemed to have lost the spirit; when in the same instant, I sprang, as by altogether supernatural impulse, to my feet, when I was aided from above to give an exhortation on the very text which my brother Williams had taken.

I told them I was like Jonah; for it had been then nearly eight years since the Lord had called me to preach his gospel to the fallen sons and daughters of Adam's race, but that I had lingered like him, and delayed to go at the bidding of the Lord, and warn those who are as deeply guilty as were the people of Ninevah.

During the exhortation, God made manifest his power in a manner sufficient to show the world that I was called to labor according to my ability, and the grace given unto me, in the vineyard of the good husbandman.

I now sat down, scarcely knowing what I had done, being frightened. I imagined, that for this indecorum, as I feared it might be called, I should be expelled from the church. But instead of this, the Bishop rose up in the assembly, and related that I had called upon him eight years before, asking to be permitted to preach, and that he had put me off; but that he now as much believed that I was called to that work, as any of the preachers present. These remarks greatly strengthened me, so that my fears of having given an offence, and made myself liable as an offender, subsided, giving place to a sweet serenity, a holy joy of a peculiar kind, untasted in my bosom until then.

Amanda Berry Smith

Born on a Maryland farm twenty miles distant from Baltimore, Amanda Berry Smith was an itinerant preacher without benefit of ordination. Not only did she travel, which was not commonplace for black women just after the era of slavery, but she traveled to exotic lands. She was endowed with a compelling voice, which uniquely affected her calling as well as her life. Her voice as much as her words impelled her hearers and brought her attention and respect. Bishop J.M. Thoburn of Calcutta, who wrote the introduction for her autobiography, described the first time he heard her give an unimpressive Bible lesson. Later in the same day, he recalled,

> I lifted my head, and . . . probably not more than two yards from me, I saw the colored sister of the morning kneeling in an upright position with her hands spread out and her face all aglow. She had suddenly broken out with a triumphant song. . . . Something like a hallowed glow seemed to rest upon the dark face before me, and I felt in a second that she was possessed of a rare degree of spiritual power. . . . She was not only a woman of faith . . . she possessed a clearness of vision which I have seldom found equalled.[1]

The music welling up within her gave her an awareness of power and of mission.

The parents of this astounding woman were slaves who lived on adjoining farms. Both were literate and her father made it a regular practice on Sunday mornings to read to his family from the Bible. Her mother helped her to learn reading before she was eight and was sent to school. The school was a private one and was in session only during the summer months. She went to another school some five miles from home when she was thirteen. Formal learning added up to hardly more than three months; for the rest she educated herself.

More controlling in the molding of her character was her father's determination to buy his family out and his strong sense of responsibility. This was furthered by his deceased master's widow, who trusted him and

---

[1]Amanda Smith, An Autobiography: the Story of the Lord's Dealings with Mrs. Amanda Smith, the Colored Evangelist . . . (Chicago, 1893), p. v.

placed the farm partly in his charge. He was given leave to use his energies, after the work of the day was done, to earn money for his own use. His mistress "allowed him so much for his work and a chance to make what extra he could for himself." A strong constitution and ·a strong motivation for securing his own freedom—and that of his wife and five children as well —enabled him to forgo sleep in order to make brooms and husk mats for the Baltimore market. As free blacks they were permitted to establish themselves in a house nearby with a lot they farmed themselves. Freedom, faith, family, and literacy were the influences of Amanda Berry's youth.

Marriage in 1859 gave her little happiness. Work as a washerwoman dejected her not at all, but she was unable to inspire her husband with her own religious fervor. Although he was a deacon of the local Methodist Episcopal Church, he did not fully share her convictions. When he died about ten years later, Amanda Smith began to preach. Her singing voice brought her recognition in her first struggles as an untrained evangelist. But she never moved from one place to another before she was sure that the divine will had so instructed. A trip to England in 1878 led her two years later to India. While in India she assisted Bishop Thoburn in religious work. To England she returned in 1881 before setting out for Africa.

The African visit lasted for eight years. Most of the time was spent in Liberia. The campaign then in progress to induce American blacks to mi-.grate to Liberia did not meet with her support. She had no objection to individual migrations, especially if one had something particular to offer the Liberians. Nativism was rampant in the America of the 1890s, and Amanda Smith succumbed to this influence in her defense of American blacks.

Her view of Africa was marked by ambivalence. Though she identified with the people in ethnic terms, she endorsed the prevailing American concept of Western cultural superiority. Christianity, Amanda Smith believed, would improve the earthly existence of "my people" while preparing them for reception into heavenly life.

I was born at Long Green, Md., Jan. 23rd, 1837. My father's name was Samuel Berry. My mother's name, Mariam. Matthews was her maiden name. My father's master's name was Darby Insor. My mother's master's name, Shadrach Green. They lived on adjoining farms. They did not own as large a number of black people, as some who lived in the neighborhood. My father

Source: Amanda Smith, An Autobiography: the Story of the Lord's Dealings with Mrs. Amanda Smith, the Colored Evangelist; Containing an Account of her Life Work of Faith, and her Travels in America, England, Ireland, Scotland, India and Africa, as an Independent Missionary (Chicago, 1893), pp. 17–36, 147–48, 156–59, 198–204, 215–23, 240–53, 378–90, 412–13, 451–52. All footnotes are the editors'.

and mother had each a good master and mistress, as was said. After my father's master died, his young master, Mr. E., and himself, had all the charge of the place. They had been boys together, but as father was the older of the two, and was a trustworthy servant, his mistress depended on him, and much was entrusted to his care. As the distance to Baltimore was only about twenty miles, more or less, my father went there with the farm produce once or twice a week, and would sell or buy, and bring the money home to his mistress. She was very kind, and was proud of him for his faithfulness, so she gave him a chance to buy himself. She allowed him so much for his work and a chance to make what extra he could for himself. So he used to make brooms and husk mats and take them to market with the produce. This work he would do nights after his day's work was done for his mistress. He was a great lime burner. Then in harvest time, after working for his mistress all day, he would walk three and four miles, and work in the harvest field till one and two o'clock in the morning, then go home and lie down and sleep for an hour or two, then up and at it again. He had an important and definite object before him, and was willing to sacrifice sleep and rest in order to accomplish it. It was not his own liberty alone, but the freedom of his wife and five children. For this he toiled day and night. He was a strong man, with an excellent constitution, and God wonderfully helped him in his struggle. After he had finished paying for himself, the next was to buy my mother and us children. There were thirteen children in all, of whom only three girls are now living. Five were born in slavery. I was the oldest girl, and my brother, William Talbart, the oldest boy. . . .

. . . My father having paid for himself was anxious to purchase his wife and children; and to show how the Lord helped in this, I must here tell of the wonderful conversion of my mother's young mistress and of her subsequent death, and the marvelous answer to my grandmother's prayers.

There was a Methodist Camp Meeting held at what was at that time called Cockey's Camp Ground. It was, I think, about twenty miles away, and the young mistress, with a number of other young people, went to this meeting. My mother went along to assist and wait on Miss Celie, as she had always done. It was an old-fashioned, red-hot Camp Meeting. These young people went just as a kind of picnic, and to have a good time looking on. They were staunch Presbyterians, and had no affinity with anything of that kind. They went more out of curiosity, to see the Methodists shout and hollow [sic], than anything else; because they did shout and hollow in those days, tremendously. Of course they were respectful. They went in to the morning meeting and sat down quietly to hear the sermon; then they purposed walking about the other part of the day, looking around, and having a pleasant time. As they sat in the congregation, the minister preached in demonstration of the Power and of the Holy Ghost. My mother said it was a wonderful time. The spirit of the Lord got hold of my young mistress, and she was mightily convicted and converted right there before she left the ground; wonderfully converted in the old-fashioned way; the shouting, hallelujah way. Of course it disgusted those who were with her. They were terribly put out. Everything was spoiled, and they did not know how to get her home. They coaxed her, but thank the Lord, she got struck through. Then they laughed at her a little. Then they scolded her, and ridiculed her; but they could not do anything with her. Then they begged her to be quiet; told her if she would just be quiet, and wait till they got home, and wait till morning, they would be satisfied. My mother was awfully glad that the Lord had answered her and grandmother's prayer. As I have heard my mother tell this story she has wept as though it had just been a few days ago. Mother had only been converted about two years before this, and had always prayed for Miss Celie, so her heart was bounding with gladness when Miss Celie was converted. . . . But when she got home she could not keep quiet, but began first thing to praise the Lord and shout. It aroused the whole house, and of course they were frightened, and thought she had lost her mind. But nay, verily, she had received the King, and there was great joy in the city. They got up and wondered what was the matter. They thought she was dreadfully excited at this meeting. They did all they could to quiet her, but they could not do much with her. But finally they did get her quiet and she went to bed. But her heart was so stirred and filled. She wanted to go then to where they would have lively meetings. She wanted to go to the Methodist church. Oh my! That was intolerable. They could not allow that. Then she wanted to go to the colored people's church. No, they would not have that. So they kept her from going. Then they separated my mother and her. They thought maybe mother might talk to her, and keep up the excitement. So they never let them be together at all, if possible. About a quarter of a mile away was the great dairy, and Miss Celie used to slip over there when she got a chance and have a good time praying with mother and grandmother. Finally they found they could do nothing with Miss Celie. So the young people decided they would get together and have a ball and get the notion out of her head. So they planned for a ball, and got all ready. The gentlemen would call on Miss Celie, she was very much admired, anyhow; and they would talk, and they did everything they could. She did not seem to take to it. . . . She used to put on her sunbonnet and slip down through the orchard and go down to the dairy and tell mother and grandmother; mother used to assist grandmother in the dairy. One day mother said she came down and said:

"Oh! Mary, I can't hold out any longer; they insist on my going to that ball, and I have decided to go. It's no use." So they had a good cry together, went off and prayed, and that was the last prayer about the ball. How strange! And yet God had that all in his infinite mercy—opening the prison to them that were bound. Just a week before the ball came off, Miss Celie was taken down with typhoid fever. They didn't think she was going to die when she was taken down, but they sent for the doctors, the best in the land. Four of them watched over her night and day. Everything was done for her that could be done. She always wanted mother with her, to sit up in the bed and hold her; she seemed only to rest comfortably then. She seemed to have sinking spells. The skill of the doctors was baffled, and they said they could not do any more. So one day after one of these sinking spells, she called them all around her bed and said: "I want to speak to you. I have one request I want to make."

They said, "Anything, my dear."

"I want you to promise me that you will let Samuel have Mariam and the children." Then they had my mother get up out of the bed at once. Of course they didn't want her to hear that; and they said:

"Now, my dear, if you will keep quiet, you may be a little better." And then she went off in a kind of sinking spell. When she said this, and they sent my mother out, she ran with all her might and told grandmother, and grandmother's faith saw the door open for the freedom of her grandchildren; and she ran out into the bush and told Jesus. Of course my mother had to hurry back so as not to be missed in the house. Miss Celie went on that way for three days, and they would quiet her down. When the second day came, and she made the request, and they sent my mother out, she ran and told grandmother that Miss Celie had made the same request; then she ran back to the house again, and grandmother went out and told Jesus. At last it came to the third and last day, and the doctor said: "She can only last such a length of time without there is a change; so what you do, you must do quickly."

Mother was in the bed behind her, holding her up. She called them all again, and said, "I want you to make me one promise; that is, that you will let Samuel have Mariam and the children."

"Oh! yes, my dear," they said, "we will do anything."

My mother was a great singer. When Miss Celie got the promise, she folded her hands together, and leaning her head upon my mother's breast she said, "Now, Mary, sing."

And as best she could, she did sing. It was hard work, for her heart was almost broken, for she loved her as one of her own children. While she sang, Miss Celie's sweet spirit swept through the gate, washed in the blood of the lamb. Hallelujah! what a Saviour. How marvelous that God should lead in this mysterious way to accomplish this end.

I often say to people that I have a right to shout more than some folks; I have been bought twice, and set free twice, and so I feel I have a good right to shout. Hallelujah!

I was quite small when my father bought us, so know nothing about the experience of slavery, because I was too young to have any trials of it. How well I remember my old mistress. She dressed very much after the Friends' style. She was very kind to me, and I was a good deal spoiled, for a little darkey. If I wanted a piece of bread, and if it was not buttered and sugared on both sides, I wouldn't have it; and when mother would get out of patience with me, and go for a switch, I would run to my old mistress and wrap myself up in her apron, and I was safe. And oh! how I loved her for that. They were getting me ready for market, but I didn't know it. I suppose that is why they allowed me to do many things that otherwise I should not have been allowed to do. They used to take me in the carriage with them to church on Sunday. How well I remember my pretty little green satin hood, lined inside with pink. How delighted I was when they used to take me. Then the young ladies would often make pretty little things and give to my mother for me. Mother was a good seamstress; she used to make all of our clothes, and all of father's every day clothes—coats, pants and vests. She had a wonderful faculty in this; she had but to see a thing of any style of dress or coat, or what-not, and she would come home and cut it out. People used to wonder at it. There were no Butterick's patterns then that she could get hold of. So one had to have a good head on them if they kept nearly in sight of things. But somehow mother was always equal to any emergency. My dear old mistress used to knit. I would follow her around. Sometimes she would walk out into the yard and sit under the trees, and I would drag the chair after her; I was too small to carry it. She would sit down awhile, and I would gather pretty flowers. When she got tired she would walk to another spot, and I would drag the chair again. So we would spend several hours in this way. My father had proposed buying us some time before, but could not be very urgent. He had to ask, and then wait a long interval before he could ask again. Two of the young ladies of our family were to be married, and as my brother and myself were the oldest of the children, one of us would have gone to one, and one to the other, as a dowry. But how God moves in a mysterious way His wonders to perform. My grandmother was a woman of deep piety and great faith. I have often heard my mother say that it was to the prayers and mighty faith of my grandmother that we owed our freedom. How I do praise the Lord for a Godly grandmother, as well as mother. She had often prayed that God would open a way so that her grandchildren might be free. The families into which these young ladies were to marry, were not considered by the black folks as good masters and mistresses as we had; and that was one of my grandmother's anxieties. And so she prayed and believed that somehow God would open a way for our deliverance. She had often tried and proved Him, and found Him to be a present help in trouble. And so in the way I have already related, the Lord did provide, and my father was permitted to purchase our freedom. . . .

After my father had got us all free and settled, he wanted to go and see his brother, who had run away for his freedom several years before my father bought himself. The laws of Maryland at that time were, that if a free man went out of the state and stayed over ten days, he lost his residence, and could be taken up and sold, unless some prominent white person interposed; and then sometimes with difficulty they might get him off. But many times poor black men were kidnapped, and would be got out of the way quick. For men who did that sort of business generally looked out for good opportunities. My mother's people all lived in Maryland. She hated to leave her mother, my dear grandmother, and so never would consent to go North.

But when my father went away to see his brother, and stayed over the ten days, she thought best to go. Poor mother! How well I remember her. After a week how anxious she was. She used to sit by the fire nearly all night. It was in the fall of the year I know, but I am not able to tell just what year it was. After my father's death, my sister, not knowing the value of the free papers, allowed them all to be destroyed. We were all recorded in the Baltimore court house. Many times I had seen my father show the papers to people. They had a large red seal—the county seal—and my father, or any of us traveling, would have to show our free papers. But those I have not got, so cannot tell the year or date. But, by and by, the ninth day came. I saw my mother walk the floor, look out of the window, and sigh. I used to get up out of my bed and sit in the corner by the fire and watch her, and see the great tears as she would wipe them away with her apron. She would say; "Amanda, why don't you stay in bed?"

I would make an excuse to stay with her. Sometimes I would cry and say I was sick. Then she would call me to her and let me lay my head in her lap; and there is no place on earth so sweet to a child as a mother's lap. I can almost feel the tender, warm, downy lap of my mother now as I write, for so it seemed to me. I loved my father, and thought he was the grandest man that ever lived. I was always the favorite of my father, and I was sorry enough when he was away, and when I saw my mother cry, I would cry, too. Ten days had passed, and father had not come yet.

Every day some of the good farmers around would call to see if "Sam" had got home yet. My father was much respected by all the best white people in that neighborhood, and many of them would not have said anything to him; but, "If nothing was said to Insor's Sam about going out of the state and staying over ten days, why all the niggers in the county would be doing the same thing!"

So this was the cause of the inquiry. Oh! no one knows the sadness and agony of my poor mother's heart. Finally the day came when father returned. Then the friends, white and black, who wished him well, advised him to leave as quickly as possible. And now the breaking up. We were doing well, and father and mother had all the work they could do. The white people in the neighborhood were kind, and gave my mother a good many things, so that we children always had plenty to eat and wear. We had a house, a good large lot, and a good garden, pigs, chickens, and turkeys. And then my mother was a great economist. She could make a little go a great ways. She was a beautiful washer and ironer, and a better cook never lifted a pot. I get my ability in that (if I have any) from my dear mother. Then withal she was an earnest Christian, and had strong faith in God, as did also my grandmother. She was deeply pious, and a woman of marvelous faith and prayer. For the reason stated my parents determined to move from Maryland, and so went to live on a farm owned by John Lowe, and situated on the Baltimore and York turnpike in the State of Pennsylvania.

My father and mother both could read. But I never remember hearing them tell how they were taught. Father was the better reader of the two. Always on Sunday morning after breakfast he would call us children around and read the Bible to us. I never knew him to sit down to a meal, no matter how scant, but what he would ask God's blessing before eating. Mother was very thoughtful and scrupulously economical. She could get up the best dinner out of almost nothing of anybody I ever saw in my life. She often cheered my father's heart when he came home at night and said: "Well, mother, how have you got on to-day?"

"Very well," she would say. It was hard planning sometimes; yet we children never had to go to bed hungry. After our evening meal, so often of nice milk and mush, she would call us children and make us all say our prayers before we went to bed. I never remember a time when I went to bed without saying the Lord's Prayer as it was taught me by my mother. Even before we were free I was taught to say my prayers.

I first went to school at the age of eight years, to the daughter of an old Methodist minister named Henry Dull; my teacher's name was Isabel Dull. She taught a little private school opposite where my mother lived, in a private house belonging to Isaac Hendricks (Bishop Hendricks' grandfather).[1] She was a great friend of my mother's, and was very pretty, and very kind to us children. She taught me my first spelling lesson. There was school only in the summer time. I had about six weeks of it. I first taught myself to read by cutting out large letters from the newspapers my father would bring home. Then I would lay them on the window and ask mother to put them together for me to make words, so that I could read. I shall never forget how delighted I was when I first read: "The house, the tree, the dog, the cow." I thought I knew it all. I would call the other children about me and show them how I could read. I did not get to go to school any more till I was about thirteen years old. Then we had to go about five miles, my brother and myself. There were but few colored people in that part of the country at that time, to go to school (white school), only about five and they were not regular; but father and mother were so anxious for us to go that they urged us on, and I was anxious also. I shall never forget one cold winter morning. The sun was bright, the snow very deep, and it was bitterly cold. My brother did not go that day, but I wanted to go. Mother thought it was too cold; she was afraid I would freeze; but I told her I could go, and after a little discussion she told me I might go. She told me I could put on my brother's heavy boots. I had on a good thick pair of stockings, a warm linsey-woolsey dress, and was well wrapped up. Off I started to my two and a half mile school house,—John Rule's school house on the Turnpike. The first half mile I got on pretty well, a good deal up hill, but O how cold I began to get, and being so wrapped up I couldn't get on so well as I thought I could. I was near freezing to death. My first thought was to go back, but I was too plucky, I

---

[1] Eugene Russell Hendrix (1847–1927), descendant of the Hendricks family of New Freedom, Pa., was elected bishop of the Methodist Episcopal Church in 1886.

was afraid if I told mother she wouldn't let me go again, so I kept still and went. When I got to the school house door, I found I couldn't open it and couldn't speak, and a white boy came up and said, "Why don't you go in?" Then I found I couldn't speak, as I tried and couldn't. He opened the door and I went in and some one came to me and took off my things and they worked with me, I can't tell how long, before I recovered from my stupor. There were a great many farmers' daughters, large girls, and boys, in the winter time, so that the school would be full, so that after coming two and a half miles, many a day I would get but one lesson, and that would be while the other scholars were taking down their dinner kettles and putting their wraps on. All the white children had to have their full lessons, and if time was left the colored children had a chance. I received in all about three months' schooling.

At thirteen years of age I lived in Strausburg, sometimes it was called Shrewsbury, about thirteen miles from York, on the Baltimore and York turnpike. I lived with a Mrs. Latimer. She was a Southern lady, was born in Savannah, Georgia. She was a widow, with five children. It was a good place, Mrs. Latimer was very kind to me and I got on nicely. It was in the spring I went there to live, and sometime in the winter a great revival broke out and went on for weeks at the Allbright Church. I was deeply interested and impressed by the spirit of the meeting. It was an old-fashioned revival, scores were converted. No colored persons went up to be prayed for; there were but few anywhere in the neighborhood. One old man named Moses Rainbow, and his two sons, Samuel and James, were the only colored people that lived anywhere within three or four miles of the town. This meeting went on for four or five weeks. When it closed a series of meetings commenced at the Methodist Church.

One of the members was Miss Mary Bloser, daughter of George Bloser, well known through all that region of country for his deep piety and Christian character, as was Miss Mary, also. She was powerful in prayer. I never heard a young person who knew how to so take hold of God for souls. She was a power for good everywhere she went. How many souls I have seen her lead to the Cross!

One night as she was speaking to persons in the congregation, she came to me, a poor colored girl sitting away back by the door, and with entreaties and tears, which I really felt, she asked me to go forward. I was the only colored girl there, but I went. She knelt beside me with her arm around me and prayed for me. O, how she prayed! I was ignorant, but prayed as best I could. The meeting closed. I went to get up, but found I could not stand. They took hold of me and stood me on my feet. My strength seemed to come to me, but I was frightened. I was afraid to step. I seemed to be so light. In my heart was peace, but I did not know how to exercise faith as I should. I went home and resolved I would be the Lord's and live for him. All the days were happy and bright. I sang and worked and thought that was all I needed to do. Then I joined the Church. I don't remember the name of the minister, but I well remember the name of my class leader was Joshua Ludrick. I liked him for his lung power, for I thought then there was a good deal of religion in loud prayers and shouts. You could hear him pray half a mile when he would get properly stirred. He was leader of the Sunday morning class, which convened after the morning preaching. My father and mother, to encourage me in my new life, joined the Church and the same class, so as to save me from going out at night. Mrs. Latimer's children, three of them, went to the Sunday School, and I must get home so as to have dinner in time for the children to get off, but I was black, so could not be led in class before a white person, must wait till the white ones were through, and I would get such a scolding when I got home, the children would all be so vexed with me, and Mrs. Latimer, and my troubles had begun. I prayed and thought it was my cross. I thought I will change my seat in the class, maybe that will help me, and sat in the first end of the pew, as the leader would always commence on the first end and go down. When I sat in the first end, then he would commence at the lower end and come up and leave me last. Then I sat between two, thinking he would lead the two above me and then lead me in turn, but he would lead the two and then jump across me and lead all the others and lead me last. I told my father I got scolded for getting home so late and making the children late for school. Father said he would speak to Mr. Ludrick about it, but if he did, it made no change, and it came to where I must decide either to give up my class or my service place. We were a large family, and father and mother thought I must keep my situation, so I had to give up my class. . . .

The name of my father's landlord was John Lowe, he was a wealthy farmer, lived between New Market and Shrewsbury, Pa. Pretty much all the farmers round about in those days were anti-slavery men; Joseph Hendricks, Clark Lowe, and a number of others. My father worked a great deal for Isaac Hendricks, who used to keep the Blueball Tavern. I and the children have gathered many a basket of apples out of the orchard, and many a pail of milk I have helped to carry to the house, and often at John Lowe's as well; I used to help them churn often. And then old Thomas Wantlen, who used to keep the store; how well I remember him. John Lowe would allow my father to do what he could in secreting the poor slaves that would get away and come to him for protection. At one time he was Magistrate, and of course did not hunt down poor slaves, and would support the law whenever things were brought before him in a proper way, but my father and mother were level headed and had good broad common sense, so they never brought him into any trouble. Our house was one of the main stations of the Under Ground Railroad. My father took the "Baltimore Weekly Sun" newspaper; that always had advertisements of runaway slaves. After giving the cut of the poor fugitive, with a little bundle on his back, going with his face northward, the advertisement would read something like this: Three thousand dollars reward! Ran away from Anerandell [sic] County, Maryland, such a date, so many feet high, scar on the right side of the forehead or some other part of the body,—belonging to Mr. A.

or B. So sometimes the excitement was so high we had to be very discreet in order not to attract suspicion. My father was watched closely.

I have known him to lead in the harvest field from fifteen to twenty men—he was a great cradler and mower in those days—and after working all day in the harvest field, he would come home at night, sleep about two hours, then start at midnight and walk fifteen or twenty miles and carry a poor slave to a place of security; sometimes a mother and child, sometimes a man and wife, other times a man or more, then get home just before day. Perhaps he could sleep an hour then go to work, and so many times baffled suspicion. Never but once was there a poor slave taken that my father ever got his hand on, and if that man had told the truth he would have been saved, but he was afraid.

There was a beautiful woods a mile from New Market on the Baltimore and York Turnpike; it was called Lowe's Camp Ground. It was about three quarters of a mile from our house. My mother was a splendid cook, so we arranged to keep a boarding house during the camp meeting time. We had melons, and pies and cakes and such like, as well. Father was very busy and had not noticed the papers for a week or two, so did not know there was any advertisement of runaways. There were living in New Market certain white men that made their living by catching runaway slaves and getting the reward. A man named Turner, who kept the post office at New Market, Ben Crout, who kept a regular Southern blood-hound for that purpose, and John Hunt. These men all lived in New Market. Then there was a Luther Amos, Jake Hedrick, Abe Samson and Luther Samson, his son. I knew them all well. Samson had a number of grey-hounds. So these fellows used to watch our house closely, trying every way to catch my father. One night during camp meeting, between twelve and one o'clock, we children were all on the pallet on the floor. It was warm weather, and father and mother slept in the bed. A man came and knocked at the door. Father asked who was there? He said "A friend. I hear you keep a boarding house and I want to get something to eat."

Father told him to come in. He had everything but hot coffee—so he went to work and got the coffee ready. Father talked with him. The man was well dressed. He had changed his clothes, he said, as he had been traveling, and it was dusty, and he was on his way to the camp meeting. This is what he said to my father. So by and by the coffee was ready, and father set him down to his supper. This man had come through New Market, and Ben Crout and John Hunt, who had read the advertisement, saw this man answered the description and hoping to catch my father, told him to come to our house and all about my father having a boarding house and all about the camp meeting. It was white people's camp meeting, but colored people went as well; it used to be the old Baltimore camp, so called, and so that was the way the poor man knew so well what to say. He had come away from Louisiana, and had been two weeks lying by in the day time and traveling at night, but had got so hungry he ventured into this town, and these men were looking for him, but he did not know it. When they saw him they knew he answered the advertisement given in the paper, for it was always explicitly given; the color, the height and scars on any part of his body. Well, just about the time the man got through with his supper, some one shouted, "Halloo!" Father went to the door. There were six or seven white men, and they said, "We want that nigger you are harboring, he is a runaway nigger."

"I am not harboring anybody," father said. Then they began to curse and swear and rushed upon him. The man jumped and ran up stairs. My mother had a small baby. Of course she was frightened and jumped up, and they were beating father and tramping all over us children on the floor. We were screaming. There stood in the middle of the floor an old fashioned ten plate stove. There was no fire in it, of course, and as my poor frightened mother ran by it trying to defend father, she caught her wrapper in the door, just as a man cut at her with a spring dirk knife; it glanced on the door instead of on mother. I have thanked God many a time for that stove door. But for it my poor mother would have been killed that night. The poor man jumped out of the window up stairs and ran about two hundred yards, when Ben Crout's blood-hound caught him and held him till they came. When they found the man was gone, they left off beating father and went for the man. That was the first and last darkey they ever got out of Sam Berry's clutches. It put a new spirit in my mother. She cried bitterly, but O, when it was all over how she had gathered courage and strength. The good white people all over the neighborhood were aroused, but he was so close to the Maryland line they had him in Baltimore a few hours from then. And, poor fellow, we never heard of him afterwards.

Some time, about three or four months after this, along in the fall, we were sleeping upstairs. One night about twelve o'clock a knock came on the fence. My father answered and went down and opened the door. Mother listened and heard them say "runaway nigger." She sprang up, and as she ran downstairs she snatched down father's cane, which had a small dirk in it; she went up and threw open the door, pushed father aside, but he got hold of her, but O, when she got through with those men! They fell back and tried to apologize, but she would hear nothing.

"I can't go to my bed and sleep at night without being hounded by you devils," she said.

Next morning father went off to work, but mother dressed herself and went to New Market; as she went she told everybody she met how she had been hounded by these men. Told all their names right out, and all the rich respectable people cried shame, and backed her up. Dr. Bell, the leading doctor in New Market, who himself owned three or four slaves,[2] stood by my

---

[2]During the 1840s aged slaves, born before 1780, were evidence of Pennsylvania's gradualism in antislavery legislation. The federal census of 1840 listed sixty-four slaves among the blacks of that state.

mother and told her to speak of it publicly; so she stood on the stepping stone at Dr. Bell's, right in front of the largest Tavern in the place. There were a lot of these men sitting out reading the news. The morning was a beautiful Fall morning, and she opened her mouth and for one hour declared unto them all the words in her heart. Not a word was said against her, but as the spectators and others looked on and listened the cry of "Shame! Shame!" could be heard; and the men skulked away here and there. By the time she got through there was not one to be seen of this tribe. That morning, as mother went to New Market, this same blood-hound of Ben Crout's was lying on the sidewalk, and as mother went on a lady she used to work for, a Mrs. Rutlidge, saw the dog and saw mother coming. She threw up her hand to indicate to her the dangerous animal. They generally kept her fastened up, but this morning she was not. Mother paid no attention but went on. Mrs. R. clasped her hands and turned her back expecting every moment to hear mother scream out. She looked around and mother was close by the dog and stepped right over her. She was so frightened she said: "O, Mary, how did you get by that dreadful dog of Ben Crout's?"

Mother was wrothy, and said, "I didn't stop to think about that dog," and passed on. And this was the wonder to everybody around. It was the great talk of the day all about the country, how that Sam Berry's wife had passed Ben Crout's blood-hound and was not hurt. Then they began to say she must have had some kind of a charm, and they were shy of her. Ever after that nobody, black or white, troubled Sam Berry's wife. It was no charm, but was God's wonderful deliverance.

About two years or more after this, the papers were full of notices of a very valuable slave who had run away. A heavy reward was offered. He had by God's mercy got to us, and by moving the poor fellow from place to place he had been kept safe for about two weeks, as there was no possible chance for father or any one to get him away, so closely were we watched. My father was a very early riser, always up and out about day dawn. Our house stood in the valley between two hills, so that the moment you struck the top of the hill, either way coming or going, you could see every move around our house. Just on the opposite side of the road there used to stand two large chestnut trees, but these had been blown down by a great storm some time before, so there was no screen to hide the house from full view. This morning, while out in the yard feeding the pigs, he saw four men coming on horseback. He knew they were strangers. He could not get in the house to tell mother, so he called to her and said: "Mother, I see four men coming; do the best you can."

She must act in a moment without being able to say a word more to father. The poor slave man was upstairs. She brought him down and put him between the cords and straw tick. As it was early in the morning her bed was not made up. In the old-fashioned houses in the country we did not have parlors. The front room downstairs was often used as the bed-room. My little brother, two years old, slept in the foot of the bed. The men rode up and spoke to my father. He was a very polite man. "Good morning, gentlemen, good morning, you are out quite early this morning."

"Yes, we are looking for a runaway nigger." Just then my father recognized the high sheriff as Mr. E., who was formerly his young master. "Why, is this is not Mr. E.?"

"Yes, Sam, didn't you know me?"

My father made a wonderful time over him, laughed heartily and said: "What in the world is up?"

"Do you know anything about this runaway?"

Another spoke up and said: "We have a search warrant and we mean to have that nigger. We want to know if you have him hid away."

"Well," father said, "if I tell you I have not, you won't believe me; if I tell you I have, it will not satisfy you, so come in and look."

He didn't know a bit what mother had done, but he knew she had a head on her, and he could trust her in an emergency. The men hesitated and said: "It is no use for us to go in, if you will just tell us if you have him or know anything about him." And father said: "You come in, gentlemen, and look."

They said, "We have heard your wife is the devil," and then, speaking very nicely, "You know, Sam, we don't want any trouble with her, you can tell us just as well."

"No, gentlemen, you will be better satisfied if you go in and see for yourselves."

Just then mother, in the most dignified and polite manner, threw open the door and said: "Good morning, gentlemen, come right in." So they laughed heartily. Two dismounted and came in, went upstairs, looked all about while one looked in the kitchen behind the chimney, in the pot closet; and my mother went to the bed and threw back the cover (she knew what cover to throw back, of course,) there lay my little brother. She said: "Look everywhere, maybe this is he?"

"My! Sam," one of them said, "here is a darkey, what will you take for him?"

"No, you have not money enough to buy him," father said. Then mother said: "Now, gentlemen, look under the bed as well: you haven't examined every thing here," and they laughed and ran out and said: "Well, Sam, we see you haven't got him."

And father said: "Well, now you are better satisfied after you have looked yourselves." So he didn't tell any lie, but he had the darkey hid just the same!

They mounted their horses and went off full tilt to York. We children were sharp enough never to show any sign of alarm. Poor me, my eyes felt like young moons. The man was safe. After they had got away, mother got the poor fellow out, and he was so weak he could scarcely stand. He trembled from head to foot, and cried like a child. Poor fellow, he thought he was gone, and but for my noble mother he would have been. We soon got him off to Canada, where, I trust, he lived to thank and praise God, who delivered him from the hand of his masters.

• • •

It was the third Sunday in November, 1890 [actually 1870]. Sister Scott, my band sister, and myself went to the Fleet street A.M.E. Church, Brooklyn. It was Communion Sunday. . . .

Brother Gould, then pastor of the Fleet Street Church, took his text. I was sitting with my eyes closed in silent prayer to God, and after he had been preaching about ten minutes, as I opened my eyes, just over his head I seemed to see a beautiful star, and as I looked at it, it seemed to form into the shape of a large white tulip; and I said, "Lord, is that what you want me to see? If so, what else?" And then I leaned back and closed my eyes. Just then I saw a large letter "G," and I said: "Lord, do you want me to read in Genesis, or in Galatians? Lord, what does this mean?"

Just then I saw the letter "O." I said, "Why, that means go." And I said "What else?" And a voice distinctly said to me "Go preach." . . .

. . . At night after Brother Holland had preached a short sermon, he called me up to exhort. As I sat in the pulpit beside him, he saw I was frightened. He leaned over and said, "Now, my child, you needn't be afraid. Lean on the Lord. He will help you."

And He did help me. There was a large congregation. The gallery was full, and every part of the house was packed. I stood up trembling. The cold chills ran over me. My heart seemed to stand still. Oh, it was a night. But the Lord gave me great liberty in speaking. After I had talked a little while the cold chills stopped, my heart began to beat naturally and all fear was gone, and I seemed to lose sight of everybody and everything but my responsibility to God and my duty to the people. The Holy Ghost fell on the people and we had a wonderful time. Souls were convicted and some converted that night. But the meeting did not go on from that.

Thursday night was the regular prayer meeting night. Brother Cooper said I was there, and would preach Thursday night. He was going to give me a chance to preach, and he wanted all the people to come out. . . .

The church was packed and crowded. I began my talk from the chapter given, with great trembling. I had gone on but a little ways when I felt the spirit of the Lord come upon me mightily. Oh! how He helped me. My soul was free. The Lord convicted sinners and backsliders and believers for holiness, and when I asked for persons to come to the altar, it was filled in a little while from the gallery and all parts of the house.

A revival broke out, and spread for twenty miles around. Oh! what a time it was. It went from the colored people to the white people. Sometimes we would go into the church at seven o'clock in the evening. I could not preach. The whole lower floor would be covered with seekers—old men, young men, old women, young women, boys and girls. Oh! glory to God!

How He put His seal on this first work to encourage my heart and establish my faith, that He indeed had chosen, and ordained and sent me. I do not know as I have ever seen anything to equal that first work, the first seal that God gave to His work at Salem. Some of the young men that were converted are in the ministry. Some have died in the triumph of faith. Others are on the way. I went on two weeks, day and night. We used to stay in the church till one and two o'clock in the morning. People could not work. Some of the young men would hire a wagon and go out in the country ten miles and bring in a load, get them converted, and then take them back. . . .

In May, '70, or '71 [actually 1872], the General Conference of the A.M.E. Church was held at Nashville, Tenn. . . . I had been laboring in Salem, where the Lord first sent me, and blessed me in winning souls; the people were not rich; they gave me a home, and something to eat; but very little money. So, before I could get back to New York, my home, I took a service place, at Mrs. Mater's, in Philadelphia, corner of Coach and Brown streets, while her servant, Mary, went to Wilmington to see her child; she was to be gone a month, but she stayed five weeks; and now the Annual Conference was in session, at the A.M.E. Union Church, near by where I was, so I had a chance to attend.

The election of delegates to the General Conference the next year was a very prominent feature of the Conference; of course every minister wanted, or hoped to be elected as delegate. As I listened, my heart throbbed. This was the first time in all these years that this religious body of black men, with a black church from beginning to end, was to be assembled south of Mason and Dixon's line.

But the great battle had been fought, and the victory won; slavery had been abolished; we were really free. There were enthusiastic speeches made on these points. Oh, how I wished I could go; and a deep desire took possession of me; but then, who was I? I had no money, no prominence at that time, except being a plain Christian woman, heard of and known by a few of the brethren, as a woman preacher, which was to be dreaded by the majority. . . . I ventured to ask one of the brethren, who had been elected delegate, to tell me how much it would cost to go to Nashville; I would like to go if it did not cost too much.

He looked at me in surprise, mingled with half disgust; the very idea of one looking like me to want to go to General Conference; they cut their eye at my big poke Quaker bonnet, with not a flower, not a feather. He said, "I tell you, Sister, it will cost money to go down there; and if you ain't got plenty of it, it's no use to go;" and turned away and smiled; another said:

"What does she want to go for?"

"Woman preacher; they want to be ordained," was the reply.

"I mean to fight that thing," said the other. "Yes, indeed, so will I," said another.

Then a slight look to see if I took it in. I did; but in spite of it all I believed God would have me go. He knew that the thought of ordination had never once entered my mind, for I had received my ordination from Him, Who said, "Ye have not chosen Me, but I have chosen you, and ordained you, that you might go and bring forth fruit, and that your fruit might remain." . . .

I was quite a curiosity to most of the visitors [at Nashville], especially the Southern brethren, in my very plain Quaker dress; I was eyed with critical suspicion as being there to agitate the question of the ordination of women. . . .

I would walk out in the afternoon alone, and to and from church alone. Several times I got ready in time and called at the parlor and asked if any of the ladies were ready; "not yet," was the usual answer; so I would walk on. After awhile, in the greatest style, would come these ladies with the good brethren.

The early mornings and the evenings were quite pleasant; so Monday evening, about six o'clock, I thought I would take a little walk; and, without knowing it, I got on the street leading to the Fisk University. As I walked on I saw a lady coming toward me; she began to smile; I thought, "I ought to know that face, but who is it?" She came up to me and said:

"Is not this Mrs. Amanda Smith?"

"Yes," I said.

"Oh, how do you do?" she said; "I'm so glad to see you. We just got home a few days ago, and we were talking about you last night; we were all in the parlor having a little sing, and we were speaking of the piece you sang with us in Music Hall, Boston."

"Oh," I said, "the Jubilee Singers." Just then I recognized her. "Why, am I anywhere near Fisk University, where the Jubilee Singers came from?"

"Yes," she said, "we are just out such a place; and you must come out and see us. Professor [George D.] White is going to invite the Conference out on Wednesday, and you must come."

This was Miss Ella Sheppard, now Mrs. Moore, wife of the faithful pastor of Lincoln Memorial Church, Washington, D.C.

When the time came there was quite an excitement about who was going. Carriages were engaged; I offered to pay for a seat in one, but there was no room; I sent out and ordered my own carriage, and paid for it myself.

While I was getting ready, a certain brother took a lady and put her in my carriage; when I went out to get in, he said, laughingly, "Mrs. Smith, Miss So and So and I want to go, and as you have room in your carriage, I thought we would get in;" but neither of them offered to pay a cent. . . .

When we got there the good brother, being a minister, took his lady and passed quite up in front and was seated. I took a seat where I could get it, back in the congregation. One or two of the bishops were on the platform, together with a number of ministers, and the fine choir of the Jubilee Singers.

The meeting was opened in the usual way—an address by one of the bishops, then a song by the choir, singing as they could sing. Miss Sheppard spied me in the audience, and told Prof. White. He looked and looked, and could not see me at first. Then he went and spoke to Miss Sheppard again. Then she pointed out the plain bonnet. Then he spied me and quickly came down and shook hands, and was so glad. They all looked astonished. Holding me by the hand, he escorted me to the platform and introduced me to the large audience, who, in the midst of overwhelming amazement, applauded. Then the good professor told how they had met me in Boston, and how I sang the grand old hymn, "All I want is a little more faith in Jesus," and what a burst of enthusiasm it created. And of all the surprised and astonished men and women you ever saw, these men and women were the most so.

While he was making these remarks, I prayed and asked God to help me. Then he said, "I'm going to ask Mrs. Smith to sing that same song she sang at Boston, and the Jubilee Singers will join in the chorus."

If ever the Lord did help me, He helped me that day. And the Spirit of the Lord seemed to fall on all the people. The preachers got happy. They wept and shouted "Amen!" "Praise the Lord!" At the close a number of them came to me and shook hands, and said, "God bless you, sister. Where did you come from? I would like to have you come on my charge." Another would say, "Look here, sister, when are you going home? God bless you. I would like to have you come to my place." And so it went. So that after that many of my brethren believed in me, especially as the question of ordination of women never was mooted in the Conference.

But how they have advanced since then. Most of them believe in the ordination of women, and I believe some have been ordained. But I am satisfied with the ordination that the Lord has given me. Praise His name! . . .

Persons often ask me how I came to think of going to Africa. While at this camp meeting [Sea Cliff, July 1872] I had my home at Mrs. Battershell's. Their beautiful cottage was the finest and largest there at that time. . . .

One day during the camp meeting they had a mission day, and as there were different speakers, some from India, some from China, some from Japan, and some from South America, I think, I went to the meeting. I heard all the speakers, and was very much interested in the meeting.

Just as they were about to close the meeting there came up a little shower of rain, and as I had no umbrella, I hurried out and on to my cottage. The meeting had made an impression on my mind, and as I walked along I kept thinking of what I had heard, and all at once it came to me that I had not heard them say anything about Africa. Then I remembered when I was quite young I had heard my father and mother talk about Africa. I remembered, too, that I used to see a large paper, away back in the forties, called "The Brother Jonathan Almanac," something like the Frank Leslie.[3] It had large pictures, and Africans in their costumes and huts, and Indians in their

---

[3]Brother Jonathan: a Weekly Compend of Belles Lettres and the Fine Arts, Standard Literature, and General Intelligence, published from 1839 to about 1845. Frank Leslie's Illustrated Newspaper was published from 1855 to 1922.

wigwams, great boa constrictors, bears, lions and panthers; and some of the pictures were horrid, as I remember them now.

Well, all the old farmers round about where we lived used to take those papers, and once in awhile father would bring home one of them for us children to look at, and my good mother would always see that it was not torn to pieces. So we had it to look at for a time, then she would carefully fold it up and put it away. I remember what a treat it was when she would say we could have it to look at again. We would spread it on the floor, and then all of us children would get down, and what times we would have over "Brother Jonathan."

So as I was walking along now, thinking of this missionary meeting, I heard some one call out, "Amanda Smith," and I turned, and a lady overtook me and said as she came up to me;

"Well, Amanda Smith, how did you like the meeting?"

"It was very nice, and I liked it. But I did not hear them say a word about Africa, and I have been wondering if all the people in Africa are converted. I remember hearing father and mother talk about them a long time ago, but I have not heard anything of them since, and I was wondering."

She smiled, and said, "Oh! I would to God they were. Have you never heard of Melville B. Cox, our first missionary of the M. E. Church to Africa?"

"No," I said, "what about him?"

Then she gave me the history as we went on together. As she told me the story, and then said what his last words were when he died at Monrovia, Africa,—"Though a thousand fall, let not Africa be given up,"—Oh! what a deep impression it made on my mind and heart. . . .

[Amanda Smith conceived the idea of educating her daughter Mazie for missionary work in Africa. She sent Mazie to Oberlin for a year, and also to Wilberforce University at Xenia, Ohio. But the expense was too great, and this effort was dropped. Meanwhile, Mrs. Smith continued her evangelical work.]

In answer to prayer, the Lord opened my way to attend Yarmouth Camp Meeting. There I heard for the first time of the landing of the Pilgrims on Plymouth Rock. It seemed the Lord had appointed that grove especially for a camp meeting grove. There I first saw the famous Hutchinson family.[4] Mr. Asa Hutchinson, his wife, two sons, and a daughter, Miss Abbie, how well I remember them; their noble, kind-heartedness. They had me sing with them several times. Although all have passed away, the precious memory of them still remains. . . .

I had been asked by the pastor of the Methodist Church, at Martha's

---

[4]A New Hampshire family deeply committed to abolition, from the 1830s on, and to temperance, women's rights, and other liberal reform movements. Their contribution took the form of singing at meetings and conventions.

Vineyard, to go to Martha's Vineyard Camp Meeting. He said he believed God would have me go, and that they had a society tent that they would put up on the camp ground, "and," said he, "you can stay with us and we will look after you." . . .

A lady from Providence, R.I., was in this tent meeting. She had come with a very definite object, to seek the blessing of a clean heart. She was called a swell lady; she was one of the ones rather up, and did not condescend to things of low estate! So as I began to sing, "All I want is a little more faith in Jesus," she walked out of the tent and said to herself, as she passed out, "I came here to seek the blessing of a clean heart, I did not come to hear a negro ditty," and the blessed Holy Spirit said to her, "Is not that your need, 'a little more faith in Jesus?' "

Then her eyes were opened, and she said, "O, Lord, I see." Then she went into her tent and there prayed, and the Lord sent the baptism and gave her the desire of her heart. . . .

I was in Brooklyn holding meetings at Fleet Street Church, Rev. J.I. Simmons, pastor. Then at Mr. Beecher's Mission, "Mayflower."[5] We had a good work, and also at the other mission, uptown. Friday afternoon the ladies' meeting in the lecture room of Plymouth. . . .

. . . Rev. Lindsey J. Parker was then pastor of old Sands Street Methodist Church. He came after me to come to Sands Street for ten days. . . .

Well, I tried my best to beg off from Mr. Parker—I told him how tired I was, and how much I needed rest. I told him I would give him the whole month of September if he would let me off.

No, he said, his official board told him he must have me come, if but for a week, and I told him I would let him know the next week. . . .

Just when we were busy talking the bell rang, and Dr. Parker was called away. Then a Miss Price, a friend of Mrs. Parker's, was there visiting. She was an English lady; had been in this country about four years, and was expecting to go home in April. She was very pleasant, and I began telling her and Mrs. Parker how I was trying to beg the Doctor to let me off for a rest. So finally Miss Price said, "Well, you do need rest; you had better come and go with me to England next month; it would be just the thing for you. The great Paris Exposition is going on, and I would take you, and we would have a real nice time, and I know the trip would do you good."

"Yes," I said, "that would be nice."

"Well," she said, "pray about it; I believe the Lord would have you go."

Just then Mr. Parker came in again. No more was said about England. He fixed on the day I was to come to Sands Street. I closed my last meeting at the "Mayflower" on Saturday night. There was a blessed work done, the result of which eternity alone will tell. . . .

---

[5]Henry Ward Beecher (1813–1887), renowned minister of Plymouth Church in Brooklyn from 1847 to the time of his death. In 1878 Mrs. Smith spent a week at each of the two Mission churches he maintained, the Bethany and the Mayflower.

. . . When I went home and got ready for bed, the thought came to me, "You know that lady told you to pray about going to England." I said, "Yes, that is so."

I thought a moment and said to myself:

"Go to England! Amanda Smith, the colored washwoman, go to England! No, I am not going to pray a bit; I have to ask the Lord for so many things that I really need, that I am not going to bother Him with what I don't need—to go to England. It does well enough for swell people to go, not for me." . . .

In the course of a week or so I went to see Miss Price off. She sailed by one of the beautiful ships of the White Star Line. It was like a floating palace. I had never seen anything like it on water; it was magnificent. I thought what a mistake I have made. "Oh, Lord, you may trust me, I will go alone if you will give me another chance." So I went home.

A week or two later I had a letter from Mrs. Mary C. Johnson [Brooklyn temperance leader and first recording secretary of the Woman's Christian Temperance Union], saying, "Mr. Johnson and I expect to sail for England such a day in May, and would be glad to take you under our wing."

Some time before, I was in Boston at Mr. Moody's[6] meeting; it was the last week of his meetings. There Mrs. Johnson told me that she had a deep conviction that the Lord had a work for me in Great Britain, but I gave no thought to it, so that Mr. and Mrs. Johnson were off in a few weeks. As soon as she got to England she wrote me and told me of the Keswick Convention, which answers to one of our holiness camp meetings in this country, but there the phraseology is changed a little, and they call it a convention for the deepening of spiritual life. . . .

. . . I went on board the steamer "Ohio," Captain Morris in command. He was a perfect gentleman and very kind to me. . . .

There were quite a number of aristocratic passengers, and I, being a colored woman and alone, there was quite a little inquiry who I was, what I was going to England for, etc. I must say I did feel somewhat embarrassed. . . .

. . . An old Quaker gentleman was the only one that really seemed to know about the leading of the Spirit, and he spoke for me on one or two occasions. . . .

The Quaker gentleman and his son were very much interested in me when they learned I was, as the Friends say, "a preacher woman." The old gentleman told me much about the usages among the Society of Friends. He said the Friends had always stood clear on the part of female preaching, and he said he was very proud of them. I had never met him before, and he did not know that colored women ever worked in that sphere. He encouraged me, and told me to go forward. Then he spoke to the captain about holding services.

---

[6]Dwight L. Moody (1837–1899), evangelist who first came to prominence in the 1870s.

There were five doctors on board, and no preacher among them. Most of the passengers were Episcopalians and Presbyterians, all very nice, but very aristocratic, so these gentlemen came and asked me if I would take the service. I told them I would if the captain thought it would be agreeable. I did not want to do anything that would not be perfectly agreeable to all. Then they went around and inquired, and everybody was willing. They thought, anything to break the monotony and have a novel entertainment.

The captain came to me himself and said he would be very glad if I would take the service. He would have the saloon arranged. I told him I would do so if he thought it would be best. He assured me that it would be all right, so everything was arranged. First bell was rung; it did seem real churchified! How the smiles and whispers went around among the passengers, "The colored woman is going to preach." All were invited down into the saloon, then the second bell was rung. Many of the second cabin and some of the steerage passengers came in. Those from the steerage were most of them Romanists, but all behaved reverently except one or two poor, ignorant persons.

The Episcopal prayer and hymn books were placed all around the long tables, and I did not know a bit how to proceed with that service, so I turned to my Quaker friend, for he and his son stood by me ready to assist in anything but to sing or pray, and he spoke to the captain, who said I should go on in my own way. So I gave out a hymn that was familiar, and they all joined as I started the tune. If I had dared to ask some one to pray I would, but if I had it would only have been an embarrassment to any one but an old time Methodist, so I looked to God for strength and prayed myself, then I sang from the Winnowed Hymns that beautiful song, "Jesus of Nazareth Passeth By."

The Lord blest the singing and it captured their attention, and before I got through I saw a number of them were touched, but how I prayed that morning for Divine help, and it surely came.

I opened my Bible at the 14th chapter of John, and said,"I will not preach, but I want to talk a little from this dear old chapter," so I talked on for over half an hour with perfect liberty and freedom. Then I prayed, and as I spoke to the Lord the several passengers came before me, those that were sick, and friends left behind, the captain and officers that had been so kind, and so on, as the Spirit prompted the prayer, so I prayed. When I got through we sang the Doxology.

Oh, how it changed the spirit of the passengers. Ladies and gentlemen that had not even said good morning to me before, came to me and thanked me for what I said, and especially for the prayer. They shook hands and were so interested, and said, "Lord bless you."

● ● ●

Old Calabar, West Africa, May 29, 1887. To-day I made my first visit to the King's Yard at Duketown. Mrs. Lisle and I, with a native Christian woman for interpreter, visited the women in the native town. Oh, the sadness, and the deplorable condition of these poor women. The wives of the kings and chiefs are not allowed to go out to church, or to go out at all without permission.

The first yard we visited was that of a big chief who has about twenty wives, and that number, or more, of slaves. The first court was the quarters and houses of these slaves. Passing out of this, up a dingy alley into a small court, then through a door into a large, open courtyard, we come to the quarters of the wives.

At the entrance of the first door are planted in the doorway four human skulls. I tried to step aside, but every way I stepped it seemed to me I stepped on one. It was a very uncomfortable feeling, but then I knew I had not done anything to the poor souls.

In the center of the yard of this large court was a tree with a little, low frame-work around it. Within this frame-work was a large American dish, such as we would use here to put a turkey on, with a human skull on. As I looked at it I thought of Daniel Webster. It was a skull quite resembling that of the great statesman; of such marvelous shape and proportions.

To the right, and very nearly in front, was the head of a goat. All had been sacrificed. I said, "When was this done?"

"Oh, years ago, men and women were offered for sacrifice; but since the missionaries have been here it has been stopped, and the skulls are a remembrance."

My second visit to the King's Yard was Sunday, June 12th. We went to four houses. I sang, and talked through an interpreter, and prayed, and told them how I found Jesus, and how He saved me. Poor things, how interested they seemed; and I saw the great tears in their eyes.

Some of the women were very good looking; good features and beautifully formed, as are also their children. Oh, how my heart longed after them for Jesus.

At the house of Ironbar, who is a big chief, the first thing we saw on entering was in one corner of the courtyard a large juju, the head of an elephant, which represents a superstition they all believe in, and which they all have, in some shape or form, in their houses. They also have the skulls of goats, numbers of human skulls, turtle shells, chicken feathers, lots of long strings, or bits of rag, hanging in strings and tied in different knots and loops, and plenty of dirty grease poured over them.

This was a big chief. He dressed like a gentleman, in English clothes, and was my first escort to the Presbyterian Church.

He had a train of servants behind him to carry his umbrella, which was large, and of different colors of silk; blue, yellow, green, red, etc., and a brass knob on top as big as a good sized teacup; two men could manage it quite well; then they would take turns. Ironbar went to church nearly every Sunday; and yet he was as full of superstition and heathenism as if he had never heard the Gospel.

At the third yard, buried at the threshold, there was a human skull, over which one must walk to get in. Oh, what horror! a human graveyard. . . . I said, "Oh, Lord, how long shall the dreadful night of heathenism last? Oh, that the day may break, and that right early. Amen."

At the fourth yard, as we passed the king's palace, to go to the court where his wives stayed, we looked in and saw the table, on which were bottles of champagne and brandy; and some eight or more of the lords, and princes, and rulers gathered around, while their servants stood ready to do their bidding; and as they drank their wine and smoked, I thought of King Belshazzar and the writing on the wall. May God hasten the time when this kingdom will be taken from them and given to the King of kings.

At the fifth yard we saw the queen; a great, fat woman, with most regular features, handsome brown skin, beautiful hands and arms, and very small feet; her hair was done up in beautiful style; she was very dignified, and tried to be pleasant, but I could see she was in no sympathy with Jesus. I ventured to give her a few words, sang a hymn, and left her. She was in full costume; about three yards of beautiful cloth about her loins was all she had on! She has slaves by the hundred.

A few days before one had hanged himself, supposed to have been kidnapped and brought in, and the horror of slavery there is, to many, as it was here, and they often kill themselves, by drowning and hanging; his head was cut off and taken to the queen as a relic. Some of the wives are girls of about fourteen. . . .

Clay-Ashland, Liberia, West Africa, July 12th, 1888. For a long time there has been a good deal of interest manifested among a number of Christians, on the subject of personal holiness; and since the revival, which has been going on for the last three weeks, this interest has been intensified, and under consideration at different times with several of the members, and with some of the leading Stewards of the church.

I suggested the propriety of having a stated meeting once a month, for the promotion of holiness, and for the benefit of those who were specially and definitely interested on the subject. And in order that the object of this meeting might be better understood, we thought it well to organize it into an association, to be called the "Clay-Ashland Holiness Association." It has the endorsement of the pastor of the church, Rev. James Cooper, and also has the benefit of his own personal experience of the blessing of entire sanctification.

It was decided that the pastor should appoint an assistant to Sister Martha Ricks, as she always had an assistant at her Friday afternoon prayer meeting; and then Sister Ricks might call anyone else to assist whom she might choose.

In order that we might help each other more, spiritually, we thought it advisable to suggest that we be very watchful, very prayerful, and devoted to God; and endeavor to lead a life of self-denial and fear of God, and, as much as lay within us, to live consistent lives, and by all means endeavor to avoid the appearance of evil; in praying for the blessing, be definite; in testimony after receiving, be definite and God will strengthen your heart, and strengthen your faith; stand together; and, with a firm faith in God, you may not fear; but trust ye in the Lord forever, for in the Lord Jehovah is everlasting strength. Amen. . . .

[Cape Mount,] Thursday, June 6th [1889]. Made several calls, and preached to a full house at night, and the Lord gave me great liberty in speaking, and helped the people.

Friday, 7th. We arranged a hammock, and walked three miles to a new settlement to visit the emigrants; and of all the sad sights I ever saw, it was those poor people; how my heart ached for them; destitute, and sick, and ignorant; there was not a house among them, that I visited, that was anything like comfortable.

Saturday, 8th. I visited at Mrs. Briley's station, the Episcopal Mission. This lady was a white missionary, and has spent a number of years in Africa, and I suppose will be there the balance of her days. This used to be a very prosperous station; but from what I saw of it, it seemed to lack about everything, and need about everything.

Sunday, 9th. I preached twice, and addressed the Sabbath School.

Monday, 10th. Six A.M. We are off to our open boats again to Monrovia. Out all night. Oh, how good the Lord is. A storm overtakes us and threatens us heavily. As I looked up to my Father, God, and called on Him to help us, He answered me speedily, and in a little while the wind seemed to subside, and the clouds passed away.

Tuesday, 11th. Still in the boat, and sick; but the morning is lovely. Praise the Lord. We get to Monrovia about eleven o'clock.

I am often asked, "What is the religion of Africa?" Well, where I was they had no real form of religion. They were what we would call devil worshipers. They say God is good; He don't make any humbug for them; so there is no need of praying to Him. But they pray, and dance, and cook large dishes of rice and fish, and set it out of a night so that the Devil can have a good meal. They think if they feed him well, and keep on good terms with him, he will give them good crops and good luck, and keep away sickness. If smallpox, or any sickness of that kind comes to their town, they say it is because somebody has made the Devil mad.

While at Baraka with Bishop Taylor,[7] I had my first experience of their laws and customs. Sister Betty Tubman, Aunt Julia Fletcher, and I, went, in company with the Bishop, to open a station at Baraka. It is a large, native town, and years ago the Methodist Church had a flourishing station right near this same town.

As Bishop Taylor had come to Africa to help my people by establishing missions and schools, I felt it was my duty to do all I could to help, and stand by the Bishop, and do what I could by looking after the little necessities.

---

[7]William Taylor, elected Methodist Episcopal missionary bishop of Africa in 1884.

I had a large canteen, as they call them in Africa; we would say lunch box here; so I would fill it with food, the best I could get; I would bake a large pone of bread, and get some tinned meats, and a ham, when I could. Five dollars was about the cheapest a ham could be got for at Cape Palmas, but even at that they didn't have to hang on the hands of the merchants; for when it comes to food, the Liberians are not stingy, and ham is not a rarity, though they don't have them every day; but generally manage when they want them specially. They can often get things of this kind, that are expensive, in trade, with coffee or palm oil. But, of course, I had nothing of this kind, and had always to pay cash for what I got at the stores.

Then I had a little kerosene stove that I took with me, and cocoa, and coffee, and a tin of condensed milk, and biscuits, or hardtack, for bread don't last very long; if you attempt to keep it, it will sour or mould; so we generally use it up while it is fresh, and fall back on hardtack.

The Lord was so good that I generally had a little cash by me. But often it was not a question of cash, and you couldn't get the things you needed; they were not to be had. But it was wonderful how I learned to manage and get on. It is said that necessity is the mother of invention; and Africa is certainly the place where it can be developed.

We used to get up in the morning early; I would boil some water and make the Bishop a cup of cocoa or coffee, and so give him an early breakfast.

The natives were always kind and hospitable; they would have their meal about nine or ten o'clock; but we would be very faint by that time, not being used to it; and, as the Bishop was a very early riser, I knew it was best for him to have something to eat before that time. And then I always took at least a cup of tea, or something before it was late in the day.

The natives would bring in, perhaps, a chicken. They didn't scald them and pick them as we do; they would kill them and swing them over a fire; and, of course, all the feathers they didn't get off, we would have to take off ourselves; then they would bring great calabashes of rice, and pepper, for they use everything very hot with pepper; that was one of the things I never could get used to, the hot pepper. But the dear old Bishop would help himself to the rice and fowl, and goat, for they would often kill a goat in the morning and cook it for breakfast.

We would set a box in the middle of the floor, and I would spread a cloth over it, and they would set these calabashes on, and we would sit down. Sometimes they would bring in three or four calabashes; we would have to eat some out of each one; they wouldn't feel pleasant at all if we sent one back without eating out of it; so we generally had plenty, if we could only eat it; one often has to acquire the taste before he can really like it. I was in Africa a whole year before I really enjoyed or relished my food. Everything seems to taste different; but some get used to it very quickly, and others take some time. I always had plenty to eat in Africa. I never saw a day but what I had plenty, though it was not always what my appetite relished.

I thought when we got to Baraka that we would make a fire outside, and we would have a real picnic time. We would cook everything the way we wanted to cook it, just as they do at picnics; for Aunt Julia and Betty, were both good cooks, and on that line I was expecting just to show the Bishop how nicely we could treat him.

But, lo, when we got there we were not allowed to make a fire outside at all; whatever cooking was done, must be done in the native house we occupied. No fire was allowed outside, except a kind of kiln, where they burned their pottery—all sorts of vessels made of clay, which are put in the fire and burned.

It is wonderful how clever they are in those things; they make all their cooking utensils; we would call it earthen ware; some of them are very pretty; they are strong and well made, and of all sizes; jars that will hold one, two, three and five gallons of water; then there are smaller utensils.

We stayed in the king's best house; a large, native house; mud floor, but dry; no windows, no chimney; there was a space in the floor where we made the fire, and did the cooking, and the smoke would ascend and go all through the thatch. I don't know how I stood it, but I got on beautifully. When the wood was wet and would smoke a good deal, I would suffer with smoke in my eyes; but, somehow, I have an idea that smoke was healthy in Africa! . . .

While we were there the old king's head wife, who was the queen wife, was tried and condemned as a witch. That meant that she was to die by drinking sassy wood.

One of the other wives of the king accused the head wife of bewitching her child. The child was a girl about fourteen years old, and while in the casava farm digging casavas she was bitten by what is called the casava snake, which is as poisonous as the cobra of India. When this child died they said it was because the head wife had bewitched her; and when any one is accused of being a witch she must die.

This poor woman ran away and was gone three months, to her people. And being the king's head wife it was what they called a great "shame palaver;" anything to happen to the king's wife—that was very bad indeed.

As the king's wife was of a very high family, they all came together, and it took them three months before they could settle it. But it was settled and she had decided to drink the sassy wood.

She had two sons, splendid young men; they were tall and graceful, just like their father, the king; they were very bright young men, and one of them could speak good English. So they told us on Friday that the mother was to drink sassy wood on Saturday. . . . So we asked them to come and tell us when the time came, and they said they would.

The mother stopped at another little native town about a half mile away from this big town. So on Saturday morning about eight o'clock the young man came and told us. Aunt Julia had gone out to look for some wood; so Betty and I went with the young man. Betty Tubman could understand the native language and talk it very well.

Just as we got to this little town we found the men and the woman going to the place of execution. The town was enclosed by a stick fence. The old woman walked through the gate into the open space just outside.

She was a woman not very tall, but very black, beautiful limbs, beautifully built, small feet, as a lady would have, and beautiful hands and arms; her head was shaved and something black rubbed over it; and she had a little grass hip cloth like a little skirt just around her loins.

As we passed through the gate I thought of the Lord Jesus, who had told us to go forth bearing his reproach. Outside the gate there was a kind of a grove, and an open space just beyond this grove. When they got to the place they stopped. There were four or five old men, and two young men.

The old men stood as witnesses. They set down a mortar. One had a calabash, and another carried the sassy wood, which is a liquid decoction. I don't know as any one has ever found what the composition of this sassy wood really is; but I am told it is a mixture of certain barks. There is a tree there which grows very tall, called the sassy wood tree; but there is something mixed with this which is very difficult to find out, and the natives do not tell what it is. They say that it is one of their medicines that they use to carry out their law for punishing witches; so you cannot find out what it is.

Though it was so warm, I felt myself get cold as I looked at the scene. My heart seemed to stop beating. Oh, how I prayed to God to save that woman. We couldn't do anything to help her; her husband couldn't help her; her sons couldn't help her; her people couldn't help her. No, she was accused of being a witch, and she must pay the penalty; and the penalty was to drink the sassy wood. If she throws it up she has gained the case.

Sometimes they do throw it up, and then they stand very high; they are raised to a higher state of dignity than ever they held before. So I prayed for the poor, dear woman, that God would make her throw it up.

I thought once I could not bear to see it; but then I held on. I remember how I clutched the limb of a tree near by when she was about to take it; and I held on and prayed. Her son stood with us and looked at his mother drink the first dose; and then ran away. The two young men dipped this decoction out of the mortar into the calabash, and set it on the ground, and then she had to pick it up and drink it.

When they had filled the basin she stood and looked at it; and then picked up three pebbles, and said something like a little prayer; then she struck on the side of the basin. I could understand when she said "Niswa, Oh, Niswa," which was to say "Oh, God." I didn't know what else she said. But she struck one of the stones on the side of the dish, threw the other in it, and the other one she threw away. Then she drank the sassy wood. She had two gallons to drink.

I turned to Betty and said: "What does she say, Betty?" And she told me the part that I could not understand. The whole prayer was this: "Oh, Niswa, if I have made witch, and this child has died, when I drink this sassy wood I must not throw it up. But if I have not made witch so that this child has died, then I must throw up the sassy wood."

So that was what she said all the time she was drinking the sassy wood. After she had swallowed the first dose they dipped out another basinful. Oh, I trembled. I said, "Lord, do make her throw it up." And just as she was going to stoop down to lift up the second basinful, I saw her give her shoulders a little twitch, and open her mouth, and if you ever saw a water plug in the street throw out water—she threw up that sassy wood, in a perfect stream!

Well, I could have shouted. I said, "Thank God." But I didn't say it very loud, for those fellows looked vengeance, and I was afraid they would drive us away.

Then she drank the second basinful, and then the third, and threw it up, and she was victor. My! didn't I come home out of that place jumping? I cannot describe how I felt.

The next morning was Sunday morning; and about eight o'clock we heard such singing and playing and beating of drums, and we wondered what in the world was up. We looked out, and here came through the town all the women, and this same woman, the king's wife, with two escorts on either side, and beautifully dressed; she had a handsome country cloth, with all sorts of colors, like Joseph's coat, wrapped about her; she was bathed and greased; she had rings in her ears, and bracelets on her wrists; her fingers were covered with rings, and rings on her toes and ankles. She looked beautiful!

They have some kind of grass they dye black, and it looks very much like hair; and she had on a head dress of this, beautifully curled, and she looked as beautiful as she could be. Then she had a great, big umbrella, red, and blue, and green and yellow striped. Oh, but she was a swell! And they took her through the town; they danced and sang; children, little boys and girls, and women.

The next day, on Monday, the men burned powder, as they called it. About five o'clock in the morning we heard a great gun firing. We didn't know but war had begun. But it was the men's day for their jollification over the victory the king's wife had gained.

I shall never forget how the poor old king came to me and wanted me to drink wine.

"No, king," I said to him, "you know I am a temperance woman. I no drink wine."

He seemed to be quite indignant. He said, "What is the matter? When my woman no die you can't drink wine a little bit with me when my heart is glad 'cause my woman no die?"

"Well," I said, "king, I am very glad, and I did pray, and believe God helped your woman so she no die. But myself I no drink wine."

Then as he went to turn away, almost with disgust, I said to him, "I tell you, king, I give you cup cocoa. I make it for you. So you drink cocoa with me."

"Yes," he said, then he smiled.

So I went to work and made a nice bowl of cocoa, and put sugar and condensed milk in it, and gave him a hardtack and some meat, which pleased him greatly. So we were friends.

The poor women of Africa, like those of India, have a hard time. As a rule, they have all the hard work to do. They have to cut and carry all the wood, carry all the water on their heads, and plant all the rice. The men and boys cut and burn the bush, with the help of the women; but sowing the rice, and planting the casava, the women have to do.

You will often see a great, big man walking ahead, with nothing in his hand but a cutlass (as they always carry that or a spear), and a woman, his wife, coming on behind, with a great big child on her back, and a load on her head.

No matter how tired she is, her lord would not think of bringing her a jar of water, to cook his supper with, or of beating the rice; no, she must do that. A great big boy would not bring water for his mother; he would say:

"Boy no tote water; that be woman's work."

If they live with missionaries, or Liberians, or anyone outside of their own native people, then they will do such things; but not for one another.

The moment a girl child is born, she belongs to somebody. The father, who has a son, makes it the highest aim of his life to see that his son has a wife; so he settles, and begins to pay a dowry for a girl for his son. Sometimes they are but a few months old, when you will see them with their betrothal jewels on.

If the fellow who buys the girl is well off, she will have about her little waist a thick roll of beads; sometimes five or six strings together; or she will have bracelets on her little wrists, sometimes of brass, sometimes only made of common iron by the native blacksmith; she will have the same on her ankles, with a little tinkle in it, like a bell, so it makes a noise when she walks.

As they grow up, they have their tastes, and their likes and dislikes. The marriageable age is from thirteen to fourteen, and sometimes younger. All these years the boy's father, or the man himself, is paying on the girl. That is why it is hard to get the girls. It is the girls that bring big money; so the more girls a father has, that much richer he is.

Girls who are bought with a bullock are high toned; that is about the highest grade. Then the next is brass kettles, and cloth and beads. The third is more ordinary; tobacco, cloth, powder, and a little gin is not objectionable. To all of these he can put as much more as he likes; but what I have named are the principal things used in buying a native girl for a wife.

Poor things, they are not consulted; they have no choice in the matter. If they don't like the man, they are obliged to go with him anyway, no matter how illy he may treat them; and sometimes they are cruelly treated. But their own father could not protect them. The laws in this are very strict. A man's wife is his wife, and no one dare interfere. . . .

At Sierra Leone, and down the coast, I think they are more advanced.

They have large markets both at Sierra Leone, and at Lagos, so the steamers take on a supply. Then all along the coast after they leave Liberia, they are supplied with fowls, eggs, pigeons, bananas, pineapples, peppers, water cress, and all sorts of vegetables in abundance; large fowls, sixpence apiece.

Further down the coast the natives make very handsome cloth. They are very clever in making their dyes; it is wonderful how they do it. They have very strong dyes, with fast colors, green, blue, red, yellow, and various colors; it is marvelous how they blend them; and some of the native cloths are really beautiful. They bring them on the steamers and sell them for different prices, ten, twenty, twenty-five, twenty-six shillings, and some for more. I bought an elegant cloth at ten shillings; but one of the officers got one at twenty, and he said it was very cheap.

Chillicothe is the place where you generally get these handsome country cloths. I also got one or two very nice pieces at Monrovia; but nothing like those that you get down the coast. They weave their cloth in strips about four or five inches wide; then they sew it together to any length or breadth they want it.

The natives are great geniuses in this way; and it is wonderful to see the number of things they can make.

Then the Liberians have other products besides those which I have named. Their coffee is very fine, and of rich flavor. There are some large planters who raise and ship thousands of pounds. Among these are, Mr. Moses Ricks, and Senator Coleman, of Clay-Ashland; Sanders Washington, of Virginia; June Moore and Saul Hill, of Arthington; and Jesse Sharpe. These are all on or near the St. Paul River. They are men who went from this country years ago, when young; men of sterling worth and push. The Ricks' were three brothers—Moses, Henry, and John; they were staunch Baptists, and good men. They always stood together, and were the stay and the backbone of the church at Clay-Ashland.

In developing mission work among the natives, so far as my observation went, the Baptists were ahead. And their churches and mission work are all self-supporting, that is, they have no foreign help, as they used to have. Then at Arthington, June Moore and Saul Hill, were classed among the men of large means. Both of these were earnest Christian men, and Deacons in the Baptist Church.

Mr. Moore, in his outward appearance, was very plain, but a man of more than ordinary intelligence, and unquestioned veracity, and moral character; and a strong temperance man. His is a beautiful character. I wish I could have found it more general.

Mr. Moore was a very good preacher. He had charge of the Baptist Church at Arthington, and had the confidence of the people, Liberians and natives. Through his sympathy and co-operation we held a temperance meeting in the Baptist Church at Arthington, and organized a Gospel Temperance Band, and, I think, made him President. Of course, the majority there, were not far advanced on the line of woman preaching. It was all right

at other churches, and they would go and hear, and get what benefit they
could. But they were generally in favor of Paul's assertion: "Let your women
keep silence in the churches."

The more liberal believe that the other statement of Paul should be
considered as well, viz.: how a woman should be adorned when praying or
prophesying.

The Lord blessed me very greatly, and I had my friends among them
all. I was never asked in a Baptist Church to take a service, while I was there;
only to address a Sabbath School. . . .

I am often asked if I favor colored people's emigrating to Liberia,
Africa.

My answer is, "Yes," and "No." . . .

Now, without there has been a vast improvement since I was there,
the Liberian government is very poor, but makes out to manage somehow.
And if educated, industrious, intelligent black men, with money, would go
there, for the love of the race, and with the love of God in their hearts, and
go with no other object than to sacrifice their lives and their money for the
good of the republic and their fellowmen (and it would take but a little
while to do that; but this is the only way for black men to go to Africa; and I
believe this is the proper way), then I say, yes, emigrate.

On the other hand, I say "No." For I don't believe it is right to take out
men and women indiscriminately, and generally of the poorest that are in the
South, or anywhere else, ignorant of the principles, and the need and duties
of the Liberian government, as the poor, ignorant Italians, or Polish Jews, or
others, with no knowledge of the country or its customs, no love for it in any
way, only what they get out of it, have not been taught, have no love of
loyalty, only as they may borrow it for selfish ends, then I say, "No, No!"

God bless the Colonization Society. It was raised up at a time of
imperative need; and so was John Knox, of Scotland; and Wesley of England. It did its work. But from the standpoint I look at it, I would move its
disbandment forthwith, and let the white people who want the Negro to
emigrate to Africa so as to make more room for the great flood of foreigners
who come to our shores, know that there is a place in the United States for
the Negro.

They are real American citizens, and at home. They have fought and
bled and died, like men, to make this country what it is. And if they have
got to suffer and die, and be lynched, and tortured, and burned at the stake, I
say they are at home.

Ann Plato

Ann Plato, a shy, introspective woman, taught school in Hartford, Connecticut. Also a writer, she published a slim volume bearing the title Essays: Including Biographies and Miscellaneous Pieces, in Prose and Poetry in 1841. Internal analysis indicates it to be the work of a young woman of about twenty. The book is mainly composed of brief sketches of the lives of friends and acquaintances. Since many of them were already dead, an elegiac tone clings to the whole. The poems are somber and colorless.

James W.C. Pennington, pastor of the Talcott Street Congregational Church of Hartford, contributed the introduction. He had also been a teacher in the North African School conducted in his church. The school for the southern district, where Ann Plato taught, was held in the Zion Methodist Church. Himself a fugitive slave, the Reverend Mr. Pennington was eager to support this fragile attempt. He encouraged Ann Plato to persevere, with the expectation that more mature work would follow. Her first literary project, however, was also her last. His introduction was more an endorsement of her piety than of her art.

Always identified with Hartford, Ann Plato was probably born in that city in the second or the third decade of the century. Hartford's black community was alert and articulate in educational matters. The "integrated" school arrangement provided earlier by Connecticut law had failed to satisfy the black population, and they had petitioned for the establishment of separate schools in 1830. No disagreement was encountered either among the city fathers or within the state legislature, and Hartford thereafter possessed two separate black schools. They were to be supported by their proportionate share of public funds.

A member of Hartford's School Society paid several visits to Ann Plato's school in 1845 and 1846. The inspections appear to have been prompted by Mr. Pennington's request for more adequate funding. After one visit the official tersely recorded, "Visited Miss Plato's School. Doing well." This unembellished compliment would have pleased Miss Plato. Despite her melancholy outlook, she was the prototype of multitudes of women, black or white, whose work was satisfying and whose compensation was the knowledge that they had done their best. Ann Plato's labor had a dominant religious theme. Struggles for freedom and for education, in her view, were preparatory to "the perfect day" to come. [1]

LINES,

Written upon Being Examined in School Studies
for the Preparation of a Teacher.

Teach me, O! Lord, the secret errors of my way,
Teach me the paths wherein I go astray,
Learn me the way to teach the word of love,
For that's the pure intelligence above.
As well as learning, give me that truth forever—
Which a mere worldly tie can never sever,
For though our bodies die, our souls will live forever.
To cultivate in every youthful mind,
Habitual grace, and sentiments refined.
Thus while I strive to govern human heart,
May I the heavenly precepts still impart;
Oh! may each youthful bosom, catch the sacred fire,
And youthful mind to virtue's throne aspire.
Now fifteen years their destined course have run,
In fast succession round the central sun;
How did the follies of that period pass,
I ask myself—are they inscribed in brass!
Oh! Recollection, speed their fresh return,
And sure 'tis mine to be ashamed and mourn.
"What shall I ask, or what refrain to say?
Where shall I point, or how conclude my lay?
So much my weakness needs—so oft thy voice,
Assures that weakness, and confirms my choice.
Oh, grant me active days of peace and truth,
Strength to my heart, and wisdom to my youth,
A sphere of usefulness—a soul to fill
That sphere with duty, and perform thy will."

---

[1]David O. White, "Hartford's African Schools, 1830–1868," *Connecticut Historical Society Bulletin* 39 (April 1974): 47–53; Thomas Robbins, *Diary of Thomas Robbins, D.D., 1796–1854*, ed. and annotated Increase N. Tarbox (Boston, 1887), I, 823.

Source: Ann Plato, *Essays; Including Biographies and Miscellaneous Pieces, in Prose and Poetry* (Hartford, 1841), pp. 94, 102–3, 114–15, 26–33.

THE INFANT CLASS.

Written in School.

This, my youngest class in school,
    Is what I do admire;
Their sweetest, ever perfect praise,
    Their eyes as sparkling fire.

How oft I've blessed them in my heart,
    Besought that every grace
And consolation, might there dwell,
    To cheer each youthful face.

I love them all as children each,
    How happy they appear:
O, may no dull unclouded path,
    Make happiness to fear.

How sweet their prayerful voices join,
    To say what I do teach:
Their infant voices, how adorn'd,
    How full of music each.

When out of school, how oft I think
    Of these, my little ones,
But when in school, how glances all,
    They shine like many suns.

They gather round me, one by one,
    Like darlings to be taught;
Ah, there behold my orphan dear,
    For me she now has sought.

Dearest, we soon must say farewell,
    May God your steps approve,
If then on earth we no more meet,
Or never do this course more greet,
    May we in Christ e'er move.

TO THE FIRST OF AUGUST.

Britannia's isles proclaim,
    That freedom is their theme;
And we do view those honor'd lands,
    With soul-delighting mien.

And unto those they held in gloom,

Gave ev'ry one their right;
They did disdain fell slavery's shade,
And trust in freedom's light.

Then unto ev'ry British blood,
Their noble worth revere,
And think them ever noble men,
And like them, hence appear.

And when on Britain's isles remote,
We're then in freedom's bounds,
And while we stand on British ground,
You're free,—you're free,—resounds.

Lift ye that country's banner high,
And may it nobly wave,
Until beneath the azure sky,
Man shall be no more a slave.

And oh! when youth's extatic [sic] hour,
When winds and torrents foam,
And passion's glowing noon are past,
To bless that free born home;

Then let us celebrate the day,
And lay the thought to heart,
And teach the rising race the way,
That they may not depart.

EDUCATION.

This appears to be the great source from which nations have become civilized, industrious, respectable and happy. A society or people are always considered as advancing, when they are found paying proper respect to education. The observer will find them erecting buildings for the establishment of schools, in various sections of their country, on different systems, where their children may at an early age commence learning, and having their habits fixed for higher attainments. Too much attention, then, can not be given to it by people, nation, society or individual. History tells us that the first settlers of our country soon made themselves conspicuous by establishing a character for the improvement, and diffusing of knowledge among them.

We hear of their inquiry, how shall our children be educated? and upon what terms or basis shall it be placed? We find their questions soon answered to that important part; and by attending to this in every stage of their advancement, with proper respect, we find them one of the most enlightened and happy nations on the globe.

It is, therefore, an unspeakable blessing to be born in those parts where wisdom and knowledge flourish; though it must be confessed there are even in these parts several poor, uninstructed persons who are but little above the late inhabitants of this country, who knew no modes of the civilized life, but wandered to and fro, over the parts of the then unknown world.

We are, some of us, very fond of knowledge, and apt to value ourselves upon any proficiency in the sciences; one science, however, there is, worth more than all the rest, and that is the science of living well—which shall remain "when tongues shall cease," and "knowledge shall vanish away."

It is owing to the preservation of books, that we are led to embrace their contents. Oral instructions can benefit but one age and one set of hearers; but these silent teachers address all ages and all nations. They may sleep for a while and be neglected; but whenever the desire of information springs up in the human breast, there they are with mild wisdom ready to instruct and please us.

No person can be considered as possessing a good education without religion. A good education is that which prepares us for our future sphere of action and makes us contented with that situation in life in which God, in his infinite mercy, has seen fit to place us, to be perfectly resigned to our lot in life, whatever it may be. Religion has been decreed as the passion of weak persons; but the Bible tells us "to seek first the kingdom of heaven, and His righteousness, and all other things shall be added unto us." This world is only a place to prepare for another and a better.

If it were not for education, how would our heathen be taught therefrom? While science and the arts boast so many illustrious names; there is another and more extended sphere of action where illustrious names and individual effort has been exerted with the happiest results, and their authors, by their deeds of charity, have won bright and imperishable crowns in the realms of bliss. Was it the united effort of nations, or of priestly synods that first sent the oracles of eternal truth to the inhospitable shores of Greenland—or placed the lamp of life in the hut of the Esquemaux—or carried a message of love to the burning climes of Africa—or that directed the deluded votaries of idolatry in that benighted land where the Ganges rolls its consecrated waters, to Calvary's Sacrifice, a sacrifice that sprinkled with blood the throne of justice, rendering it accessible to ruined, degraded man.

In proportion to the education of a nation, it is rich and powerful. To behold the wealth and power of Great Britain, and compare it with China; America with Mexico; how confused are the ideas of the latter, how narrow their conceptions, and are, as it were in an unknown world.

Education is a system which the bravest men have followed. What said Alexander about this? Said he: "I am more indebted to my tutor, Aristotle, than to my father Philip; for Philip gives me my living, but Aristotle teaches me how to live." It was Newton that threw aside the dimness of uncertainty which shrouded for so many centuries the science of astronomy; penetrated the arena of nature, and soared in his eagle-flight far, far beyond the wildest dreams of all former ages, defining with certainty the motions of those flaming worlds, and assigning laws to the fartherest star that lies on the confines of creation—that glimmers on the verge of immensity.

Knowledge is the very foundation of wealth, and of nations. Aristotle held unlimited control over the opinions of men for fifteen centuries, and governed the empire of mind where ever he was known. For knowledge, men brave every danger, they explore the sandy regions of Africa, and diminish the arena of contention and bloodshed. Where ever ignorance holds unlimited sway, the light of science, and the splendor of the gospel of truth is obscure and nearly obliterated by the gloom of monkish superstition, merged in the sable hues of idolatry and popish cruelty; no ray of glory shines on those degraded minds; "darkness covers the earth, and gross darkness the people."

Man is the noblest work in the universe of God. His excellence does not consist in the beautiful symmetry of his form, or in the exquisite structure of his complicated physical machinery; capable of intellectual and moral powers. What have been the conquests of men in the field of general science? What scholastic intrenchment is there which man would not have wished to carry—what height is there which he would not have wished to survey—what depth that he would not like to explore?—even the mountains and the earth—hidden minerals—and all that rests on the borders of creation he would like to overpower.

But shall these splendid conquests be subverted? Egypt, that once shot over the world brilliant rays of genius, is sunk in darkness. The dust of ages sleeps on the bosom of Roman warriors, poets, and orators. The glory of Greece has departed, and leaves no Demosthenes to thunder with his eloquence, [n]or Homer to soar and sing.

It is certainly true that many dull and unpromising scholars have become the most distinguished men; as Milton, Newton, Walter Scott. . . . Newton stated of himself, that his superiority to common minds was not natural, but acquired by mental discipline. Hence, we perceive that the mind is capable of wonderful improvement. The mother of Sir William Jones[1] said to him when a child: "If you wish to understand, read;" how true, that "education forms the mind."

How altogether important, then, is education; it is our guide in youth, and it will walk with us in the vale of our declining years. This knowledge we ought ever to pursue with all diligence. Our whole life is but one great

---

[1] Sir William Jones (1746–1794), English orientalist and translator; his pro-American views during the Revolution had made him widely known on this side of the Atlantic. (BJL and RB)

school; from the cradle to the grave we are all learners; nor will our education be finished until we die.

A good education is another name for happiness. Shall we not devote time and toil to learn how to be happy? It is a science which the youngest child may begin, and the wisest man is never weary of. No one should be satisfied with present attainments; we should aim high, and bend all our energies to reach the point aimed at.

We ought not to fail to combine with our clear convictions of what is right, a firmness and moral courage sufficient to enable us to "forsake every false way," and our course will be like that of the just—"brighter and brighter unto the perfect day."

III

"LET US
MAKE A MIGHTY EFFORT
AND ARISE"

Social advance is the focus of this section. Individual uplift and the elevation of a whole people were for these women two phases of a single problem,
which called for a mighty effort on the part of the blacks. It required also a
change of attitude among the whites. Hence a dual thrust is shown by most
of these women. They exhorted both their black sisters and brothers and
also the white community to mobilize for this crusade.

They were all religious women. Their emphasis, however, was largely
secular. Earthly freedom and the Christian tasks of fellowship took first
position. They visualized their work as a mode of exemplifying and
fulfilling the Biblical commandments. Relying on the churches for sanction
and support, they insisted that religion attend to the here as well as the
hereafter. They expressed the appeal of the blacks to America in the language of the prevalent religious form. They devised a new social gospel for
their race.

Maria Stewart

Maria Stewart, born in 1803, may have been the first black woman to make a public effort on behalf of black advancement. She is perhaps the earliest American-born woman of any color who delivered speeches which are still in print. The first occurred early in 1832, when she addressed the newly formed Afric-American Female Intelligence Society in Boston.

Her public career, like the founding of this educational society, was part of a movement that flourished in Northern cities in the 1830s and 1840s. "Against a background of increasing repressive legislation in the North," free blacks were growing increasingly restive and articulate. They banded together for self-improvement until late in the 1840s when this objective merged with an intensified commitment to the antislavery cause.

A freeborn New Englander who grew up in Hartford, Connecticut, Mrs. Stewart was orphaned at the age of five and "bound out" to a minister's family. Despite the lack of educational opportunity, she apparently acquired some introduction to religious rhetoric. Between her fifteenth and twentieth years, she attended "Sabbath Schools" which normally provided not merely religious education but the elements of literacy. Articulate though she was, her literacy as a young adult did not apparently match her speaking ability. As the Reverend Alexander Crummell wrote many years later, this woman "who had received but six weeks' schooling, who could not even pen her own thoughts . . . had to get a little girl ten years old to write every word of this book."

Married in 1826 and widowed three years later, Mrs. Stewart experienced a religious conversion. From this came a yearning to devote herself to "the cause of God and my brethren." She herself attributed to this moving event her moral resolve to offer up her life in the service of her race. Another event also moved her profoundly. In 1830 a black leader of the antislavery movement died. David Walker, presumably a martyr to the cause, was the author of a militant pamphlet, Walker's Appeal, several times reprinted prior to his sudden and unexplained death. Mrs. Stewart's public life in behalf of this cause and her account of it stem from her stay in Boston in the third decade of the nineteenth century.

Mrs. Stewart laid heavy burdens of duty upon the members of her audiences. Women were particularly obligated to strengthen the black com-

184 LET US MAKE A MIGHTY EFFORT AND ARISE

munity by making full use of their own inner resources. Individual initiative was to be nurtured as an instrument for ethnic advance. White women and white men were entreated to recognize the aspirations of blacks, to uphold their right to equality. While she passionately desired the abolition of slavery, she was not unmindful of the plight of the free black for whose spiritual emancipation from poverty and prejudice no effort was too great. Employment in various occupations, not only in menial work, and all the rights of citizenship were essential steps toward equality for those already free. But to "the fair daughters of Africa" she addressed some of her most stirring words. She called upon them to lift their minds above the "load of iron pots and kettles," to develop a spirit of independence in order to rise above the level of servant drudgery and attain full human potential. External change was not enough: she exhorted blacks to the moral regeneration that would merit divine aid in their righteous cause. And if God had chosen her, a woman, to speak out in public, she urged her listeners, "be no longer astonished."

Three of the Stewart speeches were printed in William Lloyd Garrison's Liberator, first published in Boston, 1 January 1831, only shortly before her public career in that city commenced. She gave due recognition to Garrison and his associate Isaac Knapp. The Liberator had earlier excerpted portions of a tract she had written on religion and announced the publication of Meditations, a pamphlet of religious poems and essays. Described by Garrison's paper as "a highly intelligent colored lady," she must also have been an impatient one. Precisely a year after the first of her "promiscuous" speeches to audiences of both men and women, she bade farewell to Boston, under the impression that she was resented for her religious exhortations and even more for her audacity as a woman. In this final speech to her Boston listeners, she appeared to have abandoned her belief in political actions, because they "strengthen the cord of prejudice." Acceptance of "our condition" as "the will of God" was the new emphasis of her religious passion.

Strangely, this forceful woman disappeared for almost half a century from the sight of her acquaintances in Boston, and from such wider view as the pages of the Liberator afforded. Without relatives, she had been deprived by wily executors of the comfortable inheritance provided by her husband's will. To this circumstance was attributed the "sad, sorrowful, and mysterious countenance" that characterized Mrs. Stewart in later years. Despite her ties with Boston's black community and white antislavery leaders, her sense of alienation persisted. Moving to New York, and "full of the greed for literature and letters," she found her way to the circle of black intellectuals there. With their help in furthering her education, she was soon a participating member of one of the city's two black literary societies for women. It was from New York that she arranged for the publication of her Boston speeches and writings.

She became a public school teacher in New York and Brooklyn, two separate cities at that time. In 1852, having lost her post in the Williamsburg

*school in Brooklyn, she migrated once more to take up teaching in Balti-
more. During the Civil War she taught in Washington. Later, while employed
there as a matron in the Freedmen's Hospital, she learned that passage of a
pension law covering veterans of the War of 1812 entitled her to a claim as
widow of a navy veteran. An astonishing reunion with the aged William
Lloyd Garrison after forty-six years was one of the consequences of her trip
to Boston to collect the necessary evidence of her marriage. Another was her
desire to bring out a new edition of her published work, which she had not
even seen for forty years. Published in 1879 in Washington with the encouragement of Garrison and others of her early friends, this edition adds a
prefatory section of biographical data on the intervening years.* [1]

I

Feeling a deep solemnity of soul, in view of our wretched and degraded
situation, and sensible of the gross ignorance that prevails among us, I have
thought proper thus publicly to express my sentiments before you. I hope
my friends will not scrutinize these pages with too severe an eye, as I have
not calculated to display either elegance or taste in their composition, but
have merely written the meditations of my heart as far as my imagination
led; and have presented them before you, in order to arouse you to exertion,
and to enforce upon your minds the great necessity of turning your attention
to knowledge and improvement.

I was born in Hartford, Connecticut, in 1803; was left an orphan at
five years of age; was bound out in a clergyman's family; had the seeds of
piety and virtue early sown in my mind; but was deprived of the advantages
of education, though my soul thirsted for knowledge. Left them at 15 years
of age; attended Sabbath Schools until I was 20; in 1826, was married to
James W. Stewart; was left a widow in 1829; was, as I humbly hope and
trust, brought to the knowledge of the truth, as it is in Jesus, in 1830; in
1831, made a public profession of my faith in Christ.

From the moment I experienced the change, I felt a strong desire, with
the help and assistance of God, to devote the remainder of my days to piety

---

[1]The Stewart quotations may be found below. The other quotations are from Leon F.
Litwack, *North of Slavery: The Negro in the Free States, 1790–1860* (Chicago, 1961), p.
235; Alexander Crummell, prefatory statement in Maria W. Stewart, *Meditations from
the Pen of Mrs. Maria W. Stewart* (Washington, D.C., 1879), p.10; *Liberator*, 17 March
1832; Crummell, p. 10.

Source: Maria W. Stewart, *Productions of Mrs. Maria W. Stewart* (Boston, 1835), pp.
3–22. This excerpt is from a pamphlet, *Religion and the Pure Principles of Morality, the
Sure Foundation on Which We Must Build*, first issued in 1831 and then partially
reprinted in the pages of the *Liberator* prior to its inclusion in the more comprehensive
Productions.

and virtue, and now possess that spirit of independence, that, were I called upon, I would willingly sacrifice my life for the cause of God and my brethren.

All the nations of the earth are crying out for Liberty and Equality. Away, away with tyranny and oppression! And shall Afric's sons be silent any longer? Far be it from me to recommend to you, either to kill, burn, or destroy. But I would strongly recommend to you, to improve your talents; let not one lie buried in the earth. Show forth your powers of mind. Prove to the world, that

> Though black your skins as shades of night,
> Your hearts are pure, your souls are white.

This is the land of freedom. The press is at liberty. Every man has a right to express his opinion. Many think, because your skins are tinged with a sable hue, that you are an inferior race of beings; but God does not consider you as such. He hath formed and fashioned you in his own glorious image, and hath bestowed upon you reason and strong powers of intellect. He hath made you to have dominion over the beasts of the field, the fowls of the air, and the fish of the sea. He hath crowned you with glory and honor; hath made you but a little lower than the angels; and, according to the Constitution of these United States, he hath made all men free and equal. Then why should one worm say to another, "Keep you down there, while I sit up yonder; for I am better than thou?" It is not the color of the skin that makes the man, but it is the principles formed within the soul.

Many will suffer for pleading the cause of oppressed Africa, and I shall glory in being one of her martyrs; for I am firmly persuaded, that the God in whom I trust is able to protect me from the rage and malice of mine enemies, and from them that will rise up against me; and if there is no other way for me to escape, he is able to take me to himself, as he did the most noble, fearless, and undaunted David Walker [see biographical sketch of Mrs. Stewart, above].

NEVER WILL VIRTUE, KNOWLEDGE, AND TRUE POLITENESS BEGIN TO FLOW, TILL THE
PURE PRINCIPLES OF RELIGION AND MORALITY ARE PUT INTO FORCE.

MY RESPECTED FRIENDS,

I feel almost unable to address you; almost incompetent to perform the task; and, at times, I have felt ready to exclaim, O that my head were waters, and mine eyes a fountain of tears, that I might weep day and night, for the transgressions of the daughters of my people. Truly, my heart's desire and prayer is, that Ethiopia might stretch forth her hands unto God. But we have a great work to do. Never, no, never will the chains of slavery and ignorance burst, till we become united as one, and cultivate among ourselves the pure principles of piety, morality and virtue. I am sensible of my ignorance; but such knowledge as God has given to me, I impart to you. I am sensible of former prejudices; but it is high time for prejudices and animosities to cease from among us. I am sensible of exposing myself to calumny and reproach; but shall I, for fear of feeble man who shall die, hold my peace? shall I for fear of scoffs and frowns, refrain my tongue? Ah, no! I speak as one that must give an account at the awful bar of God; I speak as a dying mortal, to dying mortals. O, ye daughters of Africa, awake! awake! arise! no longer sleep nor slumber, but distinguish yourselves. Show forth to the world that ye are endowed with noble and exalted faculties. O, ye daughters of Africa! what have ye done to immortalize your names beyond the grave? what examples have ye set before the rising generation? what foundation have ye laid for generations yet unborn? where are our union and love? and where is our sympathy, that weeps at another's wo[e], and hides the faults we see? And our daughters, where are they? blushing in innocence and virtue? And our sons, do they bid fair to become crowns of glory to our hoary heads? Where is the parent who is conscious of having faithfully discharged his duty, and at the last awful day of account, shall be able to say, here, Lord, is thy poor, unworthy servant, and the children thou hast given me? And where are the children that will arise, and call them blessed? Alas, O God! forgive me if I speak amiss; the minds of our tender babes are tainted as soon as they are born; they go astray, as it were, from the womb. Where is the maiden who will blush at vulgarity? and where is the youth who has written upon his manly brow a thirst for knowledge; whose ambitious mind soars above trifles, and longs for the time to come, when he shall redress the wrongs of his father, and plead the cause of his brethren? Did the daughters of our land possess a delicacy of manners, combined with gentleness and dignity; did their pure minds hold vice in abhorrence and contempt, did they frown when their ears were polluted with its vile accents, would not their influence become powerful? would not our brethren fall in love with their virtues? Their souls would become fired with a holy zeal for freedom's cause. They would become ambitious to distinguish themselves. They would become proud to display their talents. Able advocates would arise in our defence. Knowledge would begin to flow, and the chains of slavery and ignorance would melt like wax before the flames. . . .

I have been taking a survey of the American people in my own mind, and I see them thriving in arts, and sciences, and in polite literature. Their highest aim is to excel in political, moral and religious improvement. They early consecrate their children to God, and their youth indeed are blushing in artless innocence; they wipe the tears from the orphan's eyes, and they cause the widow's heart to sing for joy! and their poorest ones, who have the least wish to excel, they promote! And those that have but one talent, they encourage. But how very few are there among them that bestow one thought upon the benighted sons and daughters of Africa, who have enriched the soils of America with their tears and blood: few to promote their cause, none to encourage their talents. Under these circumstances, do not let our hearts be any longer discouraged; it is no use to murmur nor to repine; but let us promote ourselves and improve our own talents. And I am rejoiced to reflect that there are many able and talented ones among us, whose names might be recorded on the bright annals of fame. But, *"I can't,"* is a great barrier in the way. I hope it will soon be removed, and *"I will,"* resume its place.

Righteousness exalteth a nation, but sin is a reproach to any people. Why is it, my friends, that our minds have been blinded by ignorance, to the present moment? 'Tis on account of sin. Why is it that our church is involved in so much difficulty? It is on account of sin. Why is it that God has cut down, upon our right hand and upon our left, the most learned and intelligent of our men? O, shall I say, is it on account of sin! Why is it that thick darkness is mantled upon every brow, and we, as it were, look sadly upon one another? It is on account of sin. . . .

O, ye mothers, what a responsibility rests on you! You have souls committed to your charge, and God will require a strict account of you. It is you that must create in the minds of your little girls and boys a thirst for knowledge, the love of virtue, the abhorrence of vice, and the cultivation of a pure heart. The seeds thus sown will grow with their growing years; and the love of virtue thus early formed in the soul will protect their inexperienced feet from many dangers. O, do not say, you cannot make any thing of your children; but say, with the help and assistance of God, we will try. Do not indulge them in their little stubborn ways; for a child left to himself, bringeth his mother to shame. Spare not, for their crying; thou shalt beat them with a rod, and they shall not die; and thou shalt save their souls from hell. When you correct them, do it in the fear of God, and for their own good. They will not thank you for your false and foolish indulgence; they will rise up, as it were, and curse you in this world, and, in the world to come, condemn you. It is no use to say, you can't do this, or, you can't do that; you will not tell your Maker so, when you meet him at the great day of account. And you must be careful that you set an example worthy of following, for you they will imitate. There are many instances, even among us now, where parents have discharged their duty faithfully, and their children now reflect honor upon their gray hairs.

Perhaps you will say, that many parents have set pure examples at home, and they have not followed them. True, our expectations are often blasted; but let not this dishearten you. If they have faithfully discharged their duty, even after they are dead, their works may live; their prodigal children may then return to God, and become heirs of salvation; if not, their children cannot rise and condemn them at the awful bar of God.

Perhaps you will say, that you cannot send them to high schools and academies. You can have them taught in the first rudiments of useful knowledge, and then you can have private teachers, who will instruct them in the higher branches; and their intelligence will become greater than ours, and their children will attain to higher advantages, and *their* children still higher; and then, though we are dead, our works shall live: though we are mouldering, our names shall not be forgotten. . . .

I am of a strong opinion, that the day on which we unite, heart and soul, and turn our attention to knowledge and improvement, that day the hissing and reproach among the nations of the earth against us will cease. And even those who now point at us with the finger of scorn, will aid and befriend us. It is of no use for us to sit with our hands folded, hanging our heads like bulrushes, lamenting our wretched condition; but let us make a mighty effort, and arise; and if no one will promote or respect us, let us promote and respect ourselves.

The American ladies have the honor conferred on them, that by prudence and economy in their domestic concerns, and their unwearied attention in forming the minds and manners of their children, they laid the foundation of their becoming what they now are. The good women of Wethersfield, Conn. toiled in the blazing sun, year after year, weeding onions, then sold the seed and procured money enough to erect them a house of worship; and shall we not imitate their examples, as far as they are worthy of imitation? Why cannot we do something to distinguish ourselves, and contribute some of our hard earnings that would reflect honor upon our memories, and cause our children to arise and call us blessed? Shall it any longer be said of the daughters of Africa, they have no ambition, they have no force? By no means. Let every female heart become united, and let us raise a fund ourselves; and at the end of one year and a half, we might be able to lay the corner-stone for the building of a High School, that the higher branches of knowledge might be enjoyed by us; and God would raise us up, and enough to aid us in our laudable designs. Let each one strive to excel in good house-wifery, knowing that prudence and economy are the road to wealth. Let us not say, we know this, or, we know that, and practise nothing; but let us practise what we do know.

How long shall the fair daughters of Africa be compelled to bury their minds and talents beneath a load of iron pots and kettles? Until union, knowledge and love begin to flow among us. How long shall a mean set of men flatter us with their smiles, and enrich themselves with our hard earnings; their wives' fingers sparkling with rings, and they themselves laughing at our folly? Until we begin to promote and patronize each other. . . . Do you ask, what can we do? Unite and build a store of your own, if you cannot procure a license. Fill one side with dry goods, and the other with groceries. Do you ask, where is the money? We have spent more than enough for nonsense, to do what building we should want. We have never had an opportunity of displaying our talents; therefore the world thinks we know nothing. And we have been possessed of by far too mean and cowardly a disposition, though I highly disapprove of an insolent or impertinent one. Do you ask the disposition I would have you possess? Possess the spirit of independence. The Americans do, and why should not you? Possess the spirit of men, bold and enterprising, fearless and undaunted. Sue for your rights and privileges. Know the reason that you cannot attain them. Weary them with your importunities. You can but die, if you make the attempt; and we shall certainly die if you do not. The Americans have practised nothing but head-work these 200 years, and we have done their drudgery. And is it not high time for us to imitate their examples, and practise head-work too, and keep what we have got, and get what we can? We need never to think that any body is going to feel interested for us, if we do not feel interested for ourselves. That day we, as a people, hearken unto the voice of the Lord our God, and walk in his ways and ordinances, and become distinguished for our ease, elegance and grace, combined with other virtues, that day the Lord will raise us up, and enough to aid and befriend us, and we shall begin to flourish.

Did every gentleman in America realize, as one, that they had got to become bondmen, and their wives, their sons, and their daughters, servants forever, to Great Britain, their very joints would become loosened, and tremblingly would smite one against another; their countenance would be filled with horror, every nerve and muscle would be forced into action, their souls would recoil at the very thought, their hearts would die within them, and death would be far more preferable. Then why have not Afric's sons a right to feel the same? Are not their wives, their sons, and their daughters, as dear to them as those of the white man's? Certainly, God has not deprived them of the divine influences of his Holy Spirit, which is the greatest of all blessings, if they ask him. Then why should man any longer deprive his fellow-man of equal rights and privileges? Oh, America, America, foul and indelible is thy stain! Dark and dismal is the cloud that hangs over thee, for thy cruel wrongs and injuries to the fallen sons of Africa. The blood of her murdered ones cries to heaven for vengeance against thee. Thou art almost become drunken with the blood of her slain; thou hast enriched thyself through her toils and labors; and now thou refuseth to make even a small return. And thou hast caused the daughters of Africa to commit whordoms and fornications; but upon thee be their curse.

O, ye great and mighty men of America, ye rich and powerful ones, many of you will call for the rocks and mountains to fall upon you, and to hide you from the wrath of the Lamb, and from him that sitteth upon the throne; whilst many of the sable-skinned Africans you now despise, will shine in the kingdom of heaven as the stars forever and ever. Charity begins at home, and those that provide not for their own, are worse than infidels. We know that you are raising contributions to aid the gallant Poles; we know that you have befriended Greece and Ireland; and you have rejoiced with France, for her heroic deeds of valor. You have acknowledged all the nations of the earth, except Hayti; and you may publish, as far as the East is from the West, that you have two millions of negroes, who aspire no higher than to bow at your feet, and to court your smiles. You may kill, tyrannize, and oppress as much as you choose, until our cry shall come up before the throne of God; for I am firmly persuaded, that he will not suffer you to quell the proud, fearless and undaunted spirits of the Africans forever; for in his own time, he is able to plead our cause against you, and to pour out upon you the ten plagues of Egypt. We will not come out against you with swords and staves, as against a thief; but we will tell you that our souls are fired with the same love of liberty and independence with which your souls are fired. We will tell you that too much of your blood flows in our veins, and too much of your color in our skins, for us not to possess your spirits. We will tell you, that it is our gold that clothes you in fine linen and purple, and causes you to fare sumptuously every day; and it is the blood of our fathers, and the tears of our brethren that have enriched your soils. AND WE CLAIM OUR RIGHTS. We will tell you, that we are not afraid of them that kill the body, and after that can do no more; but we will tell you whom we do fear. We fear Him who is able, after he hath killed, to destroy both soul and body in hell forever. Then, my brethren, sheath your swords, and calm your angry passions. Stand still, and know that the Lord he is God. Vengeance is his, and he will repay. It is a long lane that has no turn. America has risen to her meridian. When you begin to thrive, she will begin to fall. God hath raised you up a Walker and a Garrison. Though Walker sleeps, yet he lives, and his name shall be had in everlasting remembrance. I, even I, who am but a child, inexperienced to many of you, am a living witness to testify unto you this day, that I have seen the wicked in great power, spreading himself like a green bay tree, and lo, he passed away; yea, I diligently sought him, but he could not be found; and it is God alone that has inspired my heart to feel for Afric's woes. Then fret not yourselves because of evil doers. Fret not yourselves because of the men who bring wicked devices to pass; for they shall be cut down as the grass, and wither as the green herb. Trust in the Lord, and do good; so shalt thou dwell in the land, and verily thou shalt be fed. Encourage the noble-hearted Garrison. Prove to the world that you are neither ourang-outangs, nor a species of mere animals, but that you possess the same powers of intellect as those of the proud-boasting American.

I am sensible, my brethren and friends, that many of you have been deprived of advantages, kept in utter ignorance, and that your minds are now darkened; and if any of you have attempted to aspire after high and noble enterprises, you have met with so much opposition that your souls have become discouraged. For this very cause, a few of us have ventured to expose our lives in your behalf, to plead your cause against the great; and it will be of no use, unless you feel for yourselves and your little ones, and exhibit the spirits of men. Oh, then, turn your attention to knowledge and improvement; for knowledge is power. And God is able to fill you with wisdom and understanding, and to dispel your fears. Arm yourselves with the weapons of prayer. Put your trust in the living God. Persevere strictly in the paths of virtue. Let nothing be lacking on your part; and, in God's own time, and his time is certainly the best, he will surely deliver you with a mighty hand and with an outstretched arm.

I have never taken one step, my friends, with a design to raise myself in your esteem, or to gain applause. But what I have done, has been done with an eye single to the glory of God, and to promote the good of souls. I have neither kindred nor friends. I stand alone in your midst, exposed to the fiery darts of the devil, and to the assaults of wicked men. But though all the powers of earth and hell were to combine against me, though all nature should sink into decay, still would I trust in the Lord, and joy in the God of my salvation. For I am fully persuaded, that he will bring me off conqueror, yea, more than conqueror, through him who hath loved me and given himself for me.

Boston, October, 1831.

II

Why sit ye here and die? If we say we will go to a foreign land, the famine and the pestilence are there, and there we shall die. If we sit here, we shall die. Come let us plead our cause before the whites: if they save us alive, we shall live—and if they kill us, we shall but die.

Methinks I heard a spiritual interrogation—"Who shall go forward, and take off the reproach that is cast upon the people of color? Shall it be a woman?" And my heart made this reply—"If it is thy will, be it even so, Lord Jesus!"

I have heard much respecting the horrors of slavery; but may Heaven forbid that the generality of my color throughout these United States should experience any more of its horrors than to be a servant of servants, or hewers of wood and drawers of water! Tell us no more of southern slavery; for with few exceptions, although I may be very erroneous in my opinion, yet I consider our condition but little better than that. Yet, after all, methinks there are no chains so galling as the chains of ignorance—no fetters so binding as those that bind the soul, and exclude it from the vast field of useful and scientific knowledge. O, had I received the advantages of early education, my ideas would, ere now, have expanded far and wide; but, alas! I possess nothing but moral capability—no teachings but the teachings of the Holy Spirit.

I have asked several individuals of my sex, who transact business for themselves, if providing our girls were to give them the most satisfactory references, they would not be willing to grant them an equal opportunity with others? Their reply has been—for their own part, they had no objection; but as it was not the custom, were they to take them into their employ, they would be in danger of losing the public patronage.

And such is the powerful force of prejudice. Let our girls possess what amiable qualities of soul they may; let their characters be fair and spotless as innocence itself; let their natural taste and ingenuity be what

Source: Lecture, Delivered At The Franklin Hall, Boston, 21 September 1832, in Stewart, Productions, pp.51–56, a portion of her initial lecture to a mixed audience of men and women.

they may; it is impossible for scarce an individual of them to rise above the condition of servants. Ah! why is this cruel and unfeeling distinction? Is it merely because God has made our complexion to vary? . . . Yet, after all, methinks were the American free people of color to turn their attention more assiduously to moral worth and intellectual improvement, this would be the result: prejudice would gradually diminish, and the whites would be compelled to say, unloose those fetters! . . .

Few white persons of either sex, who are calculated for any thing else, are willing to spend their lives and bury their talents in performing mean, servile labor. And such is the horrible idea that I entertain respecting a life of servitude, that if I conceived of there being no possibility of my rising above the condition of a servant, I would gladly hail death as a welcome messenger. O, horrible idea, indeed! to possess noble souls aspiring after high and honorable acquirements, yet confined by the chains of ignorance and poverty to lives of continual drudgery and toil. Neither do I know of any who have enriched themselves by spending their lives as house-domestics, washing windows, shaking carpets, brushing boots, or tending upon gentlemen's tables. I can but die for expressing my sentiments; and I am as willing to die by the sword as the pestilence; for I am a true born American; your blood flows in my veins, and your spirit fires my breast.

I observed a piece in the Liberator a few months since, stating that the colonizationists had published a work respecting us, asserting that we were lazy and idle. I confute them on that point. Take us generally as a people, we are neither lazy nor idle; and considering how little we have to excite or stimulate us, I am almost astonished that there are so many industrious and ambitious ones to be found; although I acknowledge, with extreme sorrow, that there are some who never were and never will be serviceable to society. And have you not a similar class among yourselves?

Again. It was asserted that we were "a ragged set, crying for liberty." I reply to it, the whites have so long and so loudly proclaimed the theme of equal rights and privileges, that our souls have caught the flame also, ragged as we are. As far as our merit deserves, we feel a common desire to rise above the condition of servants and drudges. I have learnt, by bitter experience, that continual hard labor deadens the energies of the soul, and benumbs the faculties of the mind; the ideas become confined, the mind barren, and, like the scorching sands of Arabia, produces nothing; or, like the uncultivated soil, brings forth thorns and thistles.

Again, continual hard labor irritates our tempers and sours our dispositions; the whole system becomes worn out with toil and fatigue; nature herself becomes almost exhausted, and we care but little whether we live or die. It is true, that the free people of color throughout these United States are neither bought nor sold, nor under the lash of the cruel driver; many obtain a comfortable support; but few, if any, have an opportunity of becoming rich and independent; and the employments we most pursue are as unprofitable to us as the spider's web or the floating bubbles that vanish into air. As servants, we are respected; but let us presume to aspire any higher, our employer regards us no longer. And were it not that the King eternal has declared that Ethiopia shall stretch forth her hands unto God, I should indeed despair.

I do not consider it derogatory, my friends, for persons to live out to service. There are many whose inclination leads them to aspire no higher; and I would highly commend the performance of almost any thing for an honest livelihood; but where constitutional strength is wanting, labor of this kind, in its mildest form, is painful. And doubtless many are the prayers that have ascended to Heaven from Afric's daughters for strength to perform their work. Oh, many are the tears that have been shed for the want of that strength! Most of our color have dragged out a miserable existence of servitude from the cradle to the grave. And what literary acquirements can be made, or useful knowledge derived, from either maps, books or charts, by those who continually drudge from Monday morning until Sunday noon? O, ye fairer sisters, whose hands are never soiled, whose nerves and muscles are never strained, go learn by experience! Had we had the opportunity that you have had, to improve our moral and mental faculties, what would have hindered our intellects from being as bright, and our manners from being as dignified as yours? Had it been our lot to have been nursed in the lap of affluence and ease, and to have basked beneath the smiles and sunshine of fortune, should we not have naturally supposed that we were never made to toil? And why are not our forms as delicate, and our constitutions as slender, as yours? Is not the workmanship as curious and complete? Have pity upon us, have pity upon us, O ye who have hearts to feel for other's woes; for the hand of God has touched us. . . .

My beloved brethren, . . . it is upon you that woman depends; she can do but little besides using her influence; and it is for her sake and yours that I have come forward and made myself a hissing and a reproach among the people; for I am also one of the wretched and miserable daughters of the descendants of fallen Africa. Do you ask, why are you wretched and miserable? I reply, look at many of the most worthy and interesting of us doomed to spend our lives in gentlemen's kitchens. Look at our young men, smart, active and energetic, with souls filled with ambitious fire; if they look forward, alas! what are their prospects? They can be nothing but the humblest laborers, on account of their dark complexions; hence many of them lose their ambition, and become worthless. Look at our middle-aged men, clad in their rusty plaids and coats; in winter, every cent they earn goes to buy their wood and pay their rents; their poor wives also toil beyond their strength, to help support their families. Look at our aged sires, whose heads are whitened with the frosts of seventy winters, with their old wood-saws on their backs. Alas, what keeps us so? Prejudice, ignorance and poverty. But ah! methinks our oppression is soon to come to an end; yea, before the Majesty of heaven, our groans and cries have reached the ears of the Lord of Sabaoth. As the prayers and tears of Christians will avail the finally impenitent nothing; neither will the prayers and tears of the friends of humanity avail us any thing, unless we possess a spirit of virtuous emulation within our breasts. Did the pilgrims, when they first landed on these shores, quietly compose themselves, and say, "the Britons have all the money and all the power, and we must continue their servants forever?" Did they sluggishly sigh and say, "our lot is hard, the Indians own the soil, and we cannot cultivate it?" No; they first made powerful efforts to raise themselves, and then God raised up those illustrious patriots, WASHINGTON and LAFAYETTE, to assist and defend them. And, my brethren, have you made a powerful effort? Have you prayed the Legislature for mercy's sake to grant you all the rights and privileges of free citizens, that your daughters may rise to that degree of respectability which true merit deserves, and your sons above the servile situations which most of them fill?

III

African rights and liberty is a subject that ought to fire the breast of every free man of color in these United States, and excite in his bosom a lively, deep, decided and heart-felt interest. When I cast my eyes on the long list of illustrious names that are enrolled on the bright annals of fame among the whites, I turn my eyes within, and ask my thoughts, "Where are the names of our illustrious ones?" It must certainly have been for the want of energy on the part of the free people of color, that they have been long willing to bear the yoke of oppression. It must have been the want of ambition and force that has given the whites occasion to say, that our natural abilities are not as good, and our capacities by nature inferior to theirs. They boldly assert, that, did we possess a natural independence of soul, and feel a love for liberty within our breasts, some one of our sable race, long before this, would have testified it, notwithstanding the disadvantages under which wo labor. We have made ourselves appear altogether unqualified to speak in our own defence, and are therefore looked upon as objects of pity and commis- eration. We have been imposed upon, insulted and derided on every side; and now, if we complain, it is considered as the height of impertinence. We have suffered ourselves to be considered as dastards, cowards, mean, faint- hearted wretches; and on this account, (not because of our complexion,) many despise us, and would gladly spurn us from their presence.

These things have fired my soul with a holy indignation, and com- pelled me thus to come forward, and endeavor to turn their attention to knowledge and improvement; for knowledge is power. I would ask, is it

Source: An Address, Delivered at the African Masonic Hall, Boston, 27 February 1833, in Stewart, Productions, pp. 63–70.

blindness of mind, or stupidity of soul, or the want of education, that has caused our men who are 60 or 70 years of age, never to let their voices be heard, nor their hands be raised in behalf of their color? Or has it been for the fear of offending the whites? If it has, O ye fearful ones, throw off your fearfulness, and come forth in the name of the Lord, and in the strength of the God of Justice, and make yourselves useful and active members in society; for they admire a noble and patriotic spirit in others; and should they not admire it in us? If you are men, convince them that you possess the spirit of men; and as your day, so shall your strength be. Have the sons of Africa no souls? feel they no ambitious desires? shall the chains of ignorance forever confine them? shall the insipid appellation of "clever negroes," or "good creatures," any longer content them? Where can we find among ourselves the man of science, or a philosopher, or an able statesman, or a counsellor at law? Show me our fearless and brave, our noble and gallant ones. Where are our lecturers on natural history, and our critics in useful knowledge? There may be a few such men among us, but they are rare. It is true, our fathers bled and died in the revolutionary war, and others fought bravely under the command of Jackson, in defence of liberty. But where is the man that has distinguished himself in these modern days by acting wholly in the defence of African rights and liberty? There was one, although he sleeps, his memory lives.

I am sensible that there are many highly intelligent gentlemen of color in these United States, in the force of whose arguments, doubtless, I should discover my inferiority; but if they are blest with wit and talent, friends and fortune, why have they not made themselves men of eminence, by striving to take all the reproach that is cast upon the people of color, and in endeavoring to alleviate the woes of their brethren in bondage? Talk, without effort, is nothing; you are abundantly capable, gentlemen, of making yourselves men of distinction; and this gross neglect, on your part, causes my blood to boil within me. Here is the grand cause which hinders the rise and progress of the people of color. It is their want of laudable ambition and requisite courage. . . .

I am informed that the agent of the Colonization Society has recently formed an association of young men, for the purpose of influencing those of us to go to Liberia who may feel disposed. The colonizationists are blind to their own interest, for should the nations of the earth make war with America, they would find their forces much weakened by our absence; or should we remain here, can our "brave soldiers," and "fellow-citizens," as they were termed in time of calamity, condescend to defend the rights of the whites, and be again deprived of their own, or sent to Liberia in return? Or, if the colonizationists are real friends to Africa, let them expend the money which they collect, in erecting a college to educate her injured sons in this land of gospel light and liberty; for it would be most thankfully received on our part, and convince us of the truth of their professions, and save time, expense and anxiety. Let them place before us noble objects, worthy of pursuit, and see if we prove ourselves to be those unambitious negroes they term us. But ah! methinks their hearts are so frozen towards us, they had rather their money should be sunk in the ocean than to administer it to our relief; and I fear, if they dared, like Pharaoh, king of Egypt, they would order every male child among us to be drowned. But the most high God is still as able to subdue the lofty pride of these white Americans, as He was the heart of that ancient rebel. They say, though we are looked upon as *things*, yet we sprang from a scientific people. Had our men the requisite force and energy, they would soon convince them by their efforts both in public and private, that they were men, or things in the shape of men. . . .

It is of no use for us to wait any longer for a generation of well educated men to arise. We have slumbered and slept too long already; the day is far spent; the night of death approaches; and you have sound sense and good judgment sufficient to begin with, if you feel disposed to make a right use of it. Let every man of color throughout the United States, who possesses the spirit and principles of a man, sign a petition to Congress, to abolish slavery in the District of Columbia, and grant you the rights and privileges of common free citizens; for if you had had faith as a grain of mustard seed, long before this the mountains of prejudice might have been removed. We are all sensible that the Anti-Slavery Society has taken hold of the arm of our whole population, in order to raise them out of the mire. Now all we have to do is, by a spirit of virtuous ambition to strive to raise ourselves; and I am happy to have it in my power thus publicly to say, that the colored inhabitants of this city, in some respects, are beginning to improve. Had the free people of color in these United States nobly and boldly contended for their rights, and showed a natural genius and talent, although not so brilliant as some; had they held up, encouraged and patronized each other, nothing could have hindered us from being a thriving and flourishing people. . . .

IV

. . . And truly, I can say with St. Paul, that at my conversion, I came to the people in the fulness of the gospel of grace. Having spent a few months in the city of——, previous, I saw the flourishing condition of their churches, and the progress they were making in their Sabbath Schools. I visited their Bible Classes and heard of the union that existed in their Female Associations. On my arrival here, not finding scarce an individual who felt interested in these subjects, and but few of the whites, except Mr. Garrison, and his friend Mr. Knapp; and hearing that those gentlemen had observed that

Source: Mrs. Stewart's Farewell Address to Her Friends in the City of Boston, 21 September 1833, in Stewart, Productions, pp.74–79.

female influence was powerful, my soul became fired with a holy zeal for your cause; every nerve and muscle in me was engaged in your behalf. I felt that I had a great work to perform; and was in haste to make a profession of my faith in Christ, that I might be about my Father's business. Soon after I made this profession, the Spirit of God came before me, and I spake before many. When going home, reflecting on what I had said, I felt ashamed, and knew not where I should hide myself. A something said within my breast, "press forward, I will be with thee." And my heart made this reply, Lord, if thou wilt be with me, then will I speak for thee so long as I live. And thus far I have every reason to believe that it is the divine influence of the Holy Spirit operating upon my heart that could possibly induce me to make the feeble and unworthy efforts that I have. . . .

. . . I believe, that for wise and holy purposes, best known to himself, he hath unloosed my tongue and put his word into my mouth, in order to confound and put all those to shame that have rose up against me. For he hath clothed my face with steel, and lined my forehead with brass. He hath put his testimony within me, and engraven his seal on my forehead. And with these weapons I have indeed set the fiends of earth and hell at defiance.

What if I am a woman; is not the God of ancient times the God of these modern days? Did he not raise up Deborah, to be a mother, and a judge in Israel? Did not queen Esther save the lives of the Jews? And Mary Magdalene first declare the resurrection of Christ from the dead? Come, said the woman of Samaria, and see a man that hath told me all things that ever I did, is not this the Christ? St. Paul declared that it was a shame for a woman to speak in public, yet our great High Priest and Advocate did not condemn the woman for a more notorious offence than this; neither will he condemn this worthless worm. The bruised reed he will not break, and the smoking flax he will not quench, till he send forth judgment unto victory. Did St. Paul but know of our wrongs and deprivations, I presume he would make no objections to our pleading in public for our rights. Again; holy women ministered unto Christ and the apostles; and women of refinement in all ages, more or less, have had a voice in moral, religious and political subjects. Again; why the Almighty hath imparted unto me the power of speaking thus, I cannot tell. "And Jesus lifted up his voice and said, I thank thee, O Father, Lord of heaven and earth, that thou hast hid these things from the wise and prudent, and hast revealed them unto babes: even so, Father, for so it seemed good in thy sight."

But to convince you of the high opinion that was formed of the capacity and ability of woman, by the ancients, I would refer you to "Sketches of the Fair Sex." Read to the 51st page, and you will find that several of the Northern nations imagined that women could look into futurity, and that they had about them, an inconceivable something, approaching to divinity. Perhaps that idea was only the effect of the sagacity common to the sex, and the advantages which their natural address gave them over rough and simple warriors. Perhaps, also, those barbarians, surprised at the influence which beauty has over force, were led to ascribe to the supernatural attraction, a charm which they could not comprehend. A belief, however, that the Deity more readily communicates himself to women, has at one time or other, prevailed in every quarter of the earth; not only among the Germans and the Britons, but all the people of Scandinavia were possessed of it. Among the Greeks, women delivered the Oracles; the respect the Romans paid to the Sybils, is well known. The Jews had their prophetesses. The prediction of the Egyptian women obtained much credit at Rome, even under the Emperors. And in the most barbarous nations, all things that have the appearance of being supernatural, the mysteries of religion, the secrets of physic, and the rites of magic, were in the possession of women.

If such women as are here described have once existed, be no longer astonished then, my brethren and friends, that God at this eventful period should raise up your own females to strive, by their example both in public and private, to assist those who are endeavoring to stop the strong current of prejudice that flows so profusely against us at present. No longer ridicule their efforts, it will be counted for sin. For God makes use of feeble means sometimes, to bring about his most exalted purposes.

In the 15th century, the general spirit of this period is worthy of observation. We might then have seen women preaching and mixing themselves in controversies. Women occupying the chairs of Philosophy and Justice; women haranguing in Latin before the Pope; women writing in Greek, and studying in Hebrew; Nuns were Poetesses, and women of quality Divines; and young girls who had studied Eloquence, would with the sweetest countenances, and the most plaintive voices, pathetically exhort the Pope and the Christian Princes, to declare war against the Turks. Women in those days devoted their leisure hours to contemplation and study. The religious spirit which has animated women in all ages, showed itself at this time. It has made them, by turns, martyrs, apostles, warriors, and concluded in making them divines and scholars.

Why cannot a religious spirit animate us now? Why cannot we become divines and scholars? Although learning is somewhat requisite, yet recollect that those great apostles, Peter and James, were ignorant and unlearned. They were taken from the fishing boat, and made fishers of men.

In the 13th century, a young lady of Bologne, devoted herself to the study of the Latin language, and of the Laws. At the age of twenty-three she pronounced a funeral oration in Latin, in the great church of Bologne. And to be admitted as an orator, she had neither need of indulgence on account of her youth or of her sex. At the age of twenty-six, she took the degree of Doctor of Laws, and began publicly to expound the Institutions of Justinian. At the age of thirty, her great reputation raised her to a chair, where she taught the law to a prodigious concourse of scholars from all nations. She joined the charms and accomplishments of a woman to all the knowledge of a man. And such was the power of her eloquence, that her beauty was only admired when her tongue was silent.

What if such women as are here described should rise among our sable race? And it is not impossible. For it is not the color of the skin that makes the man or the woman, but the principle formed in the soul. Brilliant wit will shine, come from whence it will; and genius and talent will not hide the brightness of its lustre.

But, to return to my subject; the mighty work of reformation has begun among this people. The dark clouds of ignorance are dispersing. The light of science is bursting forth. Knowledge is beginning to flow, nor will its moral influence be extinguished till its refulgent rays have spread over us from East to West, and from North to South. Thus far is this mighty work begun, but not as yet accomplished. Christians must awake from their slumbers. Religion must flourish among them before the church will be built up in its purity, or immorality be suppressed.

Yet, notwithstanding your prospects are thus fair and bright, I am about to leave you, perhaps, never more to return. For I find it is no use for me as an individual to try to make myself useful among my color in this city. It was contempt for my moral and religious opinions in private that drove me thus before a public. Had experience more plainly shown me that it was the nature of man to crush his fellow, I should not have thought it so hard. Wherefore, my respected friends, let us no longer talk of prejudice, till prejudice becomes extinct at home. Let us no longer talk of opposition, till we cease to oppose our own. For while these evils exist, to talk is like giving breath to the air, and labor to the wind. Though wealth is far more highly prized than humble merit, yet none of these things move me. Having God for my friend and portion, what have I to fear? Promotion cometh neither from the East or West, and as long as it is the will of God, I rejoice that I am as I am; for man in his best estate, is altogether vanity. Men of eminence have mostly risen from obscurity; nor will I, although a female of a darker hue, and far more obscure than they, bend my head or hang my harp upon willows; for though poor, I will virtuous prove.

Nancy Prince

Nancy Prince, who grew up in Gloucester, Massachusetts, was deeply influenced by one of her ancestors: her maternal grandfather, a slave who fought at Bunker Hill. A member of the Congregational Church, he monitored the religious instruction of his children and grandchildren. Mrs. Prince, born in 1799, may well have had a modicum of formal schooling as a young child, for her recollections refer to "pious teachers" and her grandfather's hostility toward education if "the teacher was not devoted to God." Bound out to various families from the age of eight to fourteen, she was quick to note that the ritual of family prayers in the household of employers both morning and evening did little to mitigate the exploitation of their servants. She sought in her adult life to confront heathenism with the Protestant message of faith and morals. Providing relief for destitute youth was one of her ways of making the ethical code of Protestantism explicit and concrete.

Mrs. Prince's volume is less an exhortation than a demonstration. Two points are clearly illustrated. Given opportunity, a meagerly educated domestic worker can develop strong initiative, marshal personal resources in imaginative ways, and improve, in Maria Stewart's words, the "moral and mental faculties." Second, her career documents a process of self-realization stimulated by mothering activities in various corners of the globe.

Little is known about Nancy Prince beyond what she invites us to gather from her autobiographical comments, published first in 1850, again in 1853, and in a third edition in 1856. Of mixed African and Indian ancestry, she also had an African stepfather who escaped from a slave ship and found himself on free soil. As a seaman sailing out of Massachusetts he was impressed into British service during the War of 1812 and contracted a fatal illness. Nancy, at the age of fourteen or fifteen, took the major responsibility for her mother and a large number of children. In consequence she was involved in all sorts of domestic work. Her life later took an extraordinary turn. She married a black American in the service of the Russian czar. Despite the wealth of detail with which many of her experiences are embellished, she never reveals "Mr. Prince's" Christian name.

She returned to America after a decade, as the extracts below explain, and was widowed within a short time. The Liberator mentioned her lecture

in 1839 on the "manners and customs of Russia." Two years later the
Liberator published a letter decrying the treatment she received on a voyage
from New York to Providence that summer. Garrison's introduction referred
to her as "a highly respectable, colored female (formerly of this city, but
more recently of Jamaica, where she has been acting in the capacity of a
teacher)."

The journey to Jamaica formed a third major segment of her life. Her
keen powers of observation were not thwarted there despite the frustration
of her primary goals. In October of 1854 Mrs. Prince attended the National
Woman's Rights Convention in Philadelphia, where she "invoked the blessing of God upon the notable women engaged in this enterprise." She understood, she said, "woman's wrongs better than woman's rights."[1]

I was born in Newburyport, September the 15th, 1799. My mother was born
in Gloucester, Massachusetts—the daughter of Tobias Wornton, or Backus,
so called. He was stolen from Africa, when a lad, and was a slave of Captain
Winthrop Sargent; but, although a slave, he fought for liberty. He was in the
Revolutionary army, and at the battle of Bunker Hill. He often used to tell us,
when little children, the evils of Slavery, and how he was stolen from his
native land. My grandmother was an Indian of this country; she became a
captive to the English, or their descendants. She served as a domestic in the
Parsons family. My father, Thomas Gardner, was born in Nantucket; his
parents were of African descent. He died in Newburyport, when I was three
months old. My mother was thus a second time left a widow, with her two
children, and she returned to Gloucester to her father. My mother married
her third husband, by whom she had six children. My stepfather was stolen
from Africa, and while the vessel was at anchor in one of our Eastern ports,
he succeeded in making his escape from his captors, by swimming ashore. I
have often heard him tell the tale. Having some knowledge of the English
language, he found no trouble to pass. There were two of them, and they
found, from observation, that they were in a free State. I have heard my
father describe the beautiful moon-light night when they two launched their
bodies into the deep, for liberty. When they got upon soundings, their feet
were pricked with a sea-plant that grew under water, they had to retreat,
and, at last they reached the shore. When day began to break, they laid down
under a fence, as naked as they were born—soon they heard a rattling sound,

[1]Liberator, 8 March 1839 and 17 September 1841 (the latter including Garrison's introduction); Elizabeth Cady Stanton, Susan B. Anthony, and Matilda Joslyn Gage, eds.,
History of Woman Suffrage (New York, 1881), I, 384.

Source: Nancy Prince, Narrative of the Life and Travels of Mrs. Nancy Prince, 2d ed.
(Boston, 1853), pp. 5–64. All footnotes are the editors'.

and trembling, they looked to see what it meant. In a few minutes, a man with a broad-brimmed hat on, looked over the fence and cried out, "Halloo boys! you are from that ship at anchor?" Trembling, we answered, yes. He kindly took us by the hand, and told us not to fear, for we were safe. "Jump, boys," said he, "into my cart," which we readily did. He turned about, and soon entered a large yard—we were taken to his house and carried to an apartment, where he brought us clothes and food, and cheered us with every kindness. No search was made for us; it was supposed we were drowned, as many had jumped over-board on the voyage, thinking they could get home to Africa again. I have often heard my step-father boast how brave they were, and say they stood like men and saw the ship set sail with less than half they stole from Africa. He was selling his bamboo baskets, when he was seized by white men, and put in a boat, and taken on board the ship that lay off; many such ships there were! He was called "Money Vose," and his name may be found on the Custom House books in Gloucester. His last voyage was with Captain Elias Davis, in the brig Romulus, belonging to Captain Fitz William Sargent, in whose employ he had been twelve years. During the war [the War of 1812], the brig was taken by a British privateer, and he was pressed into their service. He was sick with the dropsy a long while, and died oppressed, in the English dominions. My mother was again left a widow, with an infant six weeks old, and seven other children. When she heard of her husband's death, she exclaimed, "I thought it; what shall I do with these children?" She was young, inexperienced, with no hope in God, and without the knowledge of her Saviour. Her grief, poverty, and responsibilities, were too much for her; she never again was the mother that she had been before. I was, at this time, in Captain F.W. Sargent's family. I shall never forget the feelings I experienced, on hearing of the decease of my father-in-law [i.e., her step-father] although he was not kind to me or my sister; but, by industry a humble home was provided, for my mother and her younger children. Death had twice visited our family, in less than three months. My grandfather died before my father in law sailed. I thought I would go home a little while, and try and comfort my mother. The three oldest children were put into families.

My brother and myself stayed at home that Summer. We gathered berries and sold them in Gloucester; strawberries, raspberries, blackberries and whortleberries, were in abundance, in the stony environs, growing spontaneously. With the sale of these fruits, my brother and myself nearly supported my mother and her children, that Summer. My brother George, young as he was, caught fish and sold them, and run of errands, and was always watching for something to do, that he might help his mother. At one time he was missing; we expected he was drowned; a search was made for him in the water; the neighbors were all on the alert. Poor mother returning from a hard day's work, supposing the boy was lost, was like a lunatic. The lad was supposed to have fallen from the wharf, where he was fishing. Our friends had all given up the search—it was then eleven o'clock at night.

Mother and I locked up the children and went round to the harbor, to one Captain Warner, who traded to the Eastward. Mrs. Warner informed us that my brother came there in the morning, with his bundle, and they supposed he was sent, as the Captain wished to take him with him. He went on board, and the vessel sailed that afternoon. In three weeks, he came home, to the comfort of his mother and all of us. He brought back, for his pay, four feet of wood and three dollars.

We stayed with our mother until every resource was exhausted; we then heard of a place eight miles out of town, where a boy and girl were wanted. We both went and were engaged. We often went home with our wages, and all the comforts we could get; but we could not approach our mother as we wished. God in mercy took one little boy of seven years, who had been in a consumption one year.

My oldest sister, Silvia, was seventy miles in the country, with the family that brought her up; so we were scattered all about. Soon as the war was over, I determined to get more for my labor. I left Essex and went to Salem, in the month of April, 1814. . . . I soon found my friend that I wished, and stopped there two weeks, and then went to live with a respectable colored family. My mother was not satisfied, and came after me. I would not go to Gloucester. She left me at a friend's and this woman had a daughter, who came home from service, sick. I took her place, and thought myself fortunate to be with religious people, as I had enjoyed the happy privilege of religious instruction. My dear grandfather was a member of a Congregational Church, and a good man; he always attended meeting in the morning, and took his children with him. In the afternoon he took care of the smaller children, while my mother attended with her little group. He thought it was wrong for us to go to school where the teacher was not devoted to God. Thus I early knew the difference between right and wrong.

There were seven in the family, one sick with a fever, and another in a consumption. . . . Sabbath evening I had to prepare for the wash; soap the clothes and put them into the steamer, set the kettle of water to boiling, and then close in the steam, and let the pipe from the boiler into the steam box that held the clothes. At two o'clock, on the morning of Monday, the bell was rung for me to get up; but, that was not all, they said I was too slow, and the washing was not done well; I had to leave the tub to tend the door and wait on the family, and was not spoken kind to, at that.

Hard labor and unkindness was too much for me; in three months, my health and strength were gone. I often looked at my employers, and thought to myself, is this your religion? I did not wonder that the girl who had lived there previous to myself, went home to die. They had family prayers, morning and evening. Oh! yes, they were sanctimonious! I was a poor stranger, but fourteen years of age, imposed upon by these good people; but I must leave them. In the year 1814, they sent me to Gloucester in their chaise. . . .

In the Spring of 1815, I returned to Salem, accompanied by my eldest sister, and we obtained good places. She took it into her head to go to

Boston, as a nursery girl, where she lived a few months and was then deluded away. February 7th, 1816, a friend came to Salem and informed me of it. To have heard of her death, would not have been so painful to me, as we loved each other very much, and more particularly, as our step-father was not very kind to us. When little girls, she used to cry about it, and we used to say, when we were large enough we would go away.

It was very cold; but notwithstanding, I was so distressed about my sister that I started the next morning for Boston, on foot. . . . I was young and inexperienced, but God knew that my object was good. "In wisdom he chooses the weak things of the earth." Without his aid, how could I ever have rescued my lost sister? Mr. Brown [not otherwise identified], when he learned my errand, kindly offered to assist me. He found where my sister resided, and taking with him a large cane, he accompanied me to the house, on Sabbath evening. My sister I found seated with a number of others round a fire, the mother of harlots at the head. My sister did not see me until I clasped her round the neck. The old woman flew at me, and bid me take my hands off of her; she opened a door that led down into a cellar kitchen, and told me to come down, she attempted to take my hands off of my sister. Mr. Brown defended me with his cane; there were many men and girls there, and all was confusion. When my sister came to herself, she looked upon me and said: "Nancy, O Nancy, I am ruined!" I said, "Silvia, my dear sister, what are you here for? Will you not go with me?" She seemed thankful to get away; the enraged old woman cried out, "She owes me, she cannot go." Silvia replied, "I will go." The old woman seized her to drag her down into the kitchen; I held on to her, while Mr. Brown at my side, used his great cane; he threatened her so that she was obliged to let my sister go, who, after collecting her things, accompanied Mr. Brown and myself.

Now while I write, I am near the spot that was then the hold of all foul and unclean things. . . . Even now, I cannot refrain my feelings, although death has long separated us; but her soul is precious; she was very dear to me; she was five years older than myself, and often protected me from the blows of an unkind step-father. She often said she was not fit to live, nor fit to die. . . .

My brother George and myself were very desirous to make our mother comfortable: he went to sea for that purpose; the next April, I came to Boston to get a higher price for my labor; for we had agreed to support my mother, and hoped she would take home our little brother and take care of him, who was supported by the town. George came home, and sailed again in the same employ, leaving mother a draw bill for half his wages. My sister returned to Boston to find me, and wished to procure a place to work out. I had just changed my place for one more retired, and engaged my sister with me as a chamber maid; she tried me much. I thought it a needy time, for I had not yielded my heart to the will of God, though I had many impressions, and formed many resolutions; but the situations that I had been placed in, (having left my mother's house at the age of eight,) had not permitted me to do as I wished, although the kind counsels of my dear grandfather and pious teachers followed me wherever I went. Care after care oppressed me—my mother wandered about like a Jew—the young children who were in families were dissatisfied; all hope but in God was lost. I resolved, in my mind, to seek an interest in my Savior, and put my trust in Him; and never shall I forget the place or time when God spake to my troubled conscience. Justified by faith I found peace with God, the forgiveness of sin through Jesus Christ my Lord. After living sixteen years without hope, and without a guide, May 6th, 1819, the Rev. Thomas Paul,[1] baptized myself, and seven others, in obedience to the great command. . . .

    . . . After seven years of anxiety and toil, I made up my mind to leave my country. September 1st, 1823, Mr. Prince arrived from Russia. February 15th, 1824, we were married. April 14th, we embarked on board the Romulus, captain Epes Sargent commander, bound for Russia. May 24th, arrived at Elsinore, left the same day for Copenhagen, where we remained twelve days. We visited the king's palace, and several other extensive and beautiful buildings. We attended a number of entertainments, among the Danes and English, who were religious; observed that their manners and customs were similar; they are attentive to strangers; the Sabbath is very strictly observed; the principal religion is Lutheran and Calvinistic, but all persuasions are tolerated. The languages are Dutch, French and English. The Danes are very modest and kind, but like all other nations, they know how to take the advantage. We left Copenhagen the 7th of June, and arrived at Cronstadt on the 19th; left there the 21st for St. Petersburg, and in a few hours, were happy to find ourselves at our place of destination, through the blessing of God, in good health, and soon made welcome from all quarters. We took lodgings with a Mrs. Robinson, a native of our country, who was Patience Mott, of Providence, who left here in the year 1813, in the family of Alexander Gabriel, the man who was taken [as a temporary replacement] for Mr. Prince. There I spent six weeks very pleasantly, visiting and receiving friends, in the manner of the country. While there I attended two of their parties; there were various amusements in which I did not partake, which caused them much disappointment. I told them my religion did not allow of dancing or dice playing, which formed part of the amusements. As they were very strict in their religion, they indulged me in the same privilege. By the help of God I was ever enabled to preserve my stand.

    Mr. Prince was born in Marlborough, and lived in families in this city. In 1810 he went to Gloucester, and sailed with captain Theodore Stanwood, for Russia. He returned with him, and remained in his family, and at this time visited at my mother's. He sailed with captain Stanwood in 1812, for the last time. The Captain took with him his son Theodore, in order to place

---

[1]Reverend Thomas Paul, in 1809, gave leadership to the black Baptists of Boston in organizing their own church; he also helped to organize the forerunner of New York's Abyssinian Baptist Church.

him in School in St. Petersburg. When the Captain sailed for home, Mr. Prince went to serve the Princess Purtossof, one of the noble ladies of the Court. The palace where the imperial family reside is called the court, or the seat of Government. This magnificent building is adorned with all the ornaments that possibly can be explained; there are hundreds of people that inhabit it, besides the soldiers that guard it. There are several of these splendid edifices in the city and vicinity. The one that I was presented in, was in a village, three miles from the city. After leaving the carriage, we entered the first ward; where the usual salutation by the guards was performed. As we passed through the beautiful hall, a door was opened by two colored men in official dress. The Emperor Alexander stood on his throne, in his royal apparel. The throne is circular, elevated two steps from the floor, and covered with scarlet velvet, tasseled with gold; as I entered, the Emperor stepped forward with great politeness and condescension, and welcomed me, and asked several questions; he then accompanied us to the Empress Elizabeth; she stood in her dignity, and received me in the same manner the Emperor had. They presented me with a watch, &c. It was customary in those days, when any one married, belonging to the court, to present them with gifts, according to their standard; there was no prejudice against color; there were there all casts, and the people of all nations, each in their place.

The number of colored men that filled this station was twenty; when one dies, the number is immediately made up. Mr. Prince filled the place of one that had died. They serve in turns, four at a time, except on some great occasions, when all are employed. Provision is made for the families within or without the palace. Those without go to court at 8 o'clock in the morning; after breakfasting, they take their station in the halls, for the purpose of opening the doors, at signal given, when the Emperor and Empress pass. . . .

St. Petersburg was inundated October 9th, 1824. The water rose sixteen feet in most parts of the city; many of the inhabitants were drowned. An island between the city and Cronstadt, containing five hundred inhabitants, was inundated, and all were drowned, and great damage was done at Cron stadt. The morning of this day was fair; there was a high wind. Mr. Prince went early to the palace, as it was his turn to serve; our children boarders were gone to school; our servant had gone of an errand. I heard a cry, and to my astonishment, when I looked out to see what was the matter, the waters covered the earth. I had not then learned the language, but I beckoned to the people to come in. The waters continued to rise until 10 o'clock, A.M. The waters were then within two inches of my window, when they ebbed and went out as fast as they had come in, leaving to our view a dreadful sight. The people who came into my house for their safety retired, and I was left alone. At four o'clock in the afternoon, there was darkness that might be felt, such as I had never experienced before. My situation was the more painful, being alone, and not being able to speak. I waited until ten in the evening; I then took a lantern, and started to go to a neighbor's, whose children went to the same school with my boarders. I made my way through a long yard, over the bodies of men and beasts, and when opposite their gate I sank; I made one grasp, and the earth gave away; I grasped again, and fortunately got hold of the leg of a horse, that had been drowned. I drew myself up, covered with mire, and made my way a little further, when I was knocked down by striking against a boat, that had been washed up and left by the retiring waters; and as I had lost my lantern, I was obliged to grope my way as I could, and feeling along the walk, I at last found the door that I aimed at. My family were safe and they accompanied me home. At 12 o'clock, Mr. Prince came home, as no one was permitted to leave the palace, till his majesty had viewed the city. In the morning the children and the girl returned, and I went to view the pit into which I had sunk. It was large enough to hold a dozen like myself, where the earth had caved in. Had not the horse been there, I should never again have seen the light of day, and no one would have known my fate. Thus through the providence of God, I escaped from the flood and the pit. . . .

Should I attempt to give an account of all the holidays, it would fill volumes. The next to notice is Christmas and New Year. The first day of January a grand masquerade is given by his majesty, at the winter palace; forty thousand tickets are distributed; every thing is done in order; every gentleman wears a mask and cloak, and carries a lady with him. They are formed in a procession, and enter at the west gate; as they pass through, all the golden vessels and ornaments are displayed; these were back of a counter, which extends two hundred feet; there the company receive a cup of hot chocolate, and a paper of comfits, and a bun; a great many are in attendance, as a vast many persons are permitted to pass in and view the palace, and go out at the east gate.

The 6th of January is a still greater day, for then the water is christened; a church is built on the ice, ornamented with gold and evergreens, and a row of spruce trees, extending from the door of the palace to the church. At this time all the nobles, of different nations, make their appearance in their native costume. The Patriarch, Archbishops, and other dignitaries of the court, have a service; then they pass through and christen the water, and make it holy; then there is a great rush of the people for this holy water. On the plain an ice hill is built, eighty feet high, where the emperor and his court exercise themselves.

Februrary 10th is another holiday. Buildings are constructed on the plain for the occasion. All kinds of amusements may be found here, and all kinds of animals seen; much time and money are spent. The buildings are built in rotation. All the children of the different seminaries and institutions of education, are driven round in gilded carriages to witness the performances. After this is the great Fast, previous to the crucifixion of our Saviour. Then Christ is represented as riding into Jerusalem; branches of trees are placed on the ice, and strewed through the streets, and every performance is carried out. The Saviour is made of white marble; he is crucified and buried, and on the third day he rises, according to the Scriptures; then the cannons are fired. At the close of this forty day's Fast, they have a great feast and fair; all business is suspended, and the festivity and frolic continue for one week.

The first day of May is another great holiday. The merchant's daughters are arranged on each side of a long mall, in the beautiful gardens, and arrayed in their best clothes, under the care of an old woman known in their families; the gentlemen walk round and observe them, and if they see one they fancy, they speak to the old woman; she takes him to the parents and introduces him; if the parties agree, they prepare for the betrothal. It is their custom to marry one of their own station. All these holidays are accounted sacred. The first year I noted them all, as I was accustomed to attend them.

May, 1825. I spent some time visiting the different towns in the vicinity of St. Petersburg. In the fall of the same year, the Emperor retired to a warmer climate for the health of the Empress Elizabeth. January, 1826 [variations in dating probably stem from differences between the Russian and American calendars], the corpse of Alexander was brought in state, and was met three miles from the city by the nobles of the court; and they formed a procession, and the body was brought in state into the building where the imperial family were deposited. March, of the same year, the corpse of Elizabeth was brought in the same manner. Constantine was then king of Poland, he was next heir to the throne, and was unanimously voted by the people, but refused and resigned the crown in favor of his brother Nicholas. The day appointed the people were ordered to assemble as usual, at the ringing of the bells; they rejected Nicholas; a sign was given by the leaders that was well understood, and the people great and small rushed to the square and cried with one voice for Constantine. The emperor with his prime minister, and city governor, rode into the midst of them, entreating them to retire, without avail; they were obliged to order the cannons fired upon the mob; it was not known when they discharged them that the emperor and his ministers were in the crowd. He was wonderfully preserved, while both his friends and their horses were killed. There was a general seizing of all classes, who were taken into custody. The scene cannot be described; the bodies of the killed and mangled were cast into the river, and the snow and ice were stained with the blood of human victims; as they were obliged to drive the cannon to and fro in the midst of the crowd, the bones of those wounded, who might have been cured, were crushed. The cannon are very large, drawn by eight horses, trained for the purpose. The scene was awful; all business was stopped. This deep plot originated in 1814, in Germany, with the Russian nobility and German, under the pretence of a Free Mason's Lodge. When they returned home they increased their numbers and presented their chart to the emperor for permission, which was granted. In the year 1822, the emperor being suspicious that all was not right, took their chart from them. They carried it on in small parties, rapidly increasing, believing they would soon be able to destroy all the imperial branches, and have a republican government. Had not this taken place, undoubtedly they would at last have succeeded. So deep was the foundation of this plot laid, both males and females were engaged in it. The prison-houses were filled, and thirty of the leading men were put in solitary confinement, and twenty-six of the number died, four were burned. A stage was erected and faggots were placed underneath, each prisoner was secured by iron chains, presenting a most appalling sight to an eye-witness. A priest was in attendance to cheer their last dying moments, then fire was set to the faggots, and those brave men were consumed. Others received the knout, and even the princesses and ladies of rank were imprisoned and flogged in their own habitations. Those that survived their punishment were banished to Siberia. The mode of banishment is very imposing and very heart-rending, severing them from all dear relatives and friends, for they are never permitted to take their children. When they arrive at the gate of the city, their first sight is a guard of soldiers, then wagons with provisions, then the noblemen in their banished apparel guarded each side, then conveyances for the females, then ladies in order, guarded by soldiers. . . .

. . . The common language is a mixture of Sclavonian and Polish. The nobility make use of the modern Greek, French and English. I learned the languages in six months, so as to be able to attend to my business, and also made some proficiency in the French. My time was taken up in domestic affairs; I took two children to board, the third week after commencing housekeeping, and increased their numbers. The baby linen making and childrens' garments were in great demand. I started a business in these articles and took a journeywoman and apprentices. The present Empress is a very active one, and inquired of me respecting my business, and gave me much encouragement by purchasing of me garments for herself and children, handsomely-wrought in French and English styles, and many of the nobility also followed her example. It was to me a great blessing that we had the means of grace afforded us. The Rev. Richard Kenell, was the Protestant pastor. We had service twice every Sabbath, and evening prayer meetings, also a female society, so that I was occupied at all times.

At the time of the inundation, the Bibles and other books belonging to the society were injured. But Mr. Kenell took the liberty to purchase at full price and sell at an advance. In order that the poor might have them, we all agreed to labor for that purpose. I often visited the matron of the Empress' children, and encouraged by her I took some to the Palace, and by this means disposed of many at head quarters. Other friends without the court continued to labor until hundreds and thousands were disposed of. The old Bishop finding his religion was in danger sent a petition to the Emperor that all who were found distributing Bibles and Tracts should be punished severely. Many were taken and imprisoned, two devoted young men were banished; thus the righteous were punished, while evil practices were not forbidden, for there the sin of licentiousness is very common.

I have mentioned that the climate did not agree with me; in winter my lungs were much affected. It was the advice of the best physicians that I had better not remain in Russia during another cold season. However painful it was to me to return without my husband, yet life seemed desirable, and he flattered me and himself that he should soon follow. It is difficult for any one in the Emperor's employment to leave when they please. Mr. Prince thought it best for me to return to my native country, while he remained two years longer to accumulate a little property, and then return—but death took him away. I left St. Petersburg, August 14th, 1833, having been absent about nine years and six months. On the 17th, I sailed from Cronstadt, for New York. Arrived at Elsinore the 25th. Tuesday, 29, left. September the 2d, laid to in a gale. September 18th, made Plymouth, Old England, 19th sailed. Arrived in New York, Oct. 10th. Left there Tuesday 18th, arrived in Boston the 23d. Sabbath, Nov. 9th, I had the privilege of attending service in the old place of worship. On this day I also had the pleasure of meeting with an old friend of my grandfather, nearly one hundred years of age. I found things much changed; my mother and sister Silvia died in 1827 (that I was aware of). The Rev. T. Paul was dead, and many of my old friends were gone to their long home. The old church and society was in much confusion; I attempted to worship with them but it was in vain. The voyage was of great benefit to me. By the advice of friends I applied to a Mrs. Mott, a female physician in the city, that helped me much. I am indebted to God for his great goodness in guiding my youthful steps; my mind was directed to my fellow brethren whose circumstances were similar to my own. I found many a poor little orphan destitute and afflicted, and on account of color shut out from all the asylums for poor children. At this my heart was moved, and I proposed to my friends the necessity of a home for such, where they might be sheltered from the contaminating evils that beset their path. For this purpose I called a meeting of the people and laid before them my plan: as I had had the privilege of assisting in forming an Asylum for such a purpose in St. Petersburg, I thought it would be well to establish one on the same principles, not knowing that any person had had a thought of anything of the kind. We commenced with eight children. I gave three months of my time. A board was formed of seven females, with a committee of twelve gentlemen of standing, to superintend. At the end of three months the committee was dispensed with, and for want of funds our society soon fell through.

I passed my time in different occupations and making arrangements for the return of my husband, but death took him from me. I made my home at the Rev. J.W. Holman's, a Free Will Baptist, until I sailed for Jamaica. There had been an Anti-Slavery Society established by W.L. Garrison, Knapp,[2] and other philanthropists of the day. Their design was the amelioration of the nominally free colored people of these States, and the emancipation of the slaves in other States. These meetings I attended with much pleasure, until a contention broke out among themselves. . . .

---

[2] Isaac Knapp, associate of William Lloyd Garrison in the publication of the *Liberator.*

My mind, after the emancipation in the West Indies, was bent upon going to Jamaica. A field of usefulness seemed spread out before me. While I was thinking about it, the Rev. Mr. Ingraham,[3] who had spent seven years there, arrived in the city. He lectured in the city at the Marlboro' Chapel, on the results arising from the emancipation at the British Islands. He knew much about them, he had a station at a mountain near Kingston, and was very desirous to have persons go there to labor. He wished some one to go with him to his station. He called on me . . . to persuade me to go. I told him it was my intention to go if I could make myself useful, but that I was sensible that I was very limited in education. He told me that the moral condition of the people was very bad, and needed labor aside from any thing else.

I left America, November 16th, 1840, in the ship Scion, Captain Mansfield, bound for Jamaica, freighted with ice and machinery for the silk factory. There were on board a number of handicraftsmen and other passengers. We sailed on Monday afternoon, from Charlestown, Massachusetts. It rained continually until Saturday. Sunday, the 23d, was a fine day. Mr. De Grass, a young colored clergyman, was invited to perform divine service, which he did with much propriety. He spoke of the dangers we had escaped and the importance of being prepared to meet our God (he died of fever about three weeks after arriving at Jamaica). Some who were able to attend came on deck, and listened to him with respect, while others seemed to look on in derision; these spent the afternoon and evening in card-playing. About twelve at night a storm commenced; on Monday were in great peril; the storm continued until Friday, the 27th. On that day a sail was seen at some distance making towards us, the captain judging her to be a piratical vessel, ordered the women and children below, and the men to prepare for action. The pirates were not inclined to hazard an engagement; when they saw the deck filled with armed men they left us. Thus were we preserved from the storm and from the enemy. Sabbath, 29th, divine service,—our attention was directed to the goodness of God, in sparing us.

Monday, and we mortals are still alive. Tuesday, thus far the Lord has led us on. Wednesday, thus far his power prolongs our days. Thursday, December 3d, to-day made Turks Island. Friday, this day had a view of Hayti, its lofty mountains presented a sublime prospect. Saturday, we had a glance at Cuba. Sunday, December 6th, at six o'clock in the evening, dropped anchor at St. Ann Harbor, Jamaica. We blessed the Lord for his goodness in sparing us to see the place of our destination; and here I will mention my object in visiting Jamaica. I hoped that I might aid, in some small degree, to raise up and encourage the emancipated inhabitants, and teach the young children to read and work, to fear God, and put their trust in the Saviour. . . . On Tuesday we went on shore to see the place and the

---

[3]One of the theological students from Lane Seminary who in 1834 had withdrawn in protest against restrictions on the education of blacks.

people; my intention had been to go directly to Kingston, but the people urged me to stay with them, and I thought it my duty to comply, and wrote to Mr. Ingraham to that effect. I went first to see the minister, Mr. Abbott;[4] I thought as he was out, I had better wait his return. The people promised to pay me for my services, or send me to Kingston. When Mr. Abbott returned he made me an offer, which I readily accepted. As I lodged in the house of one of the class-leaders I attended her class a few times, and when I learned the method, I stopped. She then commenced her authority and gave me to understand if I did not comply I should not have any pay from that society. I spoke to her of the necessity of being born of the spirit of God before we become members of the church of Christ, and told her I was sorry to see the people blinded in such a way.

She was very angry with me and soon accomplished her end by complaining of me to the minister; and I soon found I was to be dismissed, unless I would yield obedience to this class-leader. I told the minister that I did not come there to be guided by a poor foolish woman. He then told me that I had spoken something about the necessity of moral conduct in church members. I told him I had, and in my opinion, I was sorry to see it so much neglected. He replied, that he hoped I would not express myself so except to him; they have the gospel, he continued, and let them into the church. I do not approve of women societies; they destroy the world's convention; the American women have too many of them.[5] I talked with him an hour. He paid me for the time I had been there. I continued with the same opinion, that something must be done for the elevation of the children, and it is for that I labor. . . .

. . . I called . . . at the market [in Kingston], and counted the different stalls. For vegetables and poultry 196, all numbered and under cover; beside 70 on the ground; these are all attended by colored women. The market is conveniently arranged, as they can close the gates and leave all safe. There are nineteen stalls for fresh fish, eighteen for pork, thirty for beef, eighteen for turtle. These are all regular built markets, and are kept by colored men and women. These are all in one place. Others also may be found, as with us, all over the city. Thus it may be hoped they are not the stupid set of beings they have been called; here surely we see industry; they are enterprising and quick in their perceptions, determined to possess themselves, and to possess property besides, and quite able to take care of themselves. They wished to know why I was so inquisitive about them. I told them we had heard in America that you are lazy, and that emancipation has been of no benefit to you; I wish to inform myself of the truth respecting you, and give a

---

[4]Probably white, because she usually specified "colored" where applicable.

[5]This seems to represent the minister's view rather than that of Mrs. Prince. The World's Anti-Slavery Convention held in London in the summer of 1840 had disclosed bitter division over the right of women to be seated as delegates and, more broadly, over the right of women to participate as speakers or agents in the antislavery movement.

true account on my return. Am I right? More than two hundred people were around me listening to what I said.

They thanked me heartily. I gave them some tracts, and told them if it so pleased God I would come back to them and bring them some more books, and try what could be done with some of the poor children to make them better. I then left them, and went to the East Market, where there are many of all nations. The Jews and Spanish looked at me very black. The colored people gathered around me. I gave them little books and tracts, and told them I hoped to see them again.

There are in this street upwards of a thousand young women and children, living in sin of every kind. From thence I went to the jail, where there were seventeen men, but no women. There were in the House of Correction three hundred culprits; they are taken from there, to work on plantations. . . .

There is in Jamaica an institution, established in 1836, called the Mico Institution. It is named after its founder, Madame Mico, who left a large sum of money to purchase (or rather to ransom, the one being a Christian act, the other a sin against the Holy Ghost, who expressly forbids such traffic). Madame Mico left this money to ransom the English who were in bondage to the Algerines [Algerian pirates]; if there was any left, it was to be devoted to the instruction of the colored people in the British Isles.

Beside the Mico establishment, there are in Jamaica twenty-seven church missionary schools, where children are taught gratis. Whole number taught, 952. London Missionary Society Schools, sixteen; the number taught not ascertained. National Schools, thirty-eight. There are also the Wesleyan, Presbyterian and Moravian Schools; it is supposed there are private schools, where three or four thousand are educated in the city of Kingston, and twice the number in the street without the means of instruction. All the children and adults taught in the above named schools, are taxed £1 a year, except the English Church School, this is the most liberal. The Rev. Mr. Horton, a Baptist minister in Kingston, told me he had sent ninety children away from the Baptist school because they did not bring their money. It is sufficient to say they had it not to bring!

Most of the people of Jamaica are emancipated slaves, many of them are old, worn out and degraded. Those who are able to work, have yet many obstacles to contend with, and very little to encourage them; every advantage is taken of their ignorance; the same spirit of cruelty is opposed to them that held them for centuries in bondage; even religious teaching is bartered for their hard earnings, while they are allowed but thirty-three cents a day, and are told if they will not work for that they shall not work at all; an extraordinary price is asked of them for every thing they may wish to purchase, even the Bibles are sold to them at a large advance on the first purchase. Where are their apologists, if they are found wanting in the strict morals that Christians ought to practice? Who kindly says, forgive them when they err. "Forgive them, this is the bitter fruit of slavery." Who has integrity sufficient to hold the balance when these poor people are to be weighed? Yet their present state is blissful, compared with slavery.

Many of the farmers bring their produce twenty or thirty miles. Some have horses or ponies, but most of them bring their burdens on their head. As I returned from St. Andrew's Mountain . . . I was overtaken by a respectable looking man on horseback; we rode about ten miles in company. The story he told me of the wrongs he and his wife had endured while in slavery, are too horrible to narrate. My heart sickens when I think of it. He asked me many questions, such as where I came from? why I came to that Isle? where had I lived, &c. I told him I was sent for by one of the missionaries to help him in his school. Indeed, said he, our color need the instruction. I asked him why the colored people did not hire for themselves? We would be very glad to, he replied, but our money is taken from us so fast we cannot. Sometimes they say we must all bring 1l.; to raise this, we have to sell at a loss or to borrow, so that we have nothing left for ourselves; the Macroon hunters take all—this is a nickname they give the missionaries and the class-leaders—a cutting sarcasm this!

Arrived at a tavern, about a mile from Kingston, I bade the man adieu, and stopped for my guide. The inn-keeper kindly invited me in; he asked me several questions, and I asked him as many. How do the people get along, said I, since the emancipation? The negroes, he replied, will have the island in spite of the d——. Do not you see how they live, and how much they can bear? We cannot do so. This man was an Englishman, with a large family of mulatto children. I returned with my mind fully made up what to do. Spent three weeks at the Mico establishment, and three with my colored friends from America. We thought something ought to be done for the poor girls that were destitute; they consulted with their friends, called a meeting, and formed a society of forty; each agreed to pay three dollars a year and collect, and provide a house, while I came back to America to raise the money for all needful articles for the school. Here I met Mr. Ingraham for the first time; he had come from the mountains, and his health had rapidly declined. Wishing to get his family home before the Lord took him away, he embarked for Baltimore in the Orb, and I sailed for Philadelphia, July 20th, 1841, twenty-one days from Jamaica, in good health. I found there, Fitz W. Sargent's family, from Gloucester, who I lived with when a little girl; they received me very kindly, and gave donations of books and money for that object.

I met the AntiSlavery Society at Mrs. Lucretia Mott's,[6] who took great interest in the cause. I visited among the friends, and spent my time very pleasantly. August 5th, I started for New York; arrived safely, and staid [sic] with an old friend; ascertained that Mr. Ingraham's family were at Newark,

[6]Lucretia Mott (1793–1880) was one of the women delegates denied a seat at the World's Anti-Slavery Convention a year earlier. Her concern with abolitionism and other reform movements was thereafter supplemented by public advocacy of woman's rights.

at Theodore Wells'.[7] He died four days after his arrival. I was invited to Mrs. Ingraham's (his cousin's widow), to spend a week. There I met with much encouragement to labor in the cause. Missionaries were coming and going, and all seemed to be interested in my object. . . .

As soon as I was able, I commenced my task of collecting funds for my Free Labor School in Jamaica. I collected in Boston and vicinity, in New York and Philadelphia, but not sufficient to make up the required sum, and I was obliged to take fifty dollars from my own purse, thinking that when I returned to Jamaica, they would refund the money to me. April 15th, embarked on board the brig Norma, of New York, for Jamaica. I arrived at Kingston May 6th, and found every thing different from what it was when I left; the people were in a state of agitation, several were hanged, and the insurrection was so great that it was found necessary to increase the army to quell it. Several had been hanged. On the very day I arrived a man was hanged for shooting a man as he passed through the street. Such was the state of things that it was not safe to be there.

A few young people met to celebrate their freedom on an open plain, where they hold their market; their former masters and mistresses, envious of their happiness, conspired against them, and thought to put them down by violence. This only served to increase their numbers; but the oppressors were powerful, and succeeded in accomplishing their revenge, although many of them were relations. There was a rule among the slave holders, to take care of the children they have by their slaves; they select them out and place them in asylums. Those who lived with their white fathers were allowed great power over their slave mothers and her slave children; my heart was often grieved to see their conduct to their poor old grand parents. Those over twenty-one were freed in 1834, all under twenty-one were to serve their masters till twenty-one. It is well known that at that time, the children, alike with others, received twenty-five dollars a head for their relatives. Were I to tell all my eyes have seen among that people, it would not be credited. It is well known that those that were freed, knowing their children were still in bondage, were not satisfied. In the year 1838, general freedom throughout the British Islands gave the death blow to the power of the master, and mothers received with joy their emancipated children; they no longer looked the picture of despair, fearing to see their mulatto son or daughter beating or abusing their younger brothers and sisters of a darker skin. On this occasion there was an outrage committed by those who were in power. What little the poor colored people had gathered during their four years of freedom, was destroyed by violence; their fences were broken down, and their horses and hogs taken from them. . . .

. . . Had there been a vessel in readiness, I should have come back immediately, it seemed useless to attempt to establish a Manual Labor

---

[7]Undoubtedly a reference to Theodore D. Weld (1803–1895), leader of the "Lane rebels" and an outstanding figure among the early abolitionists.

School, as the government was so unsettled that I could not be protected. Some of my former friends were gone as teachers to Africa, and some to other parts of the island. I called on the American Consul to consult with him, he said that although such a school was much wanted, yet every thing seemed so unsettled that I had no courage to proceed. I told him there was so much excitement that I wished to leave the island as soon as he could find me a passage, it seemed useless to spend my time there. As soon as it was known that I intended to return, a movement was made to induce me to remain. I was persuaded to try the experiment for three months, not thinking their motive was bad. Before I left the United States, I got all that was needed, within fifty dollars. The fifty dollars I got from my own purse, expecting they would pay me. It cost me ten dollars for freight, and twenty-five for passage money; these people that I had hoped to serve, were much taken up with the things I had brought, they thought that I had money, and I was continually surrounded; the thought of color was no where exhibited, much notice was taken of me. I was invited to breakfast in one place, and to dine in another, &c. A society was organized, made up of men and women of authority. A constitution was drafted by my consent, by those who were appointed to meet at my rooms. Between the time of the adjournment they altered it to suit themselves. At the time appointed we came together with a spirit apparently becoming any body of Christians; most of them were members of Christian churches. The meeting was opened with reading the Scriptures and prayer. Then said the leader, since our dear sister has left her native land and her friends to come to us, we welcome her with our hearts and hands. She will dwell among us, and we will take care of her—Brethren think of it! after which he sat down, and the constitution was called for. The Preamble held out all the flattery that a fool could desire; after which they commenced the articles, supposing that they could do as they thought best. The fourth article unveiled their design. As we have designed to take care of our sister, *we the undersigned will take charge of all she has brought;* the vote was called, every person rose in a moment except myself: every eye was upon me; one asked me why I did not vote, I made no answer—they put the vote again and again, I remained seated. Well, said the President, we can do nothing without her vote; they remained some time silent, and then broke up the meeting. The next day the deacon called to see what the state of my mind was, and some of the women proposed that we should have another meeting. I told them no, I should do no more for them. As soon as they found they could not get the things in the way they intended, they started to plunder me; but I detected their design, and was on my guard. I disposed of the articles, and made ready to leave when an opportunity presented. A more skilful plan than this, Satan never designed, but the power of God was above it. It is not surprising that this people are full of deceit and lies, this is the fruits of slavery, it makes master and slaves knaves. . . .

. . . They made another attempt to rob me, and as a passage could not be obtained for me to return home, I was obliged to go to the Mico establishment again for safety, such was the outrage. Houses were broken open and robbed every night. I came very near being shot: there was a certain place where we placed ourselves the first of the evening. A friend came to bring us some refreshments, I had just left the window when a gun was fired through it, by one that often sat with us; this was common in the time of slavery. Previous to vessels arriving, passages were engaged. I disposed of my articles and furniture at a very small profit. On the 1st of August, Capt. A. Miner arrived, and advertised for passengers. The American Consul procured me a passage, and on the 18th of August, myself and nine other passengers embarked for New York.

Harriet Tubman

"General" Harriet Tubman was a secular saver of souls. Herself a fugitive from slavery in Maryland, she made repeated forays into the South to lead other slaves to freedom. Though alert to danger, she relied on a cool head, ingenuity, and a firm belief that her plans had divine sanction. It is said that a hidden revolver gave her confidence in added measure.

A married woman—her husband was John Tubman, a black free man—she fled her past of field and house labor when her future within slavery threatened the limited security that she knew. She was almost thirty, but childless, when her young master died in 1849. Deaths, like weddings, imperiled the stability of estates; the rumor spread that she and her fellow slaves were to be sold to distant buyers. Vainly she tried to persuade her brothers to escape along with her. Only years later, on two of her furtive missions, did she bring her brothers and her aged parents out to freedom in the North. In a decade of personal daring, she made twenty trips into the slave states. The hundreds of human chattels she rescued had a large commercial value; in consequence there was a sizable price on Harriet Tubman's head.

She was in and out of Canada, shepherding illegal caravans of black travelers to safety. She was acquainted with William Still and others, black and white, who gave aid to the Underground Railroad. At St. Catherines, Ontario, she met with John Brown and took part in the plans he was making for an armed raid on Harper's Ferry in Virginia.

When the Civil War altered the context for obtaining freedom, Harriet Tubman found new patterns for her work. Fortified with credentials from her abolitionist connections, she was soon en route to Beaufort, South Carolina, to serve in the Army's Department of the South. This "gnomelike, beturbaned little woman," as a recent historian pictures her, had unique and varied skills; she was used as a nurse, a scout, and a spy. Charlotte Forten, whose work among the freedmen is included in this volume, reported a visit to the "wonderful woman—a real heroine." A raiding expedition up the Combahee River in South Carolina enlisted Harriet Tubman to fill a special role. She was to encourage the slaves on the shoreline plantations to place their trust in the Union forces and defect to freedom. Over 700 slaves were freed in this massive exodus.

A woman of action, Harriet Tubman was also in command of words. She was not a stranger to the lecture platform, but a single listener or a *small circle was her more customary audience. Sharply observant as she had to be to carry off her exploits, she conveyed conviction and emotion through the recital of homely detail. This unpolished eloquence that thrilled the middle-class reformers served equally to inspire the men and women she piloted out of slavery.*

The excerpts presented here are Harriet Tubman's words as her friend and first biographer Sarah Bradford recorded them (the attempt to demonstrate her dialect has been dropped). First printed in 1869, these selections derive from Harriet Tubman's vivid reconstruction of the high moments of her career. Her memory remained reliable into her early nineties. Only two years before her death in 1913 she retold her part in the Combahee raid, singing once more the song she had used to reassure the slaves. Wrote her visitor later, "At the refrain 'come along,' Aunt Harriet waved her withered arm with an imperious gesture. After nearly fifty years it had not lost its appeal."[1]

[On reaching free soil as a fugitive slave]

I looked at my hands, to see if I was the same person now I was free. There was such a glory over everything, the sun came like gold through the trees, and over the fields, and I felt like I was in heaven. . . .

I had crossed the line of which I had so long been dreaming. I was free; but there was no one to welcome me to the land of freedom, I was a stranger in a strange land, and my home after all was down in the old cabin quarter, with the old folks, and my brothers and sisters. But to this solemn resolution I came; I was free, and they should be free also; I would make a home for them in the North, and the Lord helping me, I would bring them all there. Oh, how I prayed then, lying all alone on the cold, damp ground; "Oh, dear Lord," I said, "I ain't got no friend but you. Come to my help, Lord, for I'm in trouble!"

[On caring for wounded soldiers during the Civil War]

I'd go to the hospital, I would, early every morning. I'd get a big chunk of ice, I would, and put it in a basin, and fill it with water; then I'd

---

[1]The quotations above are from Willie Lee Rose, *Rehearsal for Reconstruction* (New York, 1967), p. 244; Charlotte Forten Grimké, *The Journal of Charlotte L. Forten*, ed. Ray Allen Billington (New York, 1953), p. 180; and James B. Clarke, "An Hour With Harriet Tubman," in William Edgar Easton, *Christophe: A Tragedy in Prose of Imperial Haiti* (Los Angeles, 1911), p. 121.

Source: Sarah Bradford, *Harriet Tubman, The Moses of her People* (New York: Corinth Books, 1961; reprinted from the 1886 edition), pp. 30–32, 97, 100–101, 105–6.

take a sponge and begin. First man I'd come to, I'd thrash away the flies, and they'd rise, they would, like bees round a hive. Then I'd begin to bathe the wounds, and by the time I'd bathed off three or four, the fire and heat would have melted the ice and made the water warm, and it would be as red as clear blood. Then I'd go and get more ice, I would, and by the time I got to the next ones, the flies would be round the first ones black and thick as ever.

[On the Combahee River raid, June 2, 1863, in which Harriet Tubman helped Union forces carry over 700 slaves to freedom]

I never saw such a sight; we laughed, and laughed, and laughed. Here you'd see a woman with a pail on her head, rice a-smoking in it just as she'd taken it from the fire, young one hanging on behind, one hand round her forehead to hold on, the other hand digging into the rice-pot, eating with all its might; hold of her dress two or three more; down her back a bag with a pig in it. One woman brought two pigs, a white one and a black one; we took them all on board; named the white pig Beauregard, and the black pig Jeff Davis. Sometimes the women would come with twins hanging around their necks; appears like I never saw so many twins in my life; bags on their shoulders, baskets on their heads, and young ones tagging behind, all loaded; pigs squealing, chickens screaming, young ones squalling.

[Harriet Tubman's account of an ex-slave's comments at Hilton Head, S.C.]

He said, "I'd been here seventy-three years, working for my master without even a dime wages. I'd worked rain-wet sun-dry. I'd worked with my mouth full of dust, but could not stop to get a drink of water. I'd been whipped, and starved, and I was always praying, 'Oh! Lord, come and deliver us!' All that time the birds had been flying, and the ravens had been crying, and the fish had been swimming in the waters. One day I look up, and I see a big cloud; it didn't come up like as the clouds come out far yonder, but it appeared to be right over head. There was thunders out of that, and there was lightnings. Then I looked down on the water, and I see, appeared to me a big house in the water, and out of the big house came great big eggs, and the good eggs went on through the air, and fell into the fort; and the bad eggs burst before they got there. Then the Sesh Buckra [slang for Secessionist whites] begin to run, and they never stop running till they get to the swamp, and they stick there and they die there. Then I heard 'twas the Yankee ship [the *Wabash*] firing out the big eggs, and they had come to set us free. Then I praised the Lord. He came and put his little finger in the work, and the Sesh Buckra all go; and the birds stop flying, and the ravens stop crying, and when I go to catch a fish to eat with my rice, there's no fish there. The Lord Almighty had come and frightened them all out of the waters. Oh! Praise the Lord! I'd prayed seventy-three years, and now he's come and we's all free."

Sarah Parker Remond

Sarah Parker Remond belongs to the company of nineteenth-century black women although she moved within a current of special activity. Sister of Charles Lenox Remond, one of the foremost abolitionists, she was herself a well-known member of this coterie of dissidents. Her abilities, the depth of her powers, and the magnanimity of her cause associate her with other black women—Frances Watkins Harper and Charlotte Forten, for instance— who were the implacable foes of slavery. Charles Lenox Remond, known as the "Count D'Orsay of the Antislavery movement," was described as "small in stature, . . . neat wiry build, genteel appearance and pleasant voice." He was also a fine horseman, and his personal dress and appearance did not go unnoticed. Sarah Remond's character and personality were the feminine counterparts of her brother's. Both were born in Salem, Massachusetts, Sarah Remond in 1815. Their maternal grandfather had fought for American independence; their father was a free black who hailed from Curaçao.

Salem, a major center of abolitionist sentiment, was honored for the history its citizens had made and were then making. Sarah Remond grew to womanhood in a free society. Her city, her home, and her state provided an atmosphere of comparative safety and peace warmed by the companionship of a much respected brother and a rewarding life of her own. Because of its reputation as a hub of humanitarianism, Salem was marked on the itinerary of many antislavery leaders. The Remonds became the friends and acquaintances of men in the foreground of the fight for freedom, including William Lloyd Garrison. If anything marred the serenity of the Remonds' lives, it was the inequalities and inhumanities of serfdom. Regardless of their ancestry, their education, or their gentility, they were black. Acceptance by the people with whom they chose to consort or by those who wished to consort with them did not shelter the Remonds from the indignities to which they on occasion and others more constantly were subject. It did not matter that the oppressed were black; it mattered that they were human beings. The Remonds were democrats and humanitarians, for it does not matter which feeling came first, the feeling of identification with one's own group or the feeling for mankind. Wounded though the Remonds were, their efforts to destroy the slavery system gave them a modicum of tranquillity.

Miss Remond was exceptional among black females. Never a slave, never the unwilling concubine of a plantation lord, never the undeserving victim of brutality, she was well-bred, well-educated, well-clothed, and well-housed. She was accustomed to civility and generosity. Kind and informed people were her companions and confidants. She required neither protector nor sponsor; she needed but a purpose to enrich her life and she had one.

She joined her brother as a lecturer for the American Anti-Slavery Society in 1856 and became one of a team of speakers for New York State. William Lloyd Garrison, a member of the team, toured with them. The Liberator contains his report:

> Miss Sarah P. Remond, (a sister of C. L. Remond,) made her first efforts at public speaking on this extended tour, and every where commanded the respect and secured the attention of her auditors. Her calm, dignified manner, her winning personal appearance, and her earnest appeals to the conscience and heart, produced a very favorable impression. She only needs practice to become a very useful lecturer.

Away from the pleasant insulation of Salem, prejudice stabbed her pride and ignited her conscience. "Hotels," wrote another member of the group in his recollections, " . . . which would receive Miss [Susan B.] Anthony and myself, rudely denied admission to them, and solely on the ground of color." A short time later she went on a similar mission to Britain, understandably apprehensive about her reception in a strange land. She was received with warmth. When, after a lecture, she was presented with the gift of a watch as a mark of respect and admiration, she responded: "I have been removed from the degradation which overhangs all persons of my complexion; and I have felt most deeply that since I have been in Warrington and in England, I have received a sympathy I never was offered before. I had therefore no need of this testimonial of sympathy, but I receive it as the representative of my race with pleasure." The watch bore the inscription: "Presented to S. P. Remond by Englishwomen, her sisters, in Warrington, February 2nd, 1859."

The second part of her tour took her to Dublin. Relations between Ireland and the United States had been multiplied during the preceding decade. Vast numbers of Irish people, impoverished by successive failures of the potato harvest, had emigrated in search of new opportunities for survival, if not for prosperity, some to the slave states but most to the more opulent North. Sarah Remond endeavored to build antislavery sentiment among her Irish listeners, for Irishmen had a potential influence among affluent visitors from American slave states who were making the "grand tour" of the British Isles. They also had an influence upon relatives and friends already in America, some of whom had succumbed to proslavery dialectics:

> Too many who perhaps had felt persecution themselves, and had left the country filled with aspirations for human freedom, had no sooner become

residents in America and had dwelt there sufficiently long to become imbued with the all prevailing spirit of intolerance inculcated by the slave-holders, than they were to be found to go the fullest length which tyranny could desire, "going the whole ticket" in the pro-slavery interest.

Sarah Remond reached London in midsummer of 1859. Her forceful presence stimulated the formation of the London Emancipation Committee. While in London she was the guest of William and Ellen Craft, the brave couple who had escaped from slavery and who both became supporters of this project. The Leeds Young Men's Anti-Slavery Society next engaged her oratorical skills. She was beyond wearying. During the Christmas holidays, to give but a hint of her prowess, she lectured at least eight times in half a dozen cities in less than three weeks.

The coming of the Civil War infused her work with transcendent import. The United States—and therefore black men and women—needed British diplomatic support. The International Congress of Charities, Correction, and Philanthropy heard her plea. She referred to the old argument based on the similarity between enslaved blacks and English textile workers: "The free operatives of Britain are, in reality, brought into almost personal relations with slaves during their daily toil." And she added another exhortation: "Let no diplomacy of statesmen, no intimidation of slaveholders, no scarcity of cotton, no fear of slave insurrections, prevent the people of Great Britain from maintaining their position as the friend of the oppressed negro."

Home once more in 1866, she refused to allow herself pause. Slavery was no more, but former slaves, if not rescued, were certain to perish. Former slaves must therefore be transformed into free men and free women. Sarah Remond and her brother joined with Frederick Douglass and a group of whites on a New York State speaking tour. Their object was equal political rights for women and for black men. Once again she traveled to England where in 1867 she attended a celebration in honor of William Lloyd Garrison. She had done her work and done it well. America had need of her but she was surfeited with struggle. There was appeal in Europe and there were other yearnings that surged within her. Although she was now past the meridian of life, she wished to study medicine. She went to Florence to obtain a degree.[1]

---

[1]Ray Allen Billington, ed., The Journal of Charlotte L. Forten (New York, 1953), p. 16; Liberator, 6 March 1857; Aaron M. Powell, Personal Reminiscences of the Anti-Slavery and other Reforms and Reformers (New York, 1899), p. 171; Liberator, 11 March 1859; Sarah Parker Remond, "The Negroes in the United States of America," Journal of Negro History 27 (April 1942): 218. See also Dorothy B. Porter, "Sarah Parker Remond, Abolitionist and Physician," Journal of Negro History 20 (July 1935): 287–93; the biographical sketch by Dorothy B. Porter in Notable American Women, ed. Edward T. James and Janet Wilson James (Cambridge, Mass., 1971), III, 136–38; Ruth Bogin, "Sarah Parker Remond: Black Abolitionist from Salem," Essex Institute Historical Collections 110 (April 1974): 120–50.

Pursuant to announcement, a meeting of the members and friends of the Dublin Ladies' Anti-Slavery Society was held on Friday evening, the 11th of March, for the purpose of hearing a Lecture on American Slavery, from Miss S.P. Remond of Salem (Mass.), a lady of colour, whose fame had preceded her, as a gifted and zealous advocate of the cause of her oppressed race. The spacious Concert Room wherein the meeting was held, was crowded with a most respectable assemblage of citizens of both sexes, and the platform was thronged by ladies and gentlemen who are well known friends of the anti-slavery movement. Several eminent clergymen, professors of the University, and others, were present, and took part in the proceedings. The chair was taken by

James Haughton, Esq., who said, that while it gave him great pleasure to see around him so influential an assemblage, he regretted the absence of their chief magistrate, who had intended to be present and preside. His Lord-ship had written to state, that the Lady Mayoress had accepted, on his part and her own, an engagement of which he had been unaware, and which would prevent him from attending the meeting. Thus the ladies would per-ceive how great was the power they possessed, how undeniable the influence they exercised (hear, hear, and cheers).[1] He hoped they would always exercise that power in the right direction, in promoting the welfare of their fellow-creatures (cheers). It was to the Ladies' Committee of the Anti-Slavery Society that they owed the present gratifying meeting, for the purpose of hearing from the lips of a gifted lady from the other side of the Atlantic, some information on the iniquitous system of American slavery. When this subject was con-sidered in its proper light, the wonder was, that the people of this country, as well as those of all other civilized countries, were not banded together to promote its condemnation and total abolition. Although the Irish people, as a nation, always kept their hands clean from participation in the guilt of the African slave trade, that did not weaken their responsibility. It might be that our countrymen in America were sometimes misled, and their ideas perverted by the outcry of mob opinion in favour of slaveholding, but he would only say to Irishmen, in the name of their dear country, and for the honour of our race as men and Christians, let them, wherever they may be, unite earnestly and energetically with societies whose aim is to abolish slavery throughout the length and breadth of the United States.

Source: "Miss Remond's First Lecture in Dublin," *Anti-Slavery Advocate* (London), 2 (April 1859): 221–24. Paragraph structure revised by editors. All footnotes are the editors'.

[1]"Hear, hear" is a traditional phrase of approval, comparable to applause or "right on," used chiefly by audiences in the British Isles.

Miss S.P. Remond was then introduced to the meeting by the chairman, and was received with most flattering demonstrations of welcome and respect. She said she had the honour to stand before that large and influential assemblage that evening as the representative of four millions of men and women, their fellow-beings, robbed of every right, deprived of every privilege; the representative of a class so mercilessly abused, so recklessly crushed, and so ruthlessly outraged, that the story of their wrongs was a subject which should command the earnest sympathy of every friend of humanity; whilst their cause was one which should enlist the hearty cooperation of every lover of liberty, and every sincere Christian throughout the civilized world. The monster evil of American slavery—some of whose workings it should be her task to lay before the meeting—involved not alone the fate of a race, but the destiny of a nation.

It might, perhaps, be well to give some description of the position of the Northern and the Southern States as regards slavery and its influences, for they would be found to be very dissimilar. In the sixteen free States where slavery is prohibited, the law was very different and very differently administered, as contrasted with the fifteen States where slavery is sanctioned by law. In the Northern States, where wealth and intelligence abound, and where a stimulus is given to exertion by the prospect of independence, there labour is elevating, is honourable. No man or woman is degraded or thought little of who labours honestly to earn a livelihood. Not so, however, in the Southern States (hear). Where honest labour is degraded, spurned, and despised by a would-be purse-proud, self-styled aristocracy, the meanest, the most vicious, and the most contemptible in the whole world; (cheers) all people of colour are degraded and insulted, not only the miserable slave, but also the free black man—nay, the whitest skin is no protection; for many thousands of unhappy beings, whose skin is perfectly fair, in whose features or persons not a trace of African blood could be observed, are the doomed and despairing victims of American slavery.

First in the ranks of the sufferers is the poor degraded slave—a thing to be bought and sold—liable to be beaten to death with impunity, if a man; or to be made the victim of brutal licentiousness, if a female—a mere item of chattel property, having no legal right to use the intelligence or strength which God has given, save at the will and for the profit of the owners (cheers). But this was not the time for dwelling on the horrors and miseries of the lot of the poor slave. Time this evening was too precious to admit of any detail of those sickening and soul-harrowing scenes, which, alas! are too common in Slave States to command a passing notice. It might be enough to state that at the beck of a cruel master, husband and wife are continually separated and sold, never again to meet in this world; children are torn from their parents, and mothers bereaved of their beloved little ones. In numerous slave establishments, packs of bloodhounds were kept and trained for the purpose of hunting down the fugitive who loves life less than liberty (cheers). It would be indeed a sad and fearful task to give even an outline of the miseries endured by the slaves, or the brutalities practised by the inhuman slaveholders. Man degraded, lashed, and tortured even to death; womanhood defenceless, exposed to the very wantonness of insult, and without protection from the licentiousness of a brutal master. It cannot be denied that "Eliza Harris" was no fancied character, or that "Madame Cassie" was no imaginary picture. There were still in the hands of merciless and licentious slaveholders women suffering even more than those, and enduring bitterer wrong, and more cruel outrage.

Such were the results of American slavery. These facts should be impressed upon all, that those tyrants and their abettors had degraded their fellow-men to the level of the brutes. Was it not the fact that five-and-twenty thousand slaves were "raised" annually in the most northern of the Slave States, to supply the human flesh market in the South, even as herds of cattle were reared and fattened in order to supply the Southern shambles? (hear). Is it not true that in the proud city of Washington, the capital of the American Union, may be seen on stated days, numbers of enslaved human beings, group after group, in chains and fettered in pairs, driven like beasts to the auction mart to be sold like cattle to the highest bidder? (sensation.) Was it not the fact that on the first Friday of the present month, a sale of this description took place? Ay, took place in the city of Washington (hisses). The slaves were marched through the streets to the place of sale, well guarded. There were white men in front and white men in the rear, armed with loaded weapons, lest the slaves, the victims of their rapacity, goaded to desperation, might assert their God-given right as men, and regain their liberty. (Cheers.) Bitter indeed it was for the lover of the freedom of the human race (white, as well as coloured) to be compelled to avow, with shame, that America was, and deserved to be, the scorn and the reproach of all good men in every part of the civilized world (cheers). Happily, the free and enlightened denizens of this country were in a position to judge coolly, justly, and impartially on a subject so artfully slurred over and misrepresented by interested parties and their adherents, so marred by lukewarm friends and conceding philanthropists, and so opposed by the upholders of American slavery.

She (Miss Remond) would now place herself and the great cause she represented in the hands of that audience which represented so numerously and influentially the citizens of the Irish metropolis. She would ask them, without challenging the principles or feelings of a single individual amongst them, to become a jury in the issue between their fellow-immortal and his self-styled master; between the slave and his self-styled owner; between man's natural birthright of freedom derived from God, and the claim over the person of that human being, grounded on payment of a certain number of dollars, and certified by a bill of sale of a licensed appraiser of "live stock and other chattel property" (loud cheers). She (Miss Remond) would ask them to put themselves in the place of a jury, and to decide truly and give a verdict according to their conscience.

She stood there to advocate and inculcate, with all the energy of her soul, the truly noble and upright principles avowed, taught, and defended by the "ultra abolitionists" of the United States, those true friends of freedom and of the human race. She would invite her audience to imitate the energy, the zeal, the courage, and the perseverance of that noble band of philanthropists—the very salt of the American people—whose exertions and sacrifices in the cause of human liberty, and for the utter abolition of slavery in America, it was impossible to exaggerate, but which would become matter of history, yet to be read and dwelt on with pride by their descendants (cheers). It was the simple truth that many of these illustrious friends of freedom, both men and women, had devoted their time, their fortunes, and untiring personal labours to the noble cause of abolishing slavery in America (cheers). An amount of odium, obloquy, and hatred was daily visited upon them, such as no dweller in England or Ireland could have an idea of. One should be for a time in absolute contact with the American people (especially in the slaveholding States), and be a witness of the brutal acerbity prevailing against what is called the "Slave population," to comprehend the vindictive malice levelled by the slaveholders and their friends against those who would fain assert the slave's right to the equal privileges of human beings.

People here do not and cannot fathom the terrible depth and darkness of the abyss of "American slavery" (hear). There was no use in concealing or glossing over the fact. The truth was, that the honest and earnest minded abolitionists had an arduous, a terrible, task to encounter. But were they discouraged by the immensity of the obstacles opposed to them, or dismayed by the difficulties and dangers in their path? No, far from it. They were progressing—slowly perhaps, but yet steadily and surely—day after day (cheers). The abolitionists were, happily, as sincere and earnest in their efforts as the upholders of the slavery system were obstinate in their opposition. The abolitionists being true friends of freedom, were conscious that their philanthropic exertions tended not only to the rescue of the black slave from the curse of bondage, but would also be the means of eventually redeeming the very oppressors of those slaves from ruin and disaster, the inevitable results of a continuance of enforced slavery in coming times (immense cheering).

W. Lloyd Garrison, the veteran leader of the abolitionists (whose name should ever be spoken of with respect by every lover of freedom) did not ask the American people to carry out a new principle; he merely applied a new test. He did not dream, when he began his efforts to free the slaves, that he was also working for the redemption of the whites. He made his first appeal to the Christian Church, for there he felt should be his first field of effort, and possibly of success. But how was he met? At first with coolness, apathy, and indifference—then with covert sneers and injurious calumnies; and at last by open and vindictive opposition. Such had been the reception "religion" (so called) had accorded to devoted effort in the cause of human freedom (groans). Such was the case even now, because (as had been already observed) the religious as well as the literary, the commercial, the political, and other influences in the States, were in favour of the strong against the weak; in favour of rampant despotism against unoffending helplessness; it was marshalled, in short, on the side of American slavery.

She (Miss Remond) did not stand before that assemblage to advocate the cause of the slaves in America, merely because she was identified with them in complexion (an accident of which she was proud), but because they were men and women. Were they white as alabaster, they would be but men and women still, and, alas! slaves also. It was on the broad, comprehensive, and intelligible principle of that mutual love and charity which ought to exist amongst fellow-beings that she stood there to advocate the cause of the most outraged and oppressed of all God's creatures; it was because she remembered and took to heart the divine precept, *"Forasmuch as ye shall do it even to the least of these, my little ones, ye shall do it unto me"* (loud cheers). The true and sincere abolitionists in America inculcate and act on the maxim, "God is our father and the creator of us all, whatever may be our colour, complexion, race, or country. We are all equal in the sight of God." This also was a maxim taught and practically illustrated in the lives and acts of the early Christians, who worshipped the true God in secret in the catacombs of Pagan Rome (cheers). These were the sentiments which, emanating from the glowing heart of the Saviour and from his sacred lips, still characterize the acts and doings of those who were known as "ultra abolitionists" in America, who are stigmatized by every vile reproach, both as a body and individually, which vindictive malice can suggest. The abolitionists are not identified with any political party; their watch word is, "The immediate and unconditional abolition of American slavery." There is one political party (the Republicans, so called) who professed themselves to be opposed to the extension of slavery into free states or free territory, and who were to this extent hostile to the system; but they had not laid the axe to the root of the tree.

In the United States, as far as slavery is concerned, the abolitionists alone inculcate and act on the maxim that "duty to man is love to God." They assert that the emancipation of the slave would be eventually the redemption (temporally speaking) of all classes of their countrymen. They know and feel that the influence of Great Britain and Ireland on public opinion and feeling in America can hardly be overrated. (Hear.) Great Britain had now reached a degree of influence and civilization, such as had never before been attained by any country. Rome in the palmiest days of her imperial splendour had not approached it. Her navies covered the ocean; ships freighted with her merchandize crowded the harbours of the old and new world. Her colonies were flourishing in every region of the globe, and the sound of the morning and evening drums of her garrisoned troops encircled the whole earth. These facts were known and spoken of in America, and this might serve to show the estimation of British power and greatness in the minds of the American people.

Every year about forty thousand Americans visit the shores of Great Britain, penetrate to its remotest districts, and examine with curious avidity its public institutions, and the social habits of its people. Many of these visitors belong to the class who are the interested upholders of the slavery system. They mingle with society in Great Britain and do their best to promulgate their own opinions. Thus it could be felt that the spirit of American slavery had passed across the Atlantic, and thus these three hundred and forty seven thousand American slave-holders arrogate to themselves the representation of public opinion in America, and insolently assume the office of dictating to the people of Great Britain how they should feel and think, and what they should or should not do respecting it. But should they be permitted to do so? (Cries of No, No, and cheers.) No! she (Miss Remond) would repeat a thousand times No. (Cheers.) The slave-holders in America, and those who were bound up with them in the unholy system, had sought to create a community of interest and consequently of opinion throughout the civilized world in favour of slavery. They made cotton growing and the question of the supply of cotton the ground of their appeal to selfish and commercial interests. (Hear.) Yes, interest of one kind or another would be found to underlie every specious falsehood, every delusive pretext, held up in favour of American slavery. They would be told that England had nothing to do with slavery in America; but was it not criminal to encourage the existence of a crime by tacit connivance with its perpetrators?

The question the world put to the people of England was, would they or would they not range themselves on the side of the weak and the oppressed against the strong and the unjust? Would they unite with the true friends of human freedom throughout the world, in calling for sympathy and protection for the down trodden slave, and in invoking on his behalf the moral influence and exertions of good men in every land? The American advocates of that noble cause always looked for the exercise of British influence on their side. They did more than request—they demanded it. (Cheers.)

The American people were not conscious of the power which slavery had insensibly gained over themselves. Were this not the case, Mr. President Buchanan would not have officially asserted that there was no danger of the slave trade being re-opened, whilst the fact was, that scarcely had the message containing this declaration been circulated amongst the people, than authentic intelligence arrived of the landing of a cargo of African slaves on the coast of Georgia. Yes, though the traffic was declared to be "piracy" by international law, it still prevailed, despite of the measures which were taken for its suppression, and President Buchanan was compelled to acknowledge the fact; for how could he evade the truth in the face of the announcement that not less than fifteen vessels had sailed from New Orleans in pursuit of that hateful traffic? Facts upon facts too painfully true were forthcoming to prove the continued and extensive practice of this American trade in human beings; but, owing to the baneful influence of the slave-holding interest, these proofs were unheeded and the evil flourished. The futile attempts to subdue or put it down had only the effect of raising the market and enhancing the rateable value of human victims, thus giving a new stimulus to lawless enterprise, and adding increased horror to the sufferings of the wretched beings who were packed in the noisome holds of small vessels which are now used, in order the more readily to escape capture. So long as a market was kept open for the sale of God's creatures as if they were beasts of the field; so long as interested prejudice sustained the spirit and practice of American slavery, so long would mere half measures fail to ensure its abolition.

The extent of pro-slavery influence in America could not be overrated. It was deeply rooted and extensive, as it was relentless in its operation. (Hear, hear.) Surely the slave was the first and deepest sufferer. But did the evil stop there? No! thousands of enlightened and intelligent men and women, free denizens of the American States, unoffending in conduct, amiable in disposition, and deserving in every way of respect and esteem, if connected, no matter how slightly or remotely, with the proscribed race, were daily, hourly subjected to treatment such as is inflicted on the lowest criminals as the punishment of their crimes. Thus it was that the despotism of three hundred and forty seven thousand slave-holders cast its withering shadow over the free soil of America, trampling down the feelings and crushing out the very hearts of her people. Every man and woman and child of colour in the United States were held under the tyranny of a hostile opinion. Strangers in the land even of their birth, they had no rights, and were placed as it were out of the pale of society; and yet this was the law. In a recent case where this very question of the rights of the coloured race was involved, nine judges of the Supreme Court of the United States sat to examine it. Five of them were slave-holders, and the other four were not much better. Two of those four gave an opinion in accordance with that of the five slave-holders, and the other two, to save appearances and compelled by the force of public opinion in Massachusetts, pronounced an opinion apparently opposed to that of the other seven—which was to the effect "that the colored man in the United States cannot be regarded as a citizen, and that he has no rights which the white citizens are bound to respect." This is the substance of the infamous "Dred Scott decision," which is so designated as it was given on a case in which a negro whose name was Dred Scott was one of the parties. After this, what becomes of the boast that there is no country in the world wherein freedom is enjoyed so fully as in America?

But American despotism would yet have to meet a bitter day of reckoning. It would yet be quoted in solemn warning to other states and nations. It carried within itself the seeds of its own decay, and it would involve in its own destruction that of the system which has so long and so viciously upheld it. The "glorious Union" would be severed, and the sooner the better; liberty and slavery are ever incompatible, and only when the American people can be got to comprehend and appreciate genuine liberty, would the last fetter on the limbs of the slave be broken. Was it genuine love of liberty to be willing to give to those who were dear to us, the rights and the privileges which we prized and desired for ourselves? No! The genuine lovers of freedom would be ready and anxious to concede cheerfully and willingly to all their fellow-beings, belonging to no matter what race or clime, the very same rights and enjoyments that they possessed and appreciated themselves. Such was the kind of liberty which was now obtained by the Neapolitan exiles [refugees from Naples who fled to Ireland in the wake of the Revolution of 1848] who had recently taken refuge in this country (hear, hear, and cheers). This was the liberty which the abolitionists were seeking to preach and to inculcate. She (Miss Remond) was gratified that these men had landed on the shores of Ireland, rather than on the soil of America. She knew, that here they would find freedom of opinion, of thought, and of action, in its purest acceptation. She knew that slavery could not breathe in that land, whose soil the slave no sooner touches than his shackles fall. Such was not the case in America. If those men had gone there they might have fallen before the same dreadful and despotic influence, to which too many even from this country had unworthily succumbed. Too many who perhaps had felt persecution themselves, and had left the country filled with aspirations for human freedom, had no sooner become residents in America and had dwelt there sufficiently long to become imbued with the all prevailing spirit of intolerance inculcated by the slave-holders, than they were to be found to go the fullest length which tyranny could desire, "going the whole ticket" in the pro-slavery interest, and in fact, becoming basely subservient—men who glory in their iniquitous assumption of property in their fellow men.

In America it was as much as a man's reputation and social position were worth, to take up or identify himself with the cause of "Abolition." To avow one's self an Abolitionist, subjected a man to persecution such as people in this country could form no conception of. Twenty-four years ago, William Lloyd Garrison, the devoted and courageous apostle of the cause of Freedom, was attacked by an infuriate[d] mob in the city of Boston, for daring to proclaim that the black slave was a man, and an equal in the sight of God with his tyrant oppressor. He had to encounter more than once the near prospect of a martyr's death at the hands of the abettors of American slavery. The State of Georgia had offered a reward of 5,000 dollars for his head; this offer was still uncancelled; and on one occasion, to save his life, he had to seek refuge within the walls of a jail, whilst the Boston mob without were thirsting for his blood.

But now the advocates of the slave had conquered the right of free speech, and although hissed occasionally, yet they were listened to. This question was even now becoming more actively and frequently canvassed than ever in the Northern States of the Union, whilst in Congress it continually turns up and becomes the subject of discussion. The representatives of the Northern States never allowed the subject to sleep. They never lose an opportunity of raising the formidable question which, by mere iteration, was gradually forcing itself on men's minds, "Has any man a just right to enslave his fellow-being? Shall Americans continue to hold property in their fellow-men?" The Abolitionists had their task before them, and their determination was never to cease to "agitate, agitate, agitate," until justice was done to the oppressed, and the stain of human slavery was banished from the American soil.

She made her appeal to women on behalf of the female slave, the most deplorably and helplessly wretched of human sufferers. Of all who drooped and writhed under the inflictions of this horrible system, the greatest sufferer was defenceless woman (hear). For the male slave, however brutally treated, there was some resource; but for the woman slave there was neither protection nor pity. If the veriest scoundrel, the meanest coward, the most loathsome ruffian, covets the person or plots the ruin of a defenceless female, provided she be known to be, ever so remotely, of African descent, she is in his power (sensation). Remember, this did not depend upon colour. She might possess the loveliness of a sylph; she might be endowed with the dignified beauty of a Cleopatra, or have the winning grace and charming innocence of a Juliet; she might be rich in every rare gift and accomplishment which can enhance female beauty; let her skin be white as alabaster, it has only to be shown that she holds even remote affinity with the proscribed race; it has only to be known that she is the child of a slave and a slave herself, she is liable to the brutality of the vilest wretches, and may be finally auctioned and sold at any time at the will of her "master." (Miss Remond here proceeded to read an extract from a recent work, descriptive of a harrowing scene at the sale of a beautiful young female, and then proceeded.) She could go on thus furnishing a thousand painful instances, enforcing her appeal to women on behalf of the female slave, but she felt she need not; for when were the women of this country ever backward in the cause of humanity? (Cheers.) Every where woman was found ready to aid in every good work, as of old, the first at the cross and the last at the tomb. Need she name Elizabeth Fry[2] or Florence Nightingale? (cheers). Should not woman take her part in this great work also?

Miss Remond, in conclusion, thanked the assemblage for their attention, and resumed her seat amidst enthusiastic plaudits.

[A series of tributes to the speaker followod.]

Miss Remond came forward, amidst renewed plaudits, and said she wished to thank them all, Ladies and Gentlemen, for the kind attention with which they had followed her through the course of a necessarily lengthened address on a painful subject (cheers). If by any means she could have conveyed the spirit as well as the matter of this meeting to America, the slaves would take courage and rejoice in renewed hope of freedom, and their advocates would work with renewed vigor, and the slaveholders would believe that the hour of retribution was at hand, that they saw "the handwriting on the wall," and that their unholy power was passing away for ever (loud cheers).

---

[2]Elizabeth Fry (1780–1845) was an English philanthropist noted especially for her work on behalf of prison reform.

Sojourner Truth

Sojourner Truth, once a slave named Isabella, was transformed through achieving freedom and embracing mysticism. A new woman with a new name, her mission was no longer to labor for an owner but to serve her people and her God.

She was a legend during her lifetime. Extraordinary height, a powerful voice, and a flair for dramatic communication with her audiences spread her fame in the decade before the Civil War. Yet her early years had been harsh. Born a slave in New York State near the close of the eighteenth century, she was sold away from both parents while still a child. She knew heavy farm work, cruel masters, the ripping away of some of her own children.

New York's laws abolished slavery in 1827. This slave woman not only took her own freedom a year earlier, but waged a successful battle to retrieve a son illegally sold and destined for Alabama. She soon attached herself to an evangelical couple; all three joined forces with a small commune. When this venture ended, she lived in New York City for an interval, supporting herself and two small children by domestic work.

Religious fervor stirred within her. She felt impelled to spread the news of a God of love. Adopting a new name for her new life as a wandering enthusiast, she traveled into New England where she first met organized abolitionism. The encounter was of mutual significance. For Sojourner Truth the freedom movement was the secular counterpart of spiritual salvation. She brought to the abolitionists a striking and original style. Bold in spirit, intuitive in gauging hecklers and spellbound audiences alike, she electrified her listeners on numerous occasions. "As well attempt to report the seven apocalyptic thunders," wrote the reformer Parker Pillsbury, recalling a public meeting where she refuted a statement on racial inferiority.[1]

The Civil War redirected her tireless powers. She campaigned for support to the black enlistees and concerned herself with newly freed blacks. A trip to Washington brought her an interview with President Lincoln himself.

---

[1]Lillie Buffum Chace Wyman, *American Chivalry* (Boston, 1913), p. 107.

Rights for women were as urgent to Sojourner Truth as rights for slaves and freedmen. Her testimony as a former slave was comprehensive. Mere fragments of Sojourner Truth's compelling oratory survive. Never having learned to read or write, she spoke extemporaneously. Stenographic reporters or admiring friends from time to time recorded her words.

Two decades of activities are represented in the excerpts included here. The first marked her appearance at the 1851 woman's rights convention in Akron, Ohio. The second is a letter written by a friend at her dictation, describing her interview with President Lincoln in 1864. The third excerpt dates from 1867 when Sojourner Truth put her energies into the campaign of the newly formed American Equal Rights Association to eliminate both "white" and "male" from the suffrage regulations in New York State. Her opening words respond to the ovation that greeted her at the convention of this group. Following the convention Sojourner Truth remained in New York City as a guest in the home of Elizabeth Cady Stanton, a leader of the Equal Rights organization. While the Stanton youngsters read the newspapers to their house guest, their mother recorded Sojourner Truth's informal comments. Portions of these comprise the fourth selection. The final excerpts present Sojourner Truth's 1870 petition for the granting of Western lands to the freedmen congregated around Washington, and a speech to a Boston audience on New Year's Day, 1871, celebrating the eighth anniversary of the Emancipation Proclamation.

I

Well, children, where there is so much racket there must be something out of kilter. I think that 'twixt the negroes of the South and the women at the North, all talking about rights, the white men will be in a fix pretty soon. But what's all this here talking about?

That man over there says women need to be helped into carriages, and lifted over ditches, and to have the best place everywhere. Nobody ever helps me into carriages, or over mud-puddles, or gives me any best place! And ain't I a woman? Look at me! Look at my arm! I have ploughed, and planted, and gathered into barns, and no man could head me! And ain't I a woman? I could work as much and eat as much as a man—when I could get it—and bear the lash as well! And ain't I a woman? I have borne thirteen children, and seen them most all sold off to slavery, and when I cried out with my mother's grief, none but Jesus heard me! And ain't I a woman?

Source: Elizabeth Cady Stanton, Susan B. Anthony, and Matilda Joslyn Gage, eds., History of Woman Suffrage (Rochester, N.Y., 1881), I, 116. The speech was recorded in part by Mrs. Frances D. Gage, who presided over the meeting. The dialect Mrs. Gage attempted to record has been dropped.

Then they talk about this thing in the head; what's this they call it? ["Intellect," whispered someone near.] That's it, honey. What's that got to do with women's rights or negro rights? If my cup won't hold but a pint, and yours holds a quart, wouldn't you be mean not to let me have my little half-measure full?

Then that little man in black there, he says women can't have as much rights as men, because Christ wasn't a woman! Where did your Christ come from? Where did your Christ come from? From God and a woman! Man had nothing to do with Him. . . .

If the first woman God ever made was strong enough to turn the world upside down all alone, these women together ought to be able to turn it back, and get it right side up again! And now they are asking to do it, the men better let them.

II

"FREEDMAN'S VILLAGE, VA., Nov. 17, 1864.

"DEAR FRIEND:—

"I am at Freedman's Village. After visiting the president, I spent three weeks at Mrs. Swisshelm's, and held two meetings in Washington, at Rev. Mr. Garnet's Presbyterian Church, for the benefit of the Colored Soldiers' Aid Society. These meetings were successful in raising funds. One week after that I went to Mason's Island, and saw the freedmen there, and held several meetings, remained a week and was present at the celebration of the emancipation of the slaves of Maryland, and spoke on that occasion.

"It was about 8 o'clock A.M., when I called on the president. Upon entering his reception room we found about a dozen persons in waiting, among them two colored women. I had quite a pleasant time waiting until he was disengaged, and enjoyed his conversation with others; he showed as much kindness and consideration to the colored persons as to the whites—if there was any difference, more. One case was that of a colored woman who was sick and likely to be turned out of her house on account of her inability to pay her rent. The president listened to her with much attention, and spoke to her with kindness and tenderness. He said he had given so much he could give no more, but told her where to go and get the money, and asked Mrs. C——n to assist her, which she did.

"The president was seated at his desk. Mrs. C. said to him, 'This is

Source: Olive Gilbert, Narrative of Sojourner Truth, with a History of Her Labors and Correspondence, Drawn from Her "Book of Life" (Battle Creek, Mich., 1884), pp. 176–80.

Sojourner Truth, who has come all the way from Michigan to see you.' He then arose, gave me his hand, made a bow, and said, 'I am pleased to see you.'

"I said to him, Mr. President, when you first took your seat I feared you would be torn to pieces, for I likened you unto Daniel, who was thrown into the lion's den; and if the lions did not tear you into pieces, I knew that it would be God that had saved you; and I said if he spared me I would see you before the four years expired, and he has done so, and now I am here to see you for myself.

"He then congratulated me on my having been spared. Then I said, I appreciate you, for you are the best president who has ever taken the seat. He replied: 'I expect you have reference to my having emancipated the slaves in my proclamation. But,' said he, mentioning the names of several of his predecessors (and among them emphatically that of Washington), 'they were all just as good, and would have done just as I have done if the time had come. If the people over the river [pointing across the Potomac] had behaved themselves, I could not have done what I have; but they did not, which gave me the opportunity to do these things.' I then said, I thank God that you were the instrument selected by him and the people to do it. I told him that I had never heard of him before he was talked of for president. He smilingly replied, 'I had heard of you many times before that.'

"He then showed me the Bible presented to him by the colored people of Baltimore, of which you have no doubt seen a description. I have seen it for myself, and it is beautiful beyond description. After I had looked it over, I said to him, This is beautiful indeed; the colored people have given this to the head of the government, and that government once sanctioned laws that would not permit its people to learn enough to enable them to read this book. And for what? Let them answer who can.

"I must say, and I am proud to say, that I never was treated by any one with more kindness and cordiality than were shown to me by that great and good man, Abraham Lincoln, by the grace of God president of the United States for four years more. He took my little book, and with the same hand that signed the death-warrant of slavery, he wrote as follows:

" 'For Aunty Sojourner Truth,

" 'Oct. 29, 1864.   A. LINCOLN.'

"As I was taking my leave, he arose and took my hand, and said he would be pleased to have me call again. I felt that I was in the presence of a friend, and I now thank God from the bottom of my heart that I always have advocated his cause, and have done it openly and boldly. I shall feel still more in duty bound to do so in time to come. May God assist me.

"Now I must tell you something of this place. I found things quite as well as I expected. I think I can be useful and will stay. The captain in command of the guard has given me his assistance, and by his aid I have obtained a little house, and will move into it to-morrow. Will you ask Mrs. P., or any of my friends, to send me a couple of sheets and a pillow? I find many of the women very ignorant in relation to house-keeping, as most of them were instructed in field labor, but not in household duties. They all seem to think a great deal of me, and want to learn the way we live in the North. I am listened to with attention and respect, and from all things, I judge it is the will of both God and the people that I should remain.

"Now when you come to Washington, don't forget to call and see me. You may publish my whereabouts, and anything in this letter you think would interest the friends of Freedom, Justice, and Truth, in the *Standard* and *Anglo-African,* and any other paper you may see fit.

"Enclosed please find four shadows [carte de visites]. The two dollars came safely. Anything in the way of nourishment you may feel like sending, send it along. The captain sends to Washington every day. Give my love to all who inquire for me, and tell my friends to direct all things for me to the care of Capt. George B. Carse, Freedman's Village, Va. Ask Mr. Oliver Johnson to please send me the *Standard* while I am here, as many of the colored people like to hear what is going on, and to know what is being done for them. Sammy, my grandson, reads for them. We are both well, and happy, and feel that we are in good employment. I find plenty of friends.

"Your friend,   SOJOURNER TRUTH."

III

My friends, I am rejoiced that you are glad, but I don't know how you will feel when I get through. I come from another field—the country of the slave. They have got their liberty—so much good luck to have slavery partly destroyed; not entirely. I want it root and branch destroyed. Then we will all be free indeed. I feel that if I have to answer for the deeds done in my body just as much as a man, I have a right to have just as much as a man. There is a great stir about colored men getting their rights, but not a word about the colored women; and if colored men get their rights, and not colored women theirs, you see the colored men will be masters over the women, and it will be just as bad as it was before. So I am for keeping the thing going while things are stirring; because if we wait till it is still, it will take a great while to get it going again. White women are a great deal smarter, and know more than colored women, while colored women do not know scarcely anything. They go out washing, which is about as high as a colored woman gets, and their men go about idle, strutting up and down; and when the women come home, they ask for their money and take it all, and then scold because there is no food. I want you to consider on that, chil'n. I call you chil'n; you are somebody's chil'n, and I am old enough to be mother of all that is here. I want women to have their rights. In the courts women have no right, no

Source: Stanton et al., *History of Woman Suffrage,* II, 193–94.

voice; nobody speaks for them. I wish woman to have her voice there among the pettifoggers. If it is not a fit place for women, it is unfit for men to be there.

I am above eighty years old; it is about time for me to be going. I have been forty years a slave and forty years free, and would be here forty years more to have equal rights for all. I suppose I am kept here because something remains for me to do; I suppose I am yet to help to break the chain. I have done a great deal of work; as much as a man, but did not get so much pay. I used to work in the field and bind grain, keeping up with the cradler; but men doing no more, got twice as much pay; so with the German women. They work in the field and do as much work, but do not get the pay. We do as much, we eat as much, we want as much. I suppose I am about the only colored woman that goes about to speak for the rights of the colored women. I want to keep the thing stirring, now that the ice is cracked. What we want is a little money. You men know that you get as much again as women when you write, or for what you do. When we get our rights we shall not have to come to you for money, for then we shall have money enough in our own pockets; and may be you will ask us for money. But help us now until we get it. It is a good consolation to know that when we have got this battle once fought we shall not be coming to you any more. You have been having our rights so long, that you think, like a slave-holder, that you own us. I know that it is hard for one who has held the reins for so long to give up; it cuts like a knife. It will feel all the better when it closes up again. I have been in Washington about three years, seeing about these colored people. Now colored men have the right to vote. There ought to be equal rights now more than ever, since colored people have got their freedom.

IV

Children, as there is no school to-day, will you read Sojourner the reports of the Convention? I want to see whether these young sprigs of the press do me justice. You know, children, I don't read such small stuff as letters, I read men and nations. I can see through a millstone, though I can't see through a spelling-book. What a narrow idea a reading qualification is for a voter! I know and do what is right better than many big men who read. And there's that property qualification! just as bad. As if men and women themselves, who made money, were not of more value than the thing they made. If I were a delegate to the Constitutional Convention I could make suffrage as clear as daylight; but I am afraid these Republicans will "purty, purty" about

Source: Stanton et al., History of Woman Suffrage, II, 926–28, reprinting a letter from Elizabeth Cady Stanton to The World.

all manner of small things week out and week in, and never settle this foundation question after all. . . .

I'll tell you what I'm thinking. My speeches in the Convention read well. I should like to have the substance put together, improved a little, and published in tract form, headed "Sojourner Truth on Suffrage;" for if these timid men, like Greeley,[1] knew that Sojourner was out for "universal suffrage," they would not be so afraid to handle the question. Yes, children, I am going to rouse the people on equality. I must sojourn once to the ballot-box before I die. I hear the ballot-box is a beautiful glass globe, so you can see all the votes as they go in. Now, the first time I vote I'll see if a woman's vote looks any different from the rest—if it makes any stir or commotion. If it don't inside, it need not outside. . . .

V

"To the Senate and House of Representatives, in Congress assembled:—

"Whereas, From the faithful and earnest representations of Sojourner Truth (who has personally investigated the matter), we believe that the freed colored people in and about Washington, dependent upon government for support, would be greatly benefited and might become useful citizens by being placed in a position to support themselves: We, the undersigned, therefore earnestly request your honorable body to set apart for them a portion of the public land in the West, and erect buildings thereon for the aged and infirm, and otherwise legislate so as to secure the desired results."

VI

Well, children, I'm glad to see so many together. If I am eighty-three years old, I only count my age from the time that I was emancipated. Then I began to live. God is a-fulfilling, and my lost time that I lost being a slave was made up. When I was a slave I hated the white people. My mother said to me when I was to be sold from her, "I want to tell you these things that you will always know that I have told you, for there will be a great many things told you after I start out of this life into the world to come." And I say this to you all, for here is a great many people[,] that when I step

---

[1]Horace Greeley, Republican and editor of the New York Tribune, at that date was supporting suffrage for blacks but not for women. (BJL and RB)

Source (V): Gilbert, Narrative, p. 199.

Source (VI): Gilbert, Narrative, pp. 213–16, reprinting an undated report in the Boston Post. The patois rendition of Sojourner Truth's spoken words has been dropped and the paragraph structure altered.

out of this existence, that you will know what you heard old Sojourner Truth tell you.

I was bound a slave in the State of New York, Ulster County, among the low Dutch. When I was ten years old, I couldn't speak a word of English, and have no education at all. There's wonder what they have done for me. As I told you[,] when I was sold, my master died, and we was going to have a auction. We was all brought up to be sold. My mother, my father was very old, my brother younger than myself, and my mother took my hand. There opened a canopy of heaven, and she sat down and I and my brother sat down by her, and she says, "Look up to the moon and stars that shine upon your father and upon your mother when your're sold far away, and upon your brothers and sisters, that is sold away," for there was a great number of us, and was all sold away before my remembrance. I asked her who had made the moon and the stars, and she says, "God," and says I, Where is God? "Oh!" says she, "child, he sits in the sky, and he hears you when you ask him when you are away from us to make your master and mistress good, and he will do it."

When we were sold, I did what my mother told me; I said, O God, my mother told me if I asked you to make my master and mistress good, you'd do it, and they didn't get good. [Laughter.] Why, says I, God, maybe you can't do it. Kill them. [Laughter and applause.] I didn't think he could make them good. That was the idea I had. After I made such wishes my conscience burned me. Then I would say, O God, don't be mad. My master makes me wicked; and I often thought how people can do such abominable wicked things and their conscience not burn them. Now I only made wishes. I used to tell God this—I would say, "Now, God, if I was you, and you was me [laughter], and you wanted any help I'd help you;—why don't you help me? [Laughter and applause.] Well, you see I was in want, and I felt that there was no help. I know what it is to be taken in the barn and tied up and the blood drawn out of your bare back, and I tell you it would make you think about God. Yes, and then I felt, O God, if I was you and you felt like I do, and asked me for help I would help you—now why won't you help me?

Truly I don't know but God has helped me. But I got no good master until the last time I was sold, and then I found one and his name was Jesus. Oh, I tell you, didn't I find a good master when I used to feel so bad, when I used to say, O God, how can I live? I'm sorely oppressed both within and without. When God gave me that master he healed all the wounds up. My soul rejoiced. I used to hate the white people so, and I tell you when the love came in me I had so much love I didn't know what to love. Then the white people came, and I thought that love was too good for them. Then I said, Yea, God, I'll love everybody and the white people too. Ever since that, that love has continued and kept me among the white people. Well, emancipation came; we all know; can't stop to go through the whole. I go for agitating. But I believe there are works belong with agitating, too. Only think of it! Ain't it wonderful that God gives love enough to the Ethiopians [a term often used for all those of African ancestry] to love you?

Now, here is the question that I am here to-night to say. I've been to Washington, and I find out this, that the colored people that are in Washington living on the government[,] that the United States ought to give them land and move them on it. They are living on the government, and there's people taking care of them costing you so much, and it don't benefit them at all. It degrades them worse and worse. Therefore I say that these people, take and put them in the West where you can enrich them. I know the good people in the South can't take care of the negroes as they ought to, 'cause the rebels won't let them. How much better will it be for to take those colored people and give them land? We've ain't land enough for a home, and it would be a benefit for you all and God would bless the whole of you for doing it. They say, Let them take care of themselves. Why, you've taken that all away from them. Ain't got nothing left. Get these colored people out of Washington off of the government, and get the old people out and build them homes in the West, where they can feed themselves, and they would soon be able to be a people among you. That is my commission. Now agitate those people and put them there; learn them to read one part of the time and learn them to work the other part of the time. . . .

I speak these things so that when you have a paper [a reference to her petition, above] come for you to sign, you can sign it.

Frances Ellen Watkins Harper

Frances Ellen Watkins Harper viewed the life of white America with personal concern rather than tempered detachment. Beyond the struggle for the rights of blacks she was sensitive to other forms of human deprivation. An awareness of moral and spiritual impoverishment among the wealthy and the privileged stirred her; it was one of her distinctive qualities. Such intuitive knowledge was fortified by decades of teaching and lecturing which brought her into contact with many levels of society.

She was born in 1825, an only child and soon an orphan. Raised in Baltimore's free black community by an aunt and an uncle who was both a preacher and a teacher, she began domestic work at thirteen. The woman for whom she worked, intrigued by her literacy, aided in furthering it. Reading and writing, often infused with religious content, continued to form a small yet vital part of Frances Watkins' existence until, after following the dressmaker's trade, she became a teacher.

A short career of teaching in Ohio and Pennsylvania in the 1850s was a prelude to a long and full life as poet and lecturer. Her Poems on Miscellaneous Subjects was published in 1854, and in the summer of that year she gave her first address, on "The Elevation and Education of our People." Soon after, she undertook a lecture campaign for the State Anti-Slavery Society of Maine and continued the dual role of writer and speaker, traveling through New England and the other northern states and into Canada until the eve of the Civil War. Imbued with faith in the unity of Christianity and justice, she "could sing with prophetic exaltation in the darkest days." Married and settled in Ohio, she continued to write. But in the Reconstruction era, after her husband's death, she began to travel again, now familiarizing herself with the southern states and the conditions prevailing among the freedmen. She urged a thoroughgoing reconstruction involving black and white together, "getting every citizen interested in the welfare, progress and durability of the state."

Mrs. Harper earned her living as a lecturer. Frederick Douglass' paper, New National Era, carried an announcement that she was "prepared to accept calls from Lyceums and Lecturing Committees" for the 1870 lecturing season then commencing. But during her long southern sojourn, she also gave special lectures without charge to freedwomen. She strove to reach those who were isolated, impoverished, and ignorant, in the hope of elevating their lives. At this time she appeared as a distinguished guest at women's rights conventions. A strong supporter of woman suffrage and especially mindful of black women's need for the ballot, she was convinced nevertheless that the urgency of the vote for black men was even greater.

"One of the most eloquent women lecturers in the country," Frances Harper matured into an advocate for the aspirations of black women. She became a prominent speaker before widening circles of middle-class clubwomen then emerging. In 1888 she addressed the International Council of Women in Washington. At the Columbian Exposition in Chicago in 1893 she spoke on "Woman's Political Future." But it was to the National Council of Women, 23 February 1891, on the topic "Duty to Dependent Races," that she made some of her most comprehensive and persuasive remarks.[1]

I

If before sin had cast its deepest shadows or sorrow had distilled its bitterest tears, it was true that it was not good for man to be alone, it is no less true, since the shadows have deepened and life's sorrows have increased, that the world has need of all the spiritual aid that woman can give for the social advancement and moral development of the human race. The tendency of the present age, with its restlessness, religious upheavals, failures, blunders, and crimes, is toward broader freedom, an increase of knowledge, the emancipation of thought, and a recognition of the brotherhood of man; in this movement woman, as the companion of man, must be a sharer. So close is the bond between man and woman that you can not raise one without lifting the other. The world can not move without woman's sharing in the movement, and to help give a right impetus to that movement is woman's highest privilege.

If the fifteenth century discovered America to the Old World, the nineteenth is discovering woman to herself. Little did Columbus imagine, when the New World broke upon his vision like a lovely gem in the coronet of the universe, the glorious possibilities of a land where the sun should be

---

[1]Anna Julia Cooper, A Voice from the South (Xenia, Ohio, 1892), p. 140; a letter by Mrs. Harper quoted in William Still, The Underground Railroad (Philadelphia, 1872), p. 770; New National Era, 20 October 1870; Phebe Hanaford, Daughters of America; or, Women of the Century, 2d ed. (Augusta, Maine, 1882), p. 326; Philip S. Foner, ed., The Voice of Black America: Major Speeches by Negroes in the United States, 1797–1971 (New York, 1972), p. 6.

Source: Frances Ellen Watkins Harper, address, "Woman's Political Future," World's Congress of Representative Women, ed. May Wright Sewall (Chicago, 1893), pp. 433–37.

our engraver, the winged lightning our messenger, and steam our beast of burden. But as mind is more than matter, and the highest ideal always the true real, so to woman comes the opportunity to strive for richer and grander discoveries than ever gladdened the eye of the Genoese mariner.

Not the opportunity of discovering new worlds, but that of filling this old world with fairer and higher aims than the greed of gold and the lust of power, is hers. Through weary, wasting years men have destroyed, dashed in pieces, and overthrown, but to-day we stand on the threshold of woman's era, and woman's work is grandly constructive. In her hand are possibilities whose use or abuse must tell upon the political life of the nation, and send their influence for good or evil across the track of unborn ages.

As the saffron tints and crimson flushes of morn herald the coming day, so the social and political advancement which woman has already gained bears the promise of the rising of the full-orbed sun of emancipation. The result will be not to make home less happy, but society more holy; yet I do not think the mere extension of the ballot a panacea for all the ills of our national life. What we need to-day is not simply more voters, but better voters. To-day there are red-handed men in our republic, who walk unwhipped of justice, who richly deserve to exchange the ballot of the freeman for the wristlets of the felon; brutal and cowardly men, who torture, burn, and lynch their fellow-men, men whose defenselessness should be their best defense and their weakness an ensign of protection. More than the changing of institutions we need the development of a national conscience, and the upbuilding of national character. Men may boast of the aristocracy of blood, may glory in the aristocracy of talent, and be proud of the aristocracy of wealth, but there is one aristocracy which must ever outrank them all, and that is the aristocracy of character; and it is the women of a country who help to mold its character, and to influence if not determine its destiny; and in the political future of our nation woman will not have done what she could if she does not endeavor to have our republic stand foremost among the nations of the earth, wearing sobriety as a crown and righteousness as a garment and a girdle. In coming into her political estate woman will find a mass of illiteracy to be dispelled. If knowledge is power, ignorance is also power. The power that educates wickedness may manipulate and dash against the pillars of any state when they are undermined and honeycombed by injustice.

I envy neither the heart nor the head of any legislator who has been born to an inheritance of privileges, who has behind him ages of education, dominion, civilization, and Christianity, if he stands opposed to the passage of a national education bill, whose purpose is to secure education to the children of those who were born under the shadow of institutions which made it a crime to read.

To-day women hold in their hands influence and opportunity, and with these they have already opened doors which have been closed to others. By opening doors of labor woman has become a rival claimant for at least some of the wealth monopolized by her stronger brother. In the home she is the priestess, in society the queen, in literature she is a power, in legislative halls law-makers have responded to her appeals, and for her sake have humanized and liberalized their laws. The press has felt the impress of her hand. In the pews of the church she constitutes the majority; the pulpit has welcomed her, and in the school she has the blessed privilege of teaching children and youth. To her is apparently coming the added responsibility of political power; and what she now possesses should only be the means of preparing her to use the coming power for the glory of God and the good of mankind; for power without righteousness is one of the most dangerous forces in the world.

Political life in our country has plowed in muddy channels, and needs the infusion of clearer and cleaner waters. I am not sure that women are naturally so much better than men that they will clear the stream by the virtue of their womanhood; it is not through sex but through character that the best influence of women upon the life of the nation must be exerted.

I do not believe in unrestricted and universal suffrage for either men or women. I believe in moral and educational tests. I do not believe that the most ignorant and brutal man is better prepared to add value to the strength and durability of the government than the most cultured, upright, and intelligent woman. I do not think that willful ignorance should swamp earnest intelligence at the ballot-box, nor that educated wickedness, violence, and fraud should cancel the votes of honest men. The unsteady hands of a drunkard can not cast the ballot of a freeman. The hands of lynchers are too red with blood to determine the political character of the government for even four short years. The ballot in the hands of woman means power added to influence. How well she will use that power I can not foretell. Great evils stare us in the face that need to be throttled by the combined power of an upright manhood and an enlightened womanhood; and I know that no nation can gain its full measure of enlightenment and happiness if one-half of it is free and the other half is fettered. China compressed the feet of her women and thereby retarded the steps of her men. The elements of a nation's weakness must ever be found at the hearthstone.

More than the increase of wealth, the power of armies, and the strength of fleets is the need of good homes, of good fathers, and good mothers. . . .

. . . Woman coming into her kingdom will find enthroned three great evils, for whose overthrow she should be as strong in a love of justice and humanity as the warrior is in his might. She will find intemperance sending its flood of shame, and death, and sorrow to the homes of men, a fretting leprosy in our politics, and a blighting curse in our social life; the social evil sending to our streets women whose laughter is sadder than their tears, who slide from the paths of sin and shame to the friendly shelter of the grave; and lawlessness enacting in our republic deeds over which angels might weep, if heaven knows sympathy. . . .

O women of America! into your hands God has pressed one of the sublimest opportunities that ever came into the hands of the women of any race or people. It is yours to create a healthy public sentiment; to demand justice, simple justice, as the right of every race; to brand with everlasting infamy the lawless and brutal cowardice that lynches, burns, and tortures your own countrymen.

To grapple with the evils which threaten to undermine the strength of the nation and to lay magazines of powder under the cribs of future generations is no child's play.

Let the hearts of the women of the world respond to the song of the herald angels of peace on earth and good will to men. Let them throb as one heart unified by the grand and holy purpose of uplifting the human race, and humanity will breathe freer, and the world grow brighter. With such a purpose Eden would spring up in our path, and Paradise be around our way.

II

I deem it a privilege to present the negro, not as a mere dependent asking for Northern sympathy or Southern compassion, but as a member of the body politic who has a claim upon the nation for justice, simple justice, which is the right of every race, upon the government for protection, which is the rightful claim of every citizen, and upon our common Christianity for the best influences which can be exerted for peace on earth and good-will to man.

Our first claim upon the nation and government is the claim for protection to human life. That claim should lie at the basis of our civilization, not simply in theory but in fact. Outside of America, I know of no other civilized country, Catholic, Protestant, or even Mahometan, where men are still lynched, murdered, and even burned for real or supposed crimes. As long as there are such cases as moral irresponsibility, mental imbecility; as long as Potiphar's wife[1] stands in the world's pillory of shame, no man should be deprived of life or liberty without due process of law. A government which has power to tax a man in peace, and draft him in war, should have power to defend his life in the hour of peril. A government which can protect and defend its citizens from wrong and outrage and does not is vicious. A government which would do it and cannot is weak; and where

---

Source: Frances Ellen Watkins Harper, address, "Duty to Dependent Races," National Council of Women of the United States, Transactions (Philadelphia, 1891), pp. 86–91. All footnotes are the editors'.

[1]Genesis 39:14. Joseph, sold into slavery in Egypt, rebuffed the amorous entreaties of his master's wife. When he literally fled from her efforts to seduce him, leaving his garment which she had seized, she betrayed him with the allegation that he had made licentious advances. Mrs. Harper used this reference to repudiate the charges of rape or attempted rape as principal justification for the wave of lynchings that mounted in the 1880s and 1890s.

human life is insecure through either weakness or viciousness in the administration of law, there must be a lack of justice, and where this is wanting nothing can make up the deficiency.

The strongest nation on earth cannot afford to deal unjustly towards its weakest and feeblest members. A man might just as well attempt to play with the thunderbolts of heaven and expect to escape unscathed, as for a nation to trample on justice and right and evade the divine penalty. The reason our nation snapped asunder in 1861 was because it lacked the cohesion of justice; men poured out their blood like water, scattered their wealth like chaff, summoned to the field the largest armies the nation had ever seen, but they did not get their final victories which closed the rebellion till they clasped hands with the negro, and marched with him abreast to freedom and to victory. I claim for the negro protection in every right with which the government has invested him. Whether it was wise or unwise, the government has exchanged the fetters on his wrist for the ballot in his right hand, and men cannot vitiate his vote by fraud, or intimidate the voter by violence, without being untrue to the genius and spirit of our government, and bringing demoralization into their own political life and ranks. Am I here met with the objection that the negro is poor and ignorant, and the greatest amount of land, capital, and intelligence is possessed by the white race, and that in a number of States negro suffrage means negro supremacy? But is it not a fact that both North and South power naturally gravitates into the strongest hands, and is there any danger that a race who were deemed so inferior as to be only fitted for slavery, and social and political ostracism, has in less than one generation become so powerful that, if not hindered from exercising the right of suffrage, it will dominate over a people who have behind them ages of dominion, education, freedom, and civilization, a people who have had poured into their veins the blood of some of the strongest races on earth? More than a year since Mr. Grady[2] said, I believe, "We do not directly fear the political domination of blacks, but that they are ignorant and easily deluded, impulsive and therefore easily led, strong of race instinct and therefore clannish, without information and therefore without political convictions, passionate and therefore easily excited, poor, irresponsible, and with no idea of the integrity of suffrage and therefore easily bought. The fear is that this vast swarm, ignorant, purchasable, will be impacted and controlled by desperate and unscrupulous white men and made to hold the balance of power when white men are divided." Admit for one moment that every word here is true, and that the whole race should be judged by its worst, and not its best members, does any civilized country legislate to punish a man before he commits a crime?

---

[2]Henry W. Grady (1850–1889), editor of the Atlanta Constitution from 1879 to the time of his death, was a prominent spokesman for the concept that the "New South" was capable of resolving the race issue if freed from outside intervention.

It is said the negro is ignorant. But why is he ignorant? It comes with ill grace from a man who has put out my eyes to make a parade of my blindness—to reproach me for my poverty when he has wronged me of my money. If the negro is ignorant, he has lived under the shadow of an institution which, at least in part of the country, made it a crime to teach him to read the name of the ever-blessed Christ. If he is poor, what has become of the money he has been earning for the last two hundred and fifty years? Years ago it was said cotton fights and cotton conquers for American slavery. The negro helped build up that great cotton power in the South, and in the North his sigh was in the whir of its machinery, and his blood and tears upon the warp and woof of its manufactures.

But there are some rights more precious than the rights of property or the claims of superior intelligence: they are the rights of life and liberty, and to these the poorest and humblest man has just as much right as the richest and most influential man in the country. Ignorance and poverty are conditions which men outgrow. Since the sealed volume was opened by the crimson hand of war, in spite of entailed ignorance, poverty, opposition, and a heritage of scorn, schools have sprung like wells in the desert dust. It has been estimated that about two millions have learned to read. Colored men and women have gone into journalism. Some of the first magazines in the country have received contributions from them. Learned professions have given them diplomas. Universities have granted them professorships. Colored women have combined to shelter orphaned children. Tens of thousands have been contributed by colored persons for the care of the aged and infirm. Instead of the old slave-pen of former days, imposing and commodious are edifices of prayer and praise. Millions of dollars have flowed into the pockets of the race, and freed people have not only been able to provide for themselves, but reach out their hands to impoverished owners.

Has the record of the slave been such as to warrant the belief that permitting him to share citizenship with others in the country is inimical to the welfare of the nation? Can it be said that he lacks patriotism, or a readiness to make common cause with the nation in the hour of peril? In the days of the American Revolution some of the first blood which was shed flowed from the veins of a colored man, and among the latest words that died upon his lips before they paled in death was, "Crush them underfoot," meaning the British guards. To him Boston has given a monument. In or after 1812 they received from General Jackson the plaudit, "I knew you would endure hunger and thirst and all the hardships of war. I knew that you loved the land of your nativity, and that, like ourselves, you had to defend all that is most dear; but you have surpassed my hopes. I have found in you, united to all these qualities, that noble enthusiasm which impels to great deeds." And in our late civil conflict colored men threw their lives into the struggle, rallied around the old flag when others were trampling it underfoot and riddling it with bullets. Colored people learned to regard that flag as a harbinger of freedom and bring their most reliable information to the

Union army, to share their humble fare with the escaping prisoner; to be faithful when others were faithless and help turn the tide of battle in favor of the nation. While nearly two hundred thousand joined the Union army, others remained on the old plantation; widows, wives, aged men, and helpless children were left behind, when the master was at the front trying to put new rivets in their chains, and yet was there a single slave who took advantage of the master's absence to invade the privacy of his home, or wreak a summary vengeance on those whose "defenceless condition should have been their best defence?"

Instead of taking the ballot from his hands, teach him how to use it, and to add his quota to the progress, strength, and durability of the nation. Let the nation, which once consented to his abasement under a system which made it a crime to teach him to read his Bible, feel it a privilege as well as a duty to reverse the old processes of the past by supplanting his darkness with light, not simply by providing the negro, but the whole region in which he lives, with national education. No child can be blamed because he was born in the midst of squalor, poverty, and ignorance, but society is criminal if it permits him to grow up without proper efforts for ameliorating his condition.

Some months since, when I was in South Carolina, where I addressed a number of colored schools, I was informed that white children were in the factories, beginning from eight to ten years old, with working hours from six to seven o'clock; and one day, as a number of white children were wending their way apparently from the factory, I heard a colored man say, "I pity these children." It was a strange turning of the tables to hear a colored man in South Carolina bestowing pity on white children because of neglect in their education. Surely the world does move. When parents are too poor or selfish to spare the labor of their children from the factories, and the State too indifferent or short-sighted to enforce their education by law, then let the Government save its future citizens from the results of cupidity in the parents or short-sightedness in the State. If to-day there is danger from a mass of ignorance voting, may there not be a danger even greater, and that is a mass of "ignorance that does not vote"? If there is danger that an ignorant mass might be compacted to hold the balance of power where white men are divided politically, might not that same mass, if kept ignorant and disfranchised, be used by wicked men, whose weapons may be bombs and dynamite, to dash themselves against the peace and order of society? To-day the hands of the negro are not dripping with dynamite. We do not read of his flaunting the red banners of anarchy in the face of the nation, nor plotting in beer-saloons to overthrow existing institutions, nor spitting on the American flag. Once that flag was to him an ensign of freedom. Let our Government resolve that as far as that flag extends every American-born child shall be able to read upon its folds liberty for all and chains for none.

And now permit me to make my final claim, and that is a claim upon our common Christianity. . . . It is the pride of Caste which opposes the spirit of Christ, and the great work to which American Christianity is called is a work of Christly reconciliation. God has heaved up your mountains with grandeur, flooded your rivers with majesty, crowned your vales with fertility, and enriched your mines with wealth. Excluding Alaska, you have, I think, nearly three hundred millions of square miles. Be reconciled to God for making a man black, permitting him to become part of your body politic, and sharing one rood or acre of our goodly heritage. Be reconciled to the Christ of Calvary, who said, "And I, if I be lifted up, will draw all men to me," and "It is better for a man that a millstone were hanged about his neck, and he were drowned in the depths of the sea, than that he should offend one of these little ones that believe in me." Forgive the early adherents of Christianity who faced danger and difficulty and stood as victors by the side of Death, who would say, "I perceive that God is no respecter of persons." "If ye have respect of persons ye commit sin." "There is neither Greek nor Jew, circumcision nor uncircumcision, Scythian nor Barbarian, bond nor free, but Christ is all, and in all."

What I ask of American Christianity is not to show us more creeds, but more of Christ; not more rites and ceremonies, but more religion glowing with love and replete with life,—religion which will be to all weaker races an uplifting power, and not a degrading influence. Jesus Christ has given us a platform of love and duty from which all oppression and selfishness is necessarily excluded. While politicians may stumble on the barren mountains of fretful controversy and ask in strange bewilderment, "What shall we do with weaker races?" I hold that Jesus Christ answered that question nearly two thousand years since. "Whatsoever ye would that men should do to you, do you even so to them."

Ida Wells-Barnett

Ida Wells-Barnett, "pioneer of the anti-lynching crusade," deserves a memorable place in the history of the nation. She was a person of intelligence, integrity, and imaginative vigor. W.E.B. DuBois' praise is restrained, for she did in fact begin "the awakening of the conscience" of the United States about this particular barbarity. Six months before the promulgation of emancipation, Ida Wells-Barnett was born in Holly Springs, Mississippi. The Freedmen's School was her first introduction to education. Rust University, founded soon after the peace, permitted her to begin preparation for teaching.

As a child, she had a vaulting ambition to teach. But her training was suddenly interrupted by the need to earn money as a teacher. A yellow fever epidemic decimated her family when she was sixteen, and with her parents and three siblings dead, she remained the sole support of younger sisters and brothers after the small savings her father had amassed as a skilled carpenter were gone. She lengthened her dresses, passed the examination to teach in a country school, and kept the family going. While performing as a teacher, she continued her studies at Rust. By 1884 she was qualified for a more demanding post as a teacher in Memphis, where she also wrote articles for black newspapers.

Memphis and journalism gave her a new direction. She purchased a one-third interest in the Memphis Free Speech. A firsthand knowledge of black school conditions was her contribution as editor. But her outspokenness was severely criticized, and her contract was not renewed, which ended her teaching career. Journalism became her new profession and she and her associate bought out the third partner of the newspaper. Large segments of the white population were unhappy about Free Speech; they were not prepared to tolerate unvarnished condemnation of the black education, which was a token of their rectitude and generosity of spirit.

Disagreements between white communities and black communities worsened in the waning decades of the nineteenth century. A lynching in 1892 took the lives of three young black proprietors of a grocery store in Memphis. Ida Wells-Barnett declared journalistic war. The battle was lost almost before it began. Violence to the newspaper and its owners was threatened. Free Speech was an immediate casualty. Ida Wells-Barnett made a dignified retreat from Memphis. Her intellectual weapons intact, she lectured in Boston and other points in New England, particularly to black women's clubs. She published her story in the New York Age. Black women of Brooklyn and New York staged a fund-raising drive in New York's Lyric Hall, 5 October 1892, in order to reprint her articles in pamphlet form. Southern Horrors: Lynch Law in all Its Phases promptly appeared. Reprinted with minor changes, supplemental evidence, and a different title, it was issued as U. S. Atrocities in London.

The English version of the Wells-Barnett indictment was followed by British speaking tours in 1893 and 1894. An attempt was made during these visits to organize British sentiment against lynching by economic pressure on the South. There was hardly a sector of the drive against lynching in which Mrs. Wells-Barnett was not engaged. When the National Negro Conference of 1909 took place—out of which the National Association for the Advancement of Colored People emerged—she was the principal speaker on the subject on which she was expert. When a black postmaster was lynched in the South, it was Ida Wells-Barnett who on 21 March 1898 presented the petition of protest to President William McKinley at the White House. Thomas Fortune, editor of the New York Age, said of her: "She has all of a woman's tenderness in all that affects our common humanity, but she has also the courage of the great women of the past who believed that they could still be womanly while being more than ciphers in 'the world's broad field of battle.' " Nine years after her death in 1931 her name was given to a huge low-cost housing project in Chicago. The memorial was in part the work of the black clubwomen of the city. The Ida B. Wells Homes remain, as she would have wished, a tribute to them, to all other women, and to her.[1]

On Wednesday evening, May 25th, 1892, the city of Memphis, Tennessee, was filled with excitement. Editorials in the daily papers of that date caused a meeting to be held in the Cotton Exchange Building; a committee was sent for the editors of the Free Speech, an Afro-American journal published in that city, and the only reason the open threats of lynching that were made were not carried out was because the editors could not be found. The cause of all this commotion was the following editorial published in the Free Speech, May 21st, 1892, on the Saturday previous:—

"Eight Negroes lynched since last issue of Free Speech, one at Little Rock, Arkansas, last Saturday morning where the citizens broke (?) into the

---

[1]Crisis 38 (June 1931): 207; Lawson Andrew Scruggs, Women of Distinction: Remarkable in Works and Invincible in Character (Raleigh, N.C., 1893), p. 39; Ida B. Wells, Crusade for Justice: The Autobiography of Ida B. Wells, ed. Alfreda M. Duster (Chicago, 1970), passim.

Source: Ida B. Wells, U.S. Atrocities (London, 1892), pp. 1–3, 11–19. All footnotes are the editors'.

penitentiary and got their man; three near Anniston, Alabama, one near New Orleans; and three at Clarksville, Georgia, the last three for killing a white man, and five on the same old racket—the new alarm about raping white women. The same programme of hanging, then shooting bullets into the lifeless bodies, was carried out to the letter. Nobody in this section of the country believes the old thread-bare lie that Negro men rape white women. If Southern white men are not careful, they will overreach themselves and public sentiment will have a reaction; a conclusion will then be reached which will be very damaging to the moral reputation of their women."

The *Daily Commercial* of Wednesday following, May 25th, contained the following leader;—

"Those Negroes who are attempting to make the lynching of individuals of their race, a means for arousing the worst passions of their kind, are playing with a dangerous sentiment. The Negroes may as well understand that there is no mercy for the Negro rapist and little patience with his defenders. A Negro organ printed in this city, in a recent issue publishes the following atrocious paragraph: 'Nobody in this section of the country believes the old thread-bare lie that Negro men rape white women. If Southern white men are not careful they will overreach themselves, and public sentiment will have a reaction; and a conclusion will be reached which will be very damaging to the moral reputation of their women.' The fact that a black scoundrel is allowed to live and utter such loathsome and repulsive calumnies is a volume of evidence as to the wonderful patience of Southern whites. But we have had enough of it. There are some things that the Southern white man will not tolerate, and the obscene intimations of the foregoing have brought the writer to the very outermost limit of public patience. We hope we have said enough."

The *Evening Scimitar* of same date, copied the *Commercial's* editorial with these words of comment: "Patience under such circumstances is not a virtue. If the Negroes themselves do not apply the remedy without delay, it will be the duty of those whom he has attacked to tie the wretch who utters these calumnies to a stake at the intersection of Main and Madison Sts., brand him in the forehead with a hot iron, and perform upon him a surgical operation with a pair of tailor's shears."

Acting upon this advice, the leading citizens met in the Cotton Exchange Building the same evening, and threats of lynching were freely indulged—not 'by the lawless element upon which the devilry of the South is usually saddled, but by the leading business men, in their leading business centre. Mr. Fleming, the business manager and owner of a half interest in *Free Speech*, had to leave town to escape the mob, and was afterwards ordered not to return; letters and telegrams sent me in New York, where I was spending my vacation, advised me that bodily harm awaited my return. Creditors took possession of the office and sold the outfit, and the *Free Speech* was as if it had never been.

The editorial in question was prompted by the many inhuman and fiendish lynchings of Afro-Americans which have recently taken place, and was meant as a warning. Eight lynched in one week, and five of them charged with rape! The thinking public will not easily believe freedom and education more brutalising than slavery, and the world knows that the crime of rape was unknown during the four years of civil war, when the white women of the South were at the mercy of the race, which is all at once charged with being a bestial one.

Since my business has been destroyed, and I am an exile from home because of that editorial, the issue has been forced, and as the writer of it I feel that the race and the public generally should have a statement of the facts as they exist. They will serve at the same time as a defence for the Afro-American Sampsons who suffer themselves to be betrayed by white Delilahs. . . .

. . . There are many white women in the South who would marry coloured men if such an act would not place them at once beyond the pale of society, and within the clutches of the law. The miscegenation laws of the South only operate against the legitimate union of the races; they leave the white man free to seduce all the coloured girls he can, but it is death to the coloured man who yields to the force and advances of a similar attraction in white women. White men lynch the offending Afro-American not because he is a despoiler of virtue, but because he succumbs to the smiles of white women. . . .

On March 9th, 1892, there were lynched in the same city three of the best specimens of young Afro-American manhood since the war. They were peaceful, law-abiding citizens and energetic business men. They believed the problem was to be solved by eschewing politics and putting money in the purse. They owned a flourishing grocery business in a thickly populated suburb of Memphis, and a white man named Barrett had one on the opposite corner. After a personal difficulty which Barrett had sought by going into the "People's Grocery" and drawing a pistol and getting thrashed by Calvin M'Dowell, he (Barrett) threatened to "Clean them out." These men were a mile beyond the city limits and police protection; so on hearing that Barrett's crowd was coming to attack them on Saturday night, they mustered forces and prepared to defend themselves against the attack.

When Barrett came, he led a posse of officers, twelve in number who afterward claimed to be hunting a man for whom they had a warrant. [Why twelve men in citizen's clothes should think it necessary to go in the night to hunt one man who had never before been arrested, or made any record as a criminal, has never been explained.] When they entered the back door the young men thought the threatened attack was on, and fired into them. Three of the officers were wounded, and when the defending party found it was officers of the law upon whom they had fired, they ceased firing and got away. Thirty-one men were arrested and thrown in gaol as "conspirators," although they all declared more than once they did not know they were firing on officers. Excitement was at fever heat until the morning papers, two days after, announced that the wounded deputy sheriffs were recovering.

This hindered rather than helped the plans of the whites. There was no law on the statute books which would execute an Afro-American for wounding a white man, but the "unwritten law" did. Three of these men, the president, the manager, and the clerk of the grocery—"the leaders of the conspiracy"— were secretly taken from gaol and lynched in a shockingly brutal manner. "The Negroes are getting too independent," they say, "we must teach them a lesson." What lesson? The lesson of subordination. "Kill the leaders, and it will cow the Negro who dares to shoot a white man, even in self-defence."

Although the race was wild over the outrage, and the mockery of law and justice which disarmed men and locked them up in gaols where they could be easily and safely reached by the mob, the Afro-American ministers, newspapers and leaders counselled obedience to the law which did not protect them. Their counsel was heeded and not a hand was uplifted to resent the outrage; following the advice of the *Free Speech*, people left the city in great numbers.

The "dailies" and associated press reports heralded the dead men to the country as "toughs" (roughs) and "Negro desperadoes who kept a low dive." This same press service printed that a Negro who was lynched at Indianola, Mississippi, in May, had outraged the sheriff's eight-year-old daughter. This girl was more than eighteen years old, and was found by her father in this man's room, who was a servant on the place! Not content with misrepresenting the race, the mob-spirit was not to be satisfied until the paper which was doing all it could to counteract this impression was silenced. The coloured people were resenting their bad treatment in a way to make itself felt, yet gave the mob no excuse for further murder, until the appearance of the editorial which is construed as a reflection on the "honour" of the Southern white women. It is not half so libellous as that of the *Commercial* which appeared four days before, and that which has been given in these pages. They would have lynched the manager of the *Free Speech* for exercising the right of free speech (if they had found him) as quickly as they would have hung any scoundrel guilty of outrage, and been glad of the excuse to do so. The owners were ordered not to return, as *Free Speech* was suspended with as little compunction as the business of the "People's Grocery" had been broken up and its proprietors murdered. . . .

Mr. Henry W. Grady,[1] in his well-remembered speeches in New England and New York, pictured the Afro-American as incapable of self-government. Through him and other leading men the cry of the South to the country has been "Hands off! Leave us to solve our problem." To the Afro-American the South says, "The white man must and will rule." There is little difference between the Ante-bellum South and the New South. Her white citizens are wedded to any method however revolting, any measure however extreme, for the subjugation of the young manhood of the dark race. They have cheated him out of his ballot, deprived him of civil rights or

---

[1]See footnote 2 under Harper speeches, above.

redress in the Civil Courts thereof, robbed him of the fruits of his labour, and are still murdering, burning, and lynching him.

The result is a growing disregard of human life. Lynch Law has spread its insidious influence till men in New York State, Pennsylvania and on the free Western plains feel they can take the law in their own hands with impunity, especially where an Afro-American is concerned. The South is brutalised to a degree not realised by its own inhabitants, and the very foundation of government, law, and order are imperilled.

Public sentiment has had a slight "reaction," though not sufficient to stop the crusade of lawlessness and lynching. The spirit of Christianity of the great M.E. Church was sufficiently aroused by the frequent and revolting crimes against a powerless people, to pass strong condemnatory resolutions at its General Conference in Omaha last May. The spirit of justice of the grand old party asserted itself sufficiently to secure a denunciation of the wrongs, and a feeble declaration of the belief in human rights in the Republican platform at Minneapolis, June 7th. A few of the great "dailies" and "weeklies" have swung into line declaring that Lynch Law must go. The President of the United States issued a proclamation that it be not tolerated in the territories over which he has jurisdiction. Governor Northen and Chief Justice Bleckley,[2] of Georgia, have proclaimed against it. The citizens of Chattanooga, Tennessee, have set a worthy example in that they not only condemn Lynch Law, but her public men demanded a trial for Weems, who was accused of outrage, and guarded him while the trial was in progress. The trial only lasted ten minutes, and Weems chose to plead guilty, and accept twenty-one years sentence, rather than invite the certain death which awaited him outside that cordon of police if he had told the truth and shown the letters he had received from the white woman in the case.

Colonel A.S. Colyar, of Nashville, Tennessee, is so overcome with the horrible state of affairs that he addressed the following earnest letter to the Nashville *American*:—"Nothing since I have been a reading man has so impressed me with the decay of manhood among the people of Tennessee as the dastardly submission to the mob reign. We have reached the unprecedent low level; the awful criminal depravity of substituting the mob for the Court and jury, of giving up the gaol keys to the mob whenever they are demanded. We do it in the largest cities and in the country towns; we do it in midday; we do it after full, not to say formal, notice, and so thoroughly and generally is it acquiesced in that the murderers have discarded the formula of masks. They go into the town where everybody knows them, sometimes under the gaze of the governor, in the presence of the Courts, in the presence of the sheriff and his deputies, in the presence of the entire police force, take out the prisoner, take his life, often with fiendish glee, and often with acts of cruelty and barbarism which impress the reader with a

---

[2]William Jonathan Northen (1835–1913) was governor of Georgia from 1890 to 1894. Logan Edwin Bleckley (1827–1907) was Chief Justice of the Supreme Court of Georgia from 1887 to 1894.

degeneracy rapidly approaching savage life. That the State is disgraced but faintly expresses the humiliation which has settled upon the once proud people of Tennessee. The State, in its majesty, through its organised life, for which the people pay liberally, makes but one record, but one note, and that a criminal falsehood, *was hung by persons to the jury unknown*. The murder at Shelbyville is only a verification of what every intelligent man knew would come, because with a mob rumour is as good as a proof."

These efforts brought forth apologies and a short halt, but the lynching mania has raged again through the past twelve months with unabated fury. The strong arm of the law must be brought to bear upon lynchers in severe punishment, but this cannot and will not be done unless a healthy public sentiment demands and sustains such action. The men and women in the South who disapprove of lynching and remain silent on the perpetration of such outrages are *particeps criminis*—accomplices, accessories before and after the fact, equally guilty with the actual law-breakers, who would not persist if they did not know that neither the law nor militia would be employed against them. . . .

In the creation of this healthier public sentiment, the Afro-American can do for himself what no one else can do for him. The world looks on with wonder that we have conceded so much, and remain law-abiding under such great outrage and provocation.

To Northern capital and Afro-American labour the South owes its rehabilitation. If labour is withdrawn capital will not remain. The Afro-American is thus the backbone of the South. A thorough knowledge and judicious exercise of this power in lynching localities could many times effect a bloodless revolution. The white man's dollar is his god, and to stop this will be to stop outrages in many localities.

The Afro-Americans of Memphis denounced the lynching of three of their best citizens, and urged and waited for the authorities to act in the matter, and bring the lynchers to justice. No attempt was made to do so, and the black men left the city by thousands, bringing about great stagnation in every branch of business. Those who remained so injured the business of the street car company by staying off the cars, that the superintendent, manager, and treasurer called personally on the editors of the *Free Speech*, and asked them to urge our people to give them their patronage again. Other business men became alarmed over the situation, and the *Free Speech* was suppressed that the coloured people might be more easily controlled. A meeting of white citizens in June, three months after the lynching, passed resolutions for the first time condemning it. *But they did not punish the lynchers.* Every one of them was known by name because they had been selected to do the dirty work by some of the very citizens who passed these resolutions! Memphis is fast losing her black population, who proclaim as they go that there is no protection for the life and property of any Afro-American citizen in Memphis who will not be a slave.

The Afro-American citizens of Kentucky, whose intellectual and financial improvement has been phenomenal, have never had a separate car law until now. Delegations and petitions poured into the Legislature against it, yet the Bill passed, and the Jim Crow Car of Kentucky is a legalised institution. Will the great mass of Negroes continue to patronise the railroad? A special from Covington, Kentucky, says:—

"Covington, June 13th.—The railroads of the State are beginning to feel very markedly the effects of the separate coach Bill recently passed by the Legislature. No class of people in the State have so many and so largely attended excursions as the blacks. All these have been abandoned, and regular travel is reduced to a minimum." A competent authority says the loss to the various roads will reach 1,000,000 dols. this year.

A call to a State Conference in Lexington, Kentucky, last June, had delegates from every county in the State. Those delegates, the ministers, teachers, heads of secret and other orders, and the heads of families should pass the word around, for every member of the race in Kentucky to stay off railroads unless obliged to ride. If they did so, and their advice was followed persistently, the Convention would not need to petition the Legislature to repeal the law or raise money to file a suit. The railroad corporations would be so affected they would, in self defence, "lobby" to have the separate car law repealed. On the other hand, as long as the railroads can get Afro-American excursions they will always have plenty of money to fight all the suits brought against them. They will be aided in so doing by the same partisan public sentiment which passed the law. White men passed the law, and white judges and juries would pass upon the suits against the law, and render judgment in line with their prejudices, and in deference to the greater financial power.

The appeal to the white man's pocket has ever been more effectual than all the appeals ever made to his conscience. Nothing, absolutely nothing, is to be gained by a further sacrifice of manhood and self-respect. By the right exercise of his power as the industrial factor of the South, the Afro-American can demand and secure his rights, the punishment of lynchers, and a fair trial for members of his race accused of outrage.

Of the many inhuman outrages of this present year, the only case where the proposed lynching did not occur, was where the men armed themselves in Jacksonville, Florida, and Paducah, Kentucky, and prevented it. The only times an Afro-American who was assaulted got away has been when he had a gun, and used it in self-defence. The lesson this teaches, and which every Afro-American should ponder well, is that a Winchester rifle should have a place of honour in every black home, and it should be used for that protection which the law refuses to give. When the white man, who is always the aggressor, knows he runs as great risk of biting the dust every time his Afro-American victim does, he will have greater respect for Afro-American life. The more the Afro-American yields and cringes and begs, the more he has to do so, the more he is insulted, outraged, and lynched.

The assertion has been substantiated throughout these pages that the

Press contains unreliable and doctored reports of lynchings, and one of the most necessary things for the race to do is to get these facts before the public. The people must know before they can act, and there is no educator to compare with the Press.

The Afro-American papers are the only ones which will print the truth, and they lack means to employ agents and detectives to get at the facts. The race must rally a mighty host to the support of their journals, and thus enable them to do much in the way of investigation.

A lynching occurred at Port Jarvis, New York, the first week in June. A white and a coloured man were implicated in the assault upon a white girl. It was charged that the white man paid the coloured boy to make the assault, which he did on the public highway in broad day time, and was lynched. This, too, was done by "parties unknown." The white man in the case still lives. He was imprisoned, and promises to fight the case on trial. At the preliminary examination, it developed that he had been a suitor of the girl's. She had repulsed and refused him, yet had given him money, and he had sent threatening letters demanding more. The day before this examination she was so wrought up, she left home and wandered miles away. When found she said she did so because she was afraid of the man's testimony. Why should she be afraid of the prisoner? Why should she yield to his demands for money if not to prevent him exposing something he knew? It seems explainable only on the hypothesis that a *liason* existed between the coloured boy and the girl, and the white man knew of it. The press is singularly silent. Has it a motive? We owe it to ourselves to find out.

The story comes from Larned, Kansas, October 1st, that a young white lady held at bay until daylight, without alarming any one in the house, "a burly Negro," who entered her room and bed. The "burly Negro" was promptly lynched without investigation or examination of the accuracy of the statement.

A house was found burned down near Montgomery, Alabama, in Monroe County, a few weeks ago—also the burned bodies of the owners and melted piles of gold and silver. These discoveries led to the conclusion that the awful crime was not prompted by motives of robbery. The suggestion of the whites was that "brutal lust was the incentive, and as there are nearly 200 Negroes living within a radius of five miles of the place the conclusion was inevitable that some of them were the perpetrators." Upon this "suggestion," probably made by the real criminal, the mob acted upon the "conclusion," and arrested ten Afro-Americans, four of whom, they tell the world, confessed to the deed of murdering Richard L. Johnson and outraging his daughter, Jeanette. These four men, Berrell Jones, Moses Johnson, Jim and John Packer, none of them 25 years of age, upon this conclusion, were taken from gaol, hanged, shot, and burned while yet alive, the night of October 12th. The same report says that Mr. Johnson was on the best of terms with his Negro tenants.

The race thus outraged must find out the facts of this awful hurling of men into eternity on supposition, and give them to the indifferent and apathetic country. We feel this to be a garbled report, but how can we prove it?

Near Vicksburg, Mississippi, a murder was committed by a gang of burglars. Of course only Negroes could have committed the crime, and Negroes were arrested for it. It is believed that the two men, Smith Tooley and John Adams, belonged to a gang controlled by white men, who feared exposure, so on the night of July 4th they were hanged in the Court House yard by those interested in silencing them. Robberies since committed in the same vicinity have been known to be by white men who had their faces blackened. We strongly believe in the innocence of these murdered men, but we have no proof. No other news goes out to the world save that which stamps us as a race of cutthroats, robbers, and lustful wild beasts.

So great is Southern hate and prejudice, that they legally (?) hung poor little thirteen-year-old Mildred Brown at Columbia, South Carolina, October 7th, on the circumstantial evidence that she poisoned a white infant. If her guilt had been proven unmistakably, had she been white, Mildred Brown would never have been hung, the country would have been aroused and South Carolina disgraced for ever for such a crime. . . .

Nothing is more definitely settled than that he [the Afro-American] must act for himself. I have shown how he may employ the "boycott," emigration, and the Press; and I feel that by a combination of all these agencies Lynch Law—the last relic of barbarism and slavery—can be effectually stamped out. "The gods help those who help themselves." . . .

The following details of lynching from 1882 to 1891 inclusive, is proof of all that has been said, in the preceding pages. During these years the South has had full control of the political, legislative, judicial, and executive machinery. With the judges, juries, and prosecuting attorneys all Southern white men, no Negro has ever been known to escape the penalty of the law for any crime he commits. It is only the wealthy white man, with money and influence, who fails of conviction for his crimes. There is not, and never has been, any fear by the mob that a Negro would not receive full punishment for all crimes of which he is convicted. But if this state of affairs did prevail, . . . clearly the laws or those who are paid to enforce them are at fault. Hence, those who make such inoperative laws, or the officials who fail to do their duty, and not the criminals, should be lynched. But the reverse is true. The gaols, penitentiaries, and convict farms are filled with race criminals who are too poor and weak to avert such a fate. Yet of this race there were lynched in—

1882—52	1886—73	1889— 95
1883—39	1887—70	1890—100
1884—53	1888—72	1891—169
1885—77		

Of this number only 269 were charged with outrage; 253 with murder; 44 with robbery; 37 with incendiarism; 32 with reasons unstated (not necessary to give a reason for lynching a Negro); 27 with "race prejudice"; 13 with quarreling with white men; 10 with making threats; 7 with rioting; 5 with miscegenation; 4 with burglary.

Fannie Barrier Williams

Inconstancies of fortune fashioned an exclusive niche for Fannie Barrier Williams. Born in the North five years before southern Americans decreed the end of the Union, she was the daughter of parents who were "pioneer citizens" of what was then the village of Brockport, New York. Education for her was normal rather than abnormal, a regular series of progressions instead of an uneven series of contests with adversity. She attended the public schools of her locality, the Collegiate Institute of Brockport, the New England Conservatory of Music, and the School of Fine Arts in Washington, D.C. Until her marriage to S. Laing Williams, a young attorney from Chicago, she taught school in the South.

Fannie Williams' background, sensitivity, and family position account for her activity in the social and cultural life of the Chicago black community. Her gentility did not prevent taking a militant stand on the rights of blacks or the rights of women. Spokeswoman for a number of black women's organizations, she was also a member of the white Chicago Woman's Club. Appointment to the Library Board of the City of Chicago was a recognition of her race and her sex. She was the first woman to serve in that capacity and at the 1907 convention of the National American Woman's Suffrage Association, she was the only black invited to speak in eulogy of Susan B. Anthony, who had just died.

The Columbian Exposition, held in Chicago in 1893, provided Fannie Williams with a rostrum before the associated Congress of Representative Women. She earned major credit for insisting with success that black women belonged to the female species and therefore to the Congress. The meeting of the Congress coincided with mounting Jim Crow legislation. Southerners had unexampled ingenuity in making discrimination a fine sadistic art. The rising tide of lynching exhibited a savagery which the sanguine believed civilization had banished from the earth. Words can barely touch the feelings of those in direct line of the devil's fire. Black feelings were locked in fear and unbelief, but outrage found a language. Women and men demanded action to bring barbarity under the force of law. A part of the specious defense by which such behavior was condoned slandered black women. Allegations of rape by black men and of sexual immorality by black women, though less grievous than mob rule and unpremeditated murder, brought a desperate response from black women.

Fannie Williams spoke in the name of humanity. If there were moral imperfections among black women, she argued in her presentation to the ladies in Chicago, they stemmed from the existence of slavery and the prevalence of its code. No group of women, as Anna Julia Cooper had repeatedly said, is composed exclusively of heroines and the black group was no exception. Neither intelligence nor virtue was the monopoly of whites or blacks. Mrs. Williams rightly dismissed the charge of sexual immorality as "the vile imputations of a diseased public opinion." Black women have "a special sense of sympathy for all who suffer," she said, offering the other cheek of reason, since they have suffered so long and so deeply. "Our women," she asserted in gentle chastisement, "are ambitious to be contributors to all the great moral and intellectual forces that make for the greater weal of our common country." The syllogism was neat and tight; let them but have the chance and they will accomplish as much as any social group. If the record of blacks did not speak for itself, Fannie Williams spoke for it. Black women together with white women had joined to surmount cultural vestiges of the past. To release the undeveloped potential of black womanhood demanded a combined effort for the future.

Religion in America had then reached a stultifying impasse. Benevolent and effective though it was in helping blacks after the war, Christianity had to recognize that much still remained undone. American churches must cease to dissemble. They must forthrightly espouse their historic role, a role based upon "less theology and more brotherhood." "Do not," Mrs. Williams admonished with some asperity, "open the Bible too wide," for in its pages, despite the babel of tongues, love, charity, and compassion are the stern mandates for human conduct. Fannie Barrier Williams was moved by all three, and she enjoined her compatriots to live in accordance with the creeds they affirmed.[1]

---

[1]Elizabeth Lindsay Davis, ed., Lifting as They Climb (Washington, D.C., 1933), p.266. A discussion of the ideological position occupied by Fannie B. Williams and her husband in the life of Chicago's "Negro Elite" may be found in Allan H. Spear, Black Chicago: The Making of a Negro Ghetto, 1890–1920 (Chicago, 1967), pp. 66–70. Spear finds that her "background, instincts, and general inclinations disposed her toward the equal rights school of racial thought" while "the Negro power structure" dominated by Booker T. Washington "forced her" into espousal of a self-help, accommodationist viewpoint. Ibid., p. 70.

RELIGIOUS DUTY TO THE NEGRO

The strength and weakness of the Christian religion as believed, preached and practiced in the United States, is aptly illustrated in its influence as a civilizing and educational force among the colored people of this country. The negro was brought to this country by Christians, for the use of Christians, and he has ever since been treated, estimated and gauged by what are called Christian ideas of right and wrong.

• • •

The negro has been in America so long and has been so completely isolated from everything that is foreign to American notions, as to what is compatible with Christianity, that he may be fittingly said to be entirely the product of Christian influences. The vices and virtues of the American negro are the same in kind and degree as those of the men and women from whom he has been learning, by precept and example, all that he knows of God and humanity. The fetiches and crudities of the dark continent have long since ceased to be a part of his life and character,[1] he is by every mark, impulse and aspiration an American Christian, and to the American church belongs the credit and responsibility of all that he is and is to be as a man and citizen of this republic.

Religion, like every other force in America, was first used as an instrument and servant of slavery. All attempts to Christianize the negro were limited by the important fact that he was property of a valuable and peculiar sort, and that the property value must not be disturbed, even if his soul were lost. If Christianity could make the negro docile, domestic and less an independent and fighting savage, let it be preached to that extent and no further. Do not open the Bible too wide.

Such was the false, pernicious and demoralizing Gospel preached to the American slave for two hundred years. But, bad as this teaching was, it was scarcely so demoralizing as the Christian ideals held up for the negro's emulation. When mothers saw their babes sold by Christians on the auction block in order to raise money to send missionaries to foreign lands; when black Christians saw white Christians openly do everything forbidden in the Decalogue; when, indeed, they saw, as no one else could see, hypocrisy in all things triumphant everywhere, is it not remarkable if such people have any religious sense of the purities of Christianity? People who are impatient

---

Source: Fannie Barrier Williams, address, "Religious Duty to the Negro," World's Parliament of Religions, Chicago, 1893. The World's Congress of Religions (Chicago, 1894), pp. 893–97. All footnotes are the editors'.

[1]Although debate continues today over the extent to which the African cultural heritage survived in the New World, modern scholars are less prone to such derogatory value judgments of non-Christian mores. See, e.g., John Hope Franklin, From Slavery to Freedom, 3d ed. (New York, 1967), pp. 23–41.

of the moral progress of the colored people certainly are ignorant as to how far false teachings and vicious examples tended to dull the moral senses of the race.

•••

As it is there is much to be unlearned as well as to be learned. That there is something higher and better in the Christian religion than rewards and punishments is a new lesson to thousands of colored people who are still worshiping under the old dispensation of the slave Bible. But it is not an easy task to unlearn religious conceptions. "Servants, obey your masters," was preached and enforced by all the cruel instrumentalities of slavery, and by its influence the colored people were made the most valued slaves in the world. The people who in Africa resisted with terrible courage all invasions of the white races became through Christianity the most docile and defenseless of servants.[2]

Knowing full well that the religion offered to the negro was first stripped of moral instructions and suggestions, there are thousands of white church members even who charge, or are ready to believe, that the colored people are a race of moral reprobates. Fortunately the negro's career in America is radiant with evidence showing that he has always known the difference between courage and lawlessness of all forms, and anarchy in this country is not of negro origin nor a part of his history.

There was a notable period in the history of this country when the moral force of the negro character was tested to an extraordinary extent and he was not found wanting. When the country was torn asunder by the passions of civil war, and everybody thirsted for blood and revenge in every violent form, when to ravage and kill was the all-controlling passion of the hour, the negro's opportunity for retribution was ripe and at hand.

The men who degraded the race and were risking everything to continue that degradation, left their widows, their daughters, their mothers, wealth and all the precious interests of home, in the keeping of a race who had received no lessons of moral restraint. It seems but tame to say that the negro race was loyal to that trust and responsibility. Nowhere in Christendom has such nobleness of heart and moral fortitude been exampled among any people; and a recollection of the negro's conduct under this extraordinary test should save the race from the charge of being lacking in moral instincts.

---

[2]Controversy over the degree of docility induced by Christianity may be seen in two scholarly appraisals of more recent date. Benjamin E. Mays wrote in 1938, "Even in the Spirituals the Negroes did not accept without protest the social ills which they suffered." *The Negro's God as Reflected in His Literature* (Boston, 1938; reprint New York, 1968), p. 28. This interpretation is rejected in the posthumous volume of E. Franklin Frazier, *The Negro Church in America* (New York, 1963). See esp. p. 12, where the Spirituals are termed "essentially . . . other-worldly in outlook."

There is yet another notable example of the moral heroism of the colored American in spite of his lack of real religious instruction. The African Methodist Episcopal church, with its million members, vast property in churches, schools, academies, publications and learned men and women, is an enduring monument to the righteous protest of Christians to establish the mean sentiment of caste in religion and degrade us to a footstool position at the shrine of Christian worship. The colored churches of all denominations in this country are not evidences of our unfitness for religious equality, but they are so many evidences of the negro's religious heroism and self respect, that would not brook the canting assertion of mastery and superiority of those who could see the negro only as a slave, whether on earth or in heaven.

• • •

There is another and brighter side to the question as to how far the Christian religion has helped the colored people of America to realize their positions as citizens of this proud republic. Enough has already been said to show that the colored American, in spite of all the downward forces that have environed him, must have been susceptible to the higher influences of the false teachings thereof. Though the Bible was not an open book to the negro before emancipation, thousands of the enslaved men and women of the negro race learned more than was taught to them. Thousands of them realized the deeper meanings, the sweeter consolations and the spiritual awakenings that are a part of the religious experiences of all Christians. These thousands were the nucleus out of which was to grow the correct religious life of the millions.

In justification of the church it must be said that there has always been a goodly number of heroic men and saintly women who believed in the manhood and womanhood of the negro race, and at all times gave the benefit of the best religious teachings of the times. The colored people gladly acknowledge that, since emancipation, the churches of the country have almost redeemed themselves from their former sin of complicity with slavery.[3]

• • •

The churches saw these people come into the domain of citizenship stripped of all possessions, unfurnished with intelligence, untrained in the school of self-sacrifice and moral restraint, with no way out of the wilderness of their ignorance of all things, and no leadership. They saw these people with no homes or household organizations, no social order, no churches, no schools, and in the midst of people who, by training and instinct, could not recognize the manhood of the race. They saw the government give these people the certificate of freedom and citizenship without telling them what it

---

[3]Some militant black spokesmen of the 1960s have explicitly charged the churches of America with continuing complicity with racism despite Emancipation.

meant. They saw politicians count these people as so many votes, and laughed at them when pleading for schools of learning for their children.

They saw all the great business and industrial organizations of the country ignoring these people as having any possible relationship to the producing and consuming forces of the nation. They saw the whole white population looking with distrust and contempt upon these men and women, new and untried in the responsibilities of civil life. While the colored people of America were thus friendless and without status of any kind, the Christian churches came instantly, heroically and powerfully to the rescue. They began at once not only to create a sentiment favorable to the uprising of these people, but began the all-important work of building schools and churches.

They aroused the philanthropic impulse of the American people to such a degree that millions of money and an army of men and women have covered the hills of the South with agencies of regeneration of the white and black slaves of the South. The churches have vied with each other in their zeal for good work in spreading the Gospel of intelligence. Going into states that knew nothing of public school systems they have created a passion for education among both races. States that have been hostile to the idea of universal intelligence and that at one time made it a criminal offense to teach black men and women to read and write, have, under the blessed influence of the missionary work of the churches, been wonderfully converted and are now making appropriations for the education of colored children and founding and maintaining institutions that rank as normal schools, colleges and industrial schools.

Whatever may be our just grievances in the southern states, it is fitting that we acknowledge that, considering their poverty and past relationship to the negro race, they have done remarkably well for the cause of education among us. That the whole South should commit itself to the principle that the colored people have a right to be educated is an immense acquisition to the cause of popular education.

· · ·

We are grateful to the American church for this significant change of sentiment, as we are grateful to it for making our cause and needs popular at the fireside of thousands of the best homes in the country. The moral force that vouched for the expenditure of nearly $40,000,000, voluntarily given for educational and church work in the South during the last twenty-five years, is splendid testimony of the interest felt by the American people in the cause of the intellectual and moral development of the negro race. Bearing in mind all this good work done by the churches since emancipation, it is proper to ask, what can religion further do for the colored people? This question is itself significant of the important fact that colored people are beginning to think for themselves and to feel restive and conscious of every limitation to their development.

At the risk of underestimating church work in the South I must say that religion in its more blessed influences, in its wider and higher reaches of good in humanity, has made less progress in refining the life and character of the white and colored people of the South than the activity of the church interests of the South would warrant us in believing. That there is more profession than religion, more so-called church work than religious zeal, is characteristic of the American people generally, and of the southern people particularly.

More religion and less church may be accepted as a general answer to the question, "What can religion further do to advance the condition of the colored people of the South?" It is not difficult to specify wherein church interests have failed and wherein religion could have helped to improve these people. In the first place the churches have sent among us too many ministers who have had no sort of preparation and fitness for the work assigned them. With a due regard for the highly capable colored ministers of the country, I feel no hesitancy in saying that the advancement of our condition is more hindered by a large part of the ministry intrusted with leadership than by any other single cause.

Only men of moral and mental force, of a patriotic regard for the relationship of the two races, can be of real service as ministers in the South. Less theology and more of human brotherhood, less declamation and more common sense and love for truth, must be the qualifications of the new ministry that shall yet save the race from the evils of false teachings. With this new and better ministry will come the reign of that religion which ministers to the heart and gives to all our soul functions an impulse to righteousness. The tendency of creeds and doctrine to obscure religion, to make complex that which is elemental and simple, to suggest partisanship and doubt in that which is universal and certain, has seriously hindered the moral progress of the colored people of this country.

• • •

The home and social life of these people is in urgent need of the purifying power of religion. We do not yet sufficiently appreciate the fact that the heart of every social evil and disorder among the colored people, especially of the rural South, is the lack of those inherent moral potencies of home and family that are the well-springs of all the good in human society.

In nothing was slavery so savage and so relentless as in its attempted destruction of the family instincts of the negro race in America. Individuals, not families; shelters, not homes; herding, not marriages, were the cardinal sins in that system of horrors. Who can ever express in song or story the pathetic history of this race of unfortunate people when freedom came, groping about for their scattered offspring with only instinct to guide them, trying to knit together the broken ties of family kinship? It was right at this point of rehabilitation of the home life of these people that the philanthropic efforts of America should have begun. It was right here that religion in its humanitarian tendencies of love, in its moral direction and purifying force, was most needed, and still is most needed. Every preacher and every teacher in the South will tell us that preaching from the pulpit and teaching in the schoolhouse is but half done so long as the homes are uninstructed in that practical religion that can make pure and sacred every relationship it touches of man, woman and child.

Religion should not leave these people alone to learn from birds and beasts those blessed meanings of marriage, motherhood and family. Religion should not utter itself only once or twice a week through a minister from a pulpit, but should open every cabin door and get immediate contact with those who have not yet learned to translate into terms of conduct the promptings of religion.

THE INTELLECTUAL PROGRESS
OF THE COLORED WOMEN OF THE UNITED STATES
SINCE THE EMANCIPATION PROCLAMATION

Less than thirty years ago the term progress as applied to colored women of African descent in the United States would have been an anomaly. The recognition of that term to-day as appropriate is a fact full of interesting significance. That the discussion of progressive womanhood in this great assemblage of the representative women of the world is considered incomplete without some account of the colored women's status is a most noteworthy evidence that we have not failed to impress ourselves on the higher side of American life.

Less is known of our women than of any other class of Americans.

No organization of far-reaching influence for their special advancement, no conventions of women to take note of their progress, and no special literature reciting the incidents, the events, and all things interesting and instructive concerning them are to be found among the agencies directing their career. There has been no special interest in their peculiar condition as native-born American women. Their power to affect the social life of America, either for good or for ill, has excited not even a speculative interest.

Though there is much that is sorrowful, much that is wonderfully heroic, and much that is romantic in a peculiar way in their history, none of it has as yet been told as evidence of what is possible for these women. How

Source: Fannie Barrier Williams, address, "The Intellectual Progress of the Colored Women of the United States Since the Emancipation Proclamation," World's Congress of Representative Women, ed. May Wright Sewall (Chicago, 1893), pp. 696–711. This was also published as a pamphlet: Fannie Barrier Williams, The Present Status and Intellectual Progress of Colored Women (Chicago, 1893).

few of the happy, prosperous, and eager living Americans can appreciate what it all means to be suddenly changed from irresponsible bondage to the responsibility of freedom and citizenship!

The distress of it all can never be told, and the pain of it all can never be felt except by the victims, and by those saintly women of the white race who for thirty years have been consecrated to the uplifting of a whole race of women from a long-enforced degradation.

The American people have always been impatient of ignorance and poverty. They believe with Emerson that "America is another word for opportunity," and for that reason success is a virtue and poverty and ignorance are inexcusable. This may account for the fact that our women have excited no general sympathy in the struggle to emancipate themselves from the demoralization of slavery. This new life of freedom, with its far-reaching responsibilities, had to be learned by these children of darkness mostly without a guide, a teacher, or a friend. In the mean vocabulary of slavery there was no definition of any of the virtues of life. The meaning of such precious terms as marriage, wife, family, and home could not be learned in a school-house. The blue-back speller, the arithmetic, and the copy-book contain no magical cures for inherited inaptitudes for the moralities. Yet it must ever be counted as one of the most wonderful things in human history how promptly and eagerly these suddenly liberated women tried to lay hold upon all that there is in human excellence. There is a touching pathos in the eagerness of these millions of new home-makers to taste the blessedness of intelligent womanhood. The path of progress in the picture is enlarged so as to bring to view these trustful and zealous students of freedom and civilization striving to overtake and keep pace with women whose emancipation has been a slow and painful process for a thousand years. The longing to be something better than they were when freedom found them has been the most notable characteristic in the development of these women. This constant striving for equality has given an upward direction to all the activities of colored women.

Freedom at once widened their vision beyond the mean cabin life of their bondage. Their native gentleness, good cheer, and hopefulness made them susceptible to those teachings that make for intelligence and righteousness. Sullenness of disposition, hatefulness, and revenge against the master class because of two centuries of ill-treatment are not in the nature of our women.

But a better view of what our women are doing and what their present status is may be had by noticing some lines of progress that are easily verifiable.

First it should be noticed that separate facts and figures relative to colored women are not easily obtainable. Among the white women of the country independence, progressive intelligence, and definite interests have done so much that nearly every fact and item illustrative of their progress and status is classified and easily accessible. Our women, on the contrary, have had no advantage of interests peculiar and distinct and separable from those of men that have yet excited public attention and kindly recognition.

In their religious life, however, our women show a progressiveness parallel in every important particular to that of white women in all Christian churches. . . .

While there has been but little progress toward the growing rationalism in the Christian creeds, there has been a marked advance toward a greater refinement of conception, good taste, and the proprieties. It is our young women coming out of the schools and academies that have been insisting upon a more godly and cultivated ministry. It is the young women of a new generation and new inspirations that are making tramps of the ministers who once dominated the colored church, and whose intelligence and piety were mostly in their lungs. . . .

Another evidence of growing intelligence is a sense of religious discrimination among our women. Like the nineteenth century woman generally, our women find congeniality in all the creeds, from the Catholic creed to the no-creed of Emerson. There is a constant increase of this interesting variety in the religious life of our women.

Closely allied to this religious development is their progress in the work of education in schools and colleges. For thirty years education has been the magic word among the colored people of this country. That their greatest need was education in its broadest sense was understood by these people more strongly than it could be taught to them. It is the unvarying testimony of every teacher in the South that the mental development of the colored women as well as men has been little less than phenomenal. In twenty-five years, and under conditions discouraging in the extreme, thousands of our women have been educated as teachers. They have adapted themselves to the work of mentally lifting a whole race of people so eagerly and readily that they afford an apt illustration of the power of self-help. Not only have these women become good teachers in less than twenty-five years, but many of them are the prize teachers in the mixed schools of nearly every Northern city.

These women have also so fired the hearts of the race for education that colleges, normal schools, industrial schools, and universities have been reared by a generous public to meet the requirements of these eager students of intelligent citizenship. As American women generally are fighting against the nineteenth century narrowness that still keeps women out of the higher institutions of learning, so our women are eagerly demanding the best of education open to their race. They continually verify what President Rankin[4] of Howard University recently said, "Any theory of educating the Afro-American that does not throw open the golden gates of the highest culture will fail on the ethical and spiritual side."

---

[4]Dr. Jeremiah Eames Rankin (1828–1904) was a white Congregationalist minister who served as president of Howard University from 1890 to 1903.

It is thus seen that our women have the same spirit and mettle that characterize the best of American women. Everywhere they are following in the tracks of those women who are swiftest in the race for higher knowledge.

To-day they feel strong enough to ask for but one thing, and that is the same opportunity for the acquisition of all kinds of knowledge that may be accorded to other women. This granted, in the next generation these progressive women will be found successfully occupying every field where the highest intelligence alone is admissible. In less than another generation American literature, American art, and American music will be enriched by productions having new and peculiar features of interest and excellence.

The exceptional career of our women will yet stamp itself indelibly upon the thought of this country.

American literature needs for its greater variety and its deeper soundings that which will be written into it out of the hearts of these self-emancipating women.

The great problems of social reform that are now so engaging the highest intelligence of American women will soon need for their solution the reinforcement of that new intelligence which our women are developing. In short, our women are ambitious to be contributors to all the great moral and intellectual forces that make for the greater weal of our common country.

If this hope seems too extravagant to those of you who know these women only in their humbler capacities, I would remind you that all that we hope for and will certainly achieve in authorship and practical intelligence is more than prophesied by what has already been done, and more that can be done, by hundreds of Afro-American women whose talents are now being expended in the struggle against race resistance.

The power of organized womanhood is one of the most interesting studies of modern sociology. Formerly women knew so little of each other mentally, their common interests were so sentimental and gossipy, and their knowledge of all the larger affairs of human society was so meager that organization among them, in the modern sense, was impossible. Now their liberal intelligence, their contact in all the great interests of education, and their increasing influence for good in all the great reformatory movements of the age has created in them a greater respect for each other, and furnished the elements of organization for large and splendid purposes. The highest ascendancy of woman's development has been reached when they have become mentally strong enough to find bonds of association interwoven with sympathy, loyalty, and mutual trustfulness. To-day union is the watchword of woman's onward march.

If it be a fact that this spirit of organization among women generally is the distinguishing mark of the nineteenth century woman, dare we ask if the colored women of the United States have made any progress in this respect? . . .

Benevolence is the essence of most of the colored women's organizations. The humane side of their natures has been cultivated to recognize the duties they owe to the sick, the indigent and ill-fortuned. No church, school, or charitable institution for the special use of colored people has been allowed to languish or fail when the associated efforts of the women could save it. . . .

The hearts of Afro-American women are too warm and too large for race hatred. Long suffering has so chastened them that they are developing a special sense of sympathy for all who suffer and fail of justice. All the associated interests of church, temperance, and social reform in which American women are winning distinction can be wonderfully advanced when our women shall be welcomed as co-workers, and estimated solely by what they are worth to the moral elevation of all the people.

I regret the necessity of speaking to the question of the moral progress of our women, because the morality of our home life has been commented upon so disparagingly and meanly that we are placed in the unfortunate position of being defenders of our name.

It is proper to state, with as much emphasis as possible, that all questions relative to the moral progress of the colored women of America are impertinent and unjustly suggestive when they relate to the thousands of colored women in the North who were free from the vicious influences of slavery. They are also meanly suggestive as regards thousands of our women in the South whose force of character enabled them to escape the slavery taints of immorality. The question of the moral progress of colored women in the United States has force and meaning in this discussion only so far as it tells the story of how the once-enslaved women have been struggling for twenty-five years to emancipate themselves from the demoralization of their enslavement.

While I duly appreciate the offensiveness of all references to American slavery, it is unavoidable to charge to that system every moral imperfection that mars the character of the colored American. The whole life and power of slavery depended upon an enforced degradation of everything human in the slaves. The slave code recognized only animal distinctions between the sexes, and ruthlessly ignored those ordinary separations that belong to the social state.

It is a great wonder that two centuries of such demoralization did not work a complete extinction of all the moral instincts. But the recuperative power of these women to regain their moral instincts and to establish a respectable relationship to American womanhood is among the earlier evidences of their moral ability to rise above their conditions. In spite of a cursed heredity that bound them to the lowest social level, in spite of everything that is unfortunate and unfavorable, these women have continually shown an increasing degree of teachableness as to the meaning of woman's relationship to man.

Out of this social purification and moral uplift have come a chivalric sentiment and regard from the young men of the race that give to the young women a new sense of protection. I do not wish to disturb the serenity of this conference by suggesting why this protection is needed and the kind of men against whom it is needed.

It is sufficient for us to know that the daughters of women who thirty years ago were not allowed to be modest, not allowed to follow the instincts of moral rectitude, who could cry for protection to no living man, have so elevated the moral tone of their social life that new and purer standards of personal worth have been created, and new ideals of womanhood, instinct with grace and delicacy, are everywhere recognized and emulated.

This moral regeneration of a whole race of women is no idle sentiment—it is a serious business; and everywhere there is witnessed a feverish anxiety to be free from the mean suspicions that have so long underestimated the character strength of our women.

These women are not satisfied with the unmistakable fact that moral progress has been made, but they are fervently impatient and stirred by a sense of outrage under the vile imputations of a diseased public opinion. . . .

It may now perhaps be fittingly asked, What mean all these evidences of mental, social, and moral progress of a class of American women of whom you know so little? Certainly you can not be indifferent to the growing needs and importance of women who are demonstrating their intelligence and capacity for the highest privileges of freedom.

The most important thing to be noted is the fact that the colored people of America have reached a distinctly new era in their career so quickly that the American mind has scarcely had time to recognize the fact, and adjust itself to the new requirements of the people in all things that pertain to citizenship. . . .

It seems to daze the understanding of the ordinary citizen that there are thousands of men and women everywhere among us who in twenty-five years have progressed as far away from the non-progressive peasants of the "black belt" of the South as the highest social life in New England is above the lowest levels of American civilization.

This general failure of the American people to know the now generation of colored people, and to recognize this important change in them, is the cause of more injustice to our women than can well be estimated. Further progress is everywhere seriously hindered by this ignoring of their improvement.

Our exclusion from the benefits of the fair play sentiment of the country is little less than a crime against the ambitions and aspirations of a whole race of women. The American people are but repeating the common folly of history in thus attempting to repress the yearnings of progressive humanity.

In the item of employment colored women bear a distressing burden of mean and unreasonable discrimination. . . .

It is almost literally true that, except teaching in colored schools and menial work, colored women can find no employment in this free America. They are the only women in the country for whom real ability, virtue, and special talents count for nothing when they become applicants for respectable employment. Taught everywhere in ethics and social economy that merit always wins, colored women carefully prepare themselves for all kinds of occupation only to meet with stern refusal, rebuff, and disappointment. One of countless instances will show how the best as well as the meanest of American society are responsible for the special injustice to our women.

Not long ago I presented the case of a bright young woman to a well-known bank president of Chicago, who was in need of a thoroughly competent stenographer and typewriter. The president was fully satisfied with the young woman as exceptionally qualified for the position, and manifested much pleasure in commending her to the directors for appointment, and at the same time disclaimed that there could be any opposition on account of the slight tinge of African blood that identified her as a colored woman. Yet, when the matter was brought before the directors for action, these mighty men of money and business, these men whose prominence in all the great interests of the city would seem to lift them above all narrowness and foolishness, scented the African taint, and at once bravely came to the rescue of the bank and of society by dashing the hopes of this capable yet helpless young woman. . . .

Can the people of this country afford to single out the women of a whole race of people as objects of their special contempt? Do these women not belong to a race that has never faltered in its support of the country's flag in every war since Attucks fell in Boston's streets?

Are they not the daughters of men who have always been true as steel against treason to everything fundamental and splendid in the republic? In short, are these women not as thoroughly American in all the circumstances of citizenship as the best citizens of our country?

If it be so, are we not justified in a feeling of desperation against that peculiar form of Americanism that shows respect for our women as servants and contempt for them when they become women of culture? We have never been taught to understand why the unwritten law of chivalry, protection, and fair play that are everywhere the conservators of women's welfare must exclude every woman of a dark complexion.

We believe that the world always needs the influence of every good and capable woman, and this rule recognizes no exceptions based on complexion. In their complaint against hindrances to their employment colored women ask for no special favors. . . .

Another, and perhaps more serious, hindrance to our women is that nightmare known as "social equality." The term equality is the most inspiring word in the vocabulary of citizenship. It expresses the leveling quality in all the splendid possibilities of American life. It is this idea of equality that has made room in this country for all kinds and conditions of men, and made personal merit the supreme requisite for all kinds of achievement.

When the colored people became citizens, and found it written deep in the organic law of the land that they too had the right to life, liberty, and the pursuit of happiness, they were at once suspected of wishing to interpret this maxim of equality as meaning social equality.

Everywhere the public mind has been filled with constant alarm lest in some way our women shall approach the social sphere of the dominant race in this country. Men and women, wise and perfectly sane in all things else, become instantly unwise and foolish at the remotest suggestion of social contact with colored men and women. At every turn in our lives we meet this fear, and are humiliated by its aggressiveness and meanness. If we seek the sanctities of religion, the enlightenment of the university, the honors of politics, and the natural recreations of our common country, the social equality alarm is instantly given, and our aspirations are insulted. "Beware of social equality with the colored American" is thus written on all places, sacred or profane, in this blessed land of liberty. The most discouraging and demoralizing effect of this false sentiment concerning us is that it utterly ignores individual merit and discredits the sensibilities of intelligent womanhood. The sorrows and heartaches of a whole race of women seem to be matters of no concern to the people who so dread the social possibilities of these colored women.

On the other hand, our women have been wonderfully indifferent and unconcerned about the matter. The dread inspired by the growing intelligence of colored women has interested us almost to the point of amusement. It has given to colored women a new sense of importance to witness how easily their emancipation and steady advancement is disturbing all classes of American people. It may not be a discouraging circumstance that colored women can command some sort of attention, even though they be misunderstood. We believe in the law of reaction, and it is reasonably certain that the forces of intelligence and character being developed in our women will yet change mistrustfulness into confidence and contempt into sympathy and respect. It will soon appear to those who are not hopelessly monomaniacs on the subject that the colored people are in no way responsible for the social equality nonsense. We shall yet be credited with knowing better than our enemies that social equality can neither be enforced by law nor prevented by oppression. Though not philosophers, we long since learned that equality before the law, equality in the best sense of that term under our institutions, is totally different from social equality.

We know, without being exceptional students of history, that the social relationship of the two races will be adjusted equitably in spite of all fear and injustice, and that there is a social gravitation in human affairs that eventually overwhelms and crushes into nothingness all resistance based on prejudice and selfishness.

Our chief concern in this false social sentiment is that it attempts to hinder our further progress toward the higher spheres of womanhood. On account of it, young colored women of ambition and means are compelled in many instances to leave the country for training and education in the salons and studios of Europe. On many of the railroads of this country women of refinement and culture are driven like cattle into human cattle-cars lest the occupying of an individual seat paid for in a first-class car may result in social equality. This social quarantine on all means of travel in certain parts of the country is guarded and enforced more rigidly against us than the quarantine regulations against cholera.

Without further particularizing as to how this social question opposes our advancement, it may be stated that the contentions of colored women are in kind like those of other American women for greater freedom of development. Liberty to be all that we can be, without artificial hindrances, is a thing no less precious to us than to women generally.

We come before this assemblage of women feeling confident that our progress has been along high levels and rooted deeply in the essentials of intelligent humanity. We are so essentially American in speech, in instincts, in sentiments and destiny that the things that interest you equally interest us.

We believe that social evils are dangerously contagious. The fixed policy of persecution and injustice against a class of women who are weak and defenseless will be necessarily hurtful to the cause of all women. Colored women are becoming more and more a part of the social forces that must help to determine the questions that so concern women generally. In this Congress we ask to be known and recognized for what we are worth. If it be the high purpose of these deliberations to lessen the resistance to woman's progress, you can not fail to be interested in our struggles against the many oppositions that harass us.

Women who are tender enough in heart to be active in humane societies, to be foremost in all charitable activities, who are loving enough to unite Christian womanhood everywhere against the sin of intemperance, ought to be instantly concerned in the plea of colored women for justice and humane treatment. Women of the dominant race can not afford to be responsible for the wrongs we suffer, since those who do injustice can not escape a certain penalty.

But there is no wish to overstate the obstacles to colored women or to picture their status as hopeless. There is no disposition to take our place in this Congress as faultfinders or suppliants for mercy. As women of a common country, with common interests, and a destiny that will certainly bring us closer to each other, we come to this altar with our contribution of hopefulness as well as with our complaints. . . .

If the love of humanity more than the love of races and sex shall pulsate throughout all the grand results that shall issue to the world from this parliament of women, women of African descent in the United States will for the first time begin to feel the sweet release from the blighting thrall of prejudice.

The colored women, as well as all women, will realize that the inalienable right to life, liberty, and the pursuit of happiness is a maxim that will become more blessed in its significance when the hand of woman shall take it from its sepulture in books and make it the gospel of every-day life and the unerring guide in the relations of all men, women, and children.

[Following this address by Mrs. Williams and the brief comments by Anna Julia Cooper and Frances Jackson Coppin, the audience "insisted," in the words of the official report, upon a few remarks from Frederick Douglass.[5] "Mr. Douglass," the report noted, "was the only man who, after the opening session, spoke in the General Congress. The occasion was of such historical importance that the editor (May Wright Sewall) feels justified in reproducing Mr. Douglass' address here, notwithstanding the published declaration that no one would be permitted to speak in the congress whose name did not appear on the programme."]

Mr. Douglass spoke as follows:
  I have heard to night what I hardly expected ever to live to hear. I have heard refined, educated colored ladies addressing—and addressing successfully—one of the most intelligent white audiences that I ever looked upon. It is the new thing under the sun, and my heart is too full to speak; my mind is too much illuminated with hope and with expectation for the race in seeing this sign.
  Fifty years ago and more I was alone in the wilderness, telling my story of the wrongs of slavery, and imploring the justice, the humanity, the sympathy, the patriotism, and every other good quality of the American heart to do away with slavery; and you can easily see that when I hear such speeches as I have heard this evening from our women—our women—I feel a sense of gratitude to Almighty God that I have lived to see what I now see. It seems to me that we are not living in the old world I was born into, but in the one seen by John in the apocalyptic vision. A new heaven is dawning upon us, and a new earth is ours, in which all discriminations against men and women on account of color and sex is passing away, and will pass away; and as John said there would be no more sea after they had been surrounded on that desolate island so long, so I say there is a time coming when prejudices, discriminations, proscriptions, and persecutions on account of what is accidental will all pass away, and this great country of ours will be possessed by a composite nation of the grandest possible character, made up of all races, kindreds, tongues, and peoples.
  Dear friends, I am full and you are full. You have heard more to-night than you will remember, perhaps, but the grand spirit which has proceeded from this platform will live in your memory and work in your lives always.

---

[5]The remarks of Frederick Douglass appear in *World's Congress of Representative Women*, cited above, pp. 717–18. The comments of Anna Julia Cooper and Frances Jackson Coppin are excerpted below.

IV

"TO GET AN EDUCATION
AND TO TEACH MY PEOPLE"

Education was part of the effort to arise. It was a goal in itself, a privilege denied to those in bondage and even to most of the free black population. A black person who acquired some formal education also had new leverage for helping the others to inch forward.

Literacy is the fundamental tool of modern learning. To Americans in the nineteenth century it led, most importantly, to the ability to read the Bible. The right to read was the right to share more fully in the Christian fellowship. Spreading the word of God took many forms, among them spreading the skills that enabled others to read. In black communities Sabbath schools played an especially significant role.

Freedom, literacy, and religion were a trinity of interlacing values. Freedom, though primary, was not inevitably first, for literacy, even when stolen, was a move toward freedom of mind and spirit. Religion might be a source of inner freedom, the focus of communal uplift, the impetus for self-improvement.

The written word was a means of practical liberation. It enabled a slave to forge a pass, read a notice, communicate with distant family. It helped a plantation preacher to learn the whole of the Bible and not just the limited portions his master wished him to know. In freedom it was the primary step to holding a job that was not mere drudgery; to reading the terms of a contract; to knowing the law; to following the news; to learning what others had written in books. Beyond all else, it opened the way to grasp the complex culture built on alphabet and printing press.

There was a crucial distinction between those who could read and those who could not. Another step divided those with the bare rudiments of schooling from those who had found their way to study as a way of life. The women included in this section were not only well-schooled themselves but were devoted to education. Teaching was the bridge they chose between their own development and their earnest desire to serve.

Charlotte Forten Grimké

Charlotte Forten came from a background of privilege. Comfort, elegance, and dignity were its hallmarks, but so too were discrimination and protest. The comfortable pattern of living was circumscribed. Philadelphia, where she was born in 1837, knew only a limited measure of brotherly love.

Robert Forten wanted a good life for his daughter. He had money and education, a family tradition and fame not merely in his native city but far beyond. His own father was James Forten, a sailmaker known as the nation's most successful black businessman during the early nineteenth century, and known also as an outspoken antislavery leader. With wealth behind conviction James Forten had helped to sponsor William Lloyd Garrison's publication, The Liberator, voice of militant abolitionism from its start in 1831. Grandfather, father, uncles, and aunts were all articulate and active in the growing abolitionist ferment.

In this enclave, suffering the loss of her mother while still a child, Charlotte grew up much indulged and closely protected. Her grandfather's home and the nearby estate of her uncle Robert Purvis were centers for abolitionists and other reformers. From early years the child knew cosmopolitan women and men whose common ground was their commitment to act upon belief. Lucretia Mott and her husband James, distinguished Quaker reformers, were among the notables who came to dinner; Garrison stayed with the Fortens when traveling from Boston. Such contact made an education of lasting import. Private tutors supplied the formal training, for her father refused to send her to Philadelphia's segregated schools.

At once sheltered and stimulated by this "atmosphere of crusading zeal,"[1] Charlotte Forten grew into a sensitive, ladylike, serious young woman. Her stilted literary mode of expression, even in the intimate pages of a journal, was partly the outcome of her genteel education but may also have served as protective armor. She yearned for self-improvement, she longed for fuller freedom, she aspired to lead a life of purpose. Preliminary to these goals was a further education. When she was sixteen her father arranged for her to live in Salem, Massachusetts, in order to enter an integrated school. She would stay in the home of a family friend, Charles Lenox

---

[1]Ray Allen Billington, ed., The Journal of Charlotte L. Forten (New York, 1953), p. 6.

Remond. The Remonds were free black business people too. Like the Fortens, the men and even the women were in the forefront of antislavery work.

Charlotte Forten, schoolgirl, began a diary. Her entries provide rare insight into the sharp personal impact of public affairs on a nineteenth-century adolescent. At one of the hubs of intellectual and reform life, she eagerly imbibed its substance and idolized its leaders. The journal reveals the significant adults who became her models. Two women were especially important in shaping her subsequent career: Sarah Remond (included in this volume), who followed in her brother's footsteps to become an antislavery lecturer, and her "dear teacher" Mary Shepard, a white woman "thoroughly opposed" to slavery. Miss Remond inspired young Charlotte to dream of being a lecturer too, but frail health intervened. Miss Shepard overcame all impediments and enabled her student to teach.

In 1854, when she had been in the Remond household but a few weeks, Charlotte Forten's purposes were still diffuse. The distressing outcome of a fugitive slave's arrest and trial would serve her, she vowed, as "fresh incentive to more earnest study." She would fit herself "for laboring in a holy cause." Somehow she would help to alter "the condition of my oppressed and suffering people." She monitored her own emotions. Melancholy was often dominant, but she strove to find beauty in nature, books, and human behavior. Playfulness was rare. In midsummer, though, she allowed herself a bit of adventure, after the duties of school and housework were performed: "Adopted 'Bloomer' costume and ascended the highest cherry tree, . . . the first feat of the kind ever performed by me."[2]

Her teaching appointment was a milestone for Salem as much as for the new teacher herself. Charlotte Forten in 1856 became the first black teacher of white children in "this conservative, aristocratic old city of Salem."[3] Successful and appreciated, despite intermittent retreats to Philadelphia for reasons of health, she left this congenial pattern a few years later for a new challenge. Lacerated by the "cruel wrongs" of northern bigotry, she had prayed for a "day of retribution." Now it had come.

A great social experiment began at an early stage of the Civil War. Islands off the South Carolina coast had been seized by Union forces; newly liberated slaves in vast numbers were in need of work, relief, and education. Charlotte Forten was one of the many northern teachers volunteering to help. For a year and a half she knit together fragments of disparate cultures: untutored freedmen of all ages and conditions, bureaucratic idealists, young blacks in uniform, dedicated white reformers. Though she identified with blacks, she was starved for the intellectual diet of New England. Her journal was no longer her major mode of writing. She wrote articles and open letters, sharing her experiences with readers of Atlantic Monthly and The

---

[2]Ibid., p. 44.
[3]Ibid., p. 70.

Liberator. *Fatigue, ill health, and late summer's unfavorable climate prompted a vacation to the North in 1863. The following summer she went home for good.*

Intensity of living gave way to a time of quiescence, for she was worn down. Her father had died shortly after enlisting in the army in 1864. She wrote articles, she read, occasionally she did some teaching. At last she accepted a clerkship that took her to Washington. In 1878 she married Francis James Grimké, a young black minister of extraordinary connections. This natural son of a South Carolina planter, along with a brother named Archibald, had been acknowledged as nephews by the white abolitionists Angelina and Sarah Grimké, who decades earlier had rejected their family's plantation mores.

A lasting friendship formed between the Grimké couple and the Washington educator Anna Julia Cooper, who is also represented in this volume. After Charlotte Forten Grimké's death in 1914, her papers, including the diary, were safeguarded by Dr. Cooper, who later compiled a memorial volume, Life and Writings of the Grimké Family.[4] *The Journal was edited and published in 1953.*

Materials from two sources have been excerpted here. Segments from the Journal begin with the arrest of Anthony Burns in Boston as a fugitive from slavery. Charlotte Forten's letter from Port Royal to The Liberator *(19 December 1862) depicts the first Thanksgiving Day in freedom for the "contraband" community off the Carolina coast.*

Thursday, May 25, 1854. Did not intend to write this evening, but have just heard of something which is worth recording;—something which must ever rouse in the mind of every true friend of liberty and humanity, feelings of the deepest indignation and sorrow. Another fugitive from bondage has been arrested; a poor man, who for two short months has trod the soil and breathed the air of the "Old Bay State," was arrested like a criminal in the streets of her capital, and is now kept strictly guarded,—a double police force is required, the military are in readiness; and all this is done to prevent a man, whom God has created in his own image, from regaining that freedom with which, he, in common with every other human being, is endowed. I can only hope and pray most earnestly that Boston will not again disgrace herself by sending him back to a bondage worse than death; or rather that she will redeem herself from the disgrace which his arrest alone has brought upon her. . . .

---

[4]Anna Julia Cooper, *Life and Writings of the Grimké Family* (n.p., 1951).
Source: Charlotte Forten Grimké, *The Journal of Charlotte L. Forten,* ed. Ray Allen Billington (New York, 1953), pp. 34–38, 41–48, 55. The annotations give illuminating details about the arrest and trial of Anthony Burns. All footnotes are by the editors, BJL and RB.

Saturday, May 27. . . . Returned home, read the Anti-Slavery papers, and then went down to the depot to meet father; he had arrived in Boston early in the morning, regretted very much that he had not reached there the evening before to attend the great meeting at Faneuil Hall. He says that the excitement in Boston is very great; the trial of the poor man takes place on Monday. We scarcely dare to think of what may be the result; there seems to be nothing too bad for these Northern tools of slavery to do.

Tuesday, May 30. Rose very early and was busy until nine o'clock; then, at Mrs. Putnam's[1] urgent request, went to keep store for her while she went to Boston to attend the Anti-Slavery Convention. I was very anxious to go, and will certainly do so to-morrow; the arrest of the alleged fugitive will give additional interest to the meetings, I should think. His trial is still going on and I can scarcely think of anything else; read again to-day as most suitable to my feelings and to the times, "The Runaway Slave at Pilgrim's Point," by Elizabeth B. Browning; how powerfully it is written! how earnestly and touchingly does the writer portray the bitter anguish of the poor fugitive as she thinks over all the wrongs and sufferings that she has endured, and of the sin to which tyrants have driven her but which they alone must answer for! It seems as if no one could read this poem without having his sympathies roused to the utmost in behalf of the oppressed.—After a long conversation with my friends on their return, on this all-absorbing subject, we separated for the night, and I went to bed, weary and sad.

Wednesday, May 31. . . . Sarah [Remond] and I went to Boston in the morning. Everything was much quieter—outwardly than we expected, but still much real indignation and excitement prevail. We walked past the Court-House, which is now lawlessly converted into a prison, and filled with soldiers, some of whom were looking from the windows, with an air of insolent authority which made my blood boil, while I felt the strongest contempt for their cowardice and servility. We went to the meeting, but the best speakers were absent, engaged in the most arduous and untiring efforts in behalf of the poor fugitive; but though we missed the glowing eloquence of [Wendell] Phillips, [William Lloyd] Garrison, and [Theodore] Parker, still there were excellent speeches made, and our hearts responded to the exalted sentiments of Truth and Liberty which were uttered. The exciting intelligence which occasionally came in relation to the trial, added fresh zeal to the speakers, of whom Stephen [S.] Foster and his wife [Abby Kelley Foster] were the principal. The latter addressed, in the most eloquent language, the women present, entreating them to urge their husbands and brothers to action, and also to give their aid on all occasions in our just and holy cause.—I did not see father the whole day; he, of course, was deeply inter-

---

[1]Caroline Remond Putnam, a married sister of Charles Lenox Remond and Sarah Remond, had a shop for wigs and hair goods.

ested in the trial.—Dined at Mr. Garrison's; his wife is one of the loveliest persons I have ever seen, worthy of such a husband. At the table, I watched earnestly the expression of that noble face, as he spoke beautifully in support of the non-resistant principles to which he has kept firm; his is indeed the very highest Christian spirit, to which I cannot hope to reach, however, for I believe in 'resistance to tyrants,' and would fight for liberty until death. We came home in the evening, and felt sick at heart as we passed through the streets of Boston on our way to the depot, seeing the military as they rode along, ready at any time to prove themselves the minions of the South.

Thursday, June 1st. . . . The trial is over at last; the commissioner's decision will be given to-morrow. We are all in the greatest suspense; what will that decision be? Alas! that any one should have the power to decide the right of a fellow being to himself! It is thought by many that he will be acquitted of the *great crime* of leaving a life of bondage, as the legal evidence is not thought sufficient to convict him. But it is only too probable that they will sacrifice him to propitiate the South, since so many at the North dared oppose the passage of the infamous Nebraska Bill.—Miss Putnam[2] was married this evening. Mr. Frothingham performed the ceremony, and in his prayer alluded touchingly to the events of this week; he afterwards in conversation with the bridegroom, (Mr. Gilliard), spoke in the most feeling manner about this case;—his sympathies are all on the right side. The wedding was a pleasant one; the bride looked very lovely; and we enjoyed ourselves as much as is possible in these exciting times. It is impossible to be happy now.

Friday, June 2. Our worst fears are realized; the decision was against poor Burns, and he has been sent back to a bondage worse, a thousand times worse than death. Even an attempt at rescue was utterly impossible; the prisoner was completely surrounded by soldiers with bayonets fixed, a cannon loaded, ready to be fired at the slightest sign. To-day Massachusetts has again been disgraced; again has she shewed her submission to the Slave Power; and Oh! with what deep sorrow do we think of what will doubtless be the fate of that poor man, when he is again consigned to the horrors of Slavery. With what scorn must that government be regarded, which cowardly assembles thousands of soldiers to satisfy the demands of slaveholders; to deprive of his freedom a man, created in God's own image, whose sole offence is the color of his skin! And if resistance is offered to this outrage, these soldiers are to shoot down American citizens without mercy; and this by the express orders of a government which proudly boasts of being the freeest [sic] in the world; this on the very soil where the Revolution of 1776 began; in sight of the battle-field, where thousands of brave men fought and died in opposing British tyranny, which was nothing compared

---

[2]Sarah Putnam, daughter of Caroline Remond Putnam, was married by a liberal white clergyman, the Rev. O.B. Frothingham.

with the American oppression of to-day. In looking over my diary, I perceive that I did not mention that there was on the Friday night after the man's arrest, an attempt made to rescue him, but although it failed, on account of there not being men enough engaged in it, all honor should be given to those who bravely made the attempt. I can write no more. A cloud seems hanging over me, over all our persecuted race, which nothing can dispel.

Sunday, June 4. A beautiful day. The sky is cloudless, the sun shines warm and bright, and a delicious breeze fans my cheek as I sit by the window writing. How strange it is that in a world so beautiful, there can be so much wickedness; on this delightful day, while many are enjoying themselves in their happy homes, not poor Burns only,[3] but millions beside are suffering in chains; and how many Christian ministers to-day will mention him, or those who suffer with him? How many will speak from the pulpit against the cruel outrage on humanity which has just been committed; or against the many, even worse ones, which are committed in this country every day? Too well do we know that there are but very few, and these few alone deserve to be called the ministers of Christ, whose doctrine was 'Break every yoke, and let the oppressed go free.'—During the past week, we have had a vacation, which I had expected to enjoy very much, but it was of course impossible for me to do so. To-morrow school commences, and although the pleasure I shall feel in again seeing my beloved teacher, and in resuming my studies will be much saddened by recent events, yet they shall be a fresh incentive to more earnest study, to aid me in fitting myself for laboring in a holy cause, for enabling me to do much towards changing the condition of my oppressed and suffering people. Would that those with whom I shall recite to-morrow could sympathize with me in this; would that they could look upon all God's creatures without respect to color, feeling that it is character alone which makes the true man or woman! I earnestly hope that the time will come when they will feel thus. . . .

Sunday, June 25. Have been writing nearly all day.—This afternoon went to an Anti-Slavery meeting in Danvers, from which I have just returned. Mr. Foss[4] spoke eloquently, and with that warmth and sincerity which evidently come from the heart. He said he was rejoiced that the people at the North were beginning to feel that slavery is no longer confined to the black man alone, but that they too must wear the yoke; and they are becoming roused on the subject at last. He spoke of the objections made by many to the Abolitionists, on the plea of their using too violent language; they say that the slaveholders are driven by it to worse measures; what they need is mild entreaty, etc., etc. But the petition against the Nebraska Bill, couched in the

---

[3]Freed some months later through purchase by a group of abolitionists, Anthony Burns returned to the North. Charlotte Forten records that she saw him at the New England Anti-Slavery Society meeting on 30 May 1855.

[4] The Rev. Andrew D. Foss was an agent for the Massachusetts Anti-Slavery Society.

very mildest terms by the clergymen of the North, was received even less favorably by the South, than the hardest sayings of the Abolitionists; and they were abused and denounced more severely than the latter have ever been.—As we walked home, Miss [Sarah] Remond and I were wishing that we could have an anti-slavery meeting in the neighborhood every Sunday, and as well attended as this was. . . .

Sunday, July 2. A delightful day—In the morning read several chapters in the New Testament. The third verse of the last chapter of Hebrews— "Remember them that are in bonds as bound with them" suggested many thoughts to my mind: *Remember the poor slave as bound with him.* How few even of those who are opposed to slavery realize this! If they felt thus so ardent, so untiring, would be their efforts that they would soon accomplish the overthrow of this iniquitous system. All honor for the noble few who do feel for the suffering bondman *as bound with him,* and act accordingly! . . .

Sunday, July 9. Attended the meetings[5] during the day and evening. I felt sorry and disappointed to see such a small number of persons present. The intense heat of the weather perhaps accounted for this. Though for such a cause I thought much more than that might have been endured. Very eloquent and interesting speeches were made by Mr. Garrison and Mr. Foss in the afternoon and evening. After tea I went to Miss [Sarah] Remond's where Mr. Garrison had taken tea, and felt happier and better after listening to the conversation of that truly good and great man. . . .

Friday, July 28. This morning Miss Creamer, a friend of our teacher, came into the school. She is a very learned lady; a Latin teacher in Troy Seminary, and an authoress. I certainly did feel some alarm, when I saw her entering the room. But she was so very kind and pleasant that I soon felt more at ease. . . . I do think reading one's compositions before strangers is a trying task. If I were to tell Mrs. R[emond] this, I know she would ask how I could expect to become what I often say I should like to be—an Anti-Slavery lecturer. But I think that I should then trust to the inspiration of the subject.—This evening read "Poems of Phillis Wheatly [sic]," an African slave, who lived in Boston at the time of the Revolution. She was a wonderfully gifted woman, and many of her poems are very beautiful. Her character and genius afford a striking proof of the falseness of the assertion made by some that hers is an inferior race. . . .

Tuesday, August 1. To-day is the twentieth anniversary of British emancipation. The joy that we feel at an event so just and so glorious is greatly saddened by thoughts of the bitter and cruel oppression which still exists in

---

[5]In Salem, the Essex [County] Anti-Slavery Society met on Saturday and Sunday, 8 and 9 July 1854.

our own land, so proudly claiming to be "the land of the free." And how very distant seems the day when she will follow the example of "the mother country," and liberate her millions of suffering slaves! This morning I went with Mr. and Mrs. R[emond] to the celebration at Abington. The weather was delightful, and a very large number of persons was assembled in the beautiful grove. Mr. Garrison, Wendell Phillips and many other distinguished friends of freedom were present, and spoke eloquently. Mr. Garrison gave an interesting account of the rise and progress of the anti-slavery movement in Great Britain. . . . The sadness that I had felt was almost entirely dissipated by the hopeful feelings expressed by the principal speakers. And when they sang the beautiful songs for the occasion, there was something very pleasant in the blending of so many voices in the open air. And still more pleasant to think that it was for a cause so holy that they had assembled then and there. Sarah [Remond] and I had a sail in one of those charming little row-boats which are my particular favorites. It was very delightful to me to feel that I was so near the water; and I could not resist the temptation to cool my hands in the sparkling waves. I greatly enjoyed sitting under the shade of the noble pine trees and listening to the eloquent speeches in behalf of the slave; every sentiment of which met a warm response in my heart. On returning home we stopped in Boston and passed some time very pleasantly in the Common listening to the music which enlivened the stillness of the sultry night. It was quite late when we reached home. And I retired to rest feeling that this had been one of the happiest days of my life, and thinking hopefully of the happy glorious day when every fetter shall be broken, and throughout this land there shall no longer be a single slave! . . .

Tuesday, Sept. 5. . . . I have suffered much to-day,—my friends Mrs. P[utnam] and her daughters were refused admission to the Museum, after having tickets given them, solely on account of their complexion. Insulting language was used to them—Of course they felt and exhibited deep, bitter indignation; but of what avail was it? none, but to excite the ridicule of those contemptible creatures, miserable doughfaces who do not deserve the name of men. I will not attempt to write more.—No words can express my feelings. But these cruel wrongs cannot be much longer endured. A day of retribution must come. God grant that it may come very soon! . . .

Sunday, Dec. 17. This evening Sarah's husband [J. D. Gilliard] arrived from California. . . . We were very much surprised to see him. Of course Sarah is very happy. There was so much to be said, so many questions to be asked and answered, that we had nearly forgotten Lucy Stone's lecture.[6] We found the hall so much crowded that it was almost impossible to procure a seat. The lecture was earnest and impressive, and some parts of it very beautiful. It was an appeal to the noblest and warmest sympathies of our nature, in

---

[6]Lucy Stone, known widely as an advocate for women's rights, was a speaker in the lecture series of the Salem Female Anti-Slavery Society.

behalf of the oppressed. I saw many among her large and attentive audience, who had probably never attended an anti-slavery lecture before. I hope her touching appeal may not have been made in vain—that they may think rightly on this subject. And from noble *thoughts* spring noble *words* and *deeds.*

INTERESTING LETTER FROM
MISS CHARLOTTE L. FORTEN.

ST. HELENA'S ISLAND, BEAUFORT, S. C.
Nov. 27, 1862.

DEAR MR. GARRISON—I shall commence this letter in very nearly the same words used by one of your correspondents some weeks since—"To-day, for the first time since leaving home, I have been allowed the privilege of reading the *Liberator*." But I must claim that, in my case, the privilege must be a greater one than in his, for he was only in New York, while I am in South Carolina. However, we shall not be at all likely to dispute about it. I cannot tell you what a pleasure it is to see this paper. It is of an old date—Oct. 31st—but it is not the less welcome for that. It is pleasant to look upon, and familiar as the face of an old friend, here in this strange, southern land. And is it not a significant fact, that one may now sit in safety here, in the rebellious little Palmetto State, and read the *Liberator,* and display it to one's friends, rejoicing over it, in the fulness of one's heart, as a very great treasure? It is fitting that we should give it—*the pioneer paper in the cause of human rights*—a hearty welcome to the land where, until so recently, those rights have been most barbarously trampled upon. We do not forget that it is, in fact, directly traceable to the exertions of the editor of this paper, and those who have labored so faithfully with him, that Northern people now occupy in safety the South Carolina shore; that freedom now blesses it; that it is, for the first time, a place worth living in.

Perhaps it may interest you to know how we have spent this day—Thanksgiving Day—here, in the sunny South. It has been truly a "rare" day—a day worthy of October. Cool, delicious air, golden, gladdening sunlight, deep-blue sky, with soft white clouds floating over it. Had we no other causes, the glory and beauty of the day alone would make it a day to give thanks for. But we have other causes, great and glorious, that unite to make this peculiarly a day of thanksgiving and praise. You have, doubtless, ere this, read General Saxton's noble Proclamation for Thanksgiving to the people of Port Royal. I know that it will be fully appreciated by you. For

Source: *The Liberator,* 19 December 1862.

myself, I thanked God with all my heart when I heard it read. I thanked Him for giving to the freed people of these islands a governor like General Saxton—a man so thoroughly good and true, so nobly and earnestly devoted to their interests.[7] I think he is loved and appreciated as he ought to be by them.

In accordance with his Proclamation, this was observed as "a day of thanksgiving and praise." An order had been issued, that the Superintendent of each plantation should have an animal killed, that the people might, to-day, eat fresh meat, which is a great luxury to them,—and, indeed, to all of us here. This morning, a large number, superintendents, teachers, and many of the freed people, assembled in the Baptist church. Gen. Saxton, and his brother, Captain Saxton, were present. The church was crowded, and there were many outside, at the doors and windows, who could not get in. It was a sight that I shall not soon forget—that crowd of eager, happy black faces, from which the shadow of slavery had passed forever. "FOREVER FREE! FOREVER FREE!" All the time those magical words were singing themselves in my soul, and never in my life before have I felt so deeply and sincerely grateful to God. It was a moment of exultation, such as comes but seldom in one's life, that in which I sat among the people assembled on this lovely day to thank God for the most blessed and glorious of all gifts.

The singing was, as usual, very beautiful. These people have really a great deal of musical talent. It is impossible to give you an idea of many of their songs and hymns. They are so wild, so strange, and yet so invariably harmonious and sweet, they must be heard to be appreciated. And the people accompany them with a peculiar swaying motion of the body, which seems to make the singing all the more effective. There is one of their hymns—"Roll, Jordan, roll," that I never listen to without seeming to hear, almost to *feel*, the rolling of waters. There is a great rolling wave of sound through it all.

The singing, to-day, was followed by an appropriate prayer and sermon, by the Rev. Mr. Phillips,[8] who is an excellent New England man, and a minister much liked by the people. After the sermon, General Saxton made a short but very spirited speech, urging the young men of the island to enlist in the colored regiment now forming at Beaufort under Col. T. W. Higginson.[9] That was the first intimation I had had of Mr. Higginson being down here. I am greatly rejoiced thereat. He seems to me, of all fighting men, the one best fitted to command a regiment of blacks. The mention of his name recalled most vividly the happy days passed last summer in good old Mas-

---

[7]Brigadier General Rufus Saxton, whose New England abolitionist background differentiated him from most of the highly placed Army officers.

[8]Samuel D. Phillips was the nephew of the famous abolitionist and reformer Wendell Phillips. Samuel Phillips was a young medical student who had been teaching on St. Helena. He died suddenly a few days after Thanksgiving Day.

[9]Thomas Wentworth Higginson, Massachusetts author, Unitarian minister, and abolitionist, commanded the first black regiment in the Civil War.

sachusetts, when, day after day in the streets of Worcester, we used to see the indefatigable *Capt.* Higginson drilling his white company. I never saw him,— so full of life and energy, so thoroughly enjoying his work,—without thinking what a splendid general he would make. And that, too, may come about. Gen. Saxton to-day expressed the hope of seeing him one day commander of an army of black men. Gen. Saxton told the people, who listened with an eager attention, how bravely Mr. Higginson had stood by the side of Anthony Burns[10] in the old, dark days, even suffering imprisonment for his sake; and assured them that, under the leadership of such a man, they need fear no injustice. He would see to it that they were not wronged in any way. Then he told them the story of Robert Small [sic],[11] and added, "Yesterday, Robert Small came to see me. I asked him how he was getting on in the store which he was keeping for the freed people. He said he was doing very well—was making fifty dollars a week, sometimes. But, said he, 'General, I'm going to stop keeping store—I'm going to enlist.' What, said I, are you going to enlist, when you can make fifty dollars a week keeping store? 'Yes, sir,' he added, 'I'm going to enlist as a private in the black regiment. How can I expect to keep my freedom unless I fight for it? Suppose the Secesh should come back here, what good would my fifty dollars do me then? Yes, sir, I should enlist if I were making a thousand dollars a week.' " The General then told him what a victory the black soldiers had lately won on the Georgia coast, and how great a good they had done for their race in winning it. They have proved to their enemies that the black man can and will fight for his freedom.

The General's speech was a stirring one, and I trust it will prove very effective. There has been among some of the men great distrust about joining the regiment, the soldiers were formerly so unjustly treated by the government. But they trust General Saxton, and his assurances will, doubtless, have much effect. Many of the able-bodied men from these islands have already joined the regiment.

General Saxton was followed by Mrs. Frances D. Gage,[12] who spoke for a few moments very beautifully and earnestly. She told them the story of the people of Santa Cruz, how they had risen and conquered their masters, and declared themselves freemen, and nobody dared to oppose them; and how, a short time afterward, the Danish Governor rode into the marketplace, and proclaimed freedom to all the people of the Danish

---

[10]The arrest and trial of the fugitive slave Anthony Burns in 1854 had occurred just after Charlotte Forten's initial arrival in Salem. For her impressions, see her diary entries in the preceding selection.

[11]Robert Smalls, a slave trained as a steamship pilot, had escaped to Hilton Head with his family on his master's boat, which he turned over to Union authorities.

[12]Frances D. Gage, abolitionist and women's rights leader, had presided over the Ohio meeting in 1851 where Sojourner Truth had spoken so forcefully. See above, pp. 235–36. Four of Mrs. Gage's eight children were in the Union army, and she had gone South to turn her efforts to the care of freedmen.

Islands.[13] Then she made a beautiful appeal to the mothers, and urged them not to keep back their sons, fearing that they might be killed, but to send them as she had done hers, willingly and gladly to fight for liberty.

It was something very novel and strange to them, I suppose, to hear a woman speak in public, but they listened very attentively, and seemed much moved by what she said. Gen. Saxton made a few more remarks; and then the people sang, "Marching Along," with great spirit.

After church, there was a wedding. That is a ceremony that is performed here, among the freed people, nearly every Sunday. Last Sunday, there were six couples married. Some of the bridal costumes are, of course, very unique and comical, but the principal actors are happily quite unconscious of it, and look so very proud and happy while enjoying this, one of the many privileges that freedom has bestowed upon them, that it is very pleasant to see them. . . .

A mile from the Baptist church, in another beautiful grove of live oaks, is the Episcopal church, in which the aristocracy of the island used to worship. It is much smaller than the other, but possesses an organ, which, unlike the other musical instruments in this region, is not hopelessly out of order. The building is not used as a place of worship now, as it is much too small.

Our school is kept in the Baptist church. There are two ladies teaching in it, beside myself. They are earnest workers, and have done and are constantly doing a great deal for the people here, old and young. One of them, Miss T. [Laura M. Towne, Philadelphia abolitionist], is physician as well as teacher. She has a very extensive medical practice, and carries about with her everywhere her box of homeopathic medicines. The people welcome her as a ministering angel to their lowly cabins. Our school averages between eighty and ninety pupils, and later in the season we shall probably have more. It is very pleasant to see how bright, how eager to learn many of the children are. Some of them make wonderful improvement in a short time. It is a great happiness, a great privilege to be allowed to teach them. Every day I enjoy it more and more.

I cannot describe to you their singing. To me it seems wonderfully beautiful. We have just taught them the John Brown Song. I wish you could hear them sing it; it does one's soul good. How often I wish their old "secesh" masters, powerless to harm them, could hear their former chattels singing the praises of the brave old man who died for their sake! We are going to teach them "The Song of the Negro Boatmen" soon.

Although I have been here more than a month, it is at times almost impossible for me to realize that I am in South Carolina, the very last place in which, a year ago, I should have thought it desirable or possible for me to live. Sometimes it seems all like a strange wild dream. But when I see the people at work in the cotton fields, and visit their "quarters," and listen to

---

[13]In Santa Cruz, one of the Danish Virgin Islands acquired by the United States in 1917, an insurrection in 1848 successfully ended slavery.

their strange songs, it becomes more real to me. A month hence, I expect to feel quite at home here, in the very heart of Rebeldom.

I am staying at the same house in which a store is kept for the freed people by a Quaker gentleman sent here by the Philadelphia Commission. One has an excellent opportunity here for observing the negroes. I am particularly pleased with their manners. They are always perfectly courteous to each other, as well as to us. Theirs is a natural and graceful courtesy, which would put to shame many who despise them as an inferior people. As far as I have observed, they seem to me honest, industrious, and anxious to improve in every way. This is wonderful, considering the crushing and degrading system to which they have been subjected. They certainly are not the stupid, degraded people that many at the North believe them to be.

The plantation on which we live was owned by a man whom all the people unite in calling a "hard master." And his wife, it is said, was even more cruel than himself. When the negroes were ill, their scanty allowance of food was entirely withheld from them; and even after they had begun to recover, they were kept half-starved for some time—as a punishment for daring to be ill, I suppose. The whip was used freely. The people were severely whipped for the slightest offences, real or only suspected. If a fowl or anything else on the plantation was missed, and the thief could not be discovered, every slave would receive a number of lashes. They were wretchedly clothed. One poor woman had her feet and limbs so badly frozen from exposure, that she was obliged to have both legs amputated above the knee. She is living here now, and is one of the best women on the place.

From such a life as these poor people led—poorly clothed, poorly fed, worked hard, and cruelly beaten—you can imagine what a blessed change for them is the life they lead now. They are constantly rejoicing over it. Their hearts are overflowing with gratitude to the "Yankees," for coming here, and giving them their freedom. One very old man,—who came into the store this morning, dressed in a very original suit, made entirely of carpeting,—expressed to Mr. H. [John A Hunn, the Philadelphia Quaker referred to above] his delight at the new state of things:—"Don't have me feelin's hurt now, massa. Used to have me feelin's hurt all de time; but don't hab 'em hurt now, no more." And, truly, we rejoiced with the old man that he, and many like him, who have suffered so long, no longer have their "feelin's hurt," as in the old time. . . .

As I bring this letter to a close, my thoughts revert to New England— to Massachusetts, which I believe I am in the habit of considering as all New England. And I recall with pleasure the many happy Thanksgiving Days passed there. But it has been reserved for me to spend here, in South Carolina, the happiest, the most jubilant Thanksgiving Day of my life. We hear of cold weather and heavy snow storms up in the North land; but here roses and oleanders are blooming out of doors, figs are ripening, the sunlight is warm and bright, and over all shines gloriously the blessed light of freedom, freedom forevermore.

I am, dear friend, very truly yours,   C.L.F.

Lucy Craft Laney

Lucy Laney's origins were close to slavery. Born in Georgia in 1854, she had several advantages distinguishing her from most of her black contemporaries. Her parents were free and they were literate. Her father, trained in carpentry as a slave, had earned cash enough to buy himself. He also purchased his wife. They lived together as a family in their own home, with both parents going out to work each day. Lucy's father had also become an ordained Presbyterian minister.

As a child Lucy was aided in learning to read and write by her mother's employer, and the resources of a library in the house were made available to her. When she was ready for high school, there were high schools ready for her. For some blacks, Reconstruction opened up educational possibilities, and Lucy Laney was one of them. Admitted to Atlanta University, she was a member of its first graduating class in 1873. During the next ten years she taught in several of the black public schools in Georgia. In 1883, with the benediction of the Presbyterian Board of Missions for Freedmen, she opened a day and boarding school in Augusta. Three years later the school was chartered by the state and represented, in comparison with Booker T. Washington's Tuskegee Institute of Alabama, one of two approaches to black education, the academic and the industrial.

Lucy Laney appealed to the General Assembly of the Presbyterian Church for financial aid. She went to Minneapolis for that purpose. There she met Mrs. F.E.H. Haines, secretary of the Women's Executive Committee of Home Missions, whose quiet earnestness and encouragement were recognized by naming the Augusta school in her honor, the Haines Normal and Industrial Institute. Haines became a center for black students, and a number of valued teachers have come from its classrooms. One of the most notable of its teachers was Mary McLeod Bethune.

Especially interested in women, Lucy Laney was more solicitous about the education of girls than of boys. Although males were not excluded from her school, she looked primarily to women as the regenerative force to uplift the black race. In addition to the preparation of teachers and the training of students for college and university, she developed the first kindergarten in Augusta. She also initiated a program for the education of

nurses. *Lincoln University, where many of the Haines alumni went to continue their work, awarded her an honorary degree. The Lucy Craft Laney High
School, a modern academic and vocational institution, stands today in the
City of Augusta. It is a tribute to blacks, to women, and to the cause of
education. But Lucy Laney needs no landmarks of stone and mortar. The
fruits of her labors have left their mark on the land.*[1]

If the educated colored woman has a burden,—and we believe she has—
what is that burden? How can it be lightened, how may it be lifted? What it
is can be readily seen perhaps better than told, for it constantly annoys to
irritation; it bulges out as did the load of Bunyan's Christian—ignorance—
with its inseparable companions, shame and crime and prejudice.

That our position may be more readily understood, let us refer to the
past. . . . During the days of training in our first mission school—slavery—
that which is the foundation of right training and good government, the
basic rock of all true culture—the home, with its fire-side training, mother's
moulding, woman's care, was not only neglected but utterly disregarded.
There was no time in the institution for such teaching. We know that there
were, even in the first days of that school, isolated cases of men and women
of high moral character and great intellectual worth, as Phillis Wheatley,
Sojourner Truth, and John Chavers,[1] whose work and lives should have
taught, or at least suggested to their instructors, the capabilities and possibilities of their dusky slave pupils. The progress and the struggles of these
for noble things should have led their instructors to see how the souls and
minds of this people then yearned for light—the real life. But alas! these dull
teachers, like many modern pedagogues and school-keepers, failed to know
their pupils—to find out their real needs, and hence had no cause to study
methods of better and best development of the boys and girls under their
care. What other result could come from such training or want of training
than a conditioned race such as we now have?

---

[1] Mary White Ovington, *Portraits in Color* (New York, 1927), pp. 53–63; letter to the
editors from Mrs. Flora Wester, Clerk of the Board of National Missions of the United
Presbyterian Church in the United States of America, 30 November 1970; *Journal of
Negro History* 19 (January 1934): 97–102. See also the biographical sketch by Sadie
Daniel St. Clair in *Notable American Women*, ed. Edward T. James and Janet Wilson
James (Cambridge, Mass., 1971), II, 365–67.

Source: Lucy Laney, "The Burden of the Educated Colored Woman," a paper read at the
Hampton Negro Conference No. III, July 1899, *Report* (n.p., 1899), pp. 37–42. All
footnotes are the editors'

[1] Presumably this refers to John Chavis (c. 1763–1838), a free black of North Carolina
who became a minister and teacher after an education that included private study
under President Witherspoon of the College of New Jersey (now Princeton University).

For two hundred and fifty years they married, or were given in marriage. Oft times marriage ceremonies were performed for them by the learned minister of the master's church; more often there was simply a consorting by the master's consent, but it was always understood that these unions for cause, or without cause, might be more easily broken, than a divorce can be obtained in Indiana or Dakota. Without going so long a distance as from New York to Connecticut, the separated could take other companions for life, for a long or short time; for during those two hundred and fifty years there was not a single marriage legalized in a single southern state, where dwelt the mass of this people. There was something of the philosopher in the plantation preacher, who, at the close of the marriage ceremony, had the dusky couple join their right hands, and then called upon the assembled congregation to sing, as he lined it out, "Plunged in a gulf of dark despair," for well he knew the sequel of many such unions. If it so happened that a husband and wife were parted by those who owned them, such owners often consoled those thus parted with the fact that he could get another wife; she, another husband. Such was the sanctity of the marriage vow that was taught and held for over two hundred and fifty years. Habit is indeed second nature. This is the race inheritance. I thank God not of all, for we know, each of us, of instances, of holding most sacred the plighted love and keeping faithfully and sacredly the marriage vows. We know of pure homes and of growing old together. Blessed heritage! If we only had the gold there might be many "Golden Weddings." Despair not; the crushing burden of immorality which has its root in the disregard of the marriage vow, can be lightened. It must be, and the educated colored woman can and will do her part in lifting this burden.

In the old institution there was no attention given to homes and to home-making. Homes were only places in which to sleep, father had neither responsibility nor authority; mother, neither cares nor duties. She wielded no gentle sway nor influence. The character of their children was a matter of no concern to them; surroundings were not considered. It is true, house cleaning was sometimes enforced as a protection to property, but this was done at stated times and when ordered. There is no greater enemy of the race than these untidy and filthy homes; they bring not only physical disease and death, but they are very incubators of sin; they bring intellectual and moral death. The burden of giving knowledge and bringing about the practice of the laws of hygiene among a people ignorant of the laws of nature and common decency, is not a slight one. But this, too, the intelligent women can and must help to carry.

The large number of young men in the state prison is by no means the least of the heavy burdens. It is true that many of these are unjustly sentenced; that longer terms of imprisonment are given Negroes than white persons for the same offences; it is true that white criminals by the help of attorneys, money, and influence, oftener escape the prison, thus keeping small the number of prisoners recorded, for figures never lie. It is true that many are tried and imprisoned for trivial causes, such as the following, clipped from the *Tribune,* of Elberyon, Ga.: "Seven or eight Negroes were arrested and tried for stealing two fish-hooks last week. When the time of our courts is wasted in such a manner as this, it is high time to stop and consider whither we are driving. Such picayunish cases reflect on the intelligence of a community. It is fair to say the courts are not to blame in this matter." Commenting on this *The South Daily* says: "We are glad to note that the sentiment of the paper is against the injustice. Nevertheless these statistics will form the basis of some lecturer's discourse." This fact remains, that many of our youth are in prison, that large numbers of our young men are serving out long terms of imprisonment, and this is a very sore burden. Five years ago while attending a Teacher's Institute at Thomasville, Ga., I saw working on the streets in the chain gang, with rude men and ruder women, with ignorant, wicked, almost naked men, criminals, guilty of all the sins named in the decalogue, a large number of boys from ten to fifteen years of age, and two young girls between the ages of twelve and sixteen. It is not necessary that prison statistics be quoted, for we know too well the story, and we feel most sensibly this burden, the weight of which will sink us unless it is at once made lighter and finally lifted.

Last, but not least, is the burden of prejudice, heavier in that it is imposed by the strong, those from whom help, not hindrance, should come. They are making the already heavy burden of their victims heavier to bear, and yet they are commanded by One who is even the Master of all: "Bear ye one another's burdens, and thus fulfil the law." This is met with and must be borne everywhere. In the South, in public conveyances, and at all points of race contact; in the North, in hotels, at the baptismal pool, in cemeteries; everywhere, in some shape or form, it is to be borne. No one suffers under the weight of this burden as the educated Negro woman does; and she must help to lift it.

Ignorance and immorality, if they are not the prime causes, have certainly intensified prejudice. The forces to lighten and finally to lift this and all of these burdens are true culture and character, linked with that most substantial coupler, cash. We said in the beginning that the past can serve no further purpose than to give us our present bearings. It is a condition that confronts us. With this we must deal, it is this we must change. The physician of today inquires into the history of his patient, but he has to do especially with diagnosis and cure. We know the history; we think a correct diagnosis has often been made—let us attempt a cure. We would prescribe: homes—better homes, clean homes, pure homes; schools—better schools; more culture; more thrift; and work in large doses; put the patient at once on this treatment and continue through life. Can woman do this work? She can; and she must do her part, and her part is by no means small.

Nothing in the present century is more noticeable than the tendency of women to enter every hopeful field of wage-earning and philanthropy, and attempt to reach a place in every intellectual arena. Women are by nature fitted for teaching very young children; their maternal instinct makes them patient and sympathetic with their charges. Negro women of culture, as kindergartners and primary teachers have a rare opportunity to lend a hand to the lifting of these burdens, for here they may instill lessons of cleanliness, truthfulness, loving kindness, love for nature, and love for Nature's God. Here they may daily start aright hundreds of our children; here, too, they may save years of time in the education of the child; and may save many lives from shame and crime by applying the law of prevention. In the kindergarten and primary school is the salvation of the race.

For children of both sexes from six to fifteen years of age, women are more successful as teachers than men. This fact is proven by their employment. Two-thirds of the teachers in the public schools of the United States are women. It is the glory of the United States that good order and peace are maintained not by a large, standing army of well trained soldiers, but by the sentiment of her citizens, sentiments implanted and nourished by her well trained army of four hundred thousand school teachers, two-thirds of whom are women.

The educated Negro woman, the woman of character and culture, is needed in the schoolroom not only in the kindergarten, and in the primary and the secondary school; but she is needed in high school, the academy, and the college. Only those of character and culture can do successful lifting, for she who would mould character must herself possess it. Not alone in the schoolroom can the intelligent woman lend a lifting hand, but as a public lecturer she may give advice, helpful suggestions, and important knowledge that will change a whole community and start its people on the upward way. To be convinced of the good that can be done for humanity by this means one need only recall the names of Lucy Stone, Mary Livermore, Frances Harper, Frances Willard and Julia Ward Howe.[2] The refined and noble Negro woman may lift much with this lever. Women may also be most helpful as teachers of sewing schools and cooking classes, not simply in the public schools and private institutions, but in classes formed in neighborhoods that sorely need this knowledge. Through these classes girls who are not in school may be reached; and through them something may be done to better their homes, and inculcate habits of neatness and thrift. To bring the influence of the schools to bear upon these homes is the most needful thing of the hour. Often teachers who have labored most arduously, conscientiously, and intelligently have become discouraged on seeing that society had not been benefited, but sometimes positively injured by the conduct of their pupils.

The work of the schoolroom has been completely neutralized by the training of the home. Then we must have better homes, and better homes

---

[2]Frances Harper and the four white women were all associated with a variety of reform movements including temperance, woman suffrage, and women's education. For a biographical sketch of Mrs. Harper see the introduction to her speeches, above.

mean better mothers, better fathers, better born children. Emerson says, "To the well-born child all the virtues are natural, not painfully acquired."

But "The temporal life which is not allowed to open into the eternal life becomes corrupt and feeble even in its temporalness." As a teacher in the Sabbath school, as a leader in young people's meetings and missionary societies, in women's societies and Bible classes our cultured women are needed to do a great and blessed work. Here they may cause many budding lives to open into eternal life. Froebel[3] urged teachers and parents to see to the blending of the temporal and divine life when he said, "God created man in his own image; therefore man should create and bring forth like God." The young people are ready and anxiously await intelligent leadership in Christian work. The less fortunate women already assembled in churches, are ready for work. Work they do and work they will; that it may be effective work, they need the help and leadership of their more favored sisters.

A few weeks ago this country was startled by the following telegram of southern women of culture sent to Ex-Governor Northen[4] of Georgia, just before he made his Boston speech: "You are authorized to say in your address tonight that the women of Georgia, realizing the great importance to both races of early moral training of the Negro race, stand ready to undertake this work when means are supplied." But more startled was the world the next day, after cultured Boston had supplied a part of the means, $20,000, to read the glaring head lines of the southern press, "Who Will Teach the Black Babies?" because some of the cultured women who had signed the telegram had declared when interviewed, that Negro women fitted for the work could not be found, and no self-respecting southern white woman would teach a colored kindergarten. Yet already in Atlanta, Georgia, and in Athens, Georgia, southern women are at work among Negroes. There is plenty of work for all who have the proper conception of the teacher's office, who know that all men are brothers, God being their common father. But the educated Negro women must teach the "Black Babies;" she must come forward and inspire our men and boys to make a successful onslaught upon sin, shame, and crime.

---

[3]Friedrich Froebel (1782–1852) was a German educator and founder of the kindergarten concept.

[4]See footnote 2 of the Wells-Barnett selection, above.

Frances Jackson Coppin

Frances Jackson Coppin went through life proud, upright, and courageous. Of few blacks, especially black women, can it be said that the aims of adult life were achieved. While still in late adolescence, Frances Coppin framed a noble purpose: "to get an education and to teach my people." She acquired an education as good as then offered to any American woman of any color. She became a stellar teacher and a sagacious leader of her people. Rhode Island State Normal School numbers her among its graduates, and she was the second black woman to receive her collegiate degree from Oberlin College, conferred, symbolically enough, in the year of the peace between the states.

Education for all women was rare enough and Frances Coppin had a classical one. John Caldwell Calhoun, redoubtable senator from the State of South Carolina, would have suffered had he lived to see and hear Fanny Coppin. Calhoun was reputed to have said that if a Negro could conjugate a Greek verb, he would abandon the notion of black inferiority. Of course the conjugation of verbs in Greek or Sanskrit has precious little to do with intelligence, but Frances Coppin could not only conjugate but read and write Greek. More importantly, she taught other blacks, with far less formal education than she possessed, to master Greek and mathematics and a great many other things of which even the magisterial Calhoun was uninformed.

Fanny Coppin's objectives were happily balanced by intellectual candor and plasticity of mind. Praise, and there was much of it, did not deflect her from her purpose. Criticism did not sear her spirit nor mar the pleasures of rewarding effort. She was a scholar and a public servant. She was a citizen of Philadelphia to which she proffered love as well as brotherhood. She was a citizen of the Republic which she served by adding demonstrative reality to its highest ideals. No acclamation could more fully have expressed her unformed yearnings than a comment by another black woman whose aims were meshed with her own. "By common consent Mrs. Fannie [sic] Jackson Coppin ranks first in mental equipment, in natural gifts and achievements among colored teachers. . . . For more than thirty years she . . . was the most thoroughly controlling influence in moulding the lives and character of the colored people of that great city [Philadelphia]."[1]

Fanny Coppin worked hard from the beginning of her career. Chance and her own determination gave her an early education, despite her environment. A brief stint at the public High School for Negroes in Newport, Rhode Island, was followed by preparation to enter the Rhode Island State Normal School as the threshold to teaching. With this training completed, she learned about Oberlin and the prospect it offered to black women for full collegiate study.

Association with individuals who bring luster to the group is necessary to minorities, especially deprived minorities. Mrs. Coppin exulted to see her students master the intricacies of language and mathematics; she could hardly contain herself when they triumphed over Greek. Certainly the efforts of the students bore some relation to their feeling for the teacher. There are no drives more powerful in the teaching process than respect, admiration, and love; together they produce identification and transform the teacher-student polarity into a relation of reciprocity. Hostile or indifferent students may learn how to perform; students who identify with their teachers grow and therefore think.

Mrs. Coppin's honors inspired her students; their achievements honored them both. At Oberlin, her first degree still a gleaming treasure, she taught preparatory classes. Next the Institute for Colored Youth, initiated by Philadelphia Quakers to test black capacity for serious study, absorbed her energies. She became its principal and when the need arose she added a technical department to its curriculum. The Home Missionary Society of the African Methodist Episcopal Church elected her to its presidency in 1888 and she attended the London conference on the Centenary of the Mission. Married to a minister who became a bishop of the same church, she accompanied him to Africa. Missionary work for Mrs. Coppin bore no relation to an uncompromising sectarianism. "Our religious teaching," she declared, is "but an explanation of their own religious impulses."[2]

Fanny Coppin died at the age of seventy-seven. Most of these years were spent to insure the welfare of others. They were sterling years: purposive, honorable, and full. It is the record of an ex-slave girl whose body was purchased from an owner for $125 and whose learning began while she was working as a domestic in a family that befriended and encouraged her.

---

[1]Fanny Jackson Coppin, Reminiscences of School Life, and Hints on Teaching (Philadelphia, 1913), pp. 17 and 19; Fannie B. Williams, "Club Movement Among Negro Women," in John W. Gibson, The Colored American From Slavery to Honorable Citizenship (Atlanta, 1902), p. 201.

[2]Coppin, Reminscences, p. 130.

We used to call our grandmother "mammy," and one of my earliest recollections—I must have been about three years old—is, I was sent to keep my mammy company. It was in a little one-room cabin. We used to go up a ladder to the loft where we slept.

Mammy used to make a long prayer every night before going to bed; but not one word of all she said do I remember except the one word "offspring." She would ask God to bless her offspring. This word remained with me, for, I wondered what offspring meant.

Mammy had six children, three boys and three girls. One of these, Lucy, was my mother. Another one of them, Sarah, was purchased by my grandfather, who first saved money and bought himself, then four of his children. Sarah went to work at six dollars a month, saved one hundred and twenty-five dollars, and bought little Frances, having taken a great liking to her, for on account of my birth, my grandfather refused to buy my mother; and so I was left a slave in the District of Columbia, where I was born. . . .

. . . When my aunt had finally saved up the hundred and twenty-five dollars, she bought me and sent me to New Bedford, Mass., where another aunt lived, who promised to get me a place to work for my board, and get a little education if I could. She put me out to work, at a place where I was allowed to go to school when I was not at work. But I could not go on wash day, nor ironing day, nor cleaning day, and this interfered with my progress. There were no Hamptons, and no night schools then.

Finally, I found a chance to go to Newport with Mrs. Elizabeth Orr, an aunt by marriage, who offered me a home with her and a better chance at school. I went with her, but I was not satisfied to be a burden on her small resources. I was now fourteen years old, and felt that I ought to take care of myself. So I found a permanent place in the family of Mr. George H. Calvert, a great grandson of Lord Baltimore, who settled Maryland. His wife was Elizabeth Stuart, a descendant of Mary, Queen of Scots. Here I had one hour every other afternoon in the week to take some private lessons, which I did. . . . After that, I attended for a few months the public colored school. . . . I thus prepared myself to enter the examination for the Rhode Island State Normal School, . . . then located at Bristol, R. I. Here, my eyes were first opened on the subject of teaching. I said to myself, is it possible that teaching can be made so interesting as this! But, having finished the course of study there, I felt that I had just begun to learn; and, hearing of Oberlin College, I made up my mind to try and get there. I had learned a little music while at Newport, and had mastered the elementary studies of the piano and guitar. My aunt in Washington still helped me, and I was able to pay my way to Oberlin, the course of study there being the same as that at Harvard College. Oberlin

Source: Fanny Jackson Coppin, Reminiscences of School Life, and Hints on Teaching (Philadelphia, 1913), pp. 9–15, 17–31, 33–37. All footnotes are the editors'.

was then the only College in the United States where colored students[1] were permitted to study.

The faculty did not forbid a woman to take the gentleman's course, but they did not advise it. There was plenty of Latin and Greek in it, and as much mathematics as one could shoulder. Now, I took a long breath and prepared for a delightful contest. All went smoothly until I was in the junior year in College. Then, one day, the Faculty sent for me—ominous request— and I was not slow in obeying it. It was a custom in Oberlin that forty students from the junior and senior classes were employed to teach the preparatory classes. As it was now time for the juniors to begin their work, the Faculty informed me that it was their purpose to give me a class, but I was to distinctly understand that if the pupils rebelled against my teaching, they did not intend to force it. Fortunately for my training at the normal school, and my own dear love of teaching, though there was a little surprise on the faces of some when they came into the class, and saw the teacher, there were no signs of rebellion. The class went on increasing in numbers until it had to be divided, and I was given both divisions. One of the divisions ran up again, but the Faculty decided that I had as much as I could do, and it would not allow me to take any more work.

When I was within a year of graduation, an application came from a Friends' school in Philadelphia for a colored woman who could teach Greek, Latin, and higher mathematics. The answer returned was: "We have the woman, but you must wait a year for her."

Then began a correspondence with Alfred Cope,[2] a saintly character, who, having found out what my work in college was, teaching my classes in college, besides sixteen private music scholars, and keeping up my work in the senior class, immediately sent me a check for eighty dollars, which wonderfully lightened my burden as a poor student.

I shall never forget my obligation to Bishop Daniel A. Payne, of the African Methodist Episcopal Church, who gave me a scholarship of nine dollars a year upon entering Oberlin.

My obligation to the dear people of Oberlin can never be measured in words. When President Finney[3] met a new student, his first words were: "Are you a Christian? and if not, why not?" He would follow you up with an intelligent persistence that could not be resisted, until the question was settled.

When I first went to Oberlin I boarded in what was known as the Ladies' Hall, and although the food was good, yet, I think, that for lack of variety I began to run down in health. About this time I was invited to spend

---

[1]Colored *women* students; a small number of black *men* had been accepted elsewhere as well as at Oberlin.

[2]Alfred Cope (1806–1878) was a wealthy Philadelphia Quaker.

[3]Charles Grandison Finney (1792–1875), revivalist and reformer, was president of Oberlin College from 1851 to 1866.

a few weeks in the family of Professor H.E. Peck, which ended in my staying a few years, until the independence of the Republic of Hayti was recognized, under President Lincoln, and Professor Peck was sent as the first U.S. Minister to that interesting country; then the family was broken up, and I was invited by Professor and Mrs. Charles H. Churchill to spend the remainder of my time, about six months, in their family. The influence upon my life in these two Christian homes, where I was regarded as an honored member of the family circle, was a potent factor in forming the character which was to stand the test of the new and strange conditions of my life in Philadelphia. I had been so long in Oberlin that I had forgotten about my color, but I was sharply reminded of it when, in a storm of rain, a Philadelphia street car conductor forbid my entering a car that did not have on it "for colored people," so I had to wait in the storm until one came in which colored people could ride. This was my first unpleasant experience in Philadelphia. Visiting Oberlin not long after my work began in Philadelphia, President Finney asked me how I was growing in grace; I told him that I was growing as fast as the American people would let me. When told of some of the conditions which were meeting me, he seemed to think it unspeakable.

At one time, at Mrs. Peck's, when we girls were sitting on the floor getting out our Greek, Miss Sutherland, from Maine, suddenly stopped, and, looking at me, said: "Fanny Jackson, were you ever a slave?" I said yes; and she burst into tears. Not another word was spoken by us. But those tears seemed to wipe out a little of what was wrong.

I never rose to recite in my classes at Oberlin but I felt that I had the honor of the whole African race upon my shoulders. I felt that, should I fail, it would be ascribed to the fact that I was colored. At one time, when I had quite a signal triumph in Greek, the Professor of Greek concluded to visit the class in mathematics and see how we were getting along. I was particularly anxious to show him that I was as safe in mathematics as in Greek.

I, indeed, was more anxious, for I had always heard that my race was good in the languages, but stumbled when they came to mathematics. Now, I was always fond of a demonstration, and happened to get in the examination the very proposition that I was well acquainted with; and so went that day out of the class with flying colors.

I was elected class poet for the Class Day exercises, and have the kindest remembrance of the dear ones who were my classmates. I never can forget the courtesies . . . of Professor Pond, of Dr. Lucien C. Warner, . . . and others, who seemed determined that I should carry away from Oberlin nothing but most pleasant memories of my life there.[4]

---

[4]Chester H. Pond (1844–1912), together with his older brother Chauncey N. Pond, established the Union Telegraphic Institute at Oberlin during the war for the training of telegraph operators. Lucien C. Warner (1841–1925) was a fellow student and teacher in the preparatory department of Oberlin near the end of the war, later a physician, and then a corset manufacturer who became a major donor to the college.

. . . I often used to tell my aunt that if she bought me according to my weight, she certainly had made a very poor bargain. For I was not only as slim as a match, but, as the Irishman said, I was as slim as two matches. . . .

. . . It was in me to get an education and to teach my people. This idea was deep in my soul. Where it came from I cannot tell, for I had never had any exhortations, nor any lectures which influenced me to take this course. It must have been born in me. At Mrs. Calvert's, I was in contact with people of refinement and education. Mr. Calvert was a perfect gentleman, and a writer of no mean ability. They had no children, and this gave me an opportunity to come very near to Mrs. Calvert, doing for her many things which otherwise a daughter would have done. I loved her and she loved me. When I was about to leave her to go to the Normal School, she said to me: "Fanny, will money keep you?" But that deep-seated purpose to get an education and become a teacher to my people, yielded to no inducement of comfort or temporary gain. During the time that I attended the Normal School in Rhode Island, I got a chance to take some private lessons in French, and eagerly availed myself of the opportunity. French was not in the Oberlin curriculum, but there was a professor there who taught it privately, and I continued my studies under him, and so was able to complete the course and graduate with a French essay. Freedmen now began to pour into Ohio from the South, and some of them settled in the township of Oberlin. During my last year at the college, I formed an evening class for them, where they might be taught to read and write. It was deeply touching to me to see old men painfully following the simple words of spelling; so intensely eager to learn. I felt that for such people to have been kept in the darkness of ignorance was an unpardonable sin, and I rejoiced that even then I could enter measurably upon the course in life which I had long ago chosen. Mr. John M. Langston, who afterwards became Minister to Hayti, was then practicing law at Oberlin.[5] His comfortable home was always open with a warm welcome to colored students, or to any who cared to share his hospitality.

I wont to Oberlin in 1860, and was graduated in August, 1865, after having spent five and a half years.

The years 1860 and 1865 were years of unusual historic importance and activity. In '60 the immortal Lincoln was elected, and in '65 the terrible war came to a close, but not until freedom for all the slaves in America had been proclaimed, and that proclamation made valid by the victorious arms of the Union party. In the year 1863 a very bitter feeling was exhibited against the colored people of the country, because they were held responsible for the fratricidal war then going on. The riots in New York especially gave evidence of this ill feeling. It was in this year that the faculty put me to teaching.

---

[5]John M. Langston (1829–1897), black alumnus of Oberlin, was appointed minister to Haiti in 1877 and was a member of Congress from Virginia in 1890.

Of the thousands then coming to Oberlin for an education, a very few were colored. I knew that, with the exception of one here or there, all my pupils would be white; and so they were. It took a little moral courage on the part of the faculty to put me in my place against the old custom of giving classes only to white students. But, as I have said elsewhere, the matter was soon settled and became an overwhelming success. How well do I remember the delighted look on the face of Principal Fairchild[6] when he came into the room to divide my class, which then numbered over eighty. How easily a colored teacher might be put into some of the public schools. It would only take a little bravery, and might cause a little surprise, but wouldn't be even a nine days' wonder.

And now came the time for me to leave Oberlin, and start in upon my work at Philadelphia.

In the year 1837, the Friends of Philadelphia had established a school for the education of colored youth in higher learning, to make a test whether or not the Negro was capable of acquiring any considerable degree of education. For it was one of the strongest arguments in the defense of slavery, that the Negro was an inferior creation; formed by the Almighty for just the work he was doing. It is said that John C. Calhoun made the remark, that if there could be found a Negro that could conjugate a Greek verb, he would give up all his preconceived ideas of the inferiority of the Negro. Well, let's try him, and see, said the fairminded Quaker people. And for years this institution, known as the Institute for Colored Youth, was visited by interested persons from different parts of the United States and Europe. Here I was given the delightful task of teaching my own people, and how delighted I was to see them mastering Caesar, Virgil, Cicero, Horace and Xenophon's Anabasis. We also taught New Testament Greek. It was customary to have public examinations once a year, and when the teachers were through examining their classes, any interested person in the audience was requested to take it up, and ask questions. At one of such examinations, when I asked a titled Englishman to take the class and examine it, he said: "They are more capable of examining me, their proficiency is simply wonderful."

One visiting friend was so pleased with the work of the students in the difficult metres in Horace that he afterwards sent me, as a present, the Horace which he used in college. A learned Friend from Germantown, coming into a class in Greek, the first aorist, passive and middle, being so neatly and correctly written at one board, while I, at the same time, was hearing a class recite, exclaimed: "Fanny, I find thee driving a coach and six." As it is much more difficult to drive a coach and six, than a coach and one, I took it as a compliment. But I was especially glad to know that the students were doing their work so well as to justify Quakers in their fair-minded opinion of

---

[6]Edward Henry Fairchild (1815–1889) was principal of Oberlin's preparatory department from 1853 to 1869.

them. General O.C. Howard,[7] who was brought in at one time by one of the managers to hear an examination in Virgil, remarked that Negroes in trigonometry and the classics might well share in the triumphs of their brothers on the battlefield.

When I came to the School, the Principal of the Institute was Ebenezer D. Bassett, who for fourteen years had charge of the work. He was a graduate of the State Normal School of Connecticut, and was a man of unusual natural and acquired ability, and an accurate and ripe scholar; and, withal, a man of great modesty of character. Many are the reminiscences he used to give of the visits of interested persons to the school: among these was a man who had written a book to prove that the Negro was not a man. And, having heard of the wonderful achievements of this Negro school, he determined to come and see for himself what was being accomplished. He brought a friend with him, better versed in algebra than himself, and asked Mr. Bassett to bring out his highest class. There was in the class at that time Jesse Glasgow, a very black boy. All he asked was a chance. Just as fast as they gave the problems, Jesse put them on the board with the greatest ease. This decided the fate of the book, then in manuscript form, which, so far as we know, was never published. Jesse Glasgow afterwards found his way to the University of Edinburgh, Scotland.

In the year 1869, Mr. Bassett was appointed United States Minister to Hayti by President Grant; leaving the principalship of the Institute vacant. Now, Octavius V. Catto, a professor in the school, and myself, had an opportunity to keep the school up to the same degree of proficiency that it attained under its former Principal and to carry it forward as much as possible.

About this time we were visited by a delegation of school commissioners, seeking teachers for schools in Delaware, Maryland and New Jersey. These teachers were not required to know and teach the classics, but they were expected to come into an examination upon the English branches, and to have at their tongue's end the solution of any abstruse problem in the three R's which their examiners might be inclined to ask them. And now, it seemed best to give up the time spent in teaching Greek and devote it to the English studies.

As our young people were now about to find a ready field in teaching, it was thought well to introduce some text books on school management, and methods of teaching, and thoroughly prepare our students for normal work. At this time our faculty was increased by the addition of Richard T. Greener, a graduate of Harvard College, who took charge of the English Department, and Edward Bouchet, a graduate of Yale College, and also of the Sheffield Scientific School, who took charge of the scientific department. Both of these young men were admirably fitted for their work. And, with

---

[7]Oliver Otis Howard (initials given incorrectly by Mrs. Coppin) (1830–1909), Union general, Commissioner of the Freedmen's Bureau from 1865 to 1872, was a founder of Howard University and its first president, serving from 1869 to 1874.

Octavius V. Catto[8] in charge of the boys' department, and myself in charge of the girls—in connection with the principalship of the school—we had a strong working force.

I now instituted a course in normal training, which at first consisted only of a review of English studies, with the theory of teaching, school management and methods. But the inadequacy of this course was so apparent that when it became necessary to reorganize the Preparatory Departments, it was decided to put this work into the hands of the normal students, who would thus have ample practice in teaching and governing under daily direction and correction. These students became so efficient in their work that they were sought for and engaged to teach long before they finished their course of study.

Richard Humphreys, the Friend—Quaker—who gave the first endowment with which to found the school, stipulated that it should not only teach higher literary studies, but that a Mechanical and Industrial Department, including Agriculture, should come within the scope of its work. The wisdom of this thoughtful and far-seeing founder has since been amply demonstrated. At the Centennial Exhibition in 1876, the foreign exhibits of work done in trade schools opened the eyes of the directors of public education in America as to the great lack existing in our own system of education. If this deficiency was apparent as it related to the white youth of the country, it was far more so as it related to the colored.

In Philadelphia, the only place at the time where a colored boy could learn a trade, was in the House of Refuge, or the Penitentiary!

And now began an eager and intensely earnest crusade to supply this deficiency in the work of the Institute for Colored Youth.

The teachers of the Institute now vigorously applied their energies in collecting funds for the establishment of an Industrial Department, and in this work they had the encouragement of the managers of the school, who were as anxious as we that the greatly needed department should be established. . . .

The Academic Department of the Institute had been so splendidly successful in proving that the Negro youth was equally capable as others in mastering a higher education, that no argument was necessary to establish its need, but the broad ground of education by which the masses must become self-supporting was, to me, a matter of painful anxiety. Frederick Douglass once said, it was easier to get a colored boy into a lawyer's office than into a blacksmith shop; and on account of the inflexibility of the Trades Unions, this condition of affairs still continues, making it necessary for us to have our own "blacksmith shop."

The minds of our people had to be enlightened upon the necessity of industrial education.

---

[8]This young man was assassinated during election street disorders in Philadelphia in the fall of 1871.

Before all the literary societies and churches where they would hear me; in Philadelphia and the suburban towns; in New York, Washington and everywhere, when invited to speak, I made that one subject my theme. To equip an industrial plant is an expensive thing, and knowing that much money would be needed, I made it a rule to take up a collection wheresoever I spoke. But I did not urge anyone to give more than a dollar, for the reason I wanted the masses to have an opportunity to contribute their small offerings, before going to those who were able to give larger sums. . . .

In preparing for the industrial needs of the boys, the girls were not neglected. It was not difficult to find competent teachers of sewing and cooking for the girls. . . .

As the work advanced, other trades were added, and those already undertaken were expanded and perfected.

When the Industrial Department was fully established, the following trades were being taught: For boys: bricklaying, plastering, carpentry, shoemaking, printing and tailoring. For the girls: dressmaking, millinery, typewriting, stenography and classes in cooking, including both boys and girls. Stenography and typewriting were also taught the boys, as well as the girls.

Having taught certain trades, it was now necessary to find work for those who had learned them, which proved to be no easy task.

It was decided to put on exhibition, in one of the rooms of the dormitory, specimens of the work of our girls in any trade in which they had become proficient, and we thus started an Industrial Exchange for their work. Those specimens consisted of work from the sewing, millinery and cooking departments. . . .

Our white friends were invited to come and inspect the work of the Exchange. Some of the exhibits were found to be highly creditable, and many encouraging words were given to those who prepared them. There is one class of women, for whom no trades are provided, but who are expected to do their work without any special preparation; and these are the women in domestic service. I have always felt a deep sympathy with such persons, for I believe that they are capable of making a most honorable record. I therefore conceived a plan of holding some receptions for them, where the honorableness of their work and the necessity of doing it well might be discussed. I earnestly hoped that no one should be ashamed of the word servant, but should learn what great opportunity for doing good there is for those who serve others.

There is, and always must be, a large number of people who must depend upon this class of employment for a living, and there is every reason, therefore, why they should be especially prepared for it. A woman should not only know how to cook in an ordinary way, but she should have some idea of the chemical properties of the food she cooks. The health of those whom she serves depends much upon the nutritive qualities of the food which she prepares. It is possible to burn all the best out of a beefsteak, and leave a pork chop with those elements which should have been neutralized by thorough cooking.

A housemaid should know enough about sanitation to appreciate the difference between well ventilated sleeping rooms and those where impure air prevails.

I have often thought, as I sat in churches, that janitors should be better prepared for their work by being taught the difference between pure air and air with a strong infusion of coal gas. . . .

As a means of preparation for this work, which I may call an Industrial Crusade, I studied Political Economy for two years under Dr. William Elder, who was a disciple of Mr. Henry C. Carey, the eminent writer on the doctrine of Protective Tariff.

In the year 1879 the Board of Education of Philadelphia, instructed and admonished by the exhibit of work done in the schools of Europe, as exhibited in the Centennial exhibition of '76, began to consider what they were doing to train their young people in the industrial arts and trades. The comparison was not very gratifying. The old apprenticeship system had silently glided away, and merchants declared that under the pressure of competition they were not able to compete with other merchants, nor were they able to stand the waste made by those who did not know how to handle the new material economically. At a meeting of some of the public school directors and heads of some of the educational institutions, I was asked to tell what was being done in Philadelphia for the industrial education of the colored youth. It may well be understood I had a tale to tell. And I told them the only places in the city where a colored boy could learn a trade was in the House of Refuge or the Penitentiary, and the sooner he became incorrigible and got into the Refuge, or committed a crime and got into the Penitentiary, the more promising it would be for his industrial training. It was to me a serious occasion. I so expressed myself. As I saw building after building going up in this city, and not a single colored hand employed in the constructions, it made the occasion a very serious one to me. . . .

The next day Mrs. Elizabeth Whitney, the wife of one of the school directors, drove up to my school and said: Mrs. Coppin, I was there last night and heard what you had to say about the limitations of the colored youth, and I am here to say, if the colored people will go ahead and start a school for the purpose of having the colored youth taught this greatly needed education, you will find plenty of friends to help you. Here are fifty dollars to get you started, and you will find as much behind it as you need.

We only needed a feather's weight of encouragement to take up the burden. We started out at once. . . . We carried on an industrial crusade which never ended until we saw a building devoted to the purpose of teaching trades. For the managers of the Institute, seeing the need of the work, threw themselves into this new business, after their thirty previous years working for the colored youth. Our money in the end amounted to nearly three thousand dollars, and of this we have always been justly very glad. . . .

It was a delightful scene to us to pass through that school where ten trades were being taught, although in primitive fashion, the limited means of the Institute precluding the use of machinery. The managers always refused to take any money from the State, although it was frequently offered.

Many were the ejaculations of satisfaction at this busy hive of industry. "Ah," said some, "this is the way the school should have begun, the good Quaker people began at the wrong end." Not so, for when they began this school, the whole South was a great industrial plant where the fathers taught the sons and the mothers taught the daughters, but the mind was left in darkness. . . .

In the fall of the same year, namely, in November, '79, as a means of bringing the idea of industrial education and self help practically before the colored people of the United States, I undertook the work of helping an enterprise, namely, *The Christian Recorder*, edited and published by colored men at 631 Pine street, Philadelphia. I here reproduce the plea made thirty-four years ago:[9]

The Publication Department of *The Christian Recorder* is weighed down by a comparatively small debt, which cripples its usefulness and thus threatens its existence. This paper finds its way into many a dark hamlet in the South, where no one ever heard of the Philadelphia *Bulletin* or the *New York Tribune*. A persistent vitality has kept this paper alive through a good deal of thick and thin since 1852. In helping to pay this debt we shall also help to keep open an honorable vocation to colored men who, if they will be printers, must "shinny on their own side." Knowing the conditions of the masses of our people, no large sums were asked for; the people were requested to club together and send on a number of little gifts, which might be at a stated time exhibited and sold at a fair. And thus the debt liquidated by a co-operative effort would be an instructive lesson of how light a burden becomes when borne by the many instead of the few. . . . The great lesson to be taught by this fair is the value of co-operative effort to make our cents dollars, and to show us what help there is for ourselves in ourselves. That the colored people of this country have enough money to materially alter their financial condition, was clearly demonstrated by the millions of dollars deposited in the Freedmen's Bank, that they have the good sense, and the unanimity to use this power is now proven by this industrial exhibition and fair. It strikes me that much of the talk about the exodus has proceeded upon the high-handed assumption that, owing largely to the credit system of the South, the colored people there are forced to the alternative to "curse God, and die," or else "go West." Not a bit of it. The people of the South, it is true, cannot produce hundreds of dollars, but they have millions of pennies; and millions of

---

[9]This plea was first delivered as a speech at a fair organized to raise money for the periodical and at the same time to demonstrate, to both blacks and whites, the ability of the black masses to produce salable items and to band together for self-help.

pennies make tens of thousands of dollars. By clubbing together and lump-
ing their pennies, a fund might be raised in the cities of the South that the
poorer classes might fall back upon while their crops are growing, or else
by the opening of co-operative stores become their own creditors and so
effectually rid themselves of their merciless extortioners. "O, they won't do
anything; you can't get them united on anything!" The best way for a man
to prove that he can do a thing is to do it, and that is what we have done.
This fair, participated in by twenty-four States in the Union, and got up for
a purpose which is of no pecuniary benefit to those concerned in it, effectually silences all slanders about "we won't or we can't do," and teaches
its own instructive and greatly needed lessons of self-help, the best help
that any man can have, next to God's.

Those who have this matter in charge have studiously avoided preceding it with noisy and demonstrative babblings, which are so often the
vapid precursors of promises as empty as themselves; therefore in some
quarters our fair has been overlooked. It is not, we think, a presumptuous
interpretation of this great movement, to say that the voice of God now
seems to utter, "Speak to the people that they go forward." "Go forward"
in what respect? Teach the millions of poor colored laborers of the South
how much power they have in themselves, by co-operation of effort, and by
a combination of their small means to change the despairing poverty which
now drives them from their homes, and makes them a millstone around the
neck of any community, South or West. Secondly, that we shall go forward
in asking to enter the same employments which other people enter. Within
the past ten years we have made almost no advance in getting our youth
into industrial and business occupations. It is just as hard to get a boy into
a printing office now as it was ten years ago. It is simply astonishing when
we consider how many of the common vocations of life colored people are
shut out of. Colored men are not admitted to the Printers' Trade Union,
nor, with very rare exceptions, are they employed in any city of the United
States in a paid capacity as printers or writers, one of the rare exceptions
being the employment of H. Price Williams, on the Sunday Press of this
city. We are not employed as salesmen, or pharmacists, or saleswomen, or
bank clerks, or merchants' clerks, or tradesmen, or mechanics, or telegraph
operators, or to any degree as State or Government officials, and I could
keep on with the string of "ors" until tomorrow morning, but the patience
of a reader has its limit.

Slavery made us poor, and its gloomy, malicious shadow tends to
keep us so. I beg to say, kind reader, that this is not spoken in a spirit of
recrimination; we have no quarrel with our fate, and we leave your Christianity to yourself. Our faith is firmly fixed in that "Eternal Providence," that in
its own good time will "justify the ways of God to man." But, believing that
to get the right men into the right places is a "consummation most devoutly
to be wished," it is a matter of serious concern to us to see our youth, with
just as decided diversity of talent as any other people, all herded together

into three or four occupations. It is cruel to make a teacher or a preacher of a man who ought to be a printer or a blacksmith, and that is exactly what we are now obliged to do. . . .

Being determined to know whether this industrial and business ostracism was "in ourselves or in our stars," we have from time to time, knocked, shaken and kicked at these closed doors of work. A cold, metallic voice from within replies, "We do not employ colored people." Ours not to make reply, ours not to question why. . . . But we can not help wondering if some ignorant or faithless steward of God's work and God's money hasn't blundered. It seems necessary that we should make known to the good men and women who are so solicitous about our souls and our minds that we haven't quite got rid of our bodies yet, and until we do we must feed and clothe them; and this thing of keeping us out of work forces us back upon charity. . . . We do not ask that any one of our people shall be put into a position because he is a colored person, but we do most emphatically ask that he shall not be kept out of a position because he is a colored person. "An open field and no favors" is all that is requested.

[Included among those invited to comment briefly after the address by Fannie Barrier Williams at the 1893 Congress of Representative Women, Mrs. Coppin made the following statement to a predominantly white assemblage.][10]

This conference can not be indifferent to the history of the colored women of America, for if we have been able to accomplish anything whatever in what are considered the higher studies, or if we have been able to achieve anything by heroic living and thinking, all the more can you achieve it. It is an unanswerable argument for every woman's claim. If we fight the battle, all the more can you win it. Therefore you know this is not simply a side issue in which you feel that out of consideration for a certain class of people you ask them to give the history of their life. I have often thought of you when the battle went hard with me, and when it was impossible for me to gain the encouragement I might have gained by looking upon the faces of the best people of America; for whatever may be said of what we have had to suffer in this country, we have never had to suffer from the best people. The opposition, and the trials, and the oppression and depression and suppression have always come from the middle and lower classes, and that has grown out of their very poor education. And now what is the hope for the future? Every hope.

I wish by no means to be among that class of people that counsel words without knowledge. We, as a people, have suffered greatly from what

[10]World's Congress of Representative Women, ed. May Wright Sewall (Chicago, 1893), pp. 715–16. For the address of Fannie Barrier Williams, see above.

may be termed the "sizing up," and the regulation "putting down," and setting forth of what it was possible for us to do.

Our idea of getting an education did not come out of wanting to imitate any one whatever. It grew out of the uneasiness and the restlessness of the desires we felt within us; the desire to know, not just a little, but a great deal. We wanted to know how to calculate an eclipse, to know what Hesiod and Livy thought; we wished to know the best thoughts of the best minds that lived with us; not merely to gain an honest livelihood, but from a God-given love of all that is beautiful and best, and because we thought we could do it.

If black girls can calculate equations and logarithms as I saw them doing yesterday, how much more could you with your higher inheritance do? Do you consider that you owe us an obligation for that?

There was a single word used in the address that I heard this evening that I can not hear without having permission to reply. What is that word? We, as you know, are classed among the working people, and so when the days of slavery were over, and we wanted an education, people said, "What are you going to do with an education?" You know yourselves you have been met with a great many arguments of that kind. Why educate the woman—what will she do with it? An impertinent question, and an unwise one. Rather ask, "What will she be with it?" . . .

Anna Julia Cooper

Anna Julia Cooper was an educator. Individual capacity for growth through formal schooling was the cornerstone of her belief. The experience of her own potentialities unfolding through a lifelong career of teaching and learning reinforced the conviction with which she advocated educational opportunity for others.

Born a slave in or near Raleigh, North Carolina, on 10 August 1858, she was sent as a youngster to the nearby St. Augustine Normal School early in the postwar years. An Episcopalian institution preparing teachers for the rapidly multiplying schools for black children, it also provided a collegiate program for students training for the ministry. As a keen and ardent student she absorbed all that the curriculum offered and much more. In the courses designed for ministerial candidates, she noted with irritation the difference between the encouragement given the young men and the condescending toleration with which the young women were treated.

Already teaching at the age of nineteen, she herself married a minister who had come from the West Indies to teach at the school and serve as a local pastor. Widowed a scant two years later, she soon made her way north to Oberlin College. In 1884 she became one of the very few black women to hold a college degree.

In 1887 she began decades of service as teacher and later as principal at the M Street High School for black youth in Washington, D.C. (later named the Dunbar School). Here Mrs. Cooper defended the college preparatory course when strong pressures sought to deflect black aspirations from higher education into vocational training. Her efforts to secure scholarships for black students at such prestigious universities as Harvard, Yale, and Brown were logical extensions of the determined stand she took as a younger teacher. When addressing a convocation of colored Protestant Episcopal clergymen in Washington in 1886, she objected to their failure to subsidize higher education for black women as well as for black men. Such failure was ascribed to a view of girls as "a sort of tertium quid whose development may be promoted if they can pay their way and fall in with the plans mapped out for the training of the other sex."

"The very alphabet of intellectual growth," in Mrs. Cooper's creed, had a natural corollary: all impediments should be "riven asunder" so that opportunity for the fullest self-development might result. Her own life exemplified this growth. Approaching retirement age, she went to Paris where in 1925 she received a Ph.D. in Latin. The same year, she published a book entitled Le Pélérinage de Charlemagne and a study of French attitudes toward slavery. Subsequently her energies were devoted to Frelinghuysen University in Washington, a school for employed black men and women, where she served as president from 1929 to 1941. The school continued to use space in her own home until it closed a few years before her death in 1964.

   Anna Julia Cooper was a teacher with a sense of mission, a sense of urgency for the education of all her people, and a special concern for the needs of black women. She believed not only that individuals, men and women alike, deserved and required education, but that the future of the black race, degraded and deprived for centuries, depended on the development of black women together with the men. There was a broader social argument relating to the higher education of all women regardless of race. The world, she maintained, needed the education of women to unlock the feminine side of truth, as valid as the masculine side and of equal importance. A Voice From the South, which brought together some of her early speeches and essays, was widely and favorably reviewed in the black press.[1]

THE HIGHER EDUCATION OF WOMEN.

In the very first year of our century, the year 1801, there appeared in Paris a book by Silvain Marechal, entitled "Shall Woman Learn the Alphabet." The book proposes a law prohibiting the alphabet to women, and quotes authorities weighty and various, to prove that the woman who knows the alphabet has already lost part of her womanliness. The author declares that woman can use the alphabet only as Moliere predicted they would, in spelling out the verb amo; that they have no occasion to peruse Ovid's Ars Amoris, since that is already the ground and limit of their intuitive furnishing; that Madame Guion would have been far more adorable had she remained a beautiful ignoramus as nature made her; that Ruth, Naomi, the Spartan woman, the Amazons, Penelope, Andromache, Lucretia, Joan of Arc, Petrarch's Laura, the daughters of Charlemagne, could not spell their names; while Sappho, Aspasia, Madame de Maintenon, and Madame de Stael could read altogether too well for their good; finally, that if women were once permitted to read Sophocles and work with logarithms, or to nibble at any side of the apple of

---

[1]Anna Julia Cooper, A Voice From the South (Xenia, Ohio, 1892), pp. 44, 39.

Source: Anna Julia Cooper, A Voice from the South (Xenia, Ohio, 1892), pp. 48–53, 55–61, 63–79.

knowledge, there would be an end forever to their sewing on buttons and embroidering slippers.

Please remember this book was published at the *beginning* of the Nineteenth Century. At the end of its first third, (in the year 1833) one solitary college in America decided to admit women within its sacred precincts, and organized what was called a "Ladies' Course" as well as the regular B.A. or Gentlemen's course.

It was felt to be an experiment—a rather dangerous experiment—and was adopted with fear and trembling by the good fathers, who looked as if they had been caught secretly mixing explosive compounds and were guiltily expecting every moment to see the foundations under them shaken and rent and their fair superstructure shattered into fragments.

But the girls came, and there was no upheaval. They performed their tasks modestly and intelligently. Once in a while one or two were found choosing the gentlemen's course. Still no collapse; and the dear, careful, scrupulous, frightened old professors were just getting their hearts out of their throats and preparing to draw one good free breath, when they found they would have to change the names of those courses; for there were as many ladies in the gentlemen's course as in the ladies', and a distinctively Ladies' Course, inferior in scope and aim to the regular classical course, did not and could not exist.

Other colleges gradually fell into line, and to-day there are one hundred and ninety-eight colleges for women, and two hundred and seven coeducational colleges and universities in the United States alone offering the degree of B.A. to women, and sending out yearly into the arteries of this nation a warm, rich flood of strong, brave, active, energetic, well-equipped, thoughtful women—women quick to see and eager to help the needs of this needy world—women who can think as well as feel, and who feel none the less because they think—women who are none the less tender and true for the parchment scroll they bear in their hands—women who have given a deeper, richer, nobler and grander meaning to the word "womanly" than any one-sided masculine definition could ever have suggested or inspired—women whom the world has long waited for in pain and anguish till there should be at last added to its forces and allowed to permeate its thought the complement of that masculine influence which has dominated it for fourteen centuries.

Since the idea of order and subordination succumbed to barbarian brawn and brutality in the fifth century, the civilized world has been like a child brought up by his father. It has needed the great mother heart to teach it to be pitiful, to love mercy, to succor the weak and care for the lowly.

Whence came this apotheosis of greed and cruelty? Whence this sneaking admiration we all have for bullies and prize-fighters? Whence the self-congratulation of "dominant" races, as if "dominant" meant "righteous" and carried with it a title to inherit the earth? Whence the scorn of so-called weak or unwarlike races and individuals, and the very comfortable assurance that it is their manifest destiny to be wiped out as vermin before this advancing civilization? As if the possession of the Christian graces of meekness, non-resistance and forgiveness, were incompatible with a civilization professedly based on Christianity, the religion of love! Just listen to this little bit of Barbarian brag:

> "As for Far Orientals, they are not of those who will survive. Artistic attractive people that they are, their civilization is like their own tree flowers, beautiful blossoms destined never to bear fruit. If these people continue in their old course, their earthly career is closed. Just as surely as morning passes into afternoon, so surely are these races of the Far East, if unchanged, destined to disappear before the advancing nations of the West. Vanish, they will, off the face of the earth, and leave our planet the eventual possession of the dwellers where the day declines. Unless their newly imported ideas really take root, it is from this whole world that Japanese and Koreans, as well as Chinese, will inevitably be excluded. Their Nirvana is already being realized; already, it has wrapped Far Eastern Asia in its winding sheet."—*Soul of the Far East*—P. Lowell.

Delightful reflection for "the dwellers where day declines." A spectacle to make the gods laugh, truly, to see the scion of an upstart race by one sweep of his generalizing pen consigning to annihilation one-third the inhabitants of the globe—a people whose civilization was hoary headed before the parent elements that begot his race had advanced beyond nebulosity.

How like Longfellow's Iagoo, we Westerners are, to be sure! In the few hundred years, we have had to strut across our allotted territory and bask in the afternoon sun, we imagine we have exhausted the possibilities of humanity. Verily, we are the people, and after us there is none other. Our God is power; strength, our standard of excellence, inherited from barbarian ancestors through a long line of male progenitors, the Law Salic permitting no feminine modifications. . . .

As individuals, we are constantly and inevitably, whether we are conscious of it or not, giving out our real selves into our several little worlds, inexorably adding our own true ray to the flood of starlight, quite independently of our professions and our masquerading; and so in the world of thought, the influence of thinking woman far transcends her feeble declamation and may seem at times even opposed to it.

A visitor in Oberlin once said to the lady principal, "Have you no rabble in Oberlin? How is it I see no police here, and yet the streets are as quiet and orderly as if there were an officer of the law standing on every corner."

Mrs. Johnston[1] replied, "Oh, yes; there are vicious persons in Oberlin just as in other towns—*but our girls are our police.*"

---

[1]Mrs. A.A.F. Johnston was appointed principal of the Ladies' Department in 1870. (BJL and RB)

With from five to ten hundred pure-minded young women threading the streets of the village every evening unattended, vice must slink away, like frost before the rising sun: and yet I venture to say there was not one in a hundred of those girls who would not have run from a street brawl as she would from a mouse, and who would not have declared she could never stand the sight of blood and pistols.

There is, then, a real and special influence of woman. An influence subtle and often involuntary, an influence so intimately interwoven in, so intricately interpenetrated by the masculine influence of the time that it is often difficult to extricate the delicate meshes and analyze and identify the closely clinging fibers. And yet, without this influence—so long as woman sat with bandaged eyes and manacled hands, fast bound in the clamps of ignorance and inaction, the world of thought moved in its orbit like the revolutions of the moon; with one face (the man's face) always out, so that the spectator could not distinguish whether it was disc or sphere.

Now I claim that it is the prevalence of the Higher Education among women, the making it a common everyday affair for women to reason and think and express their thought, the training and stimulus which enable and encourage women to administer to the world the bread it needs as well as the sugar it cries for; in short it is the transmitting the potential forces of her soul into dynamic factors that has given symmetry and completeness to the world's agencies. So only could it be consummated that Mercy, the lesson she teaches, and Truth, the task man has set himself, should meet together: that righteousness, or *rightness*, man's ideal,—and *peace*, its necessary 'other half,' should kiss each other.

We must thank the general enlightenment and independence of woman (which we may now regard as a *fait accompli*) that both these forces are now at work in the world, and it is fair to demand from them for the twentieth century a higher type of civilization than any attained in the nineteenth. Religion, science, art, economics, have all needed the feminine flavor; and literature, the expression of what is permanent and best in all of these, may be gauged at any time to measure the strength of the feminine ingredient. You will not find theology consigning infants to lakes of unquenchable fire long after women have had a chance to grasp, master, and wield its dogmas. You will not find science annihilating personality from the government of the Universe and making of God an ungovernable, unintelligible, blind, often destructive physical force; you will not find jurisprudence formulating as an axiom the absurdity that man and wife are one, and that one the man—that the married woman may not hold or bequeath her own property save as subject to her husband's direction; you will not find political economists declaring that the only possible adjustment between laborers and capitalists is that of selfishness and rapacity—that each must get all he can and keep all that he gets, while the world cries *laissez faire* and the lawyers explain, "it is the beautiful working of the law of supply and demand;" in fine, you will not find the law of love shut out from the affairs of men after the feminine half of the world's truth is completed.

Nay, put your ear now close to the pulse of the time. What is the key-note of the literature of these days? What is the banner cry of all the activities of the last half decade? What is the dominant seventh which is to add richness and tone to the final cadences of this century and lead by a grand modulation into the triumphant harmonies of the next? Is it not compassion for the poor and unfortunate, and, as Bellamy[2] has expressed it, "indignant outcry against the failure of the social machinery as it is, to ameliorate the miseries of men!" Even Christianity is being brought to the bar of humanity and tried by the standard of its ability to alleviate the world's suffering and lighten and brighten its woe. What else can be the meaning of Matthew Arnold's[3] saddening protest, "We cannot do without Christianity," cried he, "and we cannot endure it as it is."

When went there by an age, when so much time and thought, so much money and labor were given to God's poor and God's invalids, the lowly and unlovely, the sinning as well as the suffering—homes for inebriates and homes for lunatics, shelter for the aged and shelter for babes, hospitals for the sick, props and braces for the falling, reformatory prisons and prison reformatories, all show that a "mothering" influence from some source is leavening the nation.

Now please understand me. I do not ask you to admit that these benefactions and virtues are the exclusive possession of women, or even that women are their chief and only advocates. It may be a man who formulates and makes them vocal. It may be, and often is, a man who weeps over the wrongs and struggles for the amelioration: but that man has imbibed those impulses from a mother rather than from a father and is simply materializing and giving back to the world in tangible form the ideal love and tenderness, devotion and care that have cherished and nourished the helpless period of his own existence.

All I claim is that there is a feminine as well as a masculine side to truth; that these are related not as inferior and superior, not as better and worse, not as weaker and stronger, but as complements—complements in one necessary and symmetric whole. That as the man is more noble in reason, so the woman is more quick in sympathy. That as he is indefatigable in pursuit of abstract truth, so is she in caring for the interests by the way—striving tenderly and lovingly that not one of the least of these "little ones" should perish. That while we not unfrequently see women who reason, we say, with the coolness and precision of a man, and men as considerate of helplessness as a woman, still there is a general consensus of mankind that the one trait is essentially masculine and the other is peculiarly feminine.

---

[2]Edward Bellamy (1850–1898), author and reformer, was recognized especially for his novel *Looking Backward*, published in 1888. (BJL and RB)

[3]Matthew Arnold (1822–1888) was an English critic and essayist known in America not only through his writings but from several lecture tours. (BJL and RB)

That both are needed to be worked into the training of children, in order that our boys may supplement their virility by tenderness and sensibility, and our girls may round out their gentleness by strength and self-reliance. That, as both are alike necessary in giving symmetry to the individual, so a nation or a race will degenerate into mere emotionalism on the one hand, or bully-ism on the other, if dominated by either exclusively; lastly, and most emphatically, that the feminine factor can have its proper effect only through woman's development and education so that she may fitly and intelligently stamp her force on the forces of her day, and add her modicum to the riches of the world's thought. . . .

It is true . . . that the higher education for women—in fact, the highest that the world has ever witnessed—belongs to the past; but we must remember that it was possible, down to the middle of our own century, only to a select few; and that the fashions and traditions of the times were before that all against it. There were not only no stimuli to encourage women to make the most of their powers and to welcome their development as a helpful agency in the progress of civilization, but their little aspirations, when they had any, were chilled and snubbed in embryo, and any attempt at thought was received as a monstrous usurpation of man's prerogative.

Lessing declared that "the woman who thinks is like the man who puts on rouge—ridiculous;" and Voltaire in his coarse, flippant way used to say, "Ideas are like beards—women and boys have none." Dr. Maginn remarked, "We like to hear a few words of sense from a woman sometimes, as we do from a parrot—they are so unexpected!" and even the pious Fenelon taught that virgin delicacy is almost as incompatible with learning as with vice.[4]

That the average woman retired before these shafts of wit and ridicule and even gloried in her ignorance is not surprising. . . . The ideal of the day was that "women must be pretty, dress prettily, flirt prettily, and not be too well informed;" that it was the *summum bonum* of her earthly hopes to have, as Thackeray puts it, "all the fellows battling to dance with her;" that she had no God-given destiny, no soul with unquenchable longings and inexhaustible possibilities—no work of her own to do and give to the world —no absolute and inherent value, no duty to self, transcending all pleasure-giving that may be demanded of a mere toy; but that her value was purely a relative one and to be estimated as are the fine arts—by the pleasure they give. "Woman, wine and song," as "the world's best gifts to man," were linked together in praise with as little thought of the first saying, "What doest thou," as that the wine and the song should declare, "We must be about our Father's business."

---

[4]Gotthold Ephraim Lessing (1729–1781) was a German critic and dramatist roughly contemporary with the French *philosophe* Voltaire. William Maginn (1793–1842) was an Irish scholar and author. François Salagnac de la Mothe Fénelon (1651–1715) was a French archbishop who favored education for girls. (BJL and RB)

Men believed, or pretended to believe, that the great law of self development was obligatory on their half of the human family only; that while it was the chief end of man to glorify God and put his five talents to the exchangers, gaining thereby other five, it was, or ought to be, the sole end of woman to glorify man and wrap her one decently away in a napkin, retiring into "Hezekiah Smith's lady during her natural life and Hezekiah Smith's relict on her tombstone;" that higher education was incompatible with the shape of the female cerebrum, and that even if it could be acquired it must inevitably unsex woman destroying the lisping, clinging, tenderly helpless, and beautifully dependent creatures whom men would so heroically think for and so gallantly fight for, and giving in their stead a formidable race of blue stockings with corkscrew ringlets and other spinster propensities.

But these are eighteenth century ideas.

We have seen how the pendulum has swung across our present century. The men of our time have asked with Emerson, "that woman only show us how she can best be served;" and woman has replied: the chance of the seedling and of the animalcule is all I ask—the chance for growth and self development, the permission to be true to the aspirations of my soul without incurring the blight of your censure and ridicule. . . .

Matthew Arnold during his last visit to America in '82 or '83, lectured before a certain co-educational college in the West. After the lecture he remarked, with some surprise, to a lady professor, that the young women in his audience, he noticed, paid as close attention as the men, *all the way through.* This led, of course, to a spirited discussion of the higher education for women, during which he said to his enthusiastic interlocutor, eyeing her philosophically through his English eyeglass: "But—eh—don't you think it—eh—spoils their *chawnces,* you know!"

Now, as to the result to women, this is the most serious argument ever used against the higher education. If it interferes with marriage, classical training has a grave objection to weigh and answer. . . .

I grant you that intellectual development, with the self-reliance and capacity for earning a livelihood which it gives, renders woman less dependent on the marriage relation for physical support (which, by the way, does not always accompany it). Neither is she compelled to look to sexual love as the one sensation capable of giving tone and relish, movement and vim to the life she leads. Her horizon is extended. Her sympathies are broadened and deepened and multiplied. She is in closer touch with nature. Not a bud that opens, not a dew drop, not a ray of light, not a cloud-burst or a thunderbolt, but adds to the expansiveness and zest of her soul. And if the sun of an absorbing passion be gone down, still 'tis night that brings the stars. She has remaining the mellow, less obtrusive, but none the less enchanting and inspiring light of friendship, and into its charmed circle she may gather the best the world has known. She can commune with Socrates about the *daimon* he knew and to which she too can bear witness; she can revel in the majesty of Dante, the sweetness of Virgil, the simplicity of Homer, the strength of Milton. She can listen to the pulsing heart throbs of passionate Sappho's encaged soul, as she beats her bruised wings against her prison bars and struggles to flutter out into Heaven's aether, and the fires of her own soul cry back as she listens. "Yes; Sappho, I know it all; I know it all." Here, at last, can be communion without suspicion; friendship without mis-understanding; love without jealousy.

We must admit then that Byron's picture, whether a thing of beauty or not, has faded from the canvas of to-day.

"Man's love," he wrote, "is of man's life a thing apart,
'Tis woman's whole existence.
Man may range the court, camp, church, the vessel and the mart,
Sword, gown, gain, glory offer in exchange.
Pride, fame, ambition, to fill up his heart—
And few there are whom these cannot estrange.
Men have all these resources, we *but one*—
To love again and be again undone."

This may have been true when written. *It is not true to-day.* The old, subjective, stagnant, indolent and wretched life for woman has gone. She has as many resources as men, as many activities beckon her on. As large possibilities swell and inspire her heart.

Now, then, does it destroy or diminish her capacity for loving?

Her standards have undoubtedly gone up. The necessity of speculating in 'chawnces' has probably shifted. The question is not now with the woman "How shall I so cramp, stunt, simplify and nullify myself as to make me eligible to the honor of being swallowed up into some little man?" but the problem, I trow, now rests with the man as to how he can so develop his God-given powers as to reach the ideal of a generation of women who demand the noblest, grandest and best achievements of which he is capable; and this surely is the only fair and natural adjustment of the chances. Nature never meant that the ideals and standards of the world should be dwarfing and minimizing ones, and the men should thank us for requiring of them the richest fruits which they can grow. If it makes them work, all the better for them.

As to the adaptability of the educated woman to the marriage relation, I shall simply quote from that excellent symposium of learned women that appeared recently. . . . "Admitting no longer any question as to their intellectual equality with the men whom they meet, with the simplic-ity of conscious strength, they take their place beside the men who challenge them, and fearlessly face the result of their actions. They deny that their education in any way unfits them for the duty of wifehood and maternity or primarily renders these conditions any less attractive to them than to the domestic type of woman. On the contrary, they hold that their knowledge of physiology makes them better mothers and housekeepers; their knowledge of chemistry makes them better cooks; while from their training in other natural sciences and in mathematics, they obtain an accuracy and fair-mindedness which is of great value to them in dealing with their children or employees."

So much for their willingness. Now the apple may be good for food and pleasant to the eyes, and a fruit to be desired to make one wise. Nay, it may even assure you that it has no aversion whatever to being tasted. Still, if you do not like the flavor all these recommendations are nothing. Is the intellectual woman *desirable* in the matrimonial market?

This I cannot answer. I confess my ignorance. I am no judge of such things. I have been told that strong-minded women could be, when they thought it worth their while, quite endurable, and, judging from the number of female names I find in college catalogues among the alumnae with double patronymics, I surmise that quite a number of men are willing to put up with them.

Now I would that my task ended here. Having shown that a great want of the world in the past has been a feminine force; that that force can have its full effect only through the untrammelled development of woman; that such development, while it gives her to the world and to civilization, does not necessarily remove her from the home and fireside; finally, that while past centuries have witnessed sporadic instances of this higher growth, still it was reserved for the latter half of the nineteenth century to render it common and general enough to be effective; I might close with a glowing prediction of what the twentieth century may expect from this heritage of twin forces—the masculine battered and toil-worn as a grim veteran after centuries of warfare, but still strong, active, and vigorous, ready to help with his hard-won experience the young recruit rejoicing in her newly found freedom, who so confidently places her hand in his with mutual pledges to redeem the ages.

> "And so the twain upon the skirts of Time,
> Sit side by side, full-summed in all their powers,
> Dispensing harvest, sowing the To-be,
> Self-reverent each and reverencing each."

Fain would I follow them, but duty is nearer home. The high ground of generalities is alluring but my pen is devoted to a special cause: and with a view to further enlightenment on the achievements of the century for THE HIGHER EDUCATION OF COLORED WOMEN, I wrote a few days ago to the colleges which admit women and asked how many colored women had completed the B.A. course in each during its entire history. These are the figures returned: Fisk leads the way with twelve; Oberlin next with five; Wilberforce, four; Ann Arbor and Wellesley three each, Livingstone two, Atlanta one, Howard, as yet, none.

I then asked the principal of the Washington High School[5] how many

---

[5]The M Street High School, now the Dunbar School, in Washington, D.C., is the school where Mrs. Cooper began her long teaching career in 1887. (BJL and RB)

out of a large number of female graduates from his school had chosen to go forward and take a collegiate course. He replied that but one had ever done so, and she was then in Cornell.[6]

Others ask questions too, sometimes, and I was asked a few years ago by a white friend, "How is it that the men of your race seem to outstrip the women in mental attainment?" "Oh," I said, "so far as it is true, the men, I suppose, from the life they lead, gain more by contact; and so far as it is only apparent, I think the women are more quiet. They don't feel called to mount a barrel and harangue by the hour every time they imagine they have produced an idea."

But I am sure there is another reason which I did not at that time see fit to give. The atmosphere, the standards, the requirements of our little world do not afford any special stimulus to female development.

It seems hardly a gracious thing to say, but it strikes me as true, that while our men seem thoroughly abreast of the times on almost every other subject, when they strike the woman question they drop back into sixteenth century logic. They leave nothing to be desired generally in regard to gallantry and chivalry, but they actually do not seem sometimes to have outgrown that old contemporary of chivalry—the idea that women may stand on pedestals or live in doll houses (if they happen to have them), but they must not furrow their brows with thought or attempt to help men tug at the great questions of the world. I fear the majority of colored men do not yet think it worth while that women aspire to higher education. . . . The three R's, a little music and a good deal of dancing, a first rate dress-maker and a bottle of magnolia balm, are quite enough generally to render charming any woman possessed of tact and the capacity for worshipping masculinity.

My readers will pardon my illustrating my point and also giving a reason for the fear that is in me, by a little bit of personal experience. When a child I was put into a school near home that professed to be normal and collegiate, i.e. to prepare teachers for colored youth, furnish candidates for the ministry, and offer collegiate training for those who should be ready for it. Well, I found after a while that I had a good deal of time on my hands. I had devoured what was put before me, and, like Oliver Twist, was looking around to ask for more. I constantly felt (as I suppose many an ambitious girl has felt) a thumping from within unanswered by any beckoning from without. Class after class was organized for these ministerial candidates (many of them men who had been preaching before I was born). . . .

Finally a Greek class was to be formed. My inspiring preceptor informed me that Greek had never been taught in the school, but that he was going to form a class *for the candidates for the ministry,* and if I liked I might join it. I replied—humbly I hope, as became a female of the

---

[6]Graduated from Scientific Course, June, 1890, the first colored woman to graduate from Cornell.

human species—that I would like very much to study Greek, and that I was thankful for the opportunity, and so it went on. A boy, however meager his equipment and shallow his pretentions, had only to declare a floating intention to study theology and he could get all the support, encouragement and stimulus he needed, be absolved from work and invested beforehand with all the dignity of his far away office. While a self-supporting girl had to struggle on by teaching in the summer and working after school hours to keep up with her board bills, and actually to fight her way against positive discouragements to the higher education; till one such girl one day flared out and told the principal "the only mission opening before a girl in his school was to marry one of those candidates." He said he didn't know but it was. And when at last that same girl announced her desire and intention to go to college it was received with about the same incredulity and dismay as if a brass button on one of those candidate's coats had propounded a new method for squaring the circle or trisecting the arc.

Now this is not fancy. It is a simple unvarnished photograph, and what I believe was not in those days exceptional in colored schools, and I ask the men and women who are teachers and co-workers for the highest interests of the race, that they give the girls a chance! We might as well expect to grow trees from leaves as hope to build up a civilization or a manhood without taking into consideration our women and the home life made by them, which must be the root and ground of the whole matter. Let us insist then on special encouragement for the education of our women and special care in their training. Let our girls feel that we expect something more of them than that they merely look pretty and appear well in society. Teach them that there is a race with special needs which they and only they can help; that the world needs and is already asking for their trained, efficient forces. Finally, if there is an ambitious girl with pluck and brain to take the higher education, encourage her to make the most of it. Let there be the same flourish of trumpets and clapping of hands as when a boy announces his determination to enter the lists; and then, as you know that she is physically the weaker of the two, don't stand from under and leave her to buffet the waves alone. Let her know that your heart is following her, that your hand, though she sees it not, is ready to support her. To be plain, I mean let money be raised and scholarships be founded in our colleges and universities for self-supporting, worthy young women, to offset and balance the aid that can always be found for boys who will take theology.

The earnest well trained Christian young woman, as a teacher, as a home-maker, as wife, mother, or silent influence even, is as potent a missionary agency among our people as is the theologian; and I claim that at the present stage of our development in the South she is even more important and necessary.

Let us then, here and now, recognize this force and resolve to make the most of it—not the boys less, but the girls more.

[A year after the publication of her volume of essays, Mrs. Cooper spoke to the Congress of Representative Women on the status of black women. Her short statement, reprinted below, followed a major address on the same topic by Fannie Barrier Williams.][7]

The higher fruits of civilization can not be extemporized, neither can they be developed normally, in the brief space of thirty years. It requires the long and painful growth of generations. Yet all through the darkest period of the colored women's oppression in this country her yet unwritten history is full of heroic struggle, a struggle against fearful and overwhelming odds, that often ended in a horrible death, to maintain and protect that which woman holds dearer than life. The painful, patient, and silent toil of mothers to gain a fee simple title to the bodies of their daughters, the despairing fight, as of an entrapped tigress, to keep hallowed their own persons, would furnish material for epics. That more went down under the flood than stemmed the current is not extraordinary. The majority of our women are not heroines—but I do not know that a majority of any race of women are heroines. It is enough for me to know that while in the eyes of the highest tribunal in America she was deemed no more than a chattel, an irresponsible thing, a dull block, to be drawn hither or thither at the volition of an owner, the Afro-American woman maintained ideals of womanhood unshamed by any ever conceived. Resting or fermenting in untutored minds, such ideals could not claim a hearing at the bar of the nation. The white woman could at least plead for her own emancipation; the black woman, doubly enslaved, could but suffer and struggle and be silent. I speak for the colored women of the South, because it is there that the millions of blacks in this country have watered the soil with blood and tears, and it is there too that the colored woman of America has made her characteristic history, and there her destiny is evolving. Since emancipation the movement has been at times confused and stormy, so that we could not always tell whether we were going forward or groping in a circle. We hardly knew what we ought to emphasize, whether education or wealth, or civil freedom and recognition. We were utterly destitute. Possessing no homes nor the knowledge of how to make them, no money nor the habit of acquiring it, no education, no political status, no influence, what could we do? But as Frederick Douglass had said in darker days than those, "One with God is a majority," and our ignorance had hedged us in from the fine-spun theories of agnostics. We had remaining at least a simple faith that a just God is on the throne of the universe, and that somehow—we could not see, nor did we bother our heads to try to tell how—he would in his own good time make all right that seemed most wrong.

---

[7]*World's Congress of Representative Women*, ed. May Wright Sewall (Chicago, 1893), pp. 711–15. For the address of Fannie Barrier Williams, see above.

Schools were established, not merely public day-schools, but home training and industrial schools, at Hampton, at Fisk, Atlanta, Raleigh, and other central stations, and later, through the energy of the colored people themselves, such schools as the Wilberforce, the Livingstone, the Allen, and the Paul Quinn were opened. These schools were almost without exception co-educational. Funds were too limited to be divided on sex lines, even had it been ideally desirable; but our girls as well as our boys flocked in and battled for an education. Not even then was that patient, untrumpeted heroine, the slave-mother, released from self-sacrifice, and many an unbuttered crust was eaten in silent content that she might eke out enough from her poverty to send her young folks off to school. She "never had the chance," she would tell you, with tears on her withered cheek, so she wanted them to get all they could. The work in these schools, and in such as these, has been like the little leaven hid in the measure of meal, permeating life throughout the length and breadth of the Southland, lifting up ideals of home and of womanhood; diffusing a contagious longing for higher living and purer thinking, inspiring woman herself with a new sense of her dignity in the eternal purposes of nature. To-day there are twenty-five thousand five hundred and thirty colored schools in the United States with one million three hundred and fifty-three thousand three hundred and fifty-two pupils of both sexes. This is not quite the thirtieth year since their emancipation, and the colored people hold in landed property for churches and schools twenty-five million dollars. Two and one-half million colored children have learned to read and write, and twenty-two thousand nine hundred and fifty-six colored men and women (mostly women) are teaching in these schools. According to Doctor Rankin,[8] President of Howard University, there are two hundred and forty-seven colored students (a large percentage of whom are women) now preparing themselves in the universities of Europe. . . .

Now, I think if I could crystallize the sentiment of my constituency, and deliver it as a message to this congress of women, it would be something like this: Let woman's claim be as broad in the concrete as in the abstract. We take our stand on the solidarity of humanity, the oneness of life, and the unnaturalness and injustice of all special favoritisms, whether of sex, race, country, or condition. If one link of the chain be broken, the chain is broken. A bridge is no stronger than its weakest part, and a cause is not worthier than its weakest element. Least of all can woman's cause afford to decry the weak. We want, then, as toilers for the universal triumph of justice and human rights, to go to our homes from this Congress, demanding an entrance not through a gateway for ourselves, our race, our sex, or our sect, but a grand highway for humanity. The colored woman feels that woman's cause is one and universal; and that not till the image of God, whether in parian or ebony, is sacred and inviolable; not till race, color, sex, and condi-

---

[8]See footnote 4 under Williams speeches, above. (BJL and RB)

tion are seen as the accidents, and not the substance of life; not till the universal title of humanity to life, liberty, and the pursuit of happiness is conceded to be inalienable to all; not till then is woman's lesson taught and woman's cause won—not the white woman's, nor the black woman's, nor the red woman's, but the cause of every man and of every woman who has writhed silently under a mighty wrong. Woman's wrongs are thus indissolubly linked with all undefended woe, and the acquirement of her "rights" will mean the final triumph of all right over might, the supremacy of the moral forces of reason, and justice, and love in the government of the nations of earth.

Bibliography

Works included in
BLACK WOMEN IN NINETEENTH-CENTURY AMERICAN LIFE

Annie L. Burton. *Memories of Childhood's Slavery Days.* Boston, 1909.

Anna Julia Cooper. *A Voice from the South.* Xenia, Ohio, 1892.

————. Remarks following address on "The Intellectual Progress of Colored Women of the United States Since the Emancipation Proclamation." *World's Congress of Representative Women,* ed. May Wright Sewall. Chicago, 1893.

Fanny Jackson Coppin. *Reminiscences of School Life, and Hints on Teaching.* Philadelphia, 1913. This incorporates, with minor revisions, her speech entitled "A Plea for Industrial Opportunity," which appears also in *Masterpieces of Negro Eloquence,* ed. Alice Moore Dunbar (later Alice Dunbar Nelson). New York, 1914.

————. Remarks following address on "The Intellectual Progress of Colored Women of the United States Since the Emancipation Proclamation." *World's Congress of Representative Women,* cited above.

Cornelia. "My Mother was the Smartest Black Woman in Eden." *Unwritten History of Slavery: Autobiographical Accounts of Negro Ex-Slaves,* ed. Ophelia Settle Egypt, J. Masuoka, and Charles S. Johnson. Social Science Source Documents No. 1, Fisk University Social Science Institute, Nashville, 1945, pp. 283–90. Mimeographed.

William Craft. *Running a Thousand Miles for Freedom; or, the Escape of William and Ellen Craft from Slavery.* London, 1860.

C. Wilson Larison. *Silvia Dubois. (Now 116 Years Old.) A Biography of the Slave who Whipped Her Mistress and Gained Her Freedom,* as told to C. W. Larison, M.D. Ringoes, N.J., 1883.

[Frances Whipple Greene(e)]. *Memoirs of Elleanor Eldridge.* Providence, 1838.

Elizabeth, a Colored Minister of the Gospel, born in Slavery. Philadelphia, 1889.

Charlotte Forten Grimké. *The Journal of Charlotte L. Forten,* ed. Ray Allen Billington. New York, 1953.

————. Letter to the editor, *The Liberator,* 19 December 1862.

Frances Ellen Watkins Harper. "Duty to Dependent Races." National Council of Women of the United States, *Transactions.* Philadelphia, 1891.

————. "Woman's Political Future." *World's Congress of Representative Women,* cited above.

Elizabeth Keckley. *Behind the Scenes; or, Thirty Years a Slave and Four Years in the White House.* New York, 1868.

Lucy Laney. "The Burden of the Educated Colored Woman." A paper read at the Hampton Negro Conference No. III, July 1899, *Report.* N.p., 1899.

Jarena Lee. *Religious Experience and Journal of Mrs. Jarena Lee, Giving an Account of Her Call to Preach the Gospel.* Philadelphia, 1849.

Rev. H. Mattison. *Louisa Picquet, the Octoroon: A Tale of Southern Slave Life.* New York, 1861.

Ann Plato. *Essays; Including Biographies and Miscellaneous Pieces, in Prose and Poetry.* Hartford, 1841.

Nancy Prince. *A Narrative of the Life and Travels of Mrs. Nancy Prince,* 2d ed.. Boston, 1853.

Sarah Parker Remond. Speech of 11 March 1859, recorded in "Miss Remond's First Lecture in Dublin." *Anti-Slavery Advocate* (London) 2, April 1859.

Amanda Smith. *An Autobiography: the Story of the Lord's Dealings with Mrs. Amanda Smith, the Colored Evangelist; Containing an Account of Her Life Work of Faith, and Her Travels in America, England, Ireland, Scotland, India and Africa, as an Independent Missionary*. Chicago, 1893.

Maria W. Stewart. *Productions of Mrs. Maria W. Stewart*. Boston, 1835.

Susie King Taylor. *Reminiscences of My Life in Camp with the 33rd United States Colored Troops, late 1st S.C. Volunteers*. Boston, 1902.

Sojourner Truth. Remarks at Akron, Ohio woman's rights convention, 1851, in Elizabeth Cady Stanton, Susan B. Anthony, and Matilda Joslyn Gage, eds., *History of Woman Suffrage*, I. Rochester, N.Y., 1881.

———. Speech at convention of American Equal Rights Association, 1867, and informal remarks afterward, in Stanton et al., *History of Woman Suffrage*, II. Rochester, N.Y., 1881.

———. Letter from Freedman's Village, Virginia, 17 November 1864; petition to Congress, 1870; speech in Boston, 1 January 1871, in Olive Gilbert, *Narrative of Sojourner Truth, With a History of her Labors and Correspondence, Drawn from her "Book of Life."* Battle Creek, Mich., 1884.

Harriet Tubman. Recollections. Quoted in Sarah Bradford, *Harriet Tubman, The Moses of Her People*. New York, 1886.

Ida B. Wells (later Wells-Barnett). *U.S. Atrocities*. London, 1892. British edition of *Southern Horrors*, published in New York earlier in the same year.

Fannie Barrier Williams. "Religious Duty to the Negro." *World's Parliament of Religions, Chicago, 1893: the World's Congress of Religions*, ed. John Wesley Hanson. Chicago, 1894.

———. "The Intellectual Progress of the Colored Women of the United States Since the Emancipation Proclamation." *World's Congress of Representative Women*, cited above. This address was also printed as a pamphlet, *The Present Status and Intellectual Progress of Colored Women*. Chicago, 1893.

OTHER SELECTED WRITINGS BY THESE AUTHORS

Anna Julia Cooper. *L'Attitude de la France à l'Egard de l'Esclavage pendant la Révolution*. Paris, 1925.

———. *Le Pélérinage de Charlemagne*. Paris, 1925.

———. *Equality of Races and the Democratic Movement*. Washington, D.C., 1945.

———. *Life and Writings of the Grimké Family*. N.p., 1951.

Charlotte Forten Grimké. "Glimpses of New England." *National Anti-Slavery Standard*, 3 February 1860.

———. "Life on the Sea Islands." *Atlantic Monthly* 13 (May and June 1864): 587–96, 666–76.

Frances Ellen Watkins Harper. *Poems on Miscellaneous Subjects*. Boston, 1854. Reprinted many times, including the years 1857, 1858, 1864, and 1871.

———. *Sketches of Southern Life*. Philadelphia, 1872.

———. Address at Centennial Exercises, April 14, 1875. Pennsylvania Society for Promoting the Abolition of Slavery, *Centennial Anniversary*. Philadelphia, 1875. Reprinted in Dunbar, *Masterpieces*, cited above.

———. "Coloured Women of America." *Englishwomen's Review*, n.s. 57 (15 January 1878): 10–15.

———. "The Neglected Rich." International Council of Women, *Report*. Washington, D.C., 1888.

Jarena Lee. *The Life and Religious Experience of Jarena Lee, a Coloured Lady, Giving an Account of Her Call to Preach the Gospel.* Philadelphia, 1836.

Sarah Parker Remond. "The Negroes in the United States of America." *Journal of Negro History* 27 (April 1942): 216–18. Speech delivered in London, 1862, before the International Congress of Charities, Correction, and Philanthropy.

———. *The Negroes as Freedmen and Soldiers.* London, 1864.

Maria W. Stewart. *Religion and the Pure Principles of Morality the Sure Foundation on Which we Must Build.* [N.p., 1831].

———. *Meditations.* [Boston], 1832.

———. *Speeches delivered in Boston.* Reprinted in *Liberator*, 28 April 1832; 17 November 1832; 27 April 1833; 7 May 1833.

———. *Meditations from the Pen of Mrs. Maria W. Stewart.* Washington, D.C., 1879. This volume, prepared when the author was matron of the Freedman's Hospital in Washington, reprints *Productions* (1835) in its entirety, adding new biographical material.

Ida B. Wells (later Wells-Barnett). *Southern Horrors; Lynch Law in All its Phases.* New York, 1892.

———. *A Red Record.* Chicago, 1894.

———. "Lynch Law in America." *Arena* 23 (January 1900): 15–24.

———. *Mob Rule in New Orleans.* Chicago, 1900.

———. "Lynching, the Excuse for It." *Independent*, 16 May 1901.

———. "How Enfranchisement Stops Lynchings." *Original Rights Magazine* 1 (June 1910).

———. *Crusade for Justice: The Autobiography of Ida B. Wells.* Ed. Alfreda M. Duster. Chicago, 1970.

Fannie Barrier Williams. "The Colored Woman and Her Part in Race Regeneration." In Booker T. Washington, *A New Negro for a New Century.* Chicago, 1900.

———. "Club Movement Among Negro Women." In John W. Gibson, *The Colored American From Slavery to Honorable Citizenship.* Atlanta, 1902 (reissued in 1912 under the title *Progress of a Race*).

———. "Colored Women of Chicago." *Southern Workman* 43 (October 1914): 564–66.

GUIDES TO MATERIALS

W.E.B. DuBois and Guy B. Johnson. *The Encyclopedia of the Negro: Preparatory volume with reference lists and reports.* Rev. ed. New York, 1946.

Irene Epstein. *A Bibliography on the Negro Woman in the United States.* New York, 1951. Mimeographed.

Louis Kaplan. *A Bibliography of American Autobiographies.* Madison, Wisc., 1961.

Paul Lewinson (for the Committee on Negro Studies of the American Council of Learned Societies). *A Guide to Documents in the National Archives for Negro Studies.* Washington, D.C., 1947.

Elizabeth W. Miller. *The Negro in America: A Bibliography.* Cambridge, Mass., 1966.

Daniel Murray. *Preliminary List of Books and Pamphlets by Negro Authors for Paris Exposition and Library of Congress.* Washington, D.C., 1900.

Dorothy B. Porter. "Early American Negro Writings: A Bibliographical Study." *The Papers of the Bibliographical Society of America* 39 (1945): 192–268.

Erwin A. Salk. *A Layman's Guide to Negro History.* Chicago, 1966.

Erwin K. Welsch. *The Negro in the United States: A Research Guide.* Bloomington, Ind., and London, 1965.

Monroe N. Work. *A Bibliography of the Negro in Africa and America.* New York, 1928.

GENERAL BIOGRAPHICAL SOURCES

Afro-American Artists: A Bio-Bibliographical Directory. Boston, 1973.

Richard Bardolph. "The Distinguished Negro in America, 1770–1936." *American Historical Review* 60 (April 1955): 527–47.

———. "The Negro in *Who's Who in America,* 1931–1955." *Journal of Negro History* 42 (October 1957): 261–82.

———. *The Negro Vanguard.* New York, 1959.

Benjamin G. Brawley. *Early Negro American Writers.* Chapel Hill, N.C., 1935.

———. *Negro Builders and Heroes.* Chapel Hill, N.C., 1937.

Hallie Quinn Brown. *Homespun Heroines and Other Women of Distinction.* Xenia, Ohio, 1926.

Sadie Iola Daniel. *Women Builders.* Washington, D.C., 1931.

Sylvia G. Dannett. *Profiles of Negro Womanhood.* Yonkers, N.Y., 1964.

Louis Filler. *A Dictionary of American Social Reform.* New York, 1963.

Rufus W. Griswold. *The Female Poets of America.* 2d ed. Philadelphia, 1849.

Phoebe Hanaford. *Daughters of America; or, Women of the Century.* 2d ed. Augusta, Me., 1882.

Harold Bruce Hunting. *Pioneers of Goodwill.* New York, 1929.

Edward T. James and Janet Wilson James, eds. *Notable American Women.* 3 vols. Cambridge, Mass., 1971.

Vernon Loggins. *The Negro Author, his Development in America.* New York, 1931.

Monroe A. Majors. *Noted Negro Women, their Triumphs and Activities.* Chicago, 1893.

The Negro Year Book. Tuskegee, Ala., 1912–. Issued irregularly.

Wilhelmena S. Robinson. *Historical Negro Biographies.* New York, 1967. Published under the auspices of the Association for the Study of Negro Life and History.

Lawson Andrew Scruggs. *Women of Distinction: Remarkable in Works and Invincible in Character.* Raleigh, N.C., 1893.

William J. Simmons. *Men of Mark, Eminent, Progressive, and Rising.* Cleveland, 1887.

Who's Who in Colored America. 7 vols. New York, 1927–1950.

INDIVIDUAL BIOGRAPHICAL SOURCES

Anna Julia Cooper

Mary Gibson Hundley. *The Dunbar Story (1870–1955).* New York, 1965.

Fanny Jackson Coppin

Levi Coppin. *Unwritten History, an Autobiography.* Philadelphia, 1919.

Ellen Craft

Vincent Y. Bowditch. *Life and Correspondence of Henry Ingersoll Bowditch,* II. Boston and New York, 1902.

William Wells Brown. *Sketches of Places and People Abroad.* Boston, 1855.

Henry Steele Commager. *Theodore Parker.* Boston, 1947.

The Freedman, 1 December 1865. London. (Periodical)

Marion Gleason McDougall. *Fugitive Slaves (1619–1865).* Fay House Monographs No. 3. Boston, 1891.

[Samuel May]. *The Fugitive Slave Law and its Victims*. Revised and enlarged ed. New York, 1861. (Pamphlet)
Report of the Great Anti-Slavery Meeting, Held April 9, 1851, in the Public Rooms, Broadmead, Bristol, to Receive the Fugitive Slaves, William and Ellen Craft. Bristol, England, 1851. (Pamphlet)
Marion Wilson Starling. "The Slave Narrative, Its Place in American Literary History." Unpublished Ph.D. dissertation, New York University, 1946.
William Still. *The Underground Rail Road*. Philadelphia, 1872.
John Weiss. *Life and Correspondence of Theodore Parker*, II. New York, 1864.

Silvia Dubois

C. Wilson Larison. "Preface" and "Biography." *Silvia Dubois*, cited above.

Charlotte Forten Grimké

Ray Allen Billington. "Introduction." *The Journal of Charlotte L. Forten*, cited above.
Anna Julia Cooper. *Life and Writings of the Grimké Family*, cited above.

Frances Ellen Watkins Harper

Lillian O'Connor. *Pioneer Women Orators*. New York, 1954.
Still. *The Underground Rail Road*, cited above.

Elizabeth Keckley

Ruth Painter Randall. *Mary Lincoln: Biography of a Marriage*. Boston, 1953.
John E. Washington. *They Knew Lincoln*. New York, 1942.

Lucy Laney

A. C. Griggs. "Lucy Craft Laney." *Journal of Negro History* 19 (January 1934): 97–102.
Mary White Ovington. *Portraits in Color*. New York, 1927.

Ann Plato

James W. C. Pennington. "Introduction." Plato, *Essays*, cited above.
David O. White. "Hartford's African Schools, 1830–1868." *Connecticut Historical Society Bulletin* 39 (April 1974): 47–53.

Sarah Parker Remond

The Journal of Charlotte L. Forten, ed. Ray Allen Billington, cited above.
Ruth Bogin. "Sarah Parker Remond: Black Abolitionist from Salem." *Essex Institute Historical Collections* 110 (April 1974): 120–50.
Dorothy B. Porter. "Sarah Parker Remond, Abolitionist and Physician." *Journal of Negro History* 20 (July 1935): 287–93.
Benjamin Quarles. "Ministers Without Portfolio." *Journal of Negro History* 39 (January 1954): 27–42.
——. *Black Abolitionists*. New York, 1969.

Amanda Smith

H.F. Kletzing and E.L. Kletzing. *Traits of Character Illustrated in Bible Light, together with Short Sketches of Marked and Marred Manhood and Womanhood.* Chicago, 1898.

Maria W. Stewart

Eleanor Flexner. *Century of Struggle: The Woman's Rights Movement in the United States.* Cambridge, Mass., 1959.
O'Connor, *Pioneer Women Orators,* cited above.
Dorothy B. Porter. "The Organized Educational Activities of Negro Literary Societies, 1828–46." *Journal of Negro Education* 5 (October 1936): 555–76.

Sojourner Truth

Arthur H. Fauset. *Sojourner Truth.* Chapel Hill, N.C., 1938.
Olive Gilbert. *Narrative of Sojourner Truth,* cited above.
Hertha Pauli. *Her Name was Sojourner Truth.* New York, 1962.
Lillie Buffum Chace Wyman. *American Chivalry.* Boston, 1913.

Harriet Tubman

Sarah Bradford. *Harriet Tubman,* cited above.
James B. Clarke. "An Hour With Harriet Tubman." In William Edgar Easton, *Christophe: A Tragedy in Prose of Imperial Haiti.* Los Angeles, 1911.
Earl Conrad. *Harriet Tubman.* New York, 1943.

Ida B. Wells-Barnett

Flexner. *Century of Struggle,* cited above.
Ida B. Wells. *Crusade for Justice: The Autobiography of Ida B. Wells,* ed. Alfreda M. Duster. Chicago, 1970.

Fannie Barrier Williams

Elizabeth Lindsay Davis, ed. *Lifting as They Climb.* Washington, D.C., 1933.
Charlotte Elizabeth Martin. *The Story of Brockport for One Hundred Years.* [Brockport, N.Y.], 1929.

OTHER WORKS CONSULTED

Alice Dana Adams. *The Neglected Period of Anti-Slavery in America (1808–1831).* Radcliffe College Monographs No. 14. Cambridge, Mass., 1908.
Henry Adams. *The Education of Henry Adams.* Modern Library ed. New York, 1931.
Richard Allen. *The Life, Experience, and Gospel Labors of . . . .* N.p., 1887.
American Anti-Slavery Society. *American Slavery As It Is: Testimony of a Thousand Witnesses.* New York, 1839.

American Anti-Slavery Society. *Annual Report*, 1857–58, 1859, 1860.

American Anti-Slavery Society. *Proceedings . . . at its Third Decade, Held in the City of Philadelphia, Dec. 3d and 4th, 1864* [i.e. 1863]. New York, 1864.

American Missionary Association. *History of the A.M.A.: Its Churches and Educational Institutions Among the Freedmen, Indians and Chinese.* New York, 1874.

Herbert Aptheker. *A Documentary History of the Negro People in the United States.* 2 vols. New York, 1951.

Augusta (Georgia) Chronicle, 12 May 1935; 19 June 1960.

Gilbert H. Barnes. *The Anti-Slavery Impulse, 1830–1844.* New York, 1933.

———— and Dwight L. Dumond, eds. *Letters of Theodore Dwight Weld, Angelina Grimké Weld and Sarah Grimké, 1822–1844.* II. New York, 1934.

Irving H. Bartlett. *From Slave to Citizen: The Story of the Negro in Rhode Island.* Providence, 1954.

William Bassett. *Letter to a Member of the Society of Friends in Reply to Objections Against Joining Anti-Slavery Societies.* Boston, 1837.

John F. Bayliss, ed. *Black Slave Narratives.* New York, 1970.

Mary Ritter Beard, ed. *America Through Women's Eyes.* New York, 1933.

Jessie Bernard. *Marriage and Family among Negroes.* Englewood Cliffs, N.J., 1966.

Andrew Billingsley. *Black Families in White America.* Englewood Cliffs, N.J., 1968.

John W. Blassingame. *The Slave Community: Plantation Life in the Antebellum South.* New York, 1972.

Board of Education, City of New York. *The Negro in American History.* [New York], 1964.

Horace M. Bond. *The Education of the Negro in the American Social Order.* New York, 1934.

Arna Bontemps, ed. *Great Slave Narratives.* Boston, 1969.

Benjamin A. Botkin. *Lay My Burden Down: A Folk History of Slavery.* Chicago, 1945. Based on the Slave Narrative Collection of the Federal Writers' Project, now in the Rare Book Room of the Library of Congress.

Elizabeth Hyde Botume. *First Days Among the Contrabands.* Boston, 1893.

George F. Bragg. *History of the Afro-American Group of the Episcopal Church.* Baltimore, 1922.

Benjamin Brawley. *Dr. Dillard of the Jeanes Fund.* New York, 1930.

Bristol and Clifton Ladies' Anti-Slavery Society. *Special Report . . . with a Statement of the Reasons of its Separation from the British and Foreign Anti-Slavery Society.* London and Bristol, 1852.

Bristol (England) Mercury, and Western Counties Advertiser, 12 April 1851.

Bristol (England) Mirror, 12 April 1851.

British Anti-Slavery Advocate, selected issues, 1852, 1853, 1854, 1858, 1859, 1860, 1861.

Howard Brotz, ed. *Negro Social and Political Thought, 1850–1920: Representative Texts.* New York, 1966.

Virginia W. Broughton. *Twenty Years' Experience of a Missionary.* Chicago, 1907.

Josephine Brown. *Biography of an American Bondman.* Boston, 1856.

Letitia Woods Brown. *Free Negroes in the District of Columbia, 1790–1846.* New York, 1972.

Sterling A. Brown, Arthur P. Davis, and Ulysses Lee, eds. *Negro Caravan: Writings by American Negroes.* New York, 1941.

Warren H. Brown. *Checklist of Negro Newspapers in the United States, 1827–1946.* Jefferson City, Mo., 1946.

William Wells Brown. *A Lecture Delivered Before the Female Anti-Slavery Society of Salem, at Lyceum Hall, Nov. 14, 1847.* Boston, 1847.

Henrietta Buckmaster. *Freedom Bound.* New York, 1965.

Henry Allen Bullock. *A History of Negro Education in the South: From 1619 to the Present.* Cambridge, Mass., 1967.

Nelson R. Burr. *Critical Bibliography of Religion in America.* 2 vols. Princeton, 1961.

Margaret Just Butcher. *The Negro in American Culture.* New York, 1956.

Henry J. Cadbury. "Negro Membership in the Society of Friends." *Journal of Negro History* 21 (April 1936): 151–213.

Arthur Wallace Calhoun. *A Social History of the American Family from Colonial Times to the Present.* 3 vols. Cleveland, 1917–19.

V.F. Calverton, ed. *Anthology of American Negro Literature.* New York, 1929.

Thomas Monroe Campbell. *The Movable School Goes to the Negro Farmer.* Tuskegee, Ala., 1936.

Helen S. Catterall. *Judicial Cases Concerning American Slavery and the Negro.* 5 vols. Washington, D.C., 1926–37.

Elizabeth Buffum Chace and Lucy Buffum Lovell. *Two Quaker Sisters; from the Original Diaries.* New York, 1937.

Chicago Defender, 26 October 1940.

Chicago Tribune, 17 October 1939.

Clarence C. Clendenen and Peter Duignan. *Americans in Black Africa Up to 1865.* Hoover Institution Studies No. 5. Stanford, Calif., 1964.

Levi Coffin. *Reminiscences of Levi Coffin, the Reputed President of the Underground Railroad.* Cincinnati, 1876.

James H. Cone. *The Spirituals and the Blues: An Interpretation.* New York, 1972.

Henry S. Cooley. *A Study of Slavery in New Jersey.* Baltimore, 1896.

Rossa Belle Cooley. *Homes of the Freed.* New York, 1926.

Crisis 38 (June 1931): 207.

John Wesley Cromwell. *The Negro in American History.* Washington, D.C., 1914.

Alexander Crummell. *Africa and America: Addresses and Discourses.* Springfield, Mass., 1891.

D.W. Culp, ed. *Twentieth Century Negro Literature; or, A Cyclopedia of Thought on the Vital Topics Relating to the American Negro, by One Hundred of America's Greatest Negroes.* Naperville, Ill., and Toronto, 1902.

Marion Vera Cuthbert. *Education and Marginality: a Study of the Negro Woman College Graduate.* New York, 1942.

Wendell P. Dabney. *Cincinnati's Colored Citizens: Historical, Sociological, Biographical.* Cincinnati, 1926.

Daily Worker, 1 July 1951.

John Daniels. *In Freedom's Birthplace: a Study of the Boston Negroes.* Boston and New York, 1914.

David Brion Davis. *The Problem of Slavery in Western Culture.* Ithaca, N.Y., 1966.

———. "Slavery and the Post-World War II Historians." *Daedalus* (Spring 1974): 1–16.

John P. Davis, ed. *The American Negro Reference Book.* Englewood Cliffs, N.J., 1966.

Rodolphe L. Desdunes. *Nos Hommes et Notre Histoire; Notices Biographiques Accompagnées de Réflexions et de Souvenirs Personnels, Hommage à la Population Créole, en Souvenir des Grands Hommes qu'elle a Produits et des Bonnes Choses qu'elle a Accomplies.* Montreal, 1911.

Henderson H. Donald. *The Negro Freedman: The American Negro in the Early Years after Emancipation.* New York, 1952.

Frederick Douglass. *My Bondage and My Freedom.* New York and Auburn, N.Y., 1855.

Thomas E. Drake. *Quakers and Slavery in America.* New Haven, 1950.

Martin Duberman, ed. *The Anti-Slavery Vanguard: New Essays on the Abolitionists.* Princeton, 1965.

W.E.B. DuBois. *The Philadelphia Negro.* Philadelphia, 1899.

———. *The Souls of Black Folk: Essays and Sketches.* Chicago, 1903.

———. *Darkwater: Voices from Within the Veil.* New York, 1920.

————. *The Gift of Black Folk*. Boston, 1924.

————. *Black Reconstruction*. New York, 1935.

————, ed. *The Negro American Family*. Atlanta University Publications No. 13. Atlanta, 1908.

Zilpha Elaw. *Memoirs*. London, 1846.

Stanley M. Elkins. *Slavery: A Problem in American Institutional and Intellectual Life*. Chicago, 1959.

Ralph Ellison. "A Very Stern Discipline." *Harper's Magazine* 234 (March 1967): 76–95.

Federal Writers' Project. *The Negro in Virginia*. New York, 1940.

Louis Filler. *The Crusade Against Slavery, 1830–1860*. New York, 1960.

First Mohonk Conference on the Negro Question, June 4, 5, 6, 1890. Boston, 1890.

Leslie H. Fischel, Jr., and Benjamin Quarles. *The Negro American: A Documentary History*. [Glenview, Ill.], 1967.

Fisk University Social Science Institute. *God Struck Me Dead*. Social Science Source Documents No. 2. Nashville, 1945.

Betty Fladeland. *Men and Brothers: Anglo-American Antislavery Cooperation*. Urbana, Ill., 1972.

Robert Samuel Fletcher. *A History of Oberlin College*. 2 vols. Oberlin, Ohio, 1943.

Robert William Fogel and Stanley L. Engerman. *Time on the Cross*. 2 vols. Boston, 1974.

Philip S. Foner. *The Life and Writings of Frederick Douglass*. 4 vols. New York, 1950–55.

————, ed. *The Voice of Black America: Major Speeches by Negroes in the United States 1797–1971*. New York, 1972.

Julia A. Foote. *A Brand Plucked from the Fire*. New York, 1879.

Bettiola Heloise Fortson. *Mental Pearls: Original Poems and Essays*. N.p., 1915.

John Hope Franklin. *The Free Negro in North Carolina, 1790–1860*. Chapel Hill, N.C., 1943.

————. *From Slavery to Freedom*. 3d ed. New York, 1967.

E. Franklin Frazier. *The Free Negro Family*. Nashville, 1932.

————. *The Negro Family in the United States*. Rev. and abridged ed. New York, 1948.

————. *The Negro in the United States*. Rev. ed. New York, 1957.

————. *The Negro Church in America*. New York, 1963.

Francis P. Gaines. *The Southern Plantation*. New York, 1924.

Larry Gara. *The Liberty Line: The Legend of the Underground Railroad*. Lexington, Ky., 1961.

Wendell P. Garrison and Francis J. Garrison *William Lloyd Garrison, the Story of His Life Told by His Children, 1805–1879*, II and IV. New York, 1889.

Eugene D. Genovese. "The Influence of the Black Power Movement on Historical Scholarship: Reflections of a White Historian." *Daedalus* (Spring 1970): 473–94.

————. "American Slaves and their History." *New York Review of Books*, 3 December 1970, pp. 34–43.

————. *Roll, Jordan, Roll: The World the Slaves Made*. New York, 1974.

Carol V.R. George. *Segregated Sabbaths: Richard Allen and the Emergence of Independent Black Churches, 1760–1840*. New York, 1973.

William Goodell. *The American Slave Code in Theory and Practice: Its Distinctive Features Shown by its Statutes, Judicial Decisions and Illustrative Facts*. New York, 1853.

Lorenzo J. Greene. *The Negro in Colonial New England*. New York, 1942.

Francis J. Grimké. Letter to the editor in "Communications." *Journal of Negro History* 21 (January 1936): 56–57.

Emma Azalia Hackley. *The Colored Girl Beautiful*. Kansas City, 1916.

Anna Davis Hallowell, ed. *James and Lucretia Mott: Life and Letters*. Boston, 1884.

Maud Cuney Hare. *Negro Musicians and their Music*. Washington, D.C., 1936.

Ida Husted Harper. *The Life and Work of Susan B. Anthony*, I. Indianapolis, 1908.

Albert Bushnell Hart. *Slavery and Abolition, 1831–41*. New York, 1914.

W.B. Hartgrove. "The Story of Maria Louise Moore and Fannie M. Richards." *Journal of Negro History* 1 (January 1916): 23–33.

Calvin Hernton. *Sex and Racism in America*. New York, 1966.

Theodore Hershberg. "Free Blacks in Antebellum Philadelphia: A Study of Ex-Slaves, Freeborn, and Socioeconomic Decline." *Journal of Social History* 5 (Winter 1971–72): 183–209.

Thomas Wentworth Higginson. *Army Life in a Black Regiment*. Cambridge, Mass., 1900.

Robert B. Hill. *The Strengths of Black Families*. New York, 1972.

Dwight Oliver Wendell Holmes. *Evolution of the Negro College*. New York, 1934.

Oliver Otis Howard. *Autobiography*. 2 vols. New York, 1907.

Howard University Medical Department. *A Historical, Biographical, and Statistical Souvenir*. Washington, D.C., 1900.

Julia Ward Howe. *Reminiscences, 1819–1899*. Boston and New York, 1900.

Langston Hughes and Milton Meltzer. *A Pictorial History of the Negro in America*. New York, 1963.

John Codman Hurd. *The Law of Freedom and Bondage in the United States*. 2 vols. Boston and New York, 1858–62.

Marcus W. Jernegan. *Laboring and Dependent Classes in Colonial America, 1607–1783*. Chicago, 1931.

Charles S. Johnson. *Shadow of the Plantation*. Chicago, 1934.

Winthrop D. Jordan. *White Over Black: American Attitudes Toward the Negro, 1550–1812*. Chapel Hill, N.C., 1968.

Sidney Kaplan. *The Black Presence in the Era of the American Revolution, 1770–1800*. Greenwich, Conn., 1973.

William Loren Katz. *Eyewitness: The Negro in American History*. New York, 1967.

David M. Katzman. *Before the Ghetto: Black Detroit in the Nineteenth Century*. Urbana, Ill., 1972.

Charles Flint Kellogg. *NAACP: A History of the National Association for the Advancement of Colored People*, I. Baltimore, 1967.

Frances Kemble. *Journal of a Residence on a Georgia Plantation in 1838–1839*. New York, 1864.

Herbert S. Klein. *Slavery in the Americas: A Comparative Study of Virginia and Cuba*. Chicago, 1967.

Ladies' London Emancipation Society. *Annual Report*. London, 1865.

Eugenie A. Leonard. *The Dear-Bought Heritage*. Philadephia, 1965.

Gerda Lerner. *The Grimké Sisters from South Carolina*. Boston, 1967.

———. *Black Women in White America: A Documentary History*. New York, 1972.

"Letters from Negro Women, 1827–1950." *Masses & Mainstream*, February 1951: 24–33.

Helen Matthews Lewis. *The Woman Movement and the Negro Movement: Parallel Struggles for Rights*. Charlottesville, Va., 1949.

Liberator, selected issues, 1832, 1833, 1839, 1841, 1849, 1850, 1851, 1852, 1855, 1857, 1859, 1862.

Robert J. Lifton. "Woman as Knower: Some Psychohistorical Perspectives." In *The Woman in America*, ed. Robert J. Lifton. The *Daedalus* Library. Boston, 1967.

Leon F. Litwack. *North of Slavery: The Negro in the Free States, 1790–1860*. Chicago, 1961.

———. "Free at Last." In *Anonymous Americans*, ed. Tamara K. Hareven. Englewood Cliffs, N.J., 1971.

Mary Stoughton Locke. *Anti-Slavery in America, From the Introduction of African Slaves to the Prohibition of the Slave Trade (1619–1808)*. Radcliffe College Monographs No. 11. Cambridge, Mass., 1901.

Rev. Lewis Lockwood. *Mary S. Peake: The Colored Teacher at Fortress Monroe.* Boston, n.d.

Rayford W. Logan. *The Negro in American Life and Thought: The Nadir, 1877–1901.* New York, 1954.

John Lovell, Jr. *Black Song: The Forge and the Flame.* New York, 1972.

Alma Lutz. *Crusade for Freedom: Women of the Anti-Slavery Movement.* Boston, 1968.

Edgar J. McManus. *Black Bondage in the North.* Syracuse, N.Y., 1973.

James M. McPherson. *Abolitionists and the Negro in the Civil War and Reconstruction.* Princeton, 1964.

———. *The Negro's Civil War: How American Negroes Felt and Acted During the War for the Union.* New York, 1965.

Carleton Mabee. *Black Freedom: The Nonviolent Abolitionists from 1830 through the Civil War.* New York, 1970.

Harriet Martineau. *Society in America.* 3 vols. London, 1837.

Julian D. Mason, Jr., ed. *The Poems of Phillis Wheatley.* Chapel Hill, N.C., 1966.

Massachusetts Anti-Slavery Society. *Proceedings . . . at the Annual Meetings Held in 1854, 1855, and 1856.* Boston, 1856.

Mary Elizabeth Massey. *Bonnet Brigades.* New York, 1966.

Marcia A. Mathews. *Richard Allen.* Baltimore, 1963.

Samuel J. May. *Some Recollections of our Anti-Slavery Conflict.* Boston, 1869.

Benjamin E. Mays. *The Negro's God as Reflected in His Literature.* Boston, 1938.

——— and Joseph Nicholson. *The Negro's Church.* New York, 1933.

Margaret Mead. *Male and Female: A Study of the Sexes in a Changing World.* Rev. ed. New York, 1955.

Milton Meltzer, ed. *In Their Own Words: The History of the American Negro.* 2 vols. New York, 1964–65.

T.J. Morgan. *The Negro in America and the Ideal American.* Philadelphia, 1898.

Simeon Moss. "The Persistence of Slavery and Involuntary Servitude in a Free State (1685–1866)." *Journal of Negro History* 35 (July 1950): 289–314.

Gertrude E. Mossell. *The Work of the Afro-American Woman.* Philadelphia, 1908.

Abigail Field Mott. *Biographical Sketches and Interesting Anecdotes of Persons of Color.* New York, 1837.

———. *Narratives of Colored Americans.* New York, 1875.

Daniel P. Moynihan. *The Negro Family: The Case for National Action.* Washington, D.C., 1965.

Gerald W. Mullin. *Flight and Rebellion: Slave Resistance in Eighteenth-Century Virginia.* New York, 1972.

Alexander L. Murray. "The Provincial Freeman: A New Source for the History of the Negro in Canada and the United States." *Journal of Negro History* 44 (April 1959): 123–35.

Gunnar Myrdal. *The American Dilemma.* 2 vols. New York, 1944.

National Advisory Commission on Civil Disorders. *Report* (Preliminary Kerner Report). New York, 1968.

William C. Nell. *The Colored Patriots of the American Revolution.* Boston, 1855.

Alice Dunbar Nelson. "People of Color in Louisiana." *Journal of Negro History* 1 (October 1916): 361–76 and 2 (January 1917): 51–78.

New National Era 1 (20 October 1870).

Charles H. Nichols. *Many Thousands Gone: The Ex-Slaves' Account of their Bondage and Freedom.* Leiden, 1963.

———, ed. *Black Men in Chains: Narratives by Escaped Slaves.* New York, 1972.

Jeanne L. Noble. *The Negro Woman's College Education.* Teacher's College Studies in Education. New York, 1956.

Margaretta Matilda Odell. *Memoir and Poems of Phillis Wheatley, A Native African and a Slave.* Boston, 1834.

G[reensbury] W[ashington] Offley. *A Narrative of the Life and Labors of the Rev. G.W. Offley*. Hartford, Conn., 1860.

Gilbert Osofsky, ed. *Puttin' On Ole Massa: The Slave Narratives of Henry Bibb, William Wells Brown, and Solomon Northrup*. New York, Evanston and London, 1969.

Mary White Ovington. *The Walls Came Tumbling Down*. New York, 1947.

Irvine G. Penn. *The Afro-American Press and its Editors*. Springfield, Mass., 1891.

Pennsylvania Convention Assembled to Organize a State Anti-Slavery Society at Harrisburg. *Proceedings*. Philadelphia, 1837.

Kate Pickard. *The Kidnapped and the Ransomed, Being the Personal Recollections of Peter Still and his Wife ... After Forty Years of Slavery*. Syracuse, 1856.

Dorothy B. Porter. "Early Manuscript Letters Written by Negroes." *Journal of Negro History* 24 (April 1939): 199–210.

———, ed. *Early Negro Writing, 1760–1837*. Boston, 1971.

David M. Potter. "American Women and the American Character." *Stetson University Bulletin* 62 (January 1962): 1–22, and reprinted in *American History and the Social Sciences*, ed. Edward N. Saveth. New York, 1964.

Hortense Powdermaker. *After Freedom: A Cultural Study in the Deep South*. New York, 1939.

Aaron M. Powell. *Personal Reminiscences of the Anti-Slavery and other Reforms and Reformers*. New York, 1899.

Benjamin Quarles. *The Negro in the Civil War*. Boston, 1953.

———. *The Negro in the American Revolution*. Chapel Hill, N.C., 1961.

———. "Black History Unbound." *Daedalus* (Spring 1974): 163–78.

Lee Rainwater and William L. Yancey. *The Moynihan Report and the Politics of Controversy*. Cambridge, Mass., 1967.

James G. Randall and David Donald. *The Civil War and Reconstruction*. 2d ed. Boston, 1961.

George P. Rawick. *The American Slave: A Composite Autobiography*, Vol. I: *From Sundown to Sunup: The Making of the Black Community*. Westport, Conn., 1972.

Emma S. Ray. *Twice Sold, Twice Ransomed*. Chicago, 1926.

G. Herbert Renfro. *Life and Works of Phillis Wheatley*. Washington, D.C., 1916.

Report of the Arguments of Counsel, in the case of Prudence Crandall v. State of Connecticut. Boston, 1834.

Edward Byron Reuter. *The Mulatto in the United States*. Boston, 1918.

L.E. Richards and M.H. Elliott. *Julia Ward Howe*. 2 vols. Boston, 1916.

Sidney S. Rider. "Bibliographical Memoirs of Three Rhode Island Authors." *Rhode Island Historical Tracts*, First Series, No. 11. Providence, 1880.

Frederick H. Robb, ed. *The Negro in Chicago 1779–1927; Intercollegian Wonder Book*. Chicago, 1927.

Thomas Robbins. *Diary of Thomas Robbins, D.D., 1796–1854*, ed. and annotated Increase N. Tarbox. Boston, 1887.

Willie Lee Rose. *Rehearsal for Reconstruction*. New York, 1964.

Charles Barthelemy Rousseve. *The Negro in Louisiana: Aspects of His History and His Literature*. New Orleans, 1937.

Louis D. Rubin, ed. *Teach the Freeman: The Correspondence of Rutherford B. Hayes and the Slater Fund for Negro Education, 1881–1887*. 2 vols. Baton Rouge, La., 1959.

Wilbur H. Siebert. *The Underground Railroad from Slavery to Freedom*. New York, 1898.

Samuel Sillen. *Women Against Slavery*. New York, 1955.

Francis Butler Simkins and Robert Hilliard Woody. *South Carolina During Reconstruction*. Chapel Hill, N.C., 1932.

Allan H. Spear. *Black Chicago: The Making of a Negro Ghetto, 1890–1920*. Chicago, 1967.

Melford E. Spiro. "Is the Family Universal?" *American Anthropologist* 56 (1954): 839–46, and reprinted in *Marriage, Family, and Residence,* ed. Paul Bohannan and John Middleton. Garden City, N.Y., 1968.

Rosetta Douglass Sprague. "Anna Murray-Douglass—My Mother as I Recall Her." *Journal of Negro History* 8 (January 1923): 93–101.

Kenneth M. Stampp. *The Peculiar Institution: Slavery in the Antebellum South.* New York, 1956.

———. "Rebels and Sambos: The Search for the Negro's Personality in Slavery." - *Journal of Southern History* 37 (August 1971): 367–92.

Elizabeth Cady Stanton, Susan B. Anthony, and Matilda Joslyn Gage, eds. *History of Woman Suffrage.* Vols. I–III, Rochester, N.Y., 1881–1886; Vol. IV, ed. Susan B. Anthony and Ida Husted Harper. Rochester, N.Y., 1902. This is the correct citation for the volumes consulted. The six-volume *History* was published at separate times in different places, with various editors; the two final volumes were issued in 1922.

Robert Staples, ed. *The Black Family: Essays and Studies.* Belmont, Calif., 1971.

Robert S. Starobin. "Privileged Bondsmen and the Process of Accommodation: The Role of Houseservants and Drivers as Seen in Their Own Letters." *Journal of Social History* 5 (Fall 1971): 46–70.

Dorothy Sterling, ed. *Speak Out in Thunder Tones; Letters and Other Writings by Black Northerners, 1787–1865.* Garden City, N.Y., 1973.

Susan Maria Steward. *Woman in Medicine.* Wilberforce, Ohio, 1914.

Anson Phelps Stokes. *Tuskegee Institute: the First Fifty Years.* Tuskegee, Ala., 1931.

Charles Edward Stowe, ed. *Life of Harriet Beecher Stowe.* Boston and New York, 1889.

Arvarh E. Strickland. *History of the Chicago Urban League.* Urbana, Ill., 1966.

Henry L. Swint. *Dear Ones at Home: Letters from Contraband Camps.* Nashville, 1966.

Frank Tannenbaum. *Slave and Citizen: The Negro in the Americas.* New York, 1947.

Alrutheus Ambush Taylor. *The Negro in South Carolina during the Reconstruction.* Washington, D.C., 1924.

———. *The Negro in the Reconstruction of Virginia.* Washington, D.C., 1926.

Clara Mildred Thompson. *Reconstruction in Georgia, Economic, Social, Political, 1865–1872.* New York, 1915.

Emma Lou Thornbrough. *T. Thomas Fortune: Militant Journalist.* Chicago, 1972.

Earl E. Thorpe. *The Mind of the Negro: An Intellectual History of Afro-Americans.* Baton Rouge, La., 1961.

George B. Tindall. "Southern Negroes Since Reconstruction: Dissolving the Static Image." In *Writing Southern History,* ed. Arthur S. Link and Rembert W. Patrick. Baton Rouge, La., 1965.

Frederick B. Tolles, ed. *Slavery and "The Woman Question"—Lucretia Mott's Diary of Her Visit to Great Britain to Attend the World's Anti-Slavery Convention of 1840.* Supplement No. 23 to the *Journal of the Friends' Historical Society.* Haverford, Pa., 1952.

Edward R. Turner. *The Negro in Pennsylvania, 1639–1861.* Washington, D.C., 1911.

U.S. Bureau of the Census. *Negro Population, 1790–1915.* Washington, D.C., 1918.

U.S. Department of Education. *Special Report of the Commissioner of Education on the Condition and Improvement of Public Schools in the District of Columbia . . . 1868 . . . and 1870.* Washington, D.C., 1871.

Bethany Veney. *The Narrative of Bethany Veney, a Slave Woman.* Worcester, Mass., 1889.

Richard C. Wade. *Slavery in the Cities: The South 1820–1860.* New York, 1964.

Margaret Walker. *Jubilee.* Boston, 1966.

William J. Walls. *The African Methodist Episcopal Zion Church: Reality of the Black Church.* Charlotte, N.C., 1974.

Robert A. Warner. *New Haven Negroes: A Social History.* New Haven, 1940.

Joseph R. Washington. *Black Religion.* Boston, 1964.

Washington Evening Star, 28 and 29 February 1964.

Washington Post, 29 February 1964.

Wilberforce University, *The Levi Jenkins Coppin Collection.* Wilberforce, Ohio, 1957. Mimeographed.

Bell I. Wiley. *Southern Negroes, 1861–1865.* 2d ed. New York, 1953.

George W. Williams. *History of the Negro Race in America from 1619 to 1880.* 2 vols. London and New York, 1882.

Gold Refined Wilson. "The Religion of the American Negro Slave: His Attitude Toward Life and Death." *Journal of Negro History* 8 (January 1923): 41–71.

Harvey Wish. *Slavery in the South: First-hand Accounts of the Ante-Bellum American Southland.* New York, 1964.

Woman's Era, 1894–97.

Frederick J. E. Woodbridge. *The Philosophy of History.* New York, 1916.

Carter G. Woodson. "The Negroes of Cincinnati Prior to the Civil War." *Journal of Negro History* 1 (January 1916): 1–22.

———. *Education of the Negro Prior to 1861.* Washington, D.C., 1919.

———. *The History of the Negro Church.* Washington, D.C., 1921.

———. *Free Negro Heads of Families in the United States in 1830.* Washington, D.C., 1924.

———, ed. *Negro Orators and their Orations.* Washington, D.C., 1925.

———, ed. *The Mind of the Negro as Reflected in Letters Written During the Crisis, 1800–1860.* Washington, D.C., 1926.

Helen Beal Woodward. *The Bold Women.* New York, 1953.

Thomas Woody. *A History of Women's Education in the United States.* 2 vols. New York, 1929.

Marion T. Wright. "New Jersey Laws and the Negro." *Journal of Negro History* 28 (April 1943): 156–99.

Richard Robert Wright. *Centennial Encyclopedia of the African Methodist Episcopal Church.* Philadelphia, 1916.

Norman R. Yetman, ed. *Voices from Slavery.* New York, 1970.

Arthur Zilversmit. *The First Emancipation: The Abolition of Slavery in the North.* Chicago, 1967.

Roman J. Zorn. "The New England Anti-Slavery Society: Pioneer Abolition Organization." *Journal of Negro History* 42 (July 1957): 157–76.

Index

---

*Names of women represented in this book and pages on which their selections appear are printed in boldface type.

Wesleyans, 214
West Indies. See British West Indies
Wharton, Tex., 63–69
Wheatley, Phyllis, 13, 289, 297
White, George D., 158, 159
Whitney, Elizabeth, 312
Wilberforce University, 71, 160, 326, 330
Wilkes-Barre, Pa., 46
Willard, Frances, 300
Williams family (New Orleans), 57–60, 62
Williams, Fannie Barrier, 6, 7, 15, 20, 25, 27, 29, 34, 35, **263–79,** 303n, 315, 329
Williams, H. Price, 314
Williams, Richard, 141
Williams, S. Laing, 263, 264n
Wilmington, N.C., 112, 113
Wilson, Henry, 26
Wilson, Thomas (England), 123
Witherspoon, James, 297n

Women's Christian Temperance Union, 162
Woodbridge, Frederick J.E., 3
Woodhouse, Mrs. (Savannah), 91
Woodhouse, Mary Jane, 91
Worcester, Mass., 293
World's Anti-Slavery Convention (London), 213n, 215n
World's Congress of Religions, 265n
World's Congress of Representative Women, 19, 20, 25, 36, 263, 278, 279, 315, 329
World's Parliament of Religions, 265n
Wornton, Tobias (Backus), 202

Xenia, Ohio, 55n, 160

Yale College, 309, 317
Yarmouth, Mass., 160
York, Pa., 150, 155

Zion Methodist Church (Hartford), 174